EUROPEAN ECONOMIC INTEGRATION
A Challenge in a Changing World

CONTRIBUTIONS
TO
ECONOMIC ANALYSIS

224

Honorary Editor:
J. TINBERGEN

Editors:
D. W. JORGENSON
J. -J. LAFFONT
T. PERSSON
H. K. VAN DIJK

NORTH-HOLLAND
AMSTERDAM • LONDON • NEW YORK • TOKYO

EUROPEAN ECONOMIC INTEGRATION
A Challenge in a Changing World

Mathias DEWATRIPONT
Victor GINSBURGH
Université Libre de Bruxelles
Bruxelles, Belgium

1994

NORTH-HOLLAND
AMSTERDAM • LONDON • NEW YORK • TOKYO

337.14
E894

ELSEVIER SCIENCE B.V.
Sara Burgerhartstraat 25
P.O. Box 211, 1000 AE Amsterdam, The Netherlands

ISBN: 0 444 89174 p

 This book is printed on acid-free paper.

PRINTED IN THE NETHERLANDS

INTRODUCTION TO THE SERIES

This series consists of a number of hitherto unpublished studies, which are introduced by the editors in the belief that they represent fresh contributions to economic science.

The term "economic analysis" as used in the title of the series has been adopted because it covers both the activities of the theoretical economist and the research worker.

Although the analytical methods used by the various contributors are not the same, they are nevertheless conditioned by the common origin of their studies, namely theoretical problems encountered in practical research. Since for this reason, business cycle research and national accounting, research work on behalf of economic policy, and problems of planning are the main sources of the subjects dealt with, they necessarily determine the manner of approach adopted by the authors. Their methods tend to be "practical" in the sense of not being too far remote from application to actual economic conditions. In additon they are quantitative.

It is the hope of the editors that the publication of these studies will help to stimulate the exchange of scientific information and to reinforce international cooperation in the field of economics.

The Editors

Preface

This book honours the career of Jean Waelbroeck. As students and, later on, as his colleagues, we have been able to experience both his academic and his human qualities. His constant interest for frontier research has made him an essential member of the economics department at the Université Libre de Bruxelles since 1959, first at the Department of Applied Economics (DULBEA) and then at the Centre for Econometrics and Mathematical Economics (CEME). Jean had also a profound impact on undergraduate as well as graduate students (he directed more than twenty Ph. D. theses).

His influence extends much beyond our university, despite the fact that he spent most of his time there (as a graduate student, and then as a professor). He was a visiting professor at the Massachusetts Institute of Technology, the University of British Columbia, the Université Catholique de Louvain and the Facultés Universitaires Notre-Dame de la Paix in Namur. He was also a special advisor of the research department of the World Bank.

Among other research interests, Jean was a very active "modeller." He was both at the forefront of macroeconometric modelling (as a founding member of Project Link, together with Lawrence Klein) and of applied general equilibrium modelling.

Beyond a prolific scientific career with more than 140 published papers, Jean has significantly contributed to European unification in economic science by founding, together with Herbert Glejser, the *European Economic Review*, and remaining its Editor during 21 years. Started in 1969, this journal became the official publication of the European Economic Association at its creation in 1986. It is now one of the leading journals in economics in Europe.

His lifelong interest for European academia as well as European integration in general make it natural to have asked the contributors to this volume to focus their paper on this topic.

Table of contents

Introduction

This book brings together a number of Jean Waelbroeck's friends, coauthors and colleagues. It covers topics and methods close to his centres of interest in his long and prolific career: macroeconometric and applied general equilibrium modelling, international trade and applied econometric analysis.

The contributions also share a unifying theme, that of the effects and challenges of European integration. This is a topic which has preoccupied Jean for decades. The papers were presented in a conference held in Brussels in January 1992. At that time, the Single Market was about to officially start, and the Treaty of Maastricht had just been approved by the Council of Ministers. Europe was still in the phase of "Eureuphoria" which had succeeded to the earlier phase of "Europessimism" of the early and mid-eighties. The next phase of "Europessimism" that we now experience, with the recent difficulties of ratification of the Maastricht Treaty in Denmark or France, the monetary disorders and the generalized recession, was not yet present. The tone of the book might thus sound a bit too optimistic for the current moment, but its various chapters go beyond the business cycle movements that seem to affect Europe's mood so much. In fact, all the analyses it contains focus on structural aspects of European integration, and thus address issues of greater long-term concern than the short-term movements of interest rates which make the headlines of newspapers these days.

The book tries to analyze the effects of European integration both on Europe itself and on the rest of the world. Concerning the first aspect, topics range from macroeconomic management to price convergence, industrial restructuring or the environment. As for the rest of the world, the book is concerned both with the external trade impact of European integration and with the experiences of regional integration for which Europe has been a role model. Finally, the book is concerned with Europe as a whole, including East-European transition to a West-European style market economy.

Chapter 1, by Lawrence Klein, discusses Europe's Single Market (EC92) from an American perspective. It stresses the fact that the United States has taken a typically multilateral view of international trade since the Second World War, emphasizing institutions like the GATT. This being said, American attitudes towards European integration have been largely positive, except on agricultural matters. Europe has even been taken as a role model for a North American Free Trade Association with Canada and Mexico. If NAFTA is successfully concluded, one could say that Europe should then look at it as a model for a wider Europe including the East, or even for a free-trade zone including North Africa. Such challenges, which are clearly crucial for the emergence of prosperity in the periphery of Europe, and thus for sustained dynamism in the European Community, lie ahead of us. For North America instead, opportunities for wider regional integration are clearly in Asia, with its booming markets that could be integrated in a Pacific Free Trade Area.

Chapters 2 to 5 are concerned with the internal effects of EC 92 and of the Maastricht Treaty. In a perceptive paper, Jacques Drèze argues that the convergence process implied by Maastricht focuses excessively on the fight against inflation, without sufficiently allowing for the necessary fiscal expansion in economic downturns. The paper brings together econometric evidence from a multi-country study as well as macroeconometric simulations at the European level. It advocates a "two-handed" approach combining parallel measures of wage moderation and coordinated fiscal and monetary expansion. The paper also sheds light on recent fiscal developments. The unexpectedly severe recession Europe is facing in 1993 explains why the fiscal criteria of Maastricht are being ignored by the low-public-debt countries in order to limit the growth of unemployment. In fact, the Maastricht Treaty does not rule out temporary fiscal expansion, and the current recession should not in itself threaten Monetary Union by 1999. However, the recent death of the narrow generalized EMS bands, and the potential divergence of inflationary performances within Europe add up to the unfavorable business cycle situation to raise serious doubts about the Maastricht timetable.

Chapter 3, by Anton Barten, focuses on EC92 instead of Maastricht. Using duality theory of consumer choice, he computes the welfare effect of price convergence implied by the removal of all trade barriers in Europe. His conclusion is disappointing for the supporters of the Single Market: previous price variations between countries could be explained in great part by differences in tastes. Price convergence is still a good thing, but its positive welfare effect is quite small. One should thus not expect the main benefits of EC92 to come from price convergence.

Of course, supporters of the Single Market also stress the benefits of rationalization of production. In a given market environment, there is a tradeoff between competition, which lowers price markups, and concentration, which reduces the multiplication of fixed costs. Enlarging the market provides the best of both worlds, since it allows concentration to take place without reducing the degree of competition. Partial equilibrium analyses of EC92, pioneered by Alisdair Smith and Anthony Venables, obtained significant positive effects for EC92. This book contains two applied general equilibrium analyses of EC92, which allow to take into account factor price effects of the reallocation of production implied by the Single Market. Chapter 4 is written by Jean Mercenier and Chapter 5 by Jean-Marc Burniaux and Jean Waelbroeck. Both studies share the same broad methodology, relying on static applied general equilibrium models of the world economy, which distinguish several regions and several sectors. Some of these sectors are imperfectly competitive, and the Single Market increases competition there, pushing profit margins down as well as the equilibrium number of firms in the sector. Interestingly, results end up differing significantly. Jean Mercenier finds welfare gains to be quite small (at most 1 %), whether free entry is allowed or not, and whether competition is in prices or in quantities. Such a result is derived under the assumption that EC92 simply means price convergence, but does not change consumer behavior beyond this arbitrage effect. Jean Mercenier's conclusion is that, if significant gains are to be found from the Single Market, they should come instead from dynamic effects *à la* Richard Baldwin. Instead, Jean-Marc Burniaux and Jean Waelbroeck show that much bigger static gains can be obtained if EC 92 means higher consumer price elasticities of demand in imperfectly competitive sectors. In such cases, the pro-competitive effects and the subsequent rationalization process are much more pronounced. What they have in mind is for example the entry of national firms into neighbouring markets and their building up of market shares through aggressive advertising for example, as is currently happening in many service industries. In their exercise, this is modelled in reduced form, and additional empirical work is needed to better compare the two approaches.

Chapters 6 to 8 address the issue of external trade and the consequences of European integration for the rest of the world. Helen Hughes takes, in Chapter 6, an applied general equilibrium look at East Asian prospects under alternative trade scenarios. She stresses the high level of European protectionism towards East Asia in key sectors like textile. Further protectionism under a "Fortress Europe" policy would thus have a limited impact on East Asia, given the already low bilateral trade level in these sectors. She shows that prospects for countries like China or India depend a lot more on their own domestic policies towards productivity in these sectors than on European trade policy. This reflects the lack of dynamism in trade relations between Europe and East Asia which, given the dramatic growth in that part of the world, can only be a disadvantage for Europe.

Mathew Tharakan and Jean Waelbroeck take a look at actual EC decisions in trade policy, and in particular at antidumping actions. The authors take a political economy perspective at dumping as well as injury decisions. In an econometric analysis, they highlight the importance of politics in the decision process, and thus the desirability of more transparency. For example, they show that highly concentrated sectors tend to obtain more favorable treatment, which raises antitrust concerns. Moreover, they show that Europe is tougher against producers from Japan because of aggregate trade imbalances with this country. Finally, Third World producers seem to be favored when the existence of dumping has to be ascertained, but disadvantaged once action has to be taken against those convicted of dumping, especially when they come from NIC's.

In Chapter 8, Alexis Jacquemin and André Sapir address the same issue in a broader perspective. After reviewing progress towards internal liberalization, they stress the important role of external imports as a discipline device on European producers. They argue that protection against extra-EC imports is bad for European welfare in mature sectors like agriculture, steel or cars. The case is more difficult when it comes to high-tech sectors. For example, Airbus helps promote competition! Still, they hope that European integration continues to go along the lines of "natural integration", promoting growth and thus world trade, instead of "strategic integration", which mainly results in trade diversion instead of trade creation.

The current experience of EC integration is useful to think about additional dimensions of liberalization. Chapters 9 to 11 consider some of these, with emphasis on other parts of the world (Latin America and Eastern Europe respectively) or other dimensions of economic welfare (namely, the environment). In Chapter 9, Renato Flôres focuses on Latin American integration, a topic of prospective interest right now. He argues that the agenda of integration is useful mainly in terms of stabilizing politics and of improving macroeconomic management. Current instabilities make monetary union a very challenging task, which is not realistic in the short or medium term. Convergence criteria *à la* Maastricht could however serve as a very useful domestic stimulus in all these countries. On the real side, trade flows are currently very small, and integration would take quite a while to have an impact on economic growth. Still, integration could be quite useful in increasing the bargaining power of the region as a whole in international negotiations.

Irma Adelman, Peter Berck and Dusan Vujovic focus on the transition from socialism to a market system. After a discussion where they argue for the relative superiority of gradualist reforms over a "shock therapy", they use an applied general equilibrium model to consider another reform programme which combines aspects of both gradualism and shock therapy. Namely, in a first step, they allow for complete liberalization of prices and outputs while setting taxes and subsidies so as to make production and income levels identical to their pre-reform standards. Then, they design a gradual removal of taxes and subsidies so as to minimize income losses at the individual level. In their words, such an exercise is a "possibility theorem", not a forecast of actual reform experiences. Still, this chapter shows the usefulness of applied general equilibrium analyses for systemic change.

In Chapter 11, Elisabeth Waelbroeck-Rocha combines econometric and engineering tools with market studies to analyze the economic costs and benefits of an ambitious environmental programme consisting of CO_2 taxes, circulation taxes, conservation measures, pollution reduction measures and waste management projects. The study identifies both the losing sectors (heavy polluters) as well as the gaining ones (environmental leaders). It shows that even a dramatic environmental overhaul generates limited sectoral reallocation and a small change in macroeconomic forecasts. It concludes that fears of significant outsourcing of polluting activities or losses of competitiveness are greatly exaggerated.

The book ends with two studies of consumer behavior at the European level. The Maastricht convergence criteria imply that growth should not be led by fiscal deficits. Consumer behavior is thus central in both inducing the stimulus of private consumption and in generating the savings necessary for private investment. In Chapter 12, Khalid Sekkat, Françoise Thys-Clément and Denise

Van Regemorter investigate the role of financial markets in allowing consumers to stabilize consumption over time. They identify the importance of liquidity constraints in the United Kingdom and, to a lesser extent, in Germany. Instead, French consumers seem not to suffer from such constraints. The integration of banking activities in the coming years should help improve consumer access to credit all across Europe. Finally, in Chapter 13, Anne Borsu and Herbert Glejser analyze the role of public debt in private consumption-savings decisions. They confirm the Barro-Ricardo neutrality effect in countries with large public deficits. Conversely, this means that deflationary fears coming from the strict Maastricht fiscal criteria should not be exaggerated, because consumers may be expected to react to fiscal contraction with a cut in their savings rates.

The various studies collected in this book do not exhaust the ambitious topics they address. They are however representative of the qualities that have been associated with Jean Waelbroeck's research, in that they use state-of-the-art methodology to address important economic problems of the day. As such, they may of course raise as many new questions as they provide answers. In the process, they serve a very useful stimulus to both academic researchers and policymakers.

Acknowledgements

The editors are grateful to the Fonds National de la Recherche Scientifique (FNRS), the Ministère de l'Education, de la Recherche et de la Formation, Communauté Française de Belgique, the Ministère de la Communauté Française (Direction Générale de l'Enseignement et de la Formation), the Services de la Programmation et de la Politique Scietifique under contract PAI 26, Elsevier Science Publishers B.V., the Department of Economics, the Département d'Economie Appliquée (DULBEA) and the Centre d'Economie Mathématique et d'Econométrie (CEME), all three from Université Libre de Bruxelles for their financial support, which made possible the organization of the conference at which the papers collected in this book were presented.

Special thanks are due to Dale Jorgenson, coeditor of the *Contributions to Economic Analysis* series and to Joop Dirkmaat from North-Holland-Elsevier who supported with enthusiasm the idea of the conference and the present book, published in the series for which Jean Waelbroeck served as coeditor during so many years.

The Editors
November 1993

1

The Single Market in Europe
An American Appraisal

Lawrence R. Klein

University of Pennsylvania

1 Admiration and Apprehension in North America

After the second World War the United States have had a fairly consistent overall policy viewpoint, namely that world trade should be conducted under an open multilateral system of free trade. No country has ever stood by this principle to the nth degree – even Adam Smith allowed for exceptions – but the US position has been as consistent as a major government's policy can be in an imperfect world. Leaders have varied in terms of their commitment to the principles of complete free trade. I can speak from memory of more than one meeting with Jimmy Carter, and others too, during 1975-76 when the presidential candidate seriously asked economic advisers whether we (as a nation) should try to do anything directly about the loss of American jobs to foreign companies, whether we should be concerned about foreign investments in the United States, and (later in his administration) whether we should be concerned about an external deficit.

The only answer that I ever gave or heard in these gatherings was that trade and international capital flows moved along a "two-way street" and that none of the immediate concerns should be met by restrictions, duties, or other direct intervention with the free trade principle.

Of course, there was slippage in real-world implementation of trade policy. In a political deal with the United Automobile Workers and the Chrysler Corporation, American jobs were saved in the short run through financial guarantees to the company and later quota limitations on imports of Japanese cars. This was a pure violation of the free trade principle. On the other hand, in the process of renormalization of diplomatic relations with mainland China, the Carter Administration extended most-favored-nation treatment, but this free trade gesture was accompanied by quotas on Chinese textile/apparel shipments to the United States. There were many more deals or violations of the principle in question, but the Carter Administration like most postwar administrations in the United States upheld the broad outlines of free trade.

Emerging from bilateralism, bulk commodity barter shipments, and other legacies of the wartime economy, the major economic power of the world thrived on the expansion of trade value and volume. As the return to normalcy proceeded through the 1950s, trade expanded, but literally exploded during the decade of the 1960s. Troubles in food and fuel interrupted economic progress during the 1970s, but trade expansion continues, with the main international overseeing authority resting in GATT (General Agreement on Tariffs and Trade), an organization that did not quite succeed in gaining strong authority after Bretton Woods, but played, nevertheless, a very constructive role in monitoring and assessing trends in world trade. Through the years, GATT has taken the lead in the establishment of liberal trading practices internationally, their latest efforts being devoted to extending the scope of their free-trade influences to agricultural, intellectual, and other service-oriented activities. In spoken words at least, the policy of the United States is to establish a "level playing field" along GATT lines. That does not mean that the political economy of the USA is always fully consistent with GATT rules, but the single most appropriate description is that we advocate such principles, although not without strong domestic opposition.

The economic expansion of the second half of this century is significantly related to, but not wholly dependent upon, international trade expansion. There are many dimensions to this aspect of world economic performance, but the principal interest in this paper is in the Western European expansion and its impact on the United States.

The Benelux concept served as a starting point. Customs unions and other formal types of international economic associations have been studied by scholars of international trade, and the judgment as to their desirability focuses on the issue of trade diversion vs. trade expansion. Some of these ideas date back to Jacob Viner. Over the half century or more following Viner's analysis, the same issue has arisen as Benelux broadened into the European Economic Community (EEC or "Common Market"). The EEC grew in membership and is now poised to grow in scope as well as area. What should be the American attitude to this development, both in terms of self interest and in terms of goals for the conduct of international trade or more broadly international economic relationships?

It is interesting to consider briefly the situation of New Zealand and Australia at the time of the United Kingdom's joining the EEC. Both Pacific countries enjoyed unusual trading relationships with Britain as members of the far flung Commonwealth. They sent a great deal of food, fibers, other materials, and some manufactures to Britain and became seemingly dependent on that relationship. They anticipated that intra-Market trade would gain over the years and that European goods, especially agricultural goods, would gain at their expense in established EEC markets, particularly the UK.

Britain's entry into the Common Market diverted the source of many imports from their Commonwealth partners to European exporters. But two major economic changes took place in New Zealand and Australia. Those countries changed their economic orientation away from the UK and other members of the EEC towards their Pacific neighbors. New Zealand and Australia now are firmly entrenched in Pacific Basin trading and other economic activities. The future of these two English-speaking countries lies primarily in the Asia-Pacific area. In addition they diversified a great deal into new economic activities such as financial services, technology, manufactures, and, in the case of Australia, into new primary products such as minerals and metals. The growth of the Common Market was felt by New Zealand and Australia, but they were not devastated. They have survived very well.

The American attitudes towards Common Market expansion might well be the same as those of New Zealand and Australia. They will be affected but, by no means, devastated. This holds both for the United States and Canada. There are many directions in which they can move in order to protect their own interests, as well as those of the world trading system.

American economists and citizens at large have watched the growth of the EEC from its inception. Up to this point, it has not been considered a fatal threat. The main item of contention has been agricultural trade. The United States and Canada are very large, efficient producers of grains, meat, dairy products, fruits, vegetables, and fibers. Were the members of the EEC to refrain from subsidization of agriculture, American exports could be very much larger in that market, especially for food/feed grains. This is the main item of contention in the present GATT talks-Uruguay Round. With pressure on Western Europe and Japan, we have been able to coexist with the present state of affairs, arguing regularly for concessions in a liberal direction.

The venture into the Single Market after 1992 creates something new and much more formidable than the present situation. The expanded market will be able to function more cohesively as a unified competitor. From the point of view of its population and total gross domestic product (GDP) it appears formidable. The United States or the United States and Canada will lose their position as the largest single economic entity. This, in itself, is not necessarily a bad thing; *biggest is not necessarily best*. The issue is whether the extended working of the Common Market will divert trade away from North America.

Consider exports. Two important goods that the United States exports to Common Market countries are aircraft and computers. For the moment, American comparative advantage persists, but if the enlarged market (in scope as well as area) generates stronger competition, combined Airbus facilities and also combined computer facilities could displace many US exports. This does not necessarily reduce world economic welfare, but it could be a perceived threat to the United States. It is doubtful that the EEC will soon invade the American market on a massive scale unless some goods are made much more efficiently in Europe than at present, but some latent fears could be harbored about increased imports.

Table 1.A Some indicators of size, North America and EEC, 1990[1]

	Population (mill.)	GDP ($1980) (bill.)	GDP ($1980) (per head)	Exports ($ bill.) (mdse)	Imports ($ bill.) (mdse)
North America (Canada, USA)	275	3,917	14,244	519	617
EEC	324	3,927	12,120	1,338	1,339

Table 1.B Trade Matrix, United States and EEC, 1980[2]
(FOB, Merchandise, $ mill.)

Imports into		EEC	US	ROW	Total
	EEC	385	39	266	690
Exports	US	58	0	159	217
from	Row	301	201	592	1,094
	Total	744	240	1,017	2,001

Table 1.C Trade Matrix, United States and EEC, 1990[3]
(FOB, Merchandise, $ mill.)

Imports into		EEC	US	ROW	Total
	EEC	821	96	435	1,352
Exports	US	93	0	281	374
from	Row	430	388	843	1,661
	Total	1,344	484	1,559	3,387

Even if pure economic theory suggests that the optimal international economic organization is one of unimpeded free trade with perfect knowledge, free access to information by all participants, free entry into markets, factor mobility, and peaceful relationships among nations, people in America admire the Common Market – the way it was formed, expanded, and operated. It falls short of

---

[1]Source: United Nations, *World Economic Survey*, 1991. These figures show that per capita real income of the EC is 85 percent of the North American value. Using international prices for individual EC countries, the figure (relative to the United States alone) lie mainly between 65 and 75 percent.

[2]Source: United Nations, *Monthly Bulletin of Statistics*, June 1991

[3]Source: United Nations, *Monthly Bulletin of Statistics*, June 1991. In the last decade EEC exports expanded by a larger percentage, in value, than did US exports, and the US export surplus (bilaterally) that prevailed in 1980 vanished by 1990. The largest percentage gains were in EEC's internal exports and exports to the US.

the complete world ideal because it covers only a limited number of countries, yet it has led to economic improvement and understanding in Europe. It is also impressive because of its endurance. Americans accept it as a living institution on the economic landscape.

2 A Mercantilist View of Imbalance

Against the entire EEC, the United States used to enjoy a significant trade surplus, but during the middle of the 1980s, the surplus vanished, and now we have a large merchandise deficit. Within the Common Market, our largest deficit is with West Germany, but Italy, the UK, France, and Denmark all sell more goods to us than we buy from them. There is an even larger deficit of the United States in its trade with Japan. Some of these are not transitory bilateral deficits, they have persisted for many years. Two major events caused a temporary change in the situation. The Gulf War brought the United States into temporary surplus in early 1991, but the extraordinary payments of support from Japan, Germany, and others have been made, and our accounts are reverting back towards deficit. The second event has been the unification of Germany, which caused the large prevailing worldwide surplus of West Germany to fall abruptly because of the cost of absorbing the East German economy. Eventually East Germany should become productive and efficient again, making a positive contribution to the unified economy.

There are other countries with which the United States has significant and persistent imbalance, some positive and some negative, but the amounts are not as large as in the German and Japanese cases. The surplus accounts are not under debate in the United States, but the deficits receive a great deal of attention.

Canada, of course, has traditionally been our largest trading partner, and we maintain a large deficit balance with our northern neighbor in goods trade, but service flows and investment income constitute quite another story; so our wider trade/payments relationship with Canada is not particularly unfavorable to us.

Countries in the multilateral trading network should be concerned mainly, or only, with the overall balance, the bottom line, but for many years American policy makers have focused abnormally on our deficits with West Germany and Japan. It has become a mercantilist obsession. German unification will have a longer run effect on the bilateral balance of the US than will anything that is now in sight concerning our trade with Japan.

In the case of Japan, we have been emphasizing their restrictive or idiosyncratic practices – their distribution system, e.g. – their subsidies to rice farmers, or limitations on imports of such agricultural products as beef and citrus. We have tried to limit Japan's steel, automotive and other manufactured exports to the United States, but we have sold them large amounts of grains, fibers, fuels, aircraft, and other items. We have also negotiated on the support of US defense forces stationed at Japanese bases, obtaining a larger Japanese contribution over the years.

The commodity composition of our total merchandise trade picture is quite interesting. Traditionally, the United States have maintained a large surplus in net exports of agricultural products. This is not at all bad, for we exploit our natural advantages in certain types of agriculture, as we should, and have a large exportable surplus, beyond current needs. This bothers many Americans, who would like to see the US trade balance mùove into a more favorable position with respect to manufactured goods. We used to have such a surplus but have been effectively challenged in Asia, Europe, and eventually in many other areas in several lines of manufacturing.

The agricultural surplus reached a figure as high as $25 billion in 1981, a tidy bit of support to offset part of the oil import surplus. Agricultural exports have receded, but they are still making a positive contribution, and growing again. To a large extent, agricultural exports have been destined for China and the Soviet Union, but the ability of those two countries to pay for large scale imports is limited. This is the point at which the trade relationships with the Common Market enter the picture. Our agricultural surplus could be larger were it not for the restrictive agricultural policy of Western Europe. The Uruguay Round of trade negotiations was intended, in part, to deal with the freeing up of trade in agricultural products but have run into great trouble in working out negotiations with Common Market countries. The fear of Americans is that such negotiations would be even more difficult in the European environment that is expected to prevail after 1992.

It is not only Europe that poses an obstacle for US agricultural exports. Japan subsidizes rice to such an extent that their own farmers are paid many times the world market price for their product. It would not be the United States alone who would benefit from a freeing of the Japanese rice price, to seek world levels, but we would be able to gain at least a share of that market.

Historically, the United States used to have a positive net export balance for total merchandise trade. Agriculture was one positive component, but manufactured goods constituted another. Since the recession of 1981-82 and the period of the strong (overvalued?) dollar during the first half of the 1980s, the balance in manufactured goods exports turned negative and by very large amounts. Even after the dollar fell, at the beginning of 1985, the balance on trade in manufactures has remained unfavorable. Many, but not all, members of the Common Market contributed to this turn of events, and with the Common Market, as a whole, the United States remains in deficit by a large amount for manufactured goods. That is another reason why so much attention is being paid to the issues of freer trade in agricultural goods with Western Europe and also to the general improvement in US competitiveness in manufacturing. Of course, the imbalance in manufactured goods trade is much more unfavorable with Japan and other Asia-Pacific countries than with Europe; so US trade performance will have to be improved in many directions, but the imbalance with Western Europe is large enough to cause concern in that direction and to generate fears of further deterioration after 1992.

Let us summarize the US merchandise trade position with major partners. The largest is Canada. Our overall balance with Canada is negative and is largely a result of the high value of automotive imports that came in as a result of a special bilateral agreement on trade in this industry, which was in place before the signing of the comprehensive free trade agreement in 1989. Energy products (gas and oil) are also imported from Canada on a large scale.

In the case of Japan, the next largest trading partner of the US, there is a large American export surplus in agricultural merchandise, but it could be still larger. It is, nevertheless, fairly steady. It is more than offset by a large and growing import surplus of manufactures. Coal, other minerals, and forest products are also shipped from the US to Japan.

Mexico and the rest of Latin American have close economic ties with the United States. Petroleum, tropical beverages, fruits, and substantial manufactures are imported by the United States from Latin America. It is noteworthy that the balance of trade with Latin America as a whole and with Mexico took a sudden turn, from near balance, to large deficit in 1981-82. This turn was directly associated with the emergence of the World Debt Problem, which surfaced in Mexico during 1982 and spread quickly to other major Latin American countries. An immediate response was to curtail dollar or other hard-currency imports, particularly from the United States. This problem has not been fully resolved, but by piecemeal efforts has been dealt with in a few countries – muddling through. US exports to Mexico, for example, are once again approaching their high values realized just prior to the sharp curtailments in 1982.

With the fast growing developing countries in the Far East, the US deficit has been growing rapidly. Exports to this area consisting of some foods, agricultural materials, and industrial materials along with strategic manufactures (aircraft, specialized electronics, chemicals) have grown modestly above core levels attained by the end of the 1970s, but imports of manufactures from this expansive area have accelerated once we came out of the 1981-82 recession.

Finally, we should consider OPEC in this summary. Partly, OPEC includes Latin America and Africa, but for the most part it covers the Middle East. Petroleum products, crude and refined, dominate US import figures and have been very large ever since the first oil shock of 1973-74. In turn, we ship food, feed and many manufactured goods to OPEC countries, but US exports are consistently far below imports. Also, European and other countries (Japan, South Korea, and others) have exported so extensively to the Middle East that the US have lost ground.

The United States trade everywhere in the world, but the main areas have been summarized. There may be some future importance for Eastern Europe, the USSR, the People's Republic of China, West Asia, and Africa, but the strategic decisions that must be taken, especially with regard to future competition with the EEC, will be made more with reference to our strong relationships with Canada, Japan, Mexico, the rest of Latin America, the rest of the Pacific Basin, and the oil exporting countries of the Middle East.

Before leaving the "Mercantilist View of Imbalance," we should mention the nonmerchandise components of the balance of payments, consisting of transportation, tourism, rights, other business services, and investment income.

Once the American merchandise balance shifted from positive to negative, our overall balance was preserved by a large persistent surplus on invisibles account. We are not particularly a seafaring nation, although we have extensive coastlines, and have had a consistent deficit on transport account – for both goods and people. For tourism or travel, we slipped into a large deficit position after 1982. Mexico and Canada figure importantly in this account.

The United States are beginning to realize good net export earnings for proprietary rights and other business services, but the big earner of invisible trade is in investment income, this in spite of our enormous indebtedness abroad that was built up during the 1980s. Much is said these days about the dangers of foreign investment in the United States, which focuses on acquisitions by Japanese, Europeans, and Middle Easterners. In spite of the fact that large payments must be made abroad, US receipts from our investments have grown even faster, and this keeps the US balance significantly positive. It is, however, not sufficiently positive to compensate for the much larger merchandise deficit.

Some of the items in the invisibles section of the export-import accounts are directly associated with the trade in merchandise. Shipping and related business services, even tourism, should be treated like goods in the conduct of international economic relations, and they quite naturally fall under the purview of an enhanced GATT. The concept of multilateral free trade should include the invisibles as well as the visibles.

Comparison considerations should be extended to the movement of financial capital, as assets and liabilities, among countries on a free multilateral basis. Capital ownership in the form of foreign direct investment and portfolio investment is being freed up within the EEC after 1992, and we can look for pressures to gain the same freedom on a truly global, multilateral basis. International capital ownership generates investment income flows, which are very important in the US current account. That is why many US companies are positioning themselves in Europe now. Although, mercantilist thinking publicizes concern about foreign ownership of US assets, we are heavily involved in acquiring foreign assets too, on top of already large holdings that have been accumulated over the years.

On an overall basis, not taking a mercantilist view of particular imbalances, the US position on national income and product account (NIPA) has turned from very large negative numbers to more comfortable negative values, in current prices. Depreciation of the dollar contributed to a fundamental lowering of the NIPA deficit from more than $100 billion to low 2-digit magnitudes by 1990. This is all to the good, but the NIPA balance treats all interest payments on the national debt (whether to foreigners or residents) as transfers; therefore interest payments abroad are seriously understated in comparison with figures from the current account. These are still distressingly large. The problem with the US trade and payment account on NIPA basis looks as though it has been solved, but this is not really so; the current account deficit will have to be brought close to zero before we can feel comfortable about our external position. In 1980 and 1981, the current account was slightly positive and had fluctuated by small amounts, above and below zero, for scores of peacetime years. During the 1980s, the deficit reached nearly $200 billion. In the sections to follow, we shall look at projections of the NIPA trade and current account balances, as well as the formation of new trading relationships or other policies to deal with possibilities of returning to more normal balance.

3   Some Projections from Project LINK

The LINK system of world trade and activity for some 80 countries and regions includes all the major trading partners of the United States and the EEC. This system is used regularly for projections and simulations of policy alternatives or variations about international affairs. The baseline projection to the year 2000 throws light on many of the world issues that face the US economy, particularly its relationship to the EEC. As was implied in the discussion of the preceding sections, the balances of the United States, Germany and Japan are quite important. The German balance reflects some of the problems that America faces in its dealing with the Common Market. The Japanese balance is important because it is so large and persistent, forcing American policy makers to compensate elsewhere, partly with the Common Market.

Naturally, this forecast is based on assumptions for key inputs of policy variables and those associated with general world conditions. The three major industrial countries – US, Japan, and Germany – are constrained in different ways by present circumstances. It is assumed that both the United States and Japan will lower interest rates in 1992 in order to stimulate their slow or recessionary economies. Germany, on the other hand, will keep monetary expansion in restraint because of the pressures that arise from the fiscal outlays that are being used to promote unification. By mid decade, however, the pace of world recovery should bring monetary policies of the major countries towards closer convergence. Japan is assumed to use fiscal stimulus now, to combat a cyclical slowdown, but Germany and the US are constrained, the former by the costs of unification, and the latter by the federal deficits that have been built up for the past decade.

With respect to primary producing countries, many of whom are in developmental stages, it is recognized that raw material prices, including petroleum, are at low values, which should prevail for the next two years and then rise gradually as world recovery takes hold. The oil price, in particular, is indexed

Table 2 Imbalances estimated by project Link
($ billion)

	1990	1991	1992	1993	1994	1995	1996	1997	1998	1999	2000
USA											
Mdse bal.	-133.4	-73.0	-89.3	-89.8	-93.7	-82.3	-73.3	-73.9	-72.5	-65.0	-72.9
Curr. a/c	-99.3	-0.7	-60.7	-63.3	-69.6	-59.6	-53.1	-54.1	-57.4	-51.9	-63.6
W. Germany											
Mdse bal.	70.8	67.4	66.8	61.0	57.6	51.5	47.8	44.7	42.1	43.5	37.8
Curr. a/c	37.0	32.5	33.6	28.1	27.2	22.3	20.6	19.4	17.4	17.9	13.8
Japan											
Mdse bal.	63.9	78.7	88.9	90.9	97.0	103.3	110.6	111.9	109.2	105.1	100.1
Curr. a/c	46.5	53.2	55.9	49.8	54.8	59.0	63.8	60.6	52.6	42.6	33.8
Un. Germany											
Mdse bal.	67.6	-1.1	5.1	6.1	9.3	11.1	2.4	2.1	4.1	7.8	5.8
EEC											
Mdse bal.	-1.2	0.5	-3.6	-7.9	-16.7	-23.1	-25.5	-19.2	-20.8	-17.4	-19

to inflation among OECD countries, after 1994. Also, the major efforts at restructuring among former socialist countries and several developing countries are expected to continue.

The overall balances in Table 2 – not the *bilateral* balances, which are available only for merchandise trade – show the persistence of problems throughout the decade of the 1990s.[4] There is, in this projection, little tendency towards long run convergence to equilibrium. The US deficit simply will not go away. There is an obvious improvement in connection with Desert Storm and the recession of 1991, but both the merchandise balance and the current account balance return to high values after 1992. There is some cyclical variation projected ahead but no large and lasting improvement foreseen. It is true that GDP for the US and other countries is expected to rise during this decade, by about 2.5 to 3.0 percent annually. The $5,000 billion economy is expected to become a $9,000 billion economy by the end of the decade; so the ratio of the deficits to GDP is not low enough to be called equilibrium. The average dollar exchange rate, in this projection, undergoes depreciation of about 10 percent, and perhaps this is an underestimate of what is needed to make a large improvement in trade and payments balances. It is not, however, a matter of unusual growth in economic activity because the general economic environment is not one of full-employment growth. The unemployment rate averages as high as 6.0 percent, with capacity utilization as low as 80 percent.

It should be stressed that these projections for the US and those to be commented on below for partner countries and the EEC are merely forecast values; they should not be treated as actual reported values. Also, they are forecasts over an entire decade. This has its advantages in providing a time perspective that is long enough to permit full adjustment effects to be realized, after 1992, but in all such long or medium range extrapolations there is ùmuch room for error accumulation.

West Germany shows a moderately declining trade surplus and current account surplus, although these figures are not essentially zero by the year 2000. The situation is different for unified Germany. In that case, the burden of the East brings the trade balance to a very low level, at much less that $10 billion, and even negative in 1991. At this stage, it is very difficult to model the entire current account for unified Germany. The trade figures, however, should provide a good guide. The domestic German economy is not expected to rid itself quickly of the heightened level of unemployment or of inflation that comes about with unification.

Japan, unlike Germany, quickly reverses, in the projection calculations, the declines that are now taking place in the trade and current account balances. The former is actually expected to grow a great deal, while the latter first rises and then shows an apparent tendency to recede a bit during the closing years of the decade. The Japanese surplus appears to be very stubborn and does not

---

[4]The source for this table is Project LINK model.

readily show signs of vanishing unless some unusual policies are implemented. The Japanese economy, under these circumstances, is expected to slow to an average growth rate just under 4 percent; now it is closer to 5 percent. If it turns more inward towards domestic activity rather than exporting, it may be possible to find a smaller trade surplus.

The figures in Table 2 are not bilateral balances; they are overall balances for large, key countries, but it is unlikely that better overall balance will be achieved without significant lowering of the relevant bilateral balances, particularly those vis-a-vis the US.

While Germany is expected to have a large overall surplus, the same is not true of the EEC as a whole. France, Greece, Portugal, Spain, and the UK are some large deficit countries.

4   The US in Changing Trade Relationships

Persistent problems are not going away by attrition or whatever natural market forces seem to be in motion. A preferred solution would be for the country to put its strength to work to become more efficient in an economic sense, improve productivity by much more than prevailing trends will do, and let the dollar depreciate enough to get closer to equilibrium. This will mean more austerity in consumption, more attention to capital formation (human and fixed), and more patience in letting the process work, with appropriate attention being paid to less unequal income distribution, full employment, and faster growth. These virtuous procedures have been preached over and again with little success so far. Thus, what are some institutional options open to the US after 1992, to try to improve its trade and payments position?

A natural reaction is to build an alliance in the Western Hemisphere to meet head-on competition from the extended Common Market. We have taken the first step in that direction by forging a free trade agreement with Canada. National admiration for the perceived successes of the Common Market and the enthusiasm generated by its extension seem to point to similar activity centered around the US economy. The arguments for a free trade zone and the analysis of the benefits arising from the formation of such a zone are patterned very closely from those associated with Europe after 1992. For example, the estimated benefits that would be generated by a US-Canadian trade pact are

> simplicity and speed-up at border crossings
> realization of economies of scale through enlargement of the market area
> transfer of technology
> uniformity of standards and specifications

Canadian studies suggested that there would be significant productivity gains through economies of scale and the other benefits listed above. In a detailed statistical analysis of the working of the Agreement, it was estimated that gains to Canada would occur if there were a productivity enhancement, and that crucial aspect has yet to be carefully estimated from more careful study of production functions and demand conditions.It is too early to judge the longer term effects, and those are the relevant ones to consider, but in two years there is little to show. Conclusions about effects of the agreement are clouded by implementation of the tax on goods and services and the advent of recession; most such agreements foolishly ignore the business cycle, which we have learned is always on hand to play havoc with full-employment analyses.

Canadians might say that all the benefits seem to be going to the US partners, but Canada is ready to discuss with US and Mexico a broader agreement, covering North America, as a whole. The Mexicans, in turn, are deeming the US-Canadian agreement as either so successful or so fashionable that they want to have a US-Mexican Agreement on a free trade zone and are willing to enter talks for a three-country agreement with Canada included.

The Canadian-US agreement had not only the Common Market as an indicator, but also the long standing pact on automotive product shipments between the two countries. Similarly, Mexico has the Maquiladora experience on which to build. In that arrangement, goods are produced in US operated factories or other establishments located near the border but in Mexico. Thsese plants are able to employ Mexican workers in labor-intensive activities at low wage cost. The goods that are produced can be shipped without duty or special export permission to the US for final assembly or sale. This is a thriving segment of the Mexican industrial economy and is deemed successful by both actively engaged parties but not by all concerned in the US. Entrepreneurs and workers who are directly affected in the US resent this use of cheap labor input as a competitive threat.

Without being right on the border, we have engaged in similar activities in export processing in the Far East. In those cases, the transfer of technology seemed to follow the production lines, and Mexico will probably have to implement much more foreign direct investment in order to realize the productivity gains of technology transfer. This is being done now and would be even more likely if an extended free trade pact were to be put in place.

Let us suppose that a complete free trade area can be constructed jointly among the United States, Canada, and Mexico. That would be a start in forming an effective challenge to the Common Market. Whether or not it would be beneficial in a total world welfare sense would depend on whether or not there would be a basis for international economic warfare between the European and North American zones.

The US-Canada zone is a reality, and the two countries have so much in common that the implementation of a formal agreement is merely supplementary to what is normally and naturally taking place in economic relationships between the two countries. Mexico also has much in common with the United States and the Maquiladora program was not the first form of cooperation; it was preceded by the Bracero program for Mexican workers to cross the border to take jobs in certain US industries, notably agriculture.

Steps are already being taken for the establishment of a US-Mexican Agreement and also to make it a triangular arrangement with Canada included as well. But other countries are looking for free trade pacts with the United States, and some are in South America. It is just possible that a Single Market in Europe that strongly meets European objectives will stimulate countries in South America, and maybe elsewhere in Latin America, to take up serious consideration of a Western Hemisphere trading area. This may be especially so as the EEC extends to the idea of European Economic Space. More countries from Western Europe will undoubtedly join the EEC soon, but the acceptance of East European countries will have to be worked out over time.

A wider zone than North America is definitely conceivable, but all Latin countries may not qualify for membership or even want to join; the hemispheric zone could be a good deal more powerful than North America alone.

Much has been written about the prospects for a Pacific Basin or Asia-Pacific Common Market. At first such thoughts were dismissed by the majority of economists as being simply imitative in concept without having good economic reasons for more formal integration or the political basis for an institutional arrangement. The countries of the area are considered to be highly diverse.

The thought of an Asia-Pacific institution is much less readily dismissed now. There is already a loose and informal organization that meets periodically, and there is much sentiment for an informational agency patterned along the lines of the OECD. The reason for taking up this matter in the present paper is not to emphasize that this could be the core of the *third* grouping in a tri-polar world economy. That is a much discussed configuration now, but the most relevant issue is that the United States and Canada could well participate in such an institution. This is because the economies of US and Canada are both oriented towards the Asia-Pacific Area. They have extensive Pacific, as well as Atlantic, coastlines and also have been fully participating for many years in various Pacific Basin economic groups. In a sense, the same could be said of Latin American countries that have Pacific coastlines, but the degree of participation by the US and Canada in Pacific Basin affairs is much greater. We may, therefore, find the two North American powers both in their own trade bloc and in an Asia-Pacific bloc at the same time. This can be a strategic part of the US response to an inward-looking EEC if that is the development that occurs. We would be trying to make up for European trading losses by recouping them in intra-American and Asia-Pacific trading.

5   The Monetary System and Capital Flows

Free trade within the Common Market is but one aspect of the establishment of the Single Market in Europe after 1992. Free movement of people and financial capital are two others. There is negotiation (Maastricht Treaty) also about the establishment of one currency, but that is to be implemented later.

The free movement of people does not raise an issue to which the United States should respond. The era of large scale immigration to the United States from the member countries of the EEC is a thing of the past, not necessarily forever, but for now. There will be immigration and emigration on a small scale between the US and EEC, but it should not be large enough to cause concern by either party now. It did cause a serious "brain drain" in the years after the second World War and even until the 1960s and 1970s. Also there were periods of capital flight and the presence of restrictions on capital movement, but they are not present issues. Actually, the reverse has happened with respect to financial capital. There have been large scale movements of capital into the United States in order to finance our large current account deficit. A very large portion of the capital investment flow to the United States has come from EEC countries, but more of an issue has been created by the flows from Japan and the Middle East.

A principal direct impact of the drive for the Single Market has been for US companies and general investors to seek positions in the EEC to the greatest extent possible in advance of 1992. Capital flows into and out of the United States. Presently, a good portion of the outflow is to invest in the promises of the Single Market at the very beginning while opportunity looks very attractive. This is happening across a wide variety of activities. Cars, computers, food manufactures, banking, other finance, communication, retailing, to name some outstanding cases.

As far as the implementation of the capital flows is concerned, that activity requires the use of banks, stockbrokers, investment advisers, and stock exchanges. Apart from the institutional developments in Europe, the means for market globalization are taking place anyway and anywhere. International trading in the Far East, Latin America, Europe, North America are all being pooled together in networks of international financial companies using communications systems, liberalization of rules on ownership, currency conversion, earnings repatriation, and electronic transfers. Thus, it appears that whether the Single Market does anything special about foreign activities in capital markets, it is already happening. The 24-hour global market is here, now.

The main distinctive aspect of capital flows now, and as planned ahead, in the EEC is the maintenance of a stable foreign exchange system built around the semi-fixed parities of the European Monetary System. Within the EEC, exchange rates have been stabilized, and this puts constraints on macroeconomic policy, encouraging countries to harmonize aspects of economic performance to conform to the dominant trends set in motion by the most powerful countries of the Euro-Union. This leaves the yen and dollar, as main currencies outside the European system, to fluctuate more widely in order to buffer the global system. In many respects, the world outside the EEC bears the brunt of some important international economic adjustments. The United States and Japan, in the first instance will have the responsibility. Such a responsibility increases the pressure on these two economic powers to harmonize their economic policies with those of the other main industrial countries, i.e. those in the EEC. European countries under economic stress, can, however suspend operations within the system.

2

"1 Market + 1 (tight) Money = 2 Rules of Fiscal Discipline": Europe's fiscal stance deserves another look[1]

Jacques H. Drèze

CORE, Université Catholique de Louvain

> "All econometric models are parables which stress the relevant
> features of the situation and omit the irrelevant ones."
> (V. Ginsburgh and J. Waelbroeck (1981, p. 167)).

1 Introduction

1.1 At the end of 1991, the interests of Europeans and North-Americans appear as divergent as ever – whereas their economic situations are largely analogous. Short-term interest rates are exceptionally low in the US and exceptionally high in Germany – with the expectation that these contrasting policy stands will extend into 1992. The policy debate is dominated in the US by the view that faltering growth and rising unemployment call for fiscal stimulation (increased rate of public expenditures and/or tax cuts) in addition to easy money. In Europe, where the real developments are the same, the policy debate is centered on the measures of "fiscal discipline" that should pave the way for monetary union.

Thus the "rules of fiscal discipline" approved at the summit meeting in Maastricht are essentially those proposed by the Dutch Presidency and endorsed in the *Annual Economic Report* 1991-92 of the European Commission. They call for public deficits [2] brought down from the current average level of 4.5 % to a maximum (in each participating country) of 3 % – that is, an overall tightening of fiscal stance by at least 1.5 %. The number "3 %" supposedly corresponds to a realistic long-term real growth rate or real interest rate. In addition, debt-to-GDP ratios should be brought down to 60 % (the European average) or less.

---

[1] Helpful comments by François Bourguignon are gratefully acknowledged.

[2] These are global deficits, including debt service and capital expenditures - they are not primary deficits or current account deficits.

I am surprised at limited discussion of (i) the short-run deflationary impact of the proposed rules, and (ii) the long-run logic of fixed rules. Clearly, monetary unification entails specific requirements; creating a single currency area of EC 12 size, with twelve separate national budgets (and associated revenue structures, social-security provisions a.s.o.) and with an insignificant central budget, is innovative, and carries uncertainties against which it is natural to build safeguards. Also, the preparatory documents, and the policy debate, have referred to the implications of the fiscal discipline *at the national level* – where *both* the fiscal and the monetary instruments are thus abandoned. Yet, I have seen little discussion of the relevance of the *aggregate fiscal stance* of EC 12 – the restrictive stance of the early years, the rigid inequality constraints of later years. It is as if the importance of that aggregate fiscal stance were denied or, worse still, ignored... At least one would like the issue to be raised: Does the aggregate European fiscal stance matter? Is there a sound justification for the Maastricht rules? Does there exist an alternative, possibly a superior one?

The apparent neglect of that issue, [3] which stands in sharp contrast to the continued concern about fiscal stance in the US, is probably due to two main reasons: (i) there is no tradition of European wide fiscal policy; although the advisability of cooperative fiscal measures was discussed by some a few years ago, [4] it no longer is; and the use of fiscal policy to stimulate expansion at country level has been discredited, in particular after the unsuccessful unilateral attempts by Germany in 1979 and France in 1981; thus, the relevance of the aggregate fiscal stance of EC 12 is easily ignored; (ii) the preparatory documents express concern over fiscal laxism by member states, when the current account will no longer sanction deficits; if that laxism is the only relevant concern, then rules of fiscal discipline are natural.

Yet, there are empirical as well as theoretical grounds to be concerned about the extent to which the rise and persistence of unemployment in Western Europe may have been due to an effective demand gap, a gap that may at times have been aggravated by restrictive fiscal measures or that could have been reduced by a more expansionary fiscal stance. Thus, it should be realised that net *aggregate* borrowings of general governments in Europe 9 have increased *in a single year* by 3 % in 1975 and 2.3 % in 1981. This was due, not to lavish expenditure sprees, but to the impact of external shocks. Also, aggregate borrowings have exceeded the 3 % mark in every single year from 1975 through 1988. The 3 % Maastricht rule, if taken seriously, means that external shocks affecting budgets

---

[3]Of course, the neglect is only relative, and the issue has not been *ignored altogether.* See for instance Begg *et al.* (1991), where a long section devoted to "Fiscal Rules" starts with "The Case Against Binding Rules". After this paper was written, the implications of Maastricht have been scrutinised by several authors, including Buiter (1992), Melitz (1991) or Wiplosz (1992), to name only a few. Still, more attention is devoted to the implications of the Maastricht rules for national policies than to the issue of Europe's aggregate fiscal stance as such.

[4]See in particular the annual reports of the European Commission for 1985-87 as well as those of the Macroeconomic Policy Group: Blanchard *et al.* (1985, 1986), Drèze *et al.* (1988).

negatively must imperatively lead to restrictive fiscal measures – whatever the nature of the shocks or the state of the economies. Clearly, such rules deserve more scrutiny and discussion than they have received so far.

1.2 Given the personality around whom we have the pleasure of gathering and his continued interest in macroeconomics as well as in trade issues, it would be unnatural for us to neglect the issue of aggregate fiscal stance in a discussion of the internal market. Such neglect would be all the more unfortunate, since we know that most benefits from greater integration are predicated upon faster growth and a return to full employment.

Short of having studied seriously the likely implications of the proposed rules of fiscal discipline, I would like in this paper to bring out modestly the need for a serious discussion of the place of fiscal policy in the European Community. I would hope to convince readers that we should not accept the prospect of tight money and fixed budgetary rules without a serious professional debate over its implications and its merits in comparison with potential alternatives.

To that end, I have tried to summarise in this paper what I believe to have learned about the relevance of Europe's aggregate fiscal stance, through my participation in the Macroeconomic Policy Group [5] and in the European Unemployment Program (EUP). [6] Section 2, drawing havily on the EUP findings, reviews empirical evidence about the importance of the demand side for the determination of output and employment. Section 3 reviews the theoretical prerequisites for *effectiveness* of fiscal policies. Section 4, drawing in addition on the experience of the Macroeconomic Policy Group, raises – but hardly treats – the ultimate issue of economic *efficiency* of fiscal policies. That section uses some new formulae derived in the Appendix. In order to contain this paper within a reasonable length, standard arguments are presented as concisely as possible, and no attempt is made at introducing readers to an extensive literature. I have added in Section 5 a brief presentation of simulation results from the COMPACT and QUEST models estimated at DG II of the Commission of the European Communities. That latter model may be regarded as the most up-to-date heir of the tradition created twenty years ago with DESMOS – see Waelbroeck and Dramais (1974).

---

[5] The Macroeconomic Policy Group is a group of five economists organised by the Center for European Policy Studies (CEPS) in Brussels to advise the Directorate General for Economic and Financial Affairs (DG II) at the Commission of the European Communities on macroeconomic policies. As a member in 1985-1986 and Chairman in 1987-1988, I took part in the formulation of the "Two-Handed Growth Strategy" – see Blanchard *et al.* (1985), Drèze *et al.* (1988).

[6] The European Unemployment Program was a cooperative effort by researchers in 10 countries to better understand the determination of employment as well as the causes behind the rise and persistence of unemployment in Europe since the mid 1970's. To that end, comparable econometric models, extending an earlier specification by Sneessens and Drèze (1986a,b) were estimated in the 10 countries. Results were discussed and compared during a conference held at Chelwood Gate in May 1988. See Drèze and Bean (1990, 1991), Drèze *et al.* (1991).

These are at best fragments of the knowledge that should be marshalled towards an assessment of the role of fiscal policy in the emerging new Europe. No attempt is made at identifying the policy instruments, the information requirements or institutional arrangements that might be involved in a more comprehensive approach. No attempt is made either at relating fiscal, monetary and incomes policies. Hopefully, other participants at the conference may contribute additional fragments, and enrich the debate beyond my own conclusions (Section 6). To repeat, my modest ambition is simply to convince readers that Europe's fiscal stance is an issue worthy of attention and discussion.

2   Empirical Evidence and Ambiguities

2.1 Figure 1, which I have used on several previous occasions, gives a summary picture of the underutilisation of resources in the European Community since 1972, in terms of unemployment and capacity utilisation. That picture underlies the *presumption* that the slowdown in growth rates, from 1974 on, was not due to lack of physical resources but reflected instead underutilisation of available resources – even if the capital stock of the eighties was clearly inadequate to support full employment.

In order to relate these physical observations to economic concepts, and in particular to a diagnostic of effective demand gap, an interpretative model is needed. The model used under the European Unemployment Program was precisely designed to permit that kind of diagnostic. The underlying methodology is by now well understood, and can be concisely summarised as follows.

At the heart of the model lies the recognition that for a filled job to exist three conditions must be satisfied. First, that there exists a worker in the right place and with the right skills for the job. Second that there is the capital available to employ the worker. Third that there is a demand for the worker's output. Denote respectively by LS_i the labour supply to firm i, by LC_i the number of working posts in that firm, and by LD_i the number of workers needed to produce the output demanded (at the prices posted by firm i). Actual employment L_i will then, to a first approximation and neglecting dynamics, correspond to the minimum of these three quantities:

$$L_i = \min(LD_i, LC_i, LS_i) \qquad (1)$$

Aggregation of these relations reveals that actual employment must satisfy

$$\begin{aligned} L = \Sigma_i L_i \quad &= \quad \Sigma_i min(LD_i, LC_i, LS_i) \\ &\leq \quad min(\Sigma_i LD_i, \Sigma_i LC_i, \Sigma_i LS_i) \\ &:= \quad min(LD, LC, LS). \end{aligned} \qquad (2)$$

A simple functional relationship among the aggregate variables can be derived from plausible (lognormality) assumptions about the distribution across firms of the three proximate determinants of employment, viz:

$$L = [LD^{-\rho} + LC^{-\rho} + LS^{-\rho}]^{-\frac{1}{\rho}} \tag{3}$$

where the parameter $\rho > 0$, derived from the covariance matrix of the distribution, is interpreted as a measure of "mismatch" in the distribution across firms of supply and demand. [7]

The corresponding expression for real output (GNP) is

$$Y = [YD^{-\rho} + YC^{-\rho} + YS^{-\rho}]^{-\frac{1}{\rho}} \tag{4}$$

where YD denotes effective demand, YC denotes full capacity output and YS denotes full-employment output. Thus, capacity utilisation is measured by $\frac{Y}{YC}$ and unemployment is measured by $1 - \frac{L}{LS} = 1 - \frac{Y}{YS}$. The technological choices resulting from cost minimisation at given factor prices imply technical coefficients

$$\left(\frac{YC}{K}\right) = B, \quad \left(\frac{YC}{LC}\right) = A, \tag{5}$$

where K denotes the capital stock. The core of the real part of the EUP econometric models is then given by (3)-(4)-(5), a labour supply equation, and two accounting identities

$$YD = CD + ID + GD + XD - MD \tag{6}$$

$$K = (1 - \delta)K_{-1} + I, \tag{7}$$

giving effective demand as the usual sum of consumption, investment, government expenditures and exports minus imports (with D identifying demanded as distinct from realised quantities); and updating the capital stock through depreciation and investment.

In the EUP econometric estimations for the 8 main EC Countries, Austria and the United States, it is assumed that domestic demand is never rationed. Excess demands spill over into foreign trade – so that $CD = C$, $ID = I$, $GD = G$, but $X < XD$ and $M > MD$. [8]

Thus, estimation of the technical coefficients through a production function, of the capital stock and labour supply, and of the components of effective demand, yields time series YD_t, YC_t and YS_t from which equations (3) and (4) can be estimated. Figure 2 gives an illustration from Belgian data, 1955-85; the balanced growth of the sixties and the disequilibrium features that developed after 1973 are clearly visible.

---

[7]The specific formulae (3)-(4) are used extensively in the Appendix. For the purposes of Sections 2 and 3, it suffices to assume that L is a *linear homogeneous* function of its proximate determinants; the functional form is immaterial.

[8]The ratios $\frac{X}{XD}$ and $\frac{M}{MD}$ are modeled as functions of the degree of capacity utilisation $\frac{Y}{YC}$ or as functions of the rate of excess demand for domestic output $\frac{YD}{YC}$.

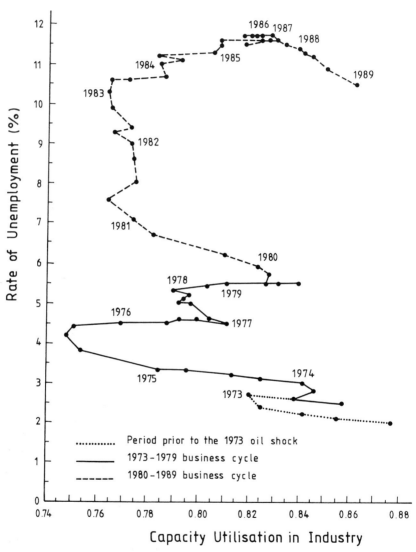

FIGURE 1. Source: European Commision, DG II, 1989.

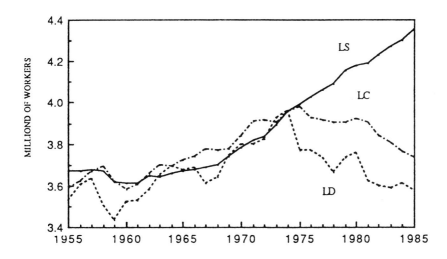

Fig. 2

Employment series: demand determined (dotted line);
capacity employment (chained line); labour supply (solid line); Belgium

Equation (4) leads to a natural decomposition of the growth rate of output into three proximate components, corresponding respectively to the growth rates of effective demand, of capacity output and of full-employment output:

$$\dot{y} = \eta_{Y \cdot YD} \; \dot{y}d + \eta_{Y \cdot YC} \; \dot{y}c + \eta_{Y \cdot YS} \; \dot{y}s \tag{8}$$

where $\eta_{Y \cdot YD}$ denotes the elasticity of output with respect to effective demand

$$\eta_{Y \cdot YD} = \frac{YD}{Y} \frac{\partial Y}{\partial YD} = \left(\frac{Y}{YD} \right)^{\rho}. \tag{9}$$

These elasticities satisfy

$$\eta_{Y \cdot YD} + \eta_{Y \cdot YC} + \eta_{Y \cdot YS} \equiv 1. \tag{10}$$

This identity has theoretical foundations in the model of aggregation underlying (3)-(4). It leads to an interpretation of the three elasticities as the proportions π_D, π_C, π_S of micromarkets where domestic output is determined by demand, by capacity and by availability of labour respectively, These proportions can also be estimated directly, for the manufacturing sector, from answers to business surveys; see Lambert (1988).

2.2 The empirical relevance of the European Unemployment Program for the present paper comes from the availability of estimated series for the proportions π_D, π_C, and π_S in ten countries over the period 1965-1986. (Unfortunately, no update of these series is available.) They are summarised in Table 1.9 of Drèze and Bean (1991), reproduced here as Table 1. Figure 3 gives a synthetic graphical presentation for 6 countries. Drèze and Bean (1991, pp.41-42) comment as follows "... the main message is the contrast between European and US patterns. In Europe the proportion of micromarkets where output is demand determined grew markedly from 1975 and especially from 1981 onward. In the United States there is little trend in the proportions; π_D moves procyclically, and π_C countercyclically.

The same message emerges in Figure 4 for the series $\pi_D \dot{y}d, \pi_C \dot{y}c$, and $\pi_S \dot{y}s$ – the decomposition of output growth into its three proximate determinants. A remarkable feature of the figure is the negligible contribution of capacity and labour supply growth to output growth in the 1980s, for most European countries and particularly for Austria, Belgium, Germany, and the United Kingdom. The proximate importance of demand for output growth since the second oil shock is clear – in contrast again to the situation in the United States, where capacity and labour supply availability retain significance."

From this first reference to empirical evidence, I feel justified in concluding – in line with Figure 1 – that the underutilisation of resources in Europe, but not in the US, from the middle seventies to the middle eighties, reflected the inadequacy of effective demand in relation to capacity output and full-employment output.

Table 1 Regime proportions

Year	Austria		Belgium		Britain		Denmark		Germany		Italy		Netherlands		Spain		United States	
	π_D	π_C	π_D	π_C	π_D	π_C	π_D	π_C	π_D	π_C	π_D	π_C	π_D	π_C	π_D	π_C	π_D	π_C
1965	0.65	0.23	0.36	0.26	0.40	0.15	0.13	0.65	0.23	0.44	0.28	0.15	0.25	0.29			0.25	0.49
1966	0.69	0.09	0.37	0.24	0.50	0.10	0.22	0.35	0.27	0.37	0.23	0.14	0.32	0.24			0.16	0.58
1967	0.46	0.21	0.54	0.16	0.72	0.08	0.34	0.18	0.54	0.18	0.42	0.18	0.55	0.08	0.22	0.20	0.12	0.61
1968	0.29	0.36	0.50	0.19	0.53	0.15	0.40	0.30	0.56	0.17	0.46	0.16	0.54	0.08	0.49	0.06	0.21	0.50
1969	0.24	0.52	0.35	0.28	0.46	0.20	0.13	0.60	0.22	0.42	0.45	0.27	0.36	0.24	0.36	0.15	0.19	0.49
1970	0.28	0.42	0.34	0.26	0.50	0.19	0.15	0.69	0.03	0.79	0.39	0.27	0.25	0.41	0.16	0.23	0.19	0.49
1971	0.28	0.53	0.43	0.20	0.71	0.14	0.28	0.46	0.09	0.69	0.58	0.27	0.36	0.31	0.18	0.14	0.41	0.33
1972	0.37	0.16	0.41	0.22	0.73	0.13	0.22	0.54	0.23	0.33	0.45	0.19	0.61	0.16	0.31	0.25	0.44	0.31
1973	0.24	0.11	0.29	0.34	0.33	0.22	0.16	0.76	0.24	0.36	0.20	0.25	0.48	0.29	0.06	0.66	0.31	0.42
1974	0.88	0.01	0.33	0.17	0.37	0.15	0.34	0.45	0.33	0.34	0.21	0.31	0.66	0.15	0.02	0.76	0.20	0.54
1975	0.91	0.01	0.67	0.23	0.75	0.07	0.88	0.03	0.73	0.13	0.61	0.26	0.79	0.13	0.13	0.63	0.31	0.45
1976	0.87	0.01	0.65	0.22	0.75	0.10	0.58	0.32	0.81	0.10	0.51	0.22	0.78	0.13	0.53	0.27	0.59	0.25
1977	0.87	0.01	0.69	0.17	0.66	0.11	0.61	0.32	0.60	0.22	0.48	0.19	0.76	0.13	0.48	0.31	0.45	0.34
1978	0.73	0.04	0.78	0.24	0.67	0.10	0.66	0.29	0.56	0.25	0.40	0.21	0.66	0.22	0.37	0.46	0.36	0.42
1979	0.77	0.04	0.71	0.24	0.65	0.12	0.30	0.63	0.47	0.31	0.35	0.20	0.41	0.48	0.50	0.43	0.28	0.49
1980	0.79	0.08	0.70	0.14	0.86	0.05	0.37	0.53	0.39	0.38	0.24	0.20	0.43	0.50	0.66	0.30	0.25	0.53
1981	0.86	0.03	0.83	0.17	0.91	0.05	0.63	0.28	0.52	0.29	0.44	0.19	0.64	0.34	0.83	0.15	0.40	0.40
1982	0.86	0.03	0.81	0.20	0.92	0.04	0.64	0.26	0.74	0.16	0.58	0.19	0.85	0.14	0.80	0.19	0.41	0.39
1983	0.74	0.06	0.79	0.28	0.86	0.09	0.52	0.34	0.84	0.12	0.73	0.19	0.83	0.16	0.70	0.29	0.65	0.24
1984	0.60	0.19	0.71	0.27	0.78	0.13	0.38	0.44	0.74	0.20	0.60	0.20	0.65	0.34	0.70	0.30	0.53	0.30
1985	0.58	0.21	0.72	0.17	0.71	0.15			0.53	0.36			0.42	0.56	0.78	0.22	0.37	0.40
1986			0.82		0.75	0.13			0.40	0.47			0.32	0.65	0.81	0.19	0.38	0.39

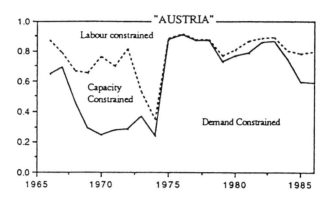

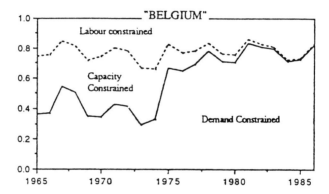

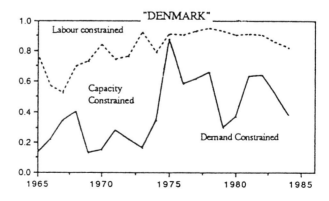

Fig. 3   Regime Proportions

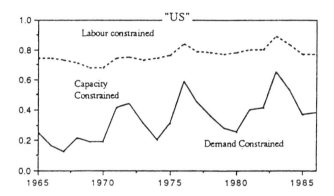

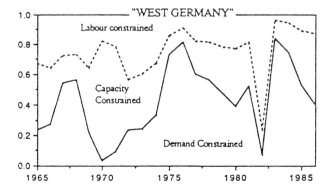

Fig. 3 (cont.)

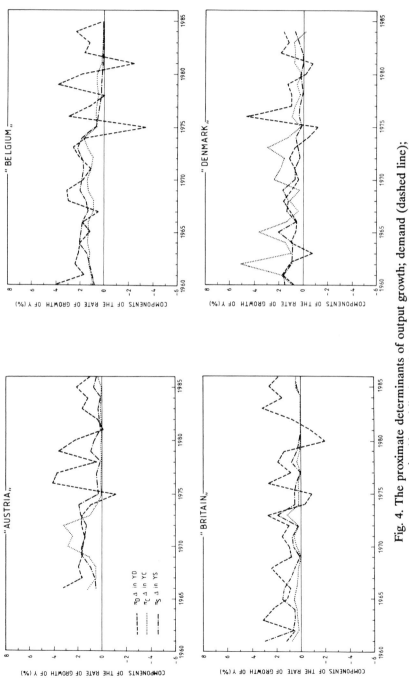

Fig. 4. The proximate determinants of output growth; demand (dashed line); capacity (dotted line); and labour force (chained line).

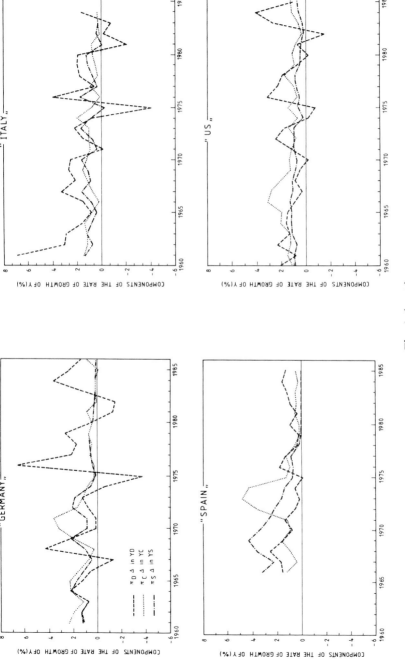

Fig. 4. (cont.)

2.3 In order to reconcile that conclusion with the widely held view that European unemployment came about through the supply shocks associated with oil prices, it is instructive to decompose the growth rates of YD into its four components

$$\dot{y}d = S_c\dot{c} + S_I\dot{i} + S_G\dot{g} + (S_X\dot{x}d - S_M\dot{m}d) \tag{11}$$

where S_C is the ratio of consumption to YD, and similarly for the other shares. That decomposition is presented in Figure 5. Drèze and Bean (1991, pp.43-52) comment as follows: "In comparison to the European experience, one might note for the United States: (1) the relatively low amplitude of the foreign trade component in that relatively closed economy, (2) the positive effect of government spending since the mid-1970s, especially in the 1980s, (3) the sustained effect of consumption, again especially in the 1980s. In Europe the amplitude of the foreign trade component is much more pronounced, especially for smaller countries such as Austria, Belgium, and Denmark.

Another striking feature shared by Europe and the United States is the amplitude of the investment contribution to GDP growth. This is somewhat surprising because investment amounts to less than 20 % of GDP; it is more volatile than the other components, so it repeatedly contributes plus or minus four percentage points to GDP growth. In particular, the sharp declines in aggregate demand in 1975 and 1981 (see Figure 4) are largely due to the collapse of investment in those years."

It is also relevant for my purpose here to note the low level of the contribution of government spending to aggregate demand in the eighties in Europe – as opposed to the United States from 1984 on. The early fiscal measures of the Reagan administration offer a vivid illustration of Keynesian stimulation, with induced effects on consumption, investment ... and the current account!

It is worth noting in addition that the resorption of inflation was more drastic in the US than in Europe, and was particularly sharp during the period of US recovery.

2.4 In trying to understand why the unemployment that arose out of the two oil shocks persisted so long, one is led to combine these observations about the demand side with an analysis of wage formation. In the absence of countercyclical budgetary measures, the only process through which unemployment could be eliminated is that of wage formation. Nowhere else indeed does unemployment play a specific autonomous role, except possibly for a negative (i.e. not self-correcting) influence on consumption.

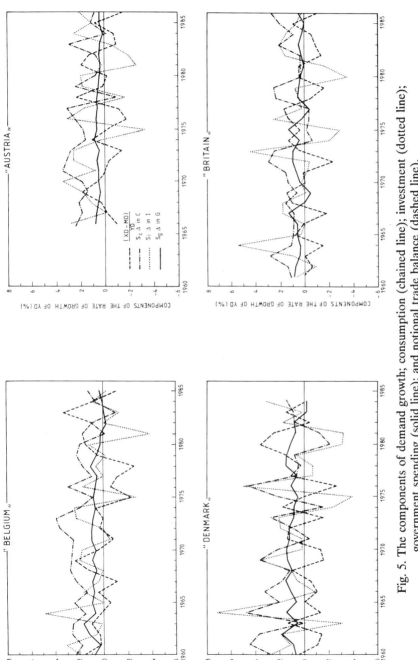

Fig. 5. The components of demand growth; consumption (chained line); investment (dotted line); government spending (solid line); and notional trade balance (dashed line).

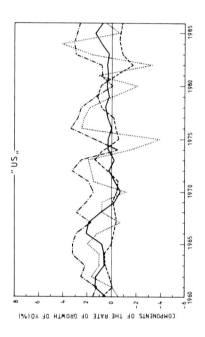

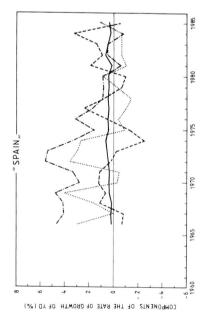

Fig. 5. (cont.)

Table 2 Adjusted wage share, total economy(% of GDP)

	1961-70	1971-80	1981-90	1990
Belgium	70.2	74.9	74.3	70.3
Germany	71.6	72.8	68.2	65.0
Spain	74.5	77.0	71.3	66.7
France	72.8	73.9	73.4	69.7
Italy	72.8	73.8	72.4	73.2
Netherlands	69.7	74.6	67.8	64.9
United Kingdom	72.7	73.8	73.1	75.4
Europe 12	73.8	74.7	72.0	70.3
United States	71.3	72.4	72.1	71.9

The wage equations estimated as part of the European Unemployment Program display two notable features, expressed as follows by Drèze and Bean (1991, p. 22): "First, with the exception of France, they all embody an error-correction mechanism that relates the *level* of real wages to the *level* of unemployment in the long run. This is in marked contrast to the traditional Phillips curve (of which the French equation is an example) which relates the unemployment rate to the *rate of change* of real wages. This level specification originates in the classic paper of Sargan (1964).

The second notable feature is that with the exception of the Danish, French, and American wage equations, the error-correction mechanisms imply that in the long run, it is essentially the share of wages in GNP (not the real wage) that is related to the unemployment rate. This would seem to correspond to the notion that in contrast to the United States, wage formation in Europe today is dominated by unions who are greatly concerned about distributional fairness." [9]

Table 2 reveals that the wage share in GNP has fallen substantially in the eighties – in Europe, but not in the United States.[10] By 1990, it had fallen to a level appreciably below that of the sixties. That lower wage share suggests – according to the EUP wage equations – that unemployment may by now have ceased to exert a persistent downwards pressure on wage dynamics. The elimination of unemployment should then result from the more indirect channels

---

[9] An error-correction mechanism relating the wage share to unemployment is confirmed by the altogether different methodology of Hendry and Mizon (1990), who submit quarterly UK data to a refined dynamic analysis and uncover a cointegrating relationship between the same variables.

[10] Source: *European Economy* 50, Statistical Annex, Table 31, p.244.

of increased profitability and increased competitiveness associated with lower wage shares. The first effect may have played a role in the investment revival of the late eighties – together with the plausible but hardly measurable "announcement effect" of the internal market. As for competitiveness, its effects are important for individual countries, but much weaker for Europe as a whole. Indeed, the trade of EC 12 with the rest of the world amounts only to some 10 % of its combined GDP, a fraction not markedly different from those prevailing in the US and Japan.

From all this, one could conclude that the current European situation is one of *underemployment equilibrium*; or alternatively that it reflects a *sluggishness of adjustment* compatible with the persistence of high unemployment for periods as long as a decade or more. In either case, the prospects for stimulation of output and employment through suitable public policies deserve attention. I now turn to these.

3 Fiscal Stance: Effectiveness

A theoretical assessment of the scope for stimulation of output and employment through debt-financed public expenditures or tax cuts, requires a more comprehensive model than could be estimated under the EUP. In particular, one needs to take into account the accumulation of public debt, its burden and its impact on private savings (the "Ricardian equivalence" issue) as well as on private investment (the "crowding out" issue).

In order to sort out the broader issues, it is helpful to distinguish a short-run analysis, where the quantity effects captured by short-run multipliers dominate (Section 3.1); and a medium-run analysis, which takes into account the adjustments of prices and wages (Section 3.2), then the impact of debt financing on savings and investment (Section 3.3).

3.1 The EUP models are interesting, for the refinement which they contribute to the evaluation of short-run multipliers. Taking into account the response of consumption and imports to changes in aggregate demand, but treating investment and government expenditures as exogenous, Drèze and Bean (1991, p. 53) obtain the following relation among growth rates:

$$\dot{y} = \frac{\pi_D}{1 + S_M \eta_{M \cdot YD} - \pi_D S_C \eta_{CY}} \cdot$$

$$\{S_I \dot{i} + S_G \dot{g} + S_X \eta_{X \cdot WT} \dot{w}_t + S_X \eta_{X \cdot (\frac{PW}{PX})} (\dot{pw} - \dot{px}) - S_M \eta_{M \cdot (\frac{PM}{P})} (\dot{pm} - \dot{p})\} \quad (12)$$

$$+ \frac{1 + S_M \eta_{M \cdot YD}}{1 + S_M \eta_{M \cdot YD} - \pi_D S_C \eta_{NY}} \{\pi_C \dot{yc} + \pi_S \dot{ys}\},$$

where $\dot{w}_t$ is the growth rate of world trade, and where PW, PX and PM denote respectively the price indices of world trade, exports and imports, with growth rates $p\dot{w}, p\dot{x}$ and $p\dot{m}$. They interpret that formula as follows:

$\dot{y} = \pi_D \times$ open-economy multiplier

$\times$ [contribution from growth rates of investment

and exogenous demand components

$+$ contributions from price effects of trade components]

$+$ contributions from $\dot{y}c$ and $\dot{y}s$.

Of particular interest is the expression for "$\pi_D \times$ open-economy multiplier"

$$\frac{\pi_D}{1 + S_M \eta_{M\cdot YD} - \pi_D \, S_C \, \eta_{CY}} = \frac{\pi_D}{1 + \frac{\partial M}{\partial YD} - \pi_D \frac{\partial C}{\partial Y}}. \tag{13}$$

Using estimates for EC 12 of $S_M = .1$, $\eta_{M \cdot YD} = 1.2$, $S_C = .62$ and $\eta_{CY} = 1$, this fraction simplifies to $[\frac{\pi_D}{1.12 - .62\pi_D}]$ and takes the values given in the first line of Table 3, as a function of π_D.

That table also includes, for comparison purposes, multiplier values for very open economies with an import share of 40 % ($S_M = .4$), like Belgium and the Netherlands; and for relatively open economies ($S_M = .25$) like France, Germany, Italy, Spain or the UK. The table thus reveals how sensitive the multiplier is, both to the state of the economy (extent of excess capacities, as measured by π_D) and to the degree of openness of the economy (as measured by S_M). A *first conclusion* (also supported by the US experience of the early eighties) is thus: *fiscal stimulation only makes sense for a relatively closed economy like* EC 12 *as distinct from even the largest member state; and only at times of substantial underutilisation of resources, capital as well as labour.*

The case for fiscal policy coordination in Europe rests precisely on this conclusion: fiscal policy makes sense for EC 12, not for individual member countries. Experience – in particular by Germany following 1978 or France following 1981 – confirms the lack of both effectiveness and sustainability (due to current account deficits) of isolated fiscal expansion. The argument is further strenghtened by the following remark. [11] In Europe, average rates or gross taxation (ratios of public receipts to GDP) are in the range of 40 % to 50 % in many countries, and marginal rates may be even higher. This implies that a country engaged in budget consolidation will tend to sterilise up to half of export-led increases in income, thereby dampening the expansionary efforts of its neighbours and reducing further their potential effectiveness.

3.2 That short-run analysis brings out the positive side of the case for coordination of fiscal stances. The negative side comes from medium-run con-

---

[11] See Drèze *et al.* (1988, Section 5.1.1).

Table 3 Open-economy multipliers

S_M		π_D	.4	.5	.6	.7	.8
.10	$\frac{\pi_D}{1.12-.62\pi_D}$		.46	.62	.80	1.02	1.28
.25	$\frac{\pi_D}{1.30-.62\pi_D}$		.38	.50	.65	.81	1.00
.40	$\frac{\pi_D}{1.48-.62\pi_D}$		.33	.43	.55	.67	.81

siderations. It has two main components: inflationary pressures (Section 3.2) and debt accumulation (Section 3.3).

The price equations estimated under the European Unemployment Program fail to validate the often heard concern that fiscal stimulation breeds demand-pull inflation. Indeed, in line with a number of earlier studies, these equations do not find evidence of demand-pull inflation – once the impact of wages and productivity is accounted for. The inflationary pressures would thus originate exclusively in the wage formation.

As noted in Section 2.4, lower unemployment means a higher equilibrium wage share, [12] presumably to be reached through higher real wages at higher nominal prices.

That understanding of price and wage formation has two important implications. First, it underscores the relevance of improving the realism of wage bargaining – to avoid the more costly route of wage-price spirals as a means of reconciling the income claims of capital and labour. Second, it means that expansionary policies aimed at reducing unemployment should not be discarded on grounds of inflationary bias, since the bias is rooted not in the fiscal instrument but rather in the very objective of the policies. In other words, a private investment boom would have exactly the same implications as the fiscal stimulation, *from the viewpoint of inflationary pressures*. To the extent that output and employment also depend upon capacity output, private investment will, of course, be more effective than public consumption – but a private investment boom would not be a natural development when unused capacities abund.

These views also underlie the so-called "two-handed approach" advocated by the EC Commission, and the Macroeconomic Policy Group, in the mid eighties: a supply-friendly cooperative fiscal expansion, with a combination of wage moderation and cuts in labour taxes aimed at improving profitability prospects. A *second conclusion* is thus: *fiscal expansion only makes sense when it is ac-*

---

[12]It was noted in Section 2.4 that the Danish and French wage equations did not fit that general pattern.

companied by measures enhancing wage moderation and labour costs reductions.

3.3 Accumulation of public debt raises one normative and two positive issues. The normative issue concerns the burden of the public debt; it is addressed in Section 4.2. The first positive issue concerns implications for private savings, the second concerns implications for interest rates and private investment.

The effectiveness of fiscal policy has been challenged by the proposition, called "Ricardian equivalence", that it makes no difference how public spending is financed – whether by taxes or borrowing – a sort of Modigliani-Miller theorem for public finance. [13] That proposition rests on the assumption that taxpayers would indifferently pay the taxes or spend the same amount on buying the bonds - thereby automatically saving whatever might be needed to pay the future taxes needed for the service of the debt.

Both logic and econometrics suggest that the extra savings generated in that reasoning will amount to a fraction only of the debt issue. Several econometric estimates suggest an order of magnitude like 25 % for the extent of offsetting through private savings; see for instance Kochin (1974), Perelman and Pestieau (1992) or Hutchinson (1992); but the multi-country analysis of Perelman and Pestieau also produces wrong signs for half the countries, and a higher propensity to consume out of government debt than out of private wealth... . Clearly, the empirical debate is far from closed!

Denoting the offsetting fraction by ψ, one could as a first approximation apply a coefficient of $(1-\psi)$ to the multiplier (13), and accept that the effectiveness of fiscal policy is reduced by a factor ψ.

Note that both the distortions associated with future taxation, and the offsetting private savings *à la* Ricardo, vanish when the public debt is issued to finance public investments yielding revenues available and sufficient to cover the service of the debt; or when the service of the debt is to be met, not through future taxation, but through future reductions of public expenditures.

A *third conclusion* is thus: *fiscal expansion is more readily justified when it corresponds to public investments yielding adequate returns; otherwise, the partial offsetting of public consumption by private savings must be taken into account.*

To the extent that public debt is not matched by voluntary savings of tax payers, it will increase the demand for financial capital, and thereby possibly raise interest rates. This, in turn, may discourage private investment – an effect usually called "crowding out". The strength of these effects depends upon the initial relationship of savings to investment in the economy and/or upon the relationship of the proposed operations to the size of the capital market (national or international) on which the debt is floated. They may also depend upon the accompanying monetary policy. An accommodating monetary policy would aim at keeping nominal interest rates unchanged, if that is possible. To the extent

---

[13] See Tobin (1980, Chap. III) for a thorough discussion.

that physical investment depends more naturally upon real rates than upon nominal rates, constancy of real rates should go a long way towards avoiding the "crowding out" effects.

There is, of course, substantial interdependence among the various considerations introduced successively in this section. Thus, if capacities are significantly underutilised, the motivation to invest is thereby reduced – as confirmed by the EUP investment functions (Drèze and Bean, 1991, Section – 5.3, p. 52). In that case, profitability of investment is enhanced by higher rates of utilisation, and the crowding out effects may be dominated by profitability effects. Actually, a positive response of private investment to fiscal stimulation is most likely when capacity utilisation is high, so that enlarging capacities through investment is needed to meet the additional demand. Still, the capacity-enlarging investments will only be undertaken if the demand expansion is perceived as recurrent, and not only as a transitory blip.

Similarly, constancy of nominal interest rates will be less unnatural if the fiscal expansion does not result in significant price inflation, which brings us back to the desirability of accompanying measures of wage moderation or labour tax reductions.

It is interesting to note, on the empirical side: (i) that the EUP researchers typically failed to identify an interest rate variable entering significantly in their investment equations; and (ii) that the simulation results reported in Section 5 find a positive effect of fiscal stimulation on private investment, when real interest rates are kept at baseline (and nominal rates are allowed to track inflation).

Tongue in cheek, I record as a *fourth conclusion: fiscal stimulation will be more effective if it does not crowd out private investment, either because it enhances profitability or because an accommodating monetary policy helps keeping real interest rates unaffected.*

3.4 Finally, and perhaps more significantly, one should be concerned about the distribution of the demand induced by the fiscal expansion (public expenditures, or private expenditures resulting from tax cuts or transfers) over the different micromarkets in the economy. What matters in the first instance is the availability of unused resources. By way of illustration, if the Belgian forestry department were to hire unskilled unemployed workers to improve the maintenance of public forests, the social cost of the measure would boil down to the real opportunity cost of the workers' time (≥ 0?) and of the imports associated with their additional consumption, but the net budgetary cost would be of the order of $1/3$ the gross outlay. If instead the same department were to improve forest maintenance by purchasing imported mechanical equipment, both the social and the net budgetary cost would be equal to the gross outlay.

This remark applies most directly to the investment collapse of 1975, following the first oil shock. In the same way that no overall wage adjustment could possibly have prevented that fall in aggregate demand, [14] similarly no general fiscal measure (like an income tax cut) could have made up for the missing investment demand. The only measure of immediate effectiveness would have consisted in public investments representing a commodity mix roughly comparable to that of the postponed or abandoned private investments. Such a mix includes investments in private housing and industrial structures, for which a public counterpart is relatively easy to imagine. But the mix also includes investments in machinery and equipment, for which a public counterpart is far from obvious; all the more so, if one recognises that the reason for private postponements (like finding out whether the oil price hike was temporary or permanent) would apply to some public investments as well (like accelerated replacement of motor vehicles).

Still, comparing the contributions of public expenditures to aggregate demand in 1975-76 and in 1981-82 for such countries as Austria, Belgium, Britain, Denmark and Germany, as shown in Figure 5, one finds prima facie evidence that the more restrictive fiscal stance which accompanied the second oil shock did contribute to magnify its impact – in spite of the more reasonable response of wages.

One intriguing issue, not addressed specifically in the foregoing, concerns the possibility of asymmetrical effects associated respectively with negative and positive demand shocks, hence possibly with fiscal contraction and fiscal expansion. Could it be the case that output and (after a lag) employment react more strongly to declines than increases in aggregate demand? I can think of at least three reasons for such an asymmetry: (i) wages and prices are more flexible upwards than downwards; (ii) it takes less time to lay off than to hire, to close down a plant than to build a new one; (iii) operating losses coupled with financial constraints are more compelling than profitability or excess liquidity. Each of these three reasons has a convincing ring, the first one being perhaps the more forceful.

4 Fiscal Stance: Efficiency

4.1 The case for interventionist fiscal policies ultimately rests on the imperfections and incompleteness of markets. The most basic imperfection is that, out of practical necessity, most manufactured goods and most services are sold by price-setting firms, instead of being auctioned at organised markets. [15] As shown by Roberts (1987, 1990), this entails the possibility for "coordina-

---

[14]Still a wage adjustment reflecting the income loss from worsened terms of trade was called for – and the fact that it did not occur at once has resulted in the loss of many jobs.

[15]Any reader unconvinced about the practical necessity is invited to consider the example, attributed to Robert Gordon, of automobile tires and parts. If these were auctioned at some Trade Center on Tuesday afternoons, what would one do in case of a blow out? Surely, some profit seeking entrepreneur would offer tires for sale at preannounced prices through a retail chain...

tion failures" resulting in underemployment equilibria... at Walrasian prices! (Macrotheorists use models of imperfectly competitive price-setting firms, not because imperfect competition is needed to model externalities and coordination failures, but because it is difficult to model the decisions of firms setting competitive prices.) The repeated underutilisation of capacity portrayed in Figure 1 most probably reflects excess supply at rationally set prices – suggesting the existence of alternative equilibria at identical prices but higher levels of activity. [16] It would be an attractive research project to establish, for a context of temporary general equilibrium with price-setting firms, the existence of a continuum of equilibria indexed by the fiscal stance...

Another source of imperfections, and of coordination failures, lies in the absence of futures markets and insurance markets (typically regrouped under the less transparent heading of "markets for contingent claims"). In the case of labour, employment contracts taking effect at a future date, either unconditionally or conditionally on specific events (like graduating three years hence), are sufficiently exceptional to be ignored! It follows that sequences of competitive equilibria on spot labour markets are not *ex ante* Pareto efficient, and are dominated on efficiency grounds alone by equilibria with downwards rigid wages, and unemployment benefits. [17] The simultaneous occurrence of extensive unemployment and high labour taxes is hard to justify on efficiency grounds, and reflects budgetary concerns. It follows that labour costs to firms grossly exaggerate the social opportunity cost of labour. Measures aimed at promoting the use of idle labour in conjunction with idle capacities are susceptible of mitigating the inefficiencies associated with the grossly distorted price signals embodied in private labour costs. If these measures are financed by public borrowing, to be offset by additional taxes at times of full use of resources, they provide scope for mitigating the intertemporal inefficiencies associated with the absence of suitable markets for intertemporal resource allocation.

4.2 Still, before concluding that efficiency gains are in sight, one must take into account the burden of the debt. I wish to argue that, other things equal (and in particular keeping constant the stock of physical capital carried forwards), the burden of internally held public debt is the deadweight loss of the taxation required to service that debt. Because additional debt is a substitute for additional taxation today, it may be viewed as a mere shifting forwards of the burden of taxation.

Intertemporal redistribution of taxation may serve two purposes. If deadweight losses are a convex function of tax rates (increasing marginal distortion), smoothing over time makes sense. [18] One should of course explain convinc-

---

[16]The *existence* of alternative equilibria at *identical* prices is precisely the theoretical result established by Roberts (1987, 1990); actual price and wage dynamics are of course more complex.

[17]See Drèze (1988), Drèze and Gollier (1990).

[18]See Barro (1979).

ingly that shifting forwards does indeed entail smoothing – not bunching at a later date! Such an explanation always entails an element of guesswork or forecasting, since the time of fiscal service and the intervening growth of nominal income are uncertain. The other purpose comes in when the deadweight loss itself depends upon the state of the economy, and that state varies over time. A relevant measure of such variation is the proportion π_D of demand-constrained firms. When π_D is very high, taxes that reduce current consumption lead to less output and employment, and the deadweight loss is high. When π_D is very low, the reduction of consumption eases off demand pressures and import spillovers, resulting in a lower deadweight loss. [19] That second purpose again rests on the hope that debt will effectively be repaid in better times (with a lower π_D). And it rests on the premise that debt-financed fiscal stimulation is sufficiently effective to be ... efficient. As suggested in Section 3, that premise is far from granted.

4.3 A complete case for fiscal policy thus requires a comprehensive assessment of its utility implications for the economic agents, balancing its current effectiveness against the prospective distortions of future debt service. A modest step in that direction is made in the Appendix, where I use the short-run framework of Section 3.1 to elicit conditions under which the overall impact of a debt financed temporary fiscal stimulus is positive, *taking into account the negative impact of the future fiscal contraction required to service the debt.*

Limited as it remains, the analysis in the Appendix is suggestive on two counts. First, it uses the theoretical specification outlined in Sections 2.1 and 3.1, which turns out to be richer (for our purposes) than alternative specifications. Second, it includes a crude attempt at dealing formally with uncertainty – a crucial consideration here – through reliance on prices for contingent claims congruent with the Capital Asset Pricing Model (CAPM).

The deterministic analysis reveals that, to a first approximation, anticipating public expenditures – say from a future date t to the present date 0 – will be efficient whenever *demand expands sufficiently faster than supply*, between 0 and t; see formulae (A.14)-(A.16) and the accompanying comments.

The logic of that conclusion was announced in Section 4.2: when π_D is lower at the time of debt service than at the time of debt-financed fiscal expansion, the reduction in output and employment associated with the contraction is quantitatively less significant than the initial expansion; and a *lower* π_D at time t than at time 0 means than aggregate demand has expanded *faster* than aggregate supply, between 0 and t. The formulae in the Appendix give a more precise content to that heuristic reasoning. They reveal that the required differential in the growth rates of demand and supply is related *positively* to the initial inadequacy of demand (π_D at time 0, denoted π_0 in the Appendix), to

---

[19]Taking price effects into account reduces somewhat the deadweight loss when π_D is high, and is apt to reduce it more significantly when π_D is low, which strenghtens the conclusion.

the real interest paid on the debt, as influenced by both the real rate and the time span (t) over which interest accrues; and to the degree of "mismatch" $(\frac{1}{\rho})$ in the economy.

The overall conclusion is not *logically* different from more traditional views which would recommend fiscal expansion at times when it will generate more output gains than price inflation, and contraction at times when it will ease off inflationary pressures; that is, views which would recommend countercyclical budgetary policies.

What the formulae bring out is the relevance of supply-side developments for an assessment of the efficiency of demand management; and the relevance of "mismatch", which reduces that efficiency (basically, for the reasons discussed in Section 3.4 above).

A further step taken in the Appendix consists in recognising that future levels of aggregate demand and supply cannot be predicted with certainty. What is the nature of the "risk premium" associated with that uncertainty about the state of the economy at the time of reimbursement (of contraction)? The Appendix throws some light on that issue, by relying on the first approximation embodied in the Capital Asset Pricing Model (CAPM). A by-product of the celebrated CAPM is a set of implicit but easily calculable "prices for contingent claims", denoted q_s in the Appendix, through which future changes in output are discounted for "time-and-state-of-the-economy". Using these prices, rather than probabilities, in weighting future developments is equivalent to introducing a proper risk premium in the analysis – at the CAPM level of approximation.

As shown in the Appendix, these considerations lead to deflate the *expected* differential between demand and supply growth by a factor equal to the *product* of a risk factor, reflecting relative risk aversion, and the expected growth rate of aggregate output – a product denoted R. $\frac{\Delta Y}{Y_0}$ in formulae (A17)-(A18). (A further adjustment, given by the risk factor times the covariance between the growth rates of output and the differential between the growth rate of demand and supply, seems to be of secondary importance).

It was by no means evident *a priori* that the risk premium should be proportional to the expected growth of aggregate output. Also, the expression so obtained suggests that the expected efficiency of fiscal policy is reduced by a factor of some 25 % or so (say 10 % to 40 %...) on account of the uncertainty – essentially because the welfare *cost* of the contraction is *negatively correlated* with the state of the economy.

Again, this conclusion is in line with traditional wisdom. If expansion today leads to contraction tomorrow *in a bad state* (due in particular to inadequate demand, as it happened in the early eighties), the cost of the contraction is higher in terms of output loss, and the output loss is compounded with the additional welfare cost of suffering the loss in a bad state. The risk premium emerging in the Appendix formulae is precisely a measure of that aggravation-through-compounding.

A simple formula bringing together all these elements says that a fiscal stimulus through debt financed expenditures at time 0 offset by a contraction at time t in the amount required to service the debt is efficient whenever

$$\left[\frac{E_0(\Delta_t Y D)}{Y D_0} - \frac{E_0(\Delta_t Y P)}{Y P_0} \right] \left[1 - R \cdot \frac{E_0(\Delta_t Y)}{Y_0} \right] > \frac{\phi_t}{\rho(1 - \pi_0)} \qquad (14)$$

where E stands for the expectation operator as of time 0, YP stands for potential output as defined by (A.7), (i.e. combining YC and YS), R is the risk factor, ϕ_t the interest payments per unit of debt and π_0 is π_D at time 0.

These are tentative results that require discussion and scrutiny. They illustrate a line of analysis insufficiently explored in the contemporary literature. And they point to an array of conclusions that could be checked against the diverse experience of European countries. Did those countries currently burdened by excessive debt (like Belgium or Italy) implicitly violate an efficiency condition like (14)? Could that condition be assessed empirically for EC 12 today, in order to reach firmer conclusions regarding the restrictive fiscal stance rule adopted in Maastricht?

As stressed in my introduction and conclusion, I advocate both more attention to, and a more open attitude towards, the definition of a proper aggregate fiscal stance for the relatively closed EC 12. Submitting that issue to a formal yet realistic efficiency analysis belongs prominently on the research agenda.

5 Some Simulation Results

5.1 Given the complexity of the theoretical discussion, it is natural to turn to econometric simulations for additional insights into the effects of fiscal policy. And it is particularly natural to look at those simulations which European policy makers might turn to. I am not aware of many attempts at simulating directly the effects of fiscal measures at the European level. One exception, dating back to 1986, comes from the COMPACT model (Dramais 1986), estimated directly from aggregate data for EC 10. A set of simulations covering the period 1986-90 were published in March 1986, leading to the crisp conclusion "that supply shocks without perspective of significant demand expansion are just about as worthless as demand shocks made without regard to their medium-term supply consequences." (Dramais, 1986, p.143). Readers were duly warned "that what is described are the properties of a still experimental model on which judgment should be applied before making any linkage to the reactions of the real world." (*ibidem*, p.135). Still, it is instructive to look at some of the results, as summarised in Table 4. In particular, these results may serve as a benchmark to interpret the more recent country simulations reviewed in Section 5.2.

The four lines of Table 4 correspond to four (out of seven) alternative exercises. The first line corresponds to a pure demand shock (public expenditures raised by 1 % of baseline GDP), sustained year after year. In line with many comparable simulations, the multiplier effects decline over time, due to rising wages, prices and interest rates; and the current account deteriorates. The budget deficit roughly mirrors the evolution of GDP, and the debt/GDP ratio deteriorates some.

The second line of Table 4 corresponds to a supply-side measure: nominal wages per employee are kept year after year 5 % below baseline – with real public expenditures kept at baseline. Given that nominal wages per employee grew on average at some 5.5 % per year over the period 1985-89 in EC 12, this simulation corresponds to a one-year wage freeze with no catching up. Also, given that the average wage share in GDP for EC 12 stood around 70 %, the associated reduction in the wage bill is of the order of 3.5 % of GDP. The results suggest a major gain on price inflation, reflecting the underlying specification in COMPACT of average cost pricing. With little change in real output, nominal GDP falls, so that the debt/GDP ratio deteriorates again.

The third and fourth lines correspond to "two-handed" policies, combining reductions in wage costs with fiscal expansion. In line 3, the same degree of wage moderation as in line 2 is combined with an adjustment in public expenditures keeping nominal GDP at baseline. If the results are to be believed, they are spectacular.

Although this policy initially causes an additional deficit of .9 % (- 1.2 % in line 3 as against -.3 % in line 2), by the fourth year the fiscal stance and debt/GDP ratio are the same. The gains on price inflation are also nearly equal. But the advantages of the "two-handed" policy for investment, output and significantly employment are substantial. The only deterioration concerns foreign reserves (- 3 % of GDP), which decline roughly by the value of the additional private investment – giving content to the idea of relying on international capital markets to finance expansion. In short, the comparison of lines 2 and 3 substantiates the claimed superiority of two-handed policies over single-handed supply-side policies.

Line 4 also corresponds to a two-handed policy, because a reduction in wage costs is financed by the public budget. Indeed, the reduction comes through the social security contributions. The simulation imposes that the reduction be reflected in prices (average cost pricing), whereas the wage formation process is unchanged. The size of the reduction in labour costs (1 % of GDP) is roughly 30 % of that in line 3, which helps explain why the gains in output and employment are also around 30 % of those in line 3.[20] The main qualitative difference relative to line 3 concerns the public deficit and debt/GDP ratio, which are directly affected by the tax cuts. The comparison of lines 1 and 4 substantiates the claimed superiority of two-handed policies over single-handed demand-side policies – and more specifically, of cuts in labour taxes over general public expenditures. (Productive public investments are another story.)

---

[20]Although it would have simplified comparisons to normalise the simulations, I did not feel justified in using linear approximations to that effect. Note however the similarity across rows of the 1989 Debt/GDP ratio.

5.2 The COMPACT model, based on aggregate data for EC 10, was an innovative attempt at exploring directly policy alternatives for Europe, while preparing a country-based final model. That model, called QUEST, is now operational – see *European Economy* (1991, 47) – and incorporates a full matrix of bilateral trade flows. From the research angle, it may be hoped that a revised version of COMPACT, mimicking the QUEST specification, will be estimated again from EC 12 aggregate data, so that results from COMPACT simulations could be compared with those from linked simulations under QUEST.

One set of QUEST simulations recently performed at DG II of the European Communities – see *European Economy* (1991, 47) – could hopefully be extended in that direction. These simulations investigate, for each of the 12 member states (except Luxemburg), the effects of a permanent increase in public expenditures[21] amounting to 1 % of GDP. These simulations correspond exactly to line 1 of Table 4. Unfortunately for my purpose here, the simulations were run country by country – in "unlinked mode". Each simulation investigates the effects within a single country of a fiscal expansion (in the form of increased public expenditure) *in the same country, keeping all external influences at baseline.* The difference from baseline in export quantities is thus entirely due to differences in export prices, at unchanged foreign demand. And the fiscal expansion is strictly country specific – with no feedback at all. Thus, if country A expands and increases its imports from country B, the "unlinked mode" ignores the fact that country B produces more and therefore imports more from country A.

Linked simulation of *simultaneous fiscal expansion* in all 12 countries would differ in two main respects: (i) each country would benefit from the expansion by its neighbours, in the form of increased demand for its exports coming close (up to 90 % as a first approximation) to matching its own additional imports; (ii) price and wage effects would be roughly symmetrical across the EC countries, so that competitiveness effects would be limited to trade with the rest of the world. Thus, the effects on output, employment, budgets and significanlty the current account should be more favourable; it is only for consumer prices that effects should be less favourable (more inflation), because each country's import prices would increase *pari passu* with the export prices of European partners.

A summary presentation of the unlinked QUEST simulations is given in Table 5, where countries are listed in decreasing order of openness. [22] It will be apparent that openness reduces short-run multipliers (the column headed "Real GDP 1990") and exposure to domestic demand-pull inflation (CPI, 1993), but increases current account deficits (reserves drain). Openness is not related in

---

[21] The publication refers to public investment – but acknowledges that the label "investment" has no specific implications yet.

[22] The measure used in the table is the ratio of imports to final demand, as published in *European Economy* (1991, 47). I would have used the ratio to GDP of "imports net of the import content of exports". The two measures are not markedly different – though not identical.

any obvious way to the other measures tabulated.

In comparing the results in Table 5 with those in the first line of Table 4, one should bear in mind the differences in geographical basis, but also in time periods (1986-89 versus 1990-93) and in model specification. Running linked simulations with QUEST, also for 1986-89, would help isolate the consequences of different model specifications.

Although stronger in Table 5 than in line 1 of Table 4, employment effects are disappointing, reflecting the sluggish adjustment of employment to output. That standard finding of econometric simulations remains to be reconciled with the surprising growth of employment over the period 1988-90: 1.4 % *per year* for EC 12, a rate never reached over the past 40 years. Yet, the average GDP growth rate was only 3.4 % for these years – rewarding, no doubt, but still well below the 4.7 % average for the period 1960-74 (over which employment grew at .2 % per year on average...). Understanding the causes and nature of the 1988-90 acceleration deserves attention from researchers.

Table 5 confirms the importance of linking fiscal stimulation with wage moderation. Although the QUEST models do ascribe some inflationary influence to changes in capacity utilisation, the main source of price inflation comes through the effect of lower unemployment on wages. The wage-price spiral does the rest – more strongly so in the less open economies (where import prices have a lower weight in the CPI). It would be interesting to run simulations with fixed nominal wages, for comparison, or with reductions in social insurance contributions.

The last column of Table 5 is taken from a parallel set of simulations where nominal interest rates are kept at baseline levels. These simulations yield more favourable results, mostly due to additional private investment. In some countries - especially Germany and the UK – the difference is sizeable. (In Germany, the additonal private investment exceeds 2 % of baseline in that case.) That column points to the relevance of an accommodating monetary policy as a complement to fiscal stimulation.

Table 4 COMPACT simulations
Shocks sustained 1986-1989

	Real GDP[a]		Employ-ment[b]	Budget balance (%GDP)[b]		Debt/GDP ratio[b,c]	Foreign reserves[b,d] (%GDP)	CPI[a]	Real priv. investm.[a] average	Nominal long term interest r.
	1986	1989	1989	1986	1989	1989	1989	1989	1986-89	1989
Public expenditures (+1% of GDP)	1.1	0.6	0.1	-0.9	-0.6	+1.7	-1.8	+1.4	1.0	+1.7
Nominal wages (5% below baseline)	-1.0	0.5	1.2	-0.3	+0.2	+2.0	+1.0	-3.2	1.4	-2.8
Nominal wages (5% below baseline) and public expenditures (keeping nominal GDP at baseline)	1.3	3.2	4.2	-1.2	+0.2	+1.8	-2.0	-3.0	2.8	-2.2
Social insurance Contributions (1% of GDP)	0.3	1.3	1.4	-0.9	-0.3	+2.4	-0.8	-1.2	1.6	-1.0

[a]Differences from baseline in percent (of baseline levels).
[b]Differences from baseline in percentage points.
[c]Calculated as $\frac{\Delta Debt}{GDP} - \frac{Debt}{GDP} \frac{\Delta GDP}{GDP}$, where $\frac{\Delta Debt}{GDP}$ is summed over four years, $\frac{\Delta GDP}{GDP}$ is the 1989 nominal figure.
[d]Algebraic sum over four years of differences (from baseline) of current account as % of GDP.

Table 5 Unlinked QUEST simulations:
Increase in public investment
by 1% of baseline GDP,
real interest rates fixed
(percentage differences from baseline)

Openness[a]	Country	Real GDP		Employ-ment[b]	Budget balance[b] (%GDP)	Debt/GDP ratio[b,c]	Foreign reserves[b,d] (%GDP)	CPI	Real priv. investm. average	ΔGDP nominal rates fixed[e]
		1990	1993	1993	1993	1993	1993	1993	1990-93	1993
0.41	Belgium	0.6	0.5	0.2	-1.2	2.6	-2.4	1.1	0.8	0.1
0.37	Netherlands	0.7	0.6	0.3	-1.1	3.1	-2.7	1.3	1.4	-
0.25	Denmark	1.1	0.6	0.4	-0.6	1.0	-0.6	0.5	0.5	0.5
0.23	Germany (West)	1.0	0.4	0.3	-1.2	2.8	-1.6	2.7	0.5	0.4
0.23	United Kingdom	0.8	-0.1	0.3	-0.6	1.4	-1.5	1.7	0.8	0.9
0.19	France	1.1	0.9	0.4	-0.9	2.2	-2.1	2.7	1.7	0.2
0.17	Spain	1.1	0.1	0.2	-0.9	2.3	-1.4	4.7	0.8	0.2
0.16	Italy	1.0	0.9	0.4	-2.9	5.1	-1.2	2.4	1.5	-
0.12	United States	1.6	0.4	0.2	-0.9	n.a.	-1.2	3.8	0.9	0.1

[a] Ratio of imports to final demand ($\frac{M}{Y+M}$).

[b] Differences from baseline in percentage points.

[c] Calculated as $\frac{\Delta Debt}{GDP} - \frac{Debt}{GDP}\frac{\Delta GDP}{GDP}$, where $\frac{\Delta Debt}{GDP}$ is summed over four years, $\frac{\Delta GDP}{GDP}$ is the 1993 nominal figure.

[d] Algebraic sum over four years of differences (from baseline) of current account as % of GDP.

[e] Should be added to column 2 to obtain the results from QUEST simulations with fixed nominal interest rates.

6   Overall Conclusion

In this paper, I have tried to summarise what I have learned over the past decade about the relevance of the fiscal stance for economic performance. There is little doubt in my mind that the fiscal stance matters, for large relatively closed economies like the US or EC 12. Models pretending to show that fiscal and monetary policies (sometimes combined in a single variable like helicopter transfers) do not affect output and employment, are misleading in their excessive simplicity. They either suppress essential mechanisms at work in the determination of equilibrium quantities, or they suppress the slow adjustment process through which equilibrium is approached. Wether one interprets Europe's persistent unemployment as evidence of underemployment equilibria, or as evidence of sluggishness protracting adjustment over a decade or more, the relevance of fiscal stance is basically the same. The empirical record is suggestive on that score. In particular, one cannot ignore the role of tax reform and public expenditures in prompting the US recovery of 1984, at a time when European Governments were trying to consolidate their budgets. Hopefully, research will unveil the nature of the European recovery of 1988, where both tax reforms and the announcement effect of the internal market may have played a role.

I have tried to argue, convincingly I hope, that *the aggregate fiscal stance of EC 12 matters* – beyond the budgetary preoccupations of individual member states. I find insufficient recognition of this feature in such Community documents as *One Market, One Money* (*European Economy*, 1990, 44). In particular, I find no recognition of the danger that rules of fiscal discipline might result in an *inefficiently restrictive* aggregate fiscal stance...

Yet, I fully realise that the case for demand management through fiscal policy is far from tight. It is one thing to argue, as I did in Section 2, that output is largely demand-determined at times of persistent underutilisation of capital and labour. It is quite another thing to establish that fiscal stimulation is apt to be effective in restoring growth of output and employment. The theoretical discussion in Section 3 reveals that the path of effective policies is narrow and hazardous. The main *conditions* for effectiveness, and associated hazards, seem to be:

(i) substantial underutilisation of resources, i.e. few supply bottlenecks;

(ii) a relatively closed economy – like EC 12, but unlike a single member state –, i.e. few import leakages;

(iii) wage moderation and/or labour tax reductions, i.e. limited risks of seeing the expansion evaporate in price inflation;

(iv) a genuine intertemporal substitution, i.e. a limited offsetting of public expenditures by increased private savings (the "Ricardian equivalence" issue) or by reduced private investment (the "crowding out" issue); this condition is more likely to be met in case of public investment (including education) than in case of public consumption; it is also more likely to be met if an accommodating monetary policy helps keeping interest rates in check;

(v) well-targeted fiscal measures, that create opportunities for releasing specific unused resources, rather than blind general measures whose effects are more apt to evaporate in import leakages and price inflation.

This is a formidable bill of requirements, and it is understandable that many would be tempted to dismiss fiscal measures altogether on grounds of inaccessible fine tuning. On the other hand, when there is evidence of unused capacities and high unemployment, supply-friendly measures of fiscal expansion, buttressed by wage moderation and concentrated on labour tax reductions or public investment, make sense at the level of the relatively closed European Community. Such measures should not be dismissed without further discussion. In particular, they should under present circumstances be retained as a credible alternative to *rules* which embody a deflationary bias. These rules should not be adopted either without further discussion. The case should not be treated as closed. Further professional debate is called for. That, in a nutshell, is the message of the present paper.

The debate – and supportive research – should aim at a better assessment of the implications of Europe's aggregate fiscal stance for effective demand, then output and employment; of the conditions for effectivenes and efficiency of fiscal policy; and of the prospects for balanced mixes of fiscal, monetary and incomes policies. At this stage, we cannot expect Europe to do better than the rather arbitrary Maastricht rules of fiscal discipline. It is important for all concerned to realise the existence of the contractionary bias, and to face the implications.

7   References

Barro, R.J. (1979), On the determinaton of the public debt, *Journal of Political Economy* 87, 940-71.

Begg, D., P.A. Chiappori, F. Giavazzi, C. Mayer, D. Neven, L. Spaventa, X. Vives and C. Wyplosz (1991), *Monitoring European Integration: The Making of a Monetary Union*, CEPR Annual Report, London.

Blanchard, O., R. Dornbusch, J.H. Drèze, H. Giersch, R. Layard and M. Monti (1985), Employment and growth in Europe: A two-handed approach, CEPS Paper 21, Bruxelles.

Blanchard O., R. Dornbusch and R. Layard (1986), *Restoring Europe's Prosperity*, Cambridge, Mass.: MIT Press.

Buiter, W.H. (1992), Should we worry about the fiscal numerology of Maastricht? CEPR Discussion Paper 668, London.

Dramais, A. (1986), Compact: A prototype macroeconomic model of the European Community in the world economy, *European Economy* 27, 111-160.

Drèze, J.H. (1988), L'arbitrage entre équité et efficacité en matière d'emploi et de salaires, 8ème Congrès des Economistes Belges de Langue Française, Commission 6, Chap IV, 121-146, 1988; reprinted in *Recherches Economiques de Louvain* 55, 1-31 (1989); also reprinted as Chapter 12 in J. H. Dréze (1991).

Drèze, J.H. (1991), *Underemployment Equilibria: Essays in Theory, Econometrics and Policy*, Cambridge: Cambridge University Press.

Drèze, J.H. and C. Bean (1990), European unemployment: Lessons from a multi-country econometric study, *Scandinavian Journal of Economics* 92, 135-165.

Drèze, J.H. and C. Bean (1991), Europe's unemployment problem: Introduction and synthesis", Chap. 1 in Drèze et al. (1991); reprinted as Chap. 16 in J.H. Drèze (1991).

Drèze, J.H., C. Bean, J.P. Lambert, F. Mehta and H. Sneessens (1991), *Europe's Unemployment Problem*, Cambridge, Mass.: MIT Press.

Drèze, J.H. and C. Gollier (1990), Risk-sharing on the labour market and second-best wage rigidities", CORE DP 9067, Louvain-la-Neuve.

Drèze, J.H., C. Wyplosz, C. Bean, F. Giavazzi and H. Giersch (1988), The two-handed growth strategy for Europe: autonomy through flexible cooperation", *Recherches Economiques de Louvain* 54, 5-52; reprinted as Chap. 18 in Drèze (1991).

Ginsburgh V.A. and J.L. Waelbroeck (1981), *Activity Analysis and General Equilibrium Modelling*, Amsterdam: North-Holland.

Hendry, D.F. and G. Mizon (1990), Evaluating dynamic econometric models by encompassing the VAR, Applied Economics Discussion Paper 102, Oxford.

Hutchinson, M.M. (1992), Budget policy and the decline of national saving revisited", BIS *Economic Papers* 33, Basel.

Kochin, L. (1974), Are future taxes anticipated by consumers, *Journal of Money, Credit and Banking*.

Lambert J.P. (1988), *Disequilibrium Macroeconomic Models, Theory and Estimation of Rationing Models Using Business Survey Data*, Cambridge: Cambridge University Press.

Mélitz, J. (1991), Brussels on a single money", *Open-Economies Review* 2, 323-336.

Perelman, S. and P. Pestieau (1992), The Determinants of the Ricardian equivalence in the OECD countries" in H. Verloon and F. Van Winden, eds., *The Political Economy of Public Debt*, Amsterdam: North-Holland.

Roberts, J. (1987), An equilibrium model with involuntary unemployment at flexible competitive prices and wages", *American Economic Review* 77, 856-74.

Roberts, J. (1990), Equilibrium without market clearing", Chap. 6 in B. Cornet and H. Tulkens, eds., *Contributions to Operations Research and Ecnometrics*, Cambridge, Mass.: MIT Press.

Sargan J. (1964), Wages and prices in the UK: A study in econometric methodology, in P. Hart, G. Mills and J. Whitaker, eds., *Econometric Analysis for Economic Planning*, London: Butterworths, London.

Sneessens H. and J.H. Drèze (1986a), "A discussion of Belgian unemployment, combining traditional concepts and disequilibrium econometrics", *Economica* 53, 89-119.

Sneessens H. and J.H. Drèze (1986b), What, if anything, have we learned from the rise of unemployment in Belgium, 1974-1983?, *Cahiers Economiques de Bruxelles* 110/111, 21-66.

Tobin J. (1980), *Asset Accumulation and Economic Activity*, Oxford: Basil Blackwell.

Waelbroeck J. and A. Dramais (1974), DESMOS: a model for the coordination of economic policies in the EEC countries, in A. Ando, R. Herring and R. Martson, eds., *International Aspects of Stabilisation Policies*, Boston: Federal Reserve Bank.

Wyplosz, C. (1992), La France et sa politique économique en UEM", mimeo, INSEAD, Fontainbleau.

8   Appendix

In this appendix, I use the model of Section 2 to spell out necessary and sufficient conditions for intertemporal efficiency of a debt-financed temporary fiscal stimulus that does not influence wages, prices and interest rates. Admittedly, this proviso is quite restrictive, and unrealistic for many practical purposes. But, to me at least, the line of analysis developed here is novel and quite instructive. See Section 4.3 above for further comments and discussion.

The exercise calls for shifting some public expenditures from a future date t to the present date 0. That is, G_0 is to be increased to $G_0 + \Delta G_0$, the increase ΔG_0 being financed by debt bearing interest at some rate ν (per period). Taxes are unchanged, and the debt is to be reimbursed at time t by reducing public expenditures then in the amount $-\Delta G_t = (1 + \nu)^t \Delta G_0$ required to cover the full service of the debt. (Thus, no provision by consumers for future taxes is needed, and the "Ricardian equivalence" issue does not arise.)

The efficiency analysis calls for combining the positive impact on output and employment from the initial fiscal stimulus with the negative impact of the fiscal contraction at time t. Note that, in a purely Keynesian model with constant multiplier, the negative future impact would exceed the immediate positive impact to the full extent of the interest charges. Indeed, by construction,

$$\Delta G_t = -(1 + \nu)^t \, \Delta G_0 < -\Delta G_0. \qquad (A.1)$$

Any justification of the stimulus would need to rely on discounting the future impact at a rate higher than that applicable to the debt. Such discounting could reflect the time preferences of consumers benefiting from the public expenditures – either directly, if the expenditures correspond to public goods; or indirectly, through the private incomes associated with the expenditures. (Note that these direct and indirect benefits may be *added*; there is no double counting, because the implications for private incomes of the future contraction are duly taken into account.) The implied discount rate is denoted λ.

In what follows, I deal exclusively with output gains, on the assumption that employment follows. It is true that a further argument could be based on differentials over time in the elasticity of employment with respect to output. Ideally, one would like to implement the stimulus $\Delta G_0 > 0$ at a time when the output-elasticity of hirings is high, and to implement the contraction $\Delta G_t < 0$ at a time when that elasticity is low.

This appendix consists of two sections, devoted successively to a deterministic analysis and then to a stochastic extension.

8.1 Deterministic Analysis

The analysis is based on the multiplier formula (13), namely:

$$\mu := \frac{dY}{dYD}\bigg|_{p,w,I,X} = \frac{\pi_D}{1 + \frac{\partial M}{\partial YD} - \pi_D \frac{\partial C}{\partial Y}} := \frac{\pi_D}{1 + m - c\,\pi_D}, \qquad (A.2)$$

where I introduce the notation μ for the multiplier, m and c respectively for the propensities to import and to consume.

The basic relations are

$$\Delta Y_0 = \mu_0 \Delta G_0 \qquad (A.3)$$

$$\Delta Y_t = \mu_t \Delta G_t = -\mu_t (1 + \nu)^t \Delta G_0 \qquad (A.4)$$

so that

$$\Delta Y_0 + (1 + \lambda)^{-t} \Delta_t Y_t \gtrless 0 \qquad (A.5)$$

according as

$$\mu_0 \gtrless \mu_t \frac{(1 + \nu)^t}{(1 + \lambda)^t} := \mu_t (1 + \phi_t) \qquad (A.6)$$

thereby defining ϕ_t as equal to $\frac{(1+\nu)^t}{(1+\lambda)^t} - 1$.

It simplifies the notation to define

$$YP = (YC^{-\rho} + YS^{-\rho})^{-\frac{1}{\rho}} \qquad (A.7)$$

so that (4) in Section 2 may be written as

$$Y = (YD^{-\rho} + YP^{-\rho})^{-\frac{1}{\rho}}. \qquad (A.8)$$

Also, (10) may now be written as

$$\eta_{Y \cdot YD} + \eta_{Y \cdot YP} \equiv 1 \equiv \pi_D + \pi_P := \pi + (1 - \pi). \qquad (10')$$

Thus, $\pi_D = \pi$ (by omission of the subscript) and $\pi_P = 1 - \pi = \pi_C + \pi_S$.

In order to translate (A.6) into operational terms, I will expand μ_t, to linear terms, as a function of YD_t and YP_t, around $\mu_0(YD_0, YP_0)$:

$$\mu_t \simeq \mu_0 + (YD_t - YD_0) \frac{\partial \mu}{\partial YD}\bigg|_{\mu_0} + (YP_t - YP_0) \frac{\partial \mu}{\partial YP}\bigg|_{\mu_0}$$

$$= \mu_0 + \frac{\partial \mu}{\partial \pi}\bigg|_{\mu_0} \left[\frac{\partial \pi}{\partial YD}\bigg|_{\pi_0} (YD_t - YD_0) + \frac{\partial \pi}{\partial YP}\bigg|_{\pi_0} (YP_t - YP_0) \right]$$

$$= \mu_0 + \frac{1 + m}{(1 + m - c\pi_0)^2} \left[\rho \left(\frac{Y_0}{YD_0} \right)^{\rho-1} \frac{\frac{\partial Y}{\partial YD} YD - Y}{YD^2}\bigg|_{Y_0} (YD_t - YD_0) \right.$$

$$\left. + \rho \left(\frac{Y_0}{YD_0} \right)^{\rho-1} \frac{1}{YD_0} \frac{\partial Y}{\partial YP}\bigg|_{Y_0} (YP_t - YP_0) \right]$$

$$= \mu_0 + \frac{1 + m}{(1 + m - c\,\pi)^2} \left[\rho\,\pi_0(\pi_0 - 1) \frac{YD_t - YD_0}{YD_0} \right. \qquad (A.9)$$

$$\left. + \rho\,\pi_0(1 - \pi_0) \frac{YP_t - YP_0}{YP_0} \right];$$

$$\frac{\mu_t - \mu_0}{\mu_0} \simeq -\frac{1 + m}{1 + m - c\,\pi_0} \rho(1 - \pi_0) \left[\frac{\Delta_t YD}{YD_0} - \frac{\Delta_t YP}{YP_0} \right]. \qquad (A.10)$$

Inserting for μ_t in (A.6) yields

$$\mu_0 \gtreqless \mu_t(1 + \phi_t)$$

according as

$$\frac{1}{1+\phi_t} \gtreqless 1 - \frac{1+m}{1+m-c\,\pi_0}\,\rho(1-\pi_0)\left[\frac{\Delta_t YD}{YD_0} - \frac{\Delta_t YP}{YP_0}\right] \qquad (A.11)$$

or equivalently

$$\frac{\Delta_t YD}{YD_0} - \frac{\Delta_t YP}{YP_0} \gtreqless \frac{1-\frac{1}{1+\phi_t}}{\rho(1-\pi_0)}\frac{1+m-c\,\pi_0}{1+m}. \qquad (A.12)$$

Sufficient conditions for efficiency of the fiscal stimulus are obtained from (A.12) through the following nested inequalities:

$$\frac{\Delta_t YD}{Y_0} - \frac{\Delta_t YP}{YP_0} > \frac{\phi_t}{\rho(1-\pi_0)} > \frac{\phi_t}{\rho(1-\pi_0)}\frac{1+m-c\,\pi_0}{1+m}$$

$$> \frac{1-\frac{1}{1+\phi_t}}{\rho(1-\pi_0)}\frac{1+m-c\,\pi_0}{1+m}. \qquad (A.13)$$

It follows from (A.13) that fiscal stimulation is warranted provided aggregate demand (YD) grows (sufficiently) faster than aggregate supply (YP) between the date of the stimulus and the date(s) of debt service.

The more noteworthy features of conditions (A.13) are

(i) the role played by capital accumulation (and growth of labour supply) in reducing the efficiency of a bond-financed fiscal stimulus;

(ii) the presence of the parameter ρ (≥ 20 in the EUP econometric estimations) in the denominator of the right-hand side of (A.13)

8.2 Stochastic analysis

Because future growth of supply and demand are inherently uncertain, it is important to extend the analysis to a formal treatment of uncertainty. Denote by $s \in S$ (a finite set) the "state of the environment" at time t, and write q_s for the value as of time 0 of a unit claim to output (real income) at time t contingent on state s. The "stochastic" counterpart to (A.5) is then

$$\Delta Y_0 + \Sigma_{s \in S}\, q_s\, \Delta Y_t(s) \gtreqless 0 \qquad (A.5')$$

where the discounting is embodied into the contingent prices q_s, which perform a "time-and-state" discounting function. The intermediate steps leading from (A.5) to (A.12) can be retraced for each state s and then pooled into

$$\Sigma_s\, q_s\left[\frac{\Delta_t YD(s)}{YD_0} - \frac{\Delta YP(s)}{YP_0}\right] \gtreqless \frac{1-\frac{1}{(1+\nu)^t}}{\rho(1-\pi_0)}\frac{1+m-c\,\Pi_0}{1+m} \qquad (A.12')$$

where $1 + \phi_t$ is replaced by $(1 + \nu)^t$ because the factor $(1 + \lambda)^t$ has dropped out of (A.5').

Assuming that the probabilities of the states are known, and denoting these by p_s, $s \in S$; writing $(1 + \lambda)^{-t}$ for $\Sigma_{s \in S} q_s$; and using the assumptions of the CAPM to obtain an explicit (approximate) expression for the prices of contingent claims, we may write, for each $s \in S$: [23]

$$q_s = \frac{1}{(1 + \lambda)^t} \, p_s \left[1 - R \cdot \frac{Y_t(s) - \overline{Y}_t}{\overline{Y}_t} \right], \qquad (A.14)$$

where $\frac{R}{\overline{Y}_t}$ is the "risk premium per unit of variance Y_t" implicit in the CAPM asset prices. Accordingly, (A.12') may be written as follows:

$$\Sigma_s \, p_s \left[1 - R \cdot \frac{Y_t(s) - \overline{Y}_t}{\overline{Y}_t} \right] \left[\frac{\Delta_t YD(s)}{YD_0} - \frac{\Delta_t YP(s)}{YP_0} \right] \gtrless \frac{1 - \frac{1}{1 + \phi_t}}{\rho(1 - \pi_0)} \, \frac{1 + m - c\, \pi_0}{1 + m}. \qquad (A.12'')$$

Explicit consideration of the uncertainty of the future thus leads to evaluate the left-hand side of (A.12''), which reduces to that of (A.12) when there is a unique state (certainty) or to a reformulation in terms of *expected values* (for $\Delta_t YD$ and $\Delta_t YP$) when $R = 0$ (risk-neutral capital markets).

Using (A.8) state-by-state to express $Y_t(s)$ as a function of $YD_t(s)$ and $YP_t(s)$, then expanding around YD_0 and YP_0, yields successively

$$Y_t(s) \simeq Y_0 + \left[YD_t(s) - YD_0 \right] \frac{\partial Y}{\partial YD} \bigg|_{Y_0} + \left[YP_t(s) - YP_0 \right] \frac{\partial Y}{\partial YP} \bigg|_{Y_0} \qquad (A.15)$$

$$\frac{Y_t(s) - Y_0}{Y_0} \simeq \frac{YD_t(s) - YD_0}{YD_0} \, \pi_0 + \frac{YP_t(s) - YP_0}{YP_0} \, (1 - \pi_0) \qquad (A.16)$$

$$\Sigma_s p_s \left[1 - R \left\{ \pi_0 \frac{YD_t(s) - YD_0}{YD_0} + (1 - \pi_0) \frac{YP_t(s) - YP_0}{YP_0} \right\} \right]$$

$$\cdot \left[\frac{YD_t(s) - YD_0}{YD_0} - \frac{YP_t(s) - YP_0}{YP_0} \right]$$

$$= \frac{E_0 \Delta_t YD(s)}{YD_0} - \frac{E_0 \Delta_t YP(s)}{YP_0}$$

$$- R \left[\pi_0 \frac{E_0 \{\Delta_t YD(s)\}^2}{YD_0^2} - (1 - \pi_0) \frac{E_0 \{\Delta_t YP(s)\}^2}{YP_0^2} \right.$$

$$+ (1 - 2\pi_0) \frac{E_0 \{\Delta_t YD(s) \cdot \Delta_t YP(s)\}}{YD_0 YP_0} \bigg]$$

$$:= \frac{\overline{\Delta_t YD}}{YD_0} - \frac{\overline{\Delta_t YP}}{YP_0}$$

---

[23] See, e.g. Drèze (1982), Section 2.3.4.

$$-R\left[\pi_0\left\{\left(\frac{\overline{\Delta_t YD}}{YD_0}\right)^2 + \text{var}\left(\frac{\Delta_t YD}{YD_0}\right)\right\}\right.$$

$$-(1-\pi_0)\left\{\left(\frac{\overline{\Delta_t YP}}{YP_0}\right)^2 + \text{var}\left(\frac{\Delta_t YP}{YP_0}\right)\right\}$$

$$\left.+(1-2\pi_0)\left\{\frac{\overline{\Delta_t YD}}{YD_0}\frac{\overline{\Delta_t YP}}{YP_0} + \text{cov}\left(\frac{\Delta_t YD}{YD_0},\frac{\Delta_t YP}{YP_0}\right)\right\}\right]$$

$$= \left(\frac{\overline{\Delta_t YD}}{YD_0} - \frac{\overline{\Delta_t YP}}{YP_0}\right)\left[1 - R\left\{\pi_0\frac{\overline{\Delta_t YD}}{YD_0} + (1-\pi_0)\frac{\overline{\Delta_t YP}}{YP_0}\right\}\right]$$

$$-R\left[\pi_0\,\text{var}\left(\frac{\Delta_t YD}{YD_0}\right) + (1-\pi_0)\,\text{var}\left(\frac{\Delta_t YP}{YP_0}\right)\right.$$

$$\left.+(1-2\pi_0)\,\text{cov}\left(\frac{\Delta_t YD}{YD_0},\frac{\Delta_t YP}{YP_0}\right)\right]$$

$$:= \left(\frac{\overline{\Delta_t YD}}{YD_0} - \frac{\overline{\Delta_t YP}}{YP_0}\right)\left[1 - R\frac{\overline{\Delta_t Y}}{Y_0}\right] - R\,\text{cov}\left(\frac{\Delta_t Y}{Y_0}\frac{\Delta_t YD}{YD_0} - \frac{\Delta_t YP}{YP_0}\right)$$

$$= \left(\frac{\overline{\Delta_t YD}}{YD_0} - \frac{\overline{\Delta_t YP}}{YP_0}\right)\left[1 - R\frac{\overline{\Delta_t Y}}{Y_0}\left\{1 + \frac{\text{cov}\left(\frac{\Delta_t Y}{Y_0},\frac{\Delta_t YD}{YD_0} - \frac{\Delta_t YP}{YP_0}\right)}{\frac{\overline{\Delta_t Y}}{Y_0}\cdot\left(\frac{\overline{\Delta_t YD}}{YD_0} - \frac{\overline{\Delta_t YP}}{YP_0}\right)}\right\}\right] \quad (A.17)$$

where use has been made of (A.16) to obtain the last two lines.

The right-hand side of (A.17) may finally be substituted for the left-hand side of (A.12) and (A.13) to define necessary and sufficient conditions for *ex ante* efficiency of a debt-financed temporary fiscal stimulus. The explicit consideration of uncertainty leads to deflate the excess of demand growth over supply growth by a factor which is the product of (i) the market risk premium per unit of variance Y, namely R; (ii) the expected growth rate of aggregate output, $\frac{\overline{\Delta_t Y}}{Y_0}$; and (iii) a covariance term.

For *growth rates*, variances and covariances are apt to represent a small fraction of the corresponding expectations. If we neglect the covariance term as a first approximation, then we obtain as a counterpart to (A.13)

$$\left(\frac{\overline{\Delta_t YD}}{YD_0} - \frac{\overline{\Delta_t YP}}{YP_0}\right)\left(1 - R\frac{\overline{\Delta_t Y}}{Y_0}\right) > \frac{\phi_t}{\rho(1-\Pi_0)}. \quad (A.18)$$

The numerical value of the factor $R\frac{\overline{\Delta_t Y}}{Y_0}$ would fall in the range of 10 to 40% as R ranges, say, from 2 to 4 and $\frac{\overline{\Delta_t Y}}{Y_0}$ ranges from 5 % to 10 % (corresponding to expected growth of real output over a span of 3 to 4 years). The correction for uncertainty is thus far from negligible.

As for the covariance between $\frac{\Delta_t Y}{Y_0}$ and $\left(\frac{\Delta_t Y D}{Y D_0} - \frac{\Delta_t Y P}{Y P_0} \right)$, it is a statistic that has never been considered, to the best of my knowledge. There is no *a priori* reason why it should rather be positive than negative. Empirical investigation is called for. (That covariance could easily be evaluated retrospectively from the EUP estimates.)

It may also be relevant to note that estimation uncertainty, in particular about R, but also ϕ, ρ, and the covariance, could be brought into a more ambitious treatment of uncertainty.

3

Measuring the Welfare Effects of European Price Convergence[1]

Anton P. Barten

Catholic University Louvain

1 Introduction

In the context of European integration it seems to be natural that (relative) prices are the same everywhere in the European Economic Community. Harmonization of indirect taxation is then a logical component of a move in that direction. In equilibrium, prices clear the market, hence reflect demand and supply conditions. Those conditions are not necessarily the same across countries.

On the *supply* side one may distinguish between tradables and nontradables. As for the tradables arbitrage may result in virtually identical absolute prices at the official parity. Given the increasing importance of nontradables this is small comfort. For the comparison of prices of nontradables the official parity is moreover not very adequate. In general, differences in availability of natural resources, in qualification of labour, in the relative scarcity of capital, in the size of the market and so on result in differences in production costs across products and countries.

On the *demand* side there are differences not only in real income but also in climate, in religion, more generally in culture and attitudes which express themselves in differences in preferences, tastes for short. In Europe some of these differences tend to vanish because of increased communication of ideas and mobility of people, but one can still expect differences in consumer behaviour not due to differences in real income and in relative prices.

Those relative prices will tend to differ across countries even in the absence of indirect taxation. Indirect taxation may mitigate differences in relative prices but it may also increase them. The welfare implications of harmonization of rates are not self evident. Such an harmonization would do away with phenom-

---

[1]Leon Bettendorf and Dirk Rober of the Center for Economic Studies of the Catholic University of Louvain have been very helpful in organizing the OECD data in a form useful for the application of this study. The author, however, bears all blame for its shortcomings.

ena like tanking petrol just across the border because taxes or excise-duties are less there, but these are of minor importance.

Given international differences in relative price systems it becomes of interest to compare those systems and to investigate whether a move towards their convergence will be a good thing or not. For example, one can ask the question whether the British relative prices are more attractive to the French consumer than the relative prices of France itself or whether the opposite holds. Imagine that one finds that Italian relative prices are more favourable in all European countries than the domestic relative prices. All countries would then adopt the Italian price system using indirect taxes to compensate for differences in supply conditions.

In the next section some evidence about differences in relative price structures is presented. We then turn to the question of how to interpret the relative attractiveness of a price system. The answer to that is supplied by the expenditure function approach. Section 4 shows how this approach can be applied using systems of demand functions which are not explicitly integrable. Section 5 discusses the estimation of systems of demand functions, one each for five European countries: Belgium, F.R. of Germany, France, United Kingdom and Italy. The data used are described in the Appendix on data documentation. Section 6 presents an attempt to estimate a single demand system for five countries together. Section 7 returns from this detour to the actual calculation of the welfare gains or losses when one of the countries considered takes over the relative price system of the others. Section 8 draws the obvious conclusions from the experiment.

2 Evidence on Relative Price Differences

Eurostat (1988) reports on the 1985 purchasing power parities for the twelve countries of the European Economic Community (EEC) and also for Austria, United States and Japan. Here the focus is on Belgium (BE), the Federal Republic of Germany (DE), France (FR), United Kingdom (GB) and Italy (IT) because for those countries collateral time series are available from OECD sources.

Of special interest for our purpose is Table 8 of Eurostat (1988) giving per EEC country a price level index for *inter alia* Total national consumption and its eight components. This table is reproduced here as Table 1 for the countries considered in the present analysis. The price indexes are scaled such that the twelve EEC country average (EUR-12) is 100, for aggregate consumption as well as for the eight components. For example, the price index of total national consumption for DE is 115.2 meaning that consumption prices in Germany were in 1985 15 % higher than the EEC average. The price index for Gross rent, fuel and power for IT is 77.5. Rents and the like are in Italy 77.5% of the EEC average for that class.

Table 1 Relative price structure

Consumption class	Country					
	BE	DE	FR	GB	IT	EU
1. Food, beverages, tobacco	100.8	103.0	101.3	101.1	93.7	100
2. Clothing and footwear	118.1	105.5	107.5	84.1	97.8	100
3. Gross rent, fuel and power	112.6	147.2	128.4	93.4	77.5	100
4. Furniture, household equipment	99.8	101.2	111.1	101.5	98.1	100
5. Medical care and health services	80.3	125.7	100.2	82.7	105.4	100
6. Transport and communication	99.4	103.5	108.9	108.5	90.9	100
7. Recreation and cultural activities	110.2	116.4	114.9	96.4	87.3	100
8. Miscellaneous goods and services	103.5	114.0	109.3	102.2	89.3	100
Total national consumption	102.4	115.2	109.8	97.3	90.8	100

Such a price index indicates what has to be paid in country X in ECU, say, for a quantity of a good, that could be bought in EUR-12 for 100 ECU. (The currency unit is of no importance here). Clearly, these prices indexes are relative vis-à-vis EUR-12. They can also be used as indicators for relative prices across the eight consumption categories of country X. For that purpose consider as the unit of quantity the amount which can be bought for 100 ECU in EUR-12. The 105.4 ECU which has to be paid in IT for such a unit of Medical care and health services can then be compared with the 77.5 ECU that the unit of rents *etcetera* costs. The relative price of Medical care in terms of the price of Rents *etcetera* is 100x105.4/77.5=136.

Table 1 indicates that there are considerable price variations across products per country. Gross rent *etcetera* displays considerable variation over the countries. In DE it is the most expensive product, in IT it is by far the cheapest one. It is, of course, a typical nontradable for which one would expect some cross-country variation. Still, the divergence of the relative prices for Clothing and footwear, an easily transportable item, is not inconsequential. The variation in the prices of medical care and health services is presumably due to the differences in the health insurance schemes across countries.

One may conclude that in spite of proximity and cultural similarity relative price systems differ considerably over the EEC countries studied. How important are these differences for consumer behaviour?

3   Comparison on Relative Price Systems

The theory of cost-of-living index numbers uses constant utility price indexes to evaluate the difference between two price systems, represented by two n-vectors of prices, say p_1 and p_2. One starts off from the *expenditure function*

$$e(v, p_1) = min_q(m = p_1'q|u(q) = v) \qquad (1)$$

where q is the n-vector of quantities and $u(q)$ is a well-behaved utility function. The expenditure function expresses the minimum amount needed to finance the purchase of a vector of quantities which will allow the consumer to obtain utility level $u(q) = v$ with price system p_1.

Let p_2 be a different price system. Then $e(v, p_2)$ is what is needed to maintain the original utility level v with the prices p_2. This will imply a different vector of quantities than the one underlying $e(v, p_1)$. The difference between $e(v, p_2)$ and $e(v, p_1)$ can be positive or negative. If it is positive the change is unfavourable to the consumer, because without an increase in means he will not be able to afford the old utility level and has to do with less. If it is negative the opposite prevails.

Part of the effect of the change from p_1 to p_2 is due to the change in the general price level. The expenditure function is homogeneous of degree one in the prices. The relative change in the general price level would express itself in an identical relative change in $e(v, p)$. Since our interest is in the effect of relative prices we will have to neutralize the difference in the general price level between p_1 and p_2 by rescaling p_2 in such a way that the general price level that the rescaled p_2 implies is the same as that of p_1.

The change in relative price systems will cause a change in the optimal quantities demanded, say from q_1 to q_2. The change in the minimal expenditure is then $m_2 - m_1 = p_2'q_2 - p_1'q_1$. In log-differential form one has

$$dlnm = \sum_i w_i dlnq_i + \sum_i w_i dlnp_i \qquad (2)$$

where $w_i = p_i q_i/m$, the budget share of good i, is evaluated at suitable values for the prices. (Note that $\sum_i w_i = 1$).

The first term on the right-hand side is related to the change in utility. Indeed, one has

$$du(q) = \sum_i \frac{\partial u}{\partial q_i} \, dq_i = \lambda \sum_i p_i dq_i = \lambda m \sum_i w_i dlnq_i \qquad (3)$$

where $\partial u/\partial q_i$ is the marginal utility of q_i, which in the optimum is equal to λp_i. Here λ is a positive Lagrangean multiplier, also interpreted as the marginal utility of m. Keeping utility constant implies then $\sum_i w_i dlnq_i = 0$.

The second term on the right-hand side of (2) can be seen as the change in the logarithmic general price index. If the general price level is the same for the two price vectors then this term is also zero.

The finding that the terms on the right-hand side of (2) are basically zero does not imply that $lnm_2 - lnm_1$ is zero too. The transition from differentials to finite changes involves higher order terms. The size of the higher order terms depends *inter alia* on the size of the changes in the relative price systems. It is difficult to say *a priori* how important the change in minimal expenditure will be.

Even if the change in minimal expenditure is small the associated quantity changes may be considerable. Keeping utility constant means that an increase in the demand for one good is compensated by a decrease in the demand for one or more of the other goods. Thus the overall effect on total expenditure is limited.

4 Measuring Minimal Expenditure

The minimal expenditure generated by the expenditure function is equal to the sum of the products of the quantities demanded and their prices. Starting from any systems of demand equations generating optimal demands one can then calculate their cost. This procedure amounts to integrating the demand functions numerically.

The advantage of such numerical integration over an analytical one is the possible use of a wider class of demand systems than those that are analytically integrable but which might be lacking in empirical quality, as pointed out by Porter-Hudak and Hayes (1991).

In the present case the so-called CBS system of Keller and Van Driel (1985) of the Dutch Central Bureau of Statistics (CBS) was used to generate the optimal demands. This system has demonstrated its empirical superiority over other similar models - see Barten (1989), Barten and McAleer (1991), Barten (1991). A typical equation of this system reads

$$\overline{w}_{ic}(\Delta lnq_{ic} - \Delta lnQ_c) = a_i + c_i \Delta lnQ_c + \sum_j s_{ij}\Delta lnp_{jc} \tag{4}$$

Here $\overline{w}_{ic} = (w_{ic} + w_{io})/2$, with o indicating the base line situation and c the case of the alternative price system. Moreover,

$$\Delta lnQ_c = \sum_i \overline{w}_{ic}\Delta lnq_{ic}$$

$$\Delta lnq_{ic} = lnq_{ic} - lnq_{io}$$

$$\Delta lnp_{jc} = lnp_{jc} - lnp_{jo}$$

For simulating the optimal demands the a_i, c_i and s_{ij} are replaced by their estimates, which satisfy the conditions

$$\sum_i a_i = 0, \sum_i c_i = 0, \sum_i s_{ij} = 0, s_{ij} = s_{ji} \qquad (5)$$

As is evident from (3) $\Delta ln Q_c$ corresponds to the change in utility. It is set at zero for the determination of the change in minimal expenditure. More generally, take it to be fixed. Then the right-hand side of (4) is given. Let it be z_i.

To elaborate the left-hand side one can start from

$$\Delta ln w_{ic} = \Delta ln q_{ic} + \Delta ln p_{ic} - \Delta ln m_c \qquad (6)$$

where $\Delta ln m_c = ln m_c - ln m_o$ and $\Delta ln w_{ic} = ln w_{ic} - ln w_{io}$. Multiply both sides of (6) by $\overline{w}_{ic}$ and add-up over i

$$\sum_i \overline{w}_{ic} \Delta ln w_{ic} = \sum_i \overline{w}_{ic} \Delta ln q_{ic} + \sum_i \overline{w}_{ic} \Delta 1 n p_{ic} - \Delta 1 n m_c \qquad (7)$$

where use is made of the property that $\sum_i \overline{w}_{ic} = 1$. In obvious notation (7) is rewritten as

$$\Delta ln W_c = \Delta ln Q_c + \Delta ln P_c - \Delta ln m_c \qquad (8)$$

Using (6) and (8) the left-hand side of (4) can be expressed for $i = 1, ..., n$ as

$$\overline{w}_{ic}(\Delta ln w_{ic} - \Delta ln p_{ic} + \Delta ln m_c - \Delta ln Q_c)$$
$$= \overline{w}_{ic}[(\Delta ln w_{ic} - \Delta ln W_c) - (\Delta ln p_{ic} - \Delta ln P_c)] \qquad (9)$$

In (9) the w_{io} are predetermined as well as p_c and p_o, the two price vectors. The w_{ic} are the unknowns. They are obtained from minimizing the sum over i of the squared difference between (9) and z_i with respect to w_{ic} under the restrictions that the w_{ic} are positive and add up to unity. One can then use (8) to establish m_c. From the solutions for w_{ic} one can obtain the q_{ic} as $w_{ic} m_c / p_{ic}$.

As already said (8) supplies $\Delta ln m_c$ once the w_{ic} are known, given $\Delta ln Q_c$ and the $\Delta ln p_{ic}$. In the case of the determination of minimal expenditure when only relative prices change both $\Delta ln Q_c$ and $\Delta ln P_c$ are zero and $\Delta ln m_c = -\Delta ln W_c = -\sum_i \overline{w}_{ic} \Delta ln w_{ic}$ which could very well be rather small.

The procedure sketched here requires knowledge of the z_i, the right-hand sides of (4). There the a_i, c_i and the s_{ij} are in principle unknown and have to be estimated. These coefficients reflect "tastes". We take them to be constant over time for a single country, but variable across countries. The next section turns to their estimation.

Table 2 Estimation results for the s_{ii}

| | Country | | | | |
Consumption class	BE	DE	FR	GB	IT
1. Food, beverages and tobacco	-.063	-.095	-.058	-.062	-.072
	(.038)	(.018)	(.009)	(.012)	(.012)
2. Clothing and footwear	-.063	-.167	-.054	-.053	-.027
	(.015)	(.022)	(.016)	(.007)	(.007)
3. Gross rent, fuel and power	-.015	-.020	-.011	-.023	-.066
	(.009)	(.004)	(.007)	(.001)	(.011)
4. Furniture, household equipment	-.008	-.176	-.015	-.060	-.026
	(.010)	(.019)	(.005)	(.006)	(.005)
5. Medical care and health services	-.015	-.010	-.024	-.004	-.012
	(.014)	(.002)	(.008)	(.002)	(.002)
6. Transport and communication	-.037	-.172	-.029	-.030	-.075
	(.018)	(.022)	(.011)	(.004)	(.015)
7. Recreation and cultural activities	-.043	-.110	-.032	-.073	-.061
	(.011)	(.020)	(.009)	(.013)	(.016)
8. Miscellaneous goods and services	-.017	-.030	-.118	-.086	-.130
	(.012)	(.015)	(.015)	(.024)	(.021)

5   Demand System Estimation

The data used for the estimation of (4), a typical equation of the CBS system, are described in detail in the Data Appendix. They derive from OECD annual national accounts publications covering the years 1960-1988 except for GB where the sample period ends with 1987. The data concern expenditure in current and in constant prices on eight mutually exclusive classes of consumer goods as listed in Table 1.

The prices have been obtained as the ratio of the current expenditures and the expenditures in constant prices. Assuming a multivariate normal distribution for the disturbance terms of the system of demand equations, the coefficients have been estimated by a maximum likelihood procedure under conditions (5) to which was added the negativity condition that $\sum_i \sum_j x_i s_{ij} x_j < 0$ for $x_i \neq x_j$ for at least one pair i, j. With eight classes the matrix of s_{ij} coefficients is 8x8. To economize on space Table 2 only reports the estimates for the diagonal elements, the s_{ii}, for the five countries considered. Standard errors are in parentheses below the coefficients. Table 3 presents the estimates for the c_i.

To interpret the coefficient estimates it is useful to relate the s_{ij} and c_i to the corresponding elasticities. Let ϵ_{ij} be the compensated or Slutsky cross price

Table 3 Estimation results for the c_i

Consumption class	Country				
	BE	DE	FR	GB	IT
1. Food, beverages and tobacco	-.152	-.131	-.153	-.089	-.070
	(.042)	(.022)	(.018)	.028)	.033)
2. Clothing and footwear	.032	.050	-.023	.039	.096
	(.025)	(.017)	(.027)	(.015)	(.022)
3. Gross rent, fuel and power	-.077	-.132	-.006	-.119	-.112
	(.039)	(.035)	(.039)	(.030)	(.032)
4. Furniture, household equipment	.078	.020	.067	.065	.067
	(.044)	(.022)	(.025)	(.010)	(.016)
5. Medical care and health services	-.025	-.009	-.020	.003	-.013
	(.026)	(.011)	(.022)	(.005)	(.011)
6. Transport and communication	-.015	.159	.137	.098	.087
	(.027)	(.037)	(.035)	(.040)	(.031)
7. Recreation and cultural activities	-.002	.062	.015	.006	-.032
	(.012)	(.025)	(.014)	(.024)	(.016)
8. Miscellaneous goods and services	.160	-.019	-.018	-.004	-.023
	(.057)	(.012)	(.022)	(.034)	(.018)

elasticity and η_i the income or rather budget elasticity, then

$$\epsilon_{ijc} = s_{ij}/w_{ic}$$

$$\eta_{ic} = 1 + c_i/w_{ic}$$

Note that these elasticities are not constants because the value shares w_i vary. The elasticities are evaluated at a specific set of values for w_{ic}. In Tables 4a and 4b the elasticities corresponding with the s_{ii} and c_i of Tables 2 and 3 are reported, evaluated for the 1985 observed budget shares.

One may observe that in Table 2 all entries are negative. This reflects the law of demand. As far as the negativity condition was not respected spontaneously it was imposed along the lines indicated in Barten and Geyskens (1975). With the exception of DE the s_{ii} values are small for all i. If the own prices elasticities were of the order of -1, the s_{ii} should be around $-1/n = -1/8$ with n being the number of goods. Very few s_{ii} values of Table 2 are in absolute value larger than .125. The low price sensitivity can also be seen from the entries of Table 4b for the compensated own price elasticities. There are very few ϵ_{ii} smaller than -1. These are only found for Germany. The relative precision of the estimates of s_{ii} is somewhat weak for BE but in general reasonable.

Table 4a 1985 values for income elasticities

	Country				
Consumption class	BE	DE	FR	GB	IT
1. Food, beverages, tobacco	.37	.44	.26	.54	.72
2. Clothing and footwear	1.50	1.57	.67	1.56	2.00
3. Gross rent, fuel and power	.58	.39	.97	.42	.28
4. Furniture, household equipment	1.65	1.22	1.80	1.97	1.79
5. Medical care and health services	.73	.71	.76	1.22	.75
6. Transport and communication	.88	2.03	1.82	1.60	1.70
7. Recreation and cultural activities	.97	1.64	1.22	1.06	.60
8. Miscellaneous goods and services	2.33	.76	.87	.98	.85

Turning to the c_i of Table 3 it is recalled that a positive c_i means a budget elasticity greater than one. It indicates a "luxury". Class 4, Furniture and household equipment, is a luxury in all five countries considered. The coefficients of Class 1, Food, beverages, tobacco, are all negative. The budget elasticities are less than one, the value shares are declining with the size of the budget. The results reflect the Law of Engel. Somewhat surprising is the necessity nature for all five countries of Class 3, Gross rent, fuel and power. The budget elasticities for 1985 can be found in Table 4a.

Both the budget elasticities η_i and the c_i appear to be similar across countries per consumption class. Still, the differences are not inconsequential. The standard errors of the point estimates are rather large, however. The question of the significance of the differences is a natural one. Its answer is the topic of the next section.

6 An Aside: A Multicountry Demand System

Differences in tastes are reflected in the differences in the coefficients of the demand systems. As is clear from Tables 2 and 3 there are differences among the c_j and the s_{ii} across the various countries. Also the a_i and the s_{ij} $(i \neq j)$ display variation from one country to the other. Are these differences significantly different from zero? Otherwise said, are tastes basically the same across Europe? Can one replace the five models, one for each country, by a single one, common to all five countries considered?

This issue can be approached by pooling the data and estimating a single CBS model for the five countries together. One imposes then the restriction that the coefficients are the same for all five countries. One also implicitly assumes that the covariance matrices of the disturbances are the same for those countries.

Table 4b 1985 values for compensated own price elasticities

Consumption class	Country				
	BE	DE	FR	GB	IT
1. Food, beverages, tobacco	-.26	-.40	-.28	-.32	-.28
2. Clothing and footwear	-.98	-1.88	-.77	-.76	-.28
3. Gross rent, fuel and power	-.08	-.09	-.06	-.11	-.43
4. Furniture, household equipment	-.06	-1.90	-.18	-.89	-.30
5. Medical care and health services	-.16	-.31	-.29	-.32	-.23
6. Transport and communication	-.29	-1.12	-.17	-.19	-.61
7. Recreation and cultural activities	-.88	-1.12	-.46	-.78	-.76
8. Miscellaneous goods and services	-.14	-.37	-.90	-.44	-.85

These covariance matrices reflect the variability in tastes. It is in keeping with the hypothesis of identical tastes across countries to also use identical covariance matrices.

The results of the estimation experiment with the pooled data set are presented in Table 5 along the same lines as those of Tables 2, 3, 4a and 4b.

The s_{ii} do not differ drastically from those of Table 2. They are also rather small. The standard errors of the s_{ii} of Table 5 are not really smaller than those of Table 2 contrary to one's expectation since five times more data is used. The c_i values reported in Table 5 are also similar to those of Table 3. Four goods are luxuries, four goods are necessities. Here the standard errors are smaller than those of Table 3, but not by very much. The elasticities in Table 5 have been obtained for the average budget shares per good for the whole sample.

The results of Table 5 are only of interest if the common model is not too restrictive. To test the null hypothesis that this is not the case the likelihood ratio test statistic (LRT) can be used.

The log-likelihood value for the model with the pooled data is 4631.87. It involves the joint estimation of 42 coefficients of the deterministic part of the model. For the covariance matrix 28 variances and covariances had to be estimated. The number of observation points is 139, 27 for GB and 28 each for the four other countries.

The unconstrained alternative is the set of models estimated separately for each of the five countries. The sum of the five log-likelihood values is 5035.09 obtained while estimating 5 x 42 = 210 coefficients for the deterministic part and 5 covariance matrices with each 28 (independent) coefficients.

The traditional LRT takes 2 x (5035.09 - 4631.87) = 806.45 as the value for the test statistic. Under the null of validity of the common model it is asymptotically distributed as χ^2 with 210 - 42 = 168 degrees of freedom. The

Table 5 Results for pooled data

	Coefficients		Budget	Compensated	Average
	s_{ii}	c_i	elasticity	own elasticity	value share
1. Food, beverages, tobacco	-.056 (.013)	-.107 (.013)	.62	-.20	.28
2. Clothing and footwear	-.045 (.007)	.046 (.009)	1.52	-.61	.09
3. Gross rent, fuel and power	-.035 (.008)	-.095 (.015)	.41	-.22	.16
4. Furniture, household equipment	-.012 (.007)	.067 (.010)	1.68	-.12	.10
5. Medical care and health services	-.015 (.005)	-.002 (.007)	.95	-.32	.05
6. Transport and communication	-.076 (.013)	.077 (.016)	1.61	-.60	.13
7. Recreation and cultural activities	-.048 (.009)	-.002 (.008)	.98	-.63	.08
8. Miscellaneous goods and services	-.039 (.010)	.015 (.013)	1.12	-.32	.12

corresponding 5 per cent critical value is about 200. Similarity of tastes is being rejected. Taking into account the 112 extra degrees of freedom gained by having a single covariance matrix is of little avail. The critical χ^2 value for 280 degrees of freedom is about 320. Small sample corrections of the type proposed by Italianer (1985) are not enough to decrease the LRT to less than the five per cent critical value. Common tastes are not realistic.

Differences in tastes justify differences in relative prices in equilibrium. It is then also difficult to make international welfare comparisons. In the sequel we will limit ourselves to making such comparisons for a single country only.

7 Calculating the Costs of a Change in Relative Prices

We are now in a position to apply the scheme of section 4 to obtain the change in minimal expenditure as the consequence of a change in the relative prices. A few further specifications are in order before (4) can be applied for the purpose.

Since Eurostat (1988) supplies us with the relative prices for 1985, the year 1985 was chosen as the year for which the calculations are to be made. The

Table 6 Simulated budget shares for Italian tastes and the minimal
expenditures

Consumption class	Relative price system for 1985 for					
	IT	BE	DE	FR	GB	EU
1. Food, beverages, tobacco	.25	.24	.25	.24	.26	.25
2. Clothing and footwear	.10	.11	.09	.10	.09	.10
3. Gross rent, fuel and power	.15	.17	.19	.18	.16	.17
4. Furniture, household equipment	.08	.08	.08	.09	.09	.08
5. Medical care and health services	.05	.04	.05	.04	.05	.05
6. Transport and communication	.12	.12	.12	.12	.13	.12
7. Recreation and cultural activities	.08	.09	.08	.08	.08	.08
8. Miscellaneous goods and services	.15	.15	.15	.15	.15	.15
Minimal expenditures	6861	6862	6860	6861	6861	6861
$10^4(lnm_c - lnm_0)$	-	-1.025	-.940	.049	.187	.017

OECD 1985 total national consumption per capita in domestic currency is less
than the corresponding figure of Table 4 of the Eurostat publication. To cali-
brate the calculations the total national consumption per capita in ECUs was
taken from that table to use as the m_0 value. The relative prices for the baseline
country were taken from Eurostat Table 8. Those for the other four countries
are from the same source but are proportionally adjusted to imply the same
price level as that of the baseline country.

Next, the OECD relative price change was applied to the 1985 relative price
vector for the baseline country to obtain a corresponding price vector for 1984.
The relative change in total consumer expenditure 1985-1984 was used to obtain
the 1984 total expenditure in terms of ECUs. Residuals from the estimation were
added on the right-hand side of the demand equations. In this way simulating
the change from 1984 to 1985 resulted in the exact OECD budget shares. At
the same time the value of real income Q was obtained for the baseline country
for that year.

These values were kept constant when simulating the effects of adopting
the relative price system of another country. Table 6 presents results for the
case where IT is in the baseline position. The EU relative price vector has all
elements equal. One may note that the budget shares do not vary greatly across
different relative price systems. This is reflected in the small differences in m_c
from its value for IT. As was explained in Section 4, this difference equals minus
the weighted sum of $lnw_{ic} - lnw_{i0}$ and is consequently rather small as well. For
the other four demand systems one arrives at basically the same picture.

In Table 6 the budget shares are given using the demand system estimated

Table 7 Simulated budget shares Belgian relative prices

| | Tastes of | | | | |
Consumption class	BE	DE	FR	GB	IT
1. Food, beverages, tobacco	.24	.25	.22	.18	.24
2. Clothing and footwear	.06	.08	.07	.07	.11
3. Gross rent, fuel and power	.18	.19	.18	.22	.17
4. Furniture, household equipment	.12	.12	.08	.07	.08
5. Medical care and health services	.09	.03	.08	.01	.04
6. Transport and communication	.12	.16	.16	.14	.12
7. Recreation and cultural activities	.05	.09	.07	.09	.09
8. Miscellaneous goods and services	.13	.09	.13	.20	.15

for Italian data (Italian tastes). They are rather insensitive to changes in relative prices. In Table 7 the budget shares are given using the Belgian relative prices in the demand systems estimated for the five data sets. There is greater variation than in Table 6. Specifically Class 5 Medical care and health services displays variation, which may reflect the different set-up of the health insurance systems.

Tables like Table 6 can be drafted for the other countries than IT. They all have the same message: the change in minimal expenditure due to a variation of the relative prices of a type observed in Europe is minute: a few ECU per head. One should keep in mind that these results were obtained with imprecisely estimated coefficients and are thus to be taken with a grain of salt.

In view of what was said in Section 4 about the higher order nature of the change in minimal expenditure it comes not as a surprise that it is so small. Still, one had to wait until the empirical information about the degree of variation in the relative prices and the importance of the effects of price changes was available to actually find out that the change in minimal expenditure is negligible.

8 Conclusions

As is demonstrated in this paper changes in relative prices have a very small effect on consumers' welfare. A move towards a more uniform system of relative prices cannot claim to be in the interest of the consumer. Harmonization of indirect taxes may do away with across-the-border shopping but will make very little difference for the consumer otherwise.

A byproduct of the empirical application is the finding that tastes are not the same across the countries of Europe. They may be more responsible for differences in expenditure patterns than differences in relative price systems. Of course, also differences in real income matter, but were not further studied here.

The outcomes of the paper are basically negative: differences in relative price structures do not matter, differences in tastes do matter. Both conclusions imply little need for the common market to become an entity with the same price system.

9 References

Barten, A.P. (1989), Towards a levels version of the Rotterdam and related demand systems, in B. Cornet and H. Tulkens, eds., *Contributions to Operations Research and Economics: the Twentieth Anniversary of CORE*, Cambridge Mass.:The MIT Press, 441-465.

Barten, A.P. (1993), Consumer allocation models: choice of functional form, *Empirical Economics* 18, 129-158.

Barten, A.P. and E. Geyskens (1975), The negativity condition in consumer demand, *European Economic Review* 6, 227-260.

Barten, A.P. and M. McAleer (1991), Comparing the empirical performance of alternative demand systems, Center Discussion Paper 9102, Tilburg.

Eurostat (1988), *Purchasing Power Parties and Gross Domestic Product in Real Terms. Results 1985*, Luxemburg: Statistical Office of the European Communities.

Italianer, A. (1985), A small sample correction of the likelihood ratio test, *Economics Letters* 19, 315-317.

Keller, W.J. and J. Van Driel (1985), Differential consumer demand system, *European Economic Review* 27, 375-390.

Porter-Hudak, S. and K. Hayes (1991), A numerical methods approach to calculating cost-of-living indices, *Journal of Econometrics* 50, 91-105.

10 Appendix: Documenting the Time Series Data

The basic source of the OECD time series on consumption is the January 1991 Magnetic Tape release of the National Accounts Volumes I and II. The Volume II tape contains for all five countries (Belgium (BE), Federal Republic of Germany

(DE), France (FR), United Kingdom (GB) and Italy (IT)) the information on the expenditures in current prices and in constant prices for 1970-1988 for the classes specified in Table 2 of the main text. Only for GB no data were given for 1988. The base year for the prices is 1985 for GB and 1980 for the other countries. Since expenditure per capita is considered population 1960-1988 was obtained from the Volume I tape. Only for BE and GE did the Volume II tape supply data for the full period 1960-1988. For the other countries other sources had to be mobilized.

For FR the OECD National Accounts Volume I 1962-1979 contained information on the expenditures in current prices and 1970 prices on the eight classes for 1962-1970. The corresponding 1960-1971 publication contained that information for 1960-1962, with 1963 as the base year. To align the series in current prices the ratios of the 1970 tape information and the older 1970 values were used to multiply through the "old" 1962-1969 data. The ratios of the "new" 1962 data and the old 1962 numbers were used to multiply through the "old" 1960-1961 data. The Volume I tape contains total expenditure on consumption both in current and in constant prices of 1985 for the whole 1960-1988 period. It differs from the sum of the expenditures on the eight classes because of statistical discrepancies and of direct purchases abroad by resident households minus direct purchases in the domestic market by non-resident households. The 1970 ratio of the sum of the eight classes and the published total was then used to obtain adjusted totals for 1960-1969. The expenditures per year were then multiplicatively adjusted so that their sum equals the adjusted total for that year.

For the series in constant prices basically the same procedure was used. Here the first multiplicative adjustment also takes care of the difference in base years for the prices. Of course the total expenditure in 1985 prices was first converted into one in 1980 prices.

For GB the Volume II tape contained the current price expenditure from 1960 on. So no further treatment was needed there. The expenditure in 1975 prices for 1964-1970 came from Volume II 1964-1981, that in 1975 prices for 1961-1964 came from Volume II 1969-1978, while the expenditures in 1963 prices for 1960-1961 were found in Volume II, 1960-1971. All these sources also contain the relevant information in current prices. From the ratios of the current and constant price expenditures price indexes were constructed which were scaled to have 1985 for base year. These price indexes were used to deflate the 1960-1969 current expenditures of the Volume II tape to obtain the expenditures in 1985 prices for that period.

The Italian data have been processed along the same lines as those for FR.

4

Market reform in a heterogeneous world
A general equilibrium assessment of the Single Market program[1]

Jean-Marc Burniaux

OECD

Jean Waelbroeck

Université Libre de Bruxelles

1 Introduction

1.1 The unification of the European market as a process of market reform

The "EC92" program is a remarkably ambitious experiment in market reform. More than as a basically new development, it must be seen as an acceleration of a long standing effort: the European Community has been reforming trading practices since its inception. Taken together, the three hundred or so directives that have been agreed will, gradually, transform markets that were segmented along national lines into a true "Single European Market".

As this is an unprecedented experiment, it is not surprising that we are still unsure about how to analyse its impact. The European Commission's evaluation is provided in the Cecchini (1988) report and in the so-called "Blue Book"[2] which, in spite of the fact that it achieves standards of rigour that are unusual for such work, is an official "advocacy document". A number of models have been used to offer such an appraisal of the program, that are based on the

---

[1]The first author is administrator at OECD; his work was done in a private capacity. The authors are grateful for comments from Renato Flores and an anonymous referee. Of course, they only are responsible for remaining defects.
[2]Commission of the European Communities(1988).

innovative work of Cox and Harris (1985, 1986) and Harris (1984), in particular the seminal model of Smith and Venables (1988),[3] the model of Mercenier in this volume. Big Nonante Deux, the model used in this paper, is part of this line of research.

New tools are needed because the EC92 program is an attempt to make markets more perfect; its goal is to open the way to a fuller exploitation of economies of scale. It would be make no sense therefore to assess it using general equilibrium models of the traditional type and standard trade theory, both of which assume that competition is perfect and that returns to scale are non increasing. Appropriate analytical tools should take account of the fact that markets are imperfect and that (to use the phrasing of Adam Smith) "the division of labour is limited by the extent of the market.

Our work differs from earlier work in two respects.

Again and again, the European Commission has found that securing agreement on market liberalization was difficult because in some countries, the relevant market was far more hemmed in by restrictions than in others, and that the negotiators of the countries where restrictions were prevalent argued that liberalization would inflict high adjustment costs on their producers.[4] "Big Nonante Deux model" is specifically designed to highlight such asymmetries in economic structure.

Other model builders have assumed that the creation of the Single Market would enhance competition only by changing the number of competitors in particular markets. We believe that this is too restrictive: market reform does not merely change the number of competitors that confront each other in markets. In many ways, the EC92 program has made the goods produced by different firms more substitutable, and has changed the strategic response of producers to actions by their competitors.[5]

The paper is organized as follows. We first spell out how market reform changes the degree of substitutability of commodities, changes producers' perceptions of the response of others to their actions. This is followed by an analysis of important properties of imperfection competition models. The data and calibration of our Big Nonante Deux model are then described, leading to a discussion of the results of Big Nonante Deux simulations. An appendix provides a more complete description of the model's equations.

---

[3] As well as many methodological papers by Venables, too numerous to be cited here.

[4] Telecommunications in Belgium; road transport and insurance in Germany; steel in Spain, etc. Greece and the Iberic countries used this argument to secure special grace periods for the implementation of a number of directives.

[5] A similar view was taken in an earlier paper by Burniaux and Waelbroeck (1992), where this idea is implemented in a way that is quite different from the approach adopted in the present paper.

1.2 Market reform and its impact on the functioning of the economy, and in particular on the substitutability of goods and on the market strategies of producers

A review of measures that have been implemented is useful to motivate Big Nonante Deux's design.

The reforms have removed border and non border obstacles to trade that were akin to transport costs. An example is eliminating long delays of trucks at country borders. A less obvious one is the repeal of the Belgian law that required that margarine be packaged in cubes, which imposed extra costs on exporters to Belgium.

Other measures result in shifts in demand. Examples are changes in norms and miscellaneous import prohibitions. In a celebrated decision, for example, the European Court of Justice decided that the German government could not impose on French exporters of Cassis de Dijon[6] the alcohol content that German norms prescribed, which would have denatured the drink's taste. Since Cassis de Dijon is not separate item in trade statistics, but is included in a broad import category, the Court of Justice decision should be represented by a *shift in the German demand function* for aperitive drinks.

In other instances, the reform implies a change of the *price elasticity*. This is likely where a specific market segment is reserved for domestic goods. For example, it used to be that imports of strawberries were forbidden while Belgian fields were in fruit. This shifted demand, but also reduced its price elasticity by preventing competition between native and imported fruit. The Belgian strawberry market was opened long ago, but it remains true throughout the Community that foreign suppliers do not have a ready access to public contracts. By reserving for domestic firms a portion of the domestic market, this reduces the elasticity of demand in the same way as in the strawberry example.

It was sometimes not sellers but buyers that were freed. It used to be that buyers of insurance were forced to sign long term contracts. Now that this obligation is abolished, they can switch readily between domestic suppliers as well as between domestic and foreign ones. Here also, the impact was to increase price elasticities and to shift demand curves.

Market reforms have destroyed cozy cartel agreements and forced producers to give up cozy co-operative agreements, changing the perceived elasticity of demand of producers. For example, EC banks can now set up branches anywhere in the Community. A "contestable competition" situation has come into being, which has destroyed the arrangements through which domestic banks colluded to keep at low levels the interest rates that they paid to depositors

Yet another effect of market integration has been to prevent producers from segmenting EC markets along national lines. The European Court of Justice has consistently taken the view that the Treaty of Rome prohibited efforts by

---

[6]A black currant liquor that is traditionally mixed into white wine cocktails.

firms to oppose parallel imports. A variety of dispositions in the EC92 program will make such imports far easier than in the past, preventing producers from setting different prices in different countries of the Community.[7]

The Commission also hopes that the EC92 program, by allowing for economies of scale, will induce a beneficial supply shock. Sharper competition will lead to an overall reduction of consumer prices, that will boost real wages. Assuming that real wages are semi-rigid so that the labour market does not clear, this will result in a moderation of wage claims which will make it possible to increase both together employment and welfare.

1.3 Imperfectly competitive market models and their properties

Like other imperfect competition market models (ICMM), Big Nonante Deux may be seen as a perfect competition model (PCMM) where a block of industries is imperfectly competitive. Production in those industries is subject to increasing returns to scale.

Increasing returns to scale may be introduced in various ways. In the model of this paper, they arise from the assumption that a fixed setup cost must be borne before production of a differentiated good is initiated; thereafter marginal cost is constant. This generates an average cost curve that is steeply declining when production is low, and almost flat when it is high.

Utility functions are taken to be of the nested CES form, which takes the classical form in the perfectly competitive sector, and the Dixit Stiglitz (1977) form in the imperfectly competitive ones. The latter is a CES function where the number of terms equals the number of differentiated goods that are produced.[8]

Individual firms do not matter in the perfectly competitive sector, where the basic unit is the industry. This is not true in the imperfectly competitive sector, where market behaviour is quite different if a single firm dominates an industry than if a dozen firms are active. In almost all such models, a symmetry assumption implies that firms are similar in each industry and country.

Returns to scale and efficiency in long run solutions

The mechanisms through which returns to scale influence efficiency in ICMM models are somewhat paradoxical; it is useful to sketch them briefly.

Strangely, market size has no direct impact on efficiency in the long run. Since the number of firms is not constrained to be an integer in these models, N producers have the same cost of production irrespective of whether N is small or large, so that a steel producer whose market is Monaco may attain the same

---

[7]For automobiles, producers have actually had to commit themselves to keep price divergences across countries within agreed bounds.
[8]For a more detailed discussion, see below.

cost of production as one who sells to the whole of the United States. Market size influences efficiency in the long run only if through some mechanism, it increases the perceived elasticity of demand, and so changes profit margins.

The first step in showing this is to note that according to the Lerner formula, the price markup over cost is proportional to the perceived elasticity of demand by producers. How this is determined depends on the assumed producer behaviour. We shall outline the argument for the Cournot case, that characterizes the producer behaviour that is assumed in the imperfectly competitive sectors.

Assume that the elasticity of substitution between the firm's good and those produced by other firms is σ, that all firms belong to the same country which has only one industry of which the aggregate price elasticity of demand is unity. Under the assumptions just specified, it is shown in the methodological appendix (see equation (14)) that the firm's perceived elasticity of demand is a function of s, the firm's market share in the industry, and the proportional conjecture coefficient γ, as defined by equation (10) in the appendix:

$$\epsilon = \frac{\sigma}{1 + (\sigma - 1)(s + \gamma(1 - s))}$$

According to the Lerner formula, the equilibrium price markup is $1/\epsilon$. Thus, the larger the firm's market share s or the conjecture coefficient γ, the smaller the firm's perceived demand elasticity ϵ and the larger the producer markup. Gross profit is thus qp/ϵ, where q is firm's output and p, the output price. Total output is nq, where n is the number of symmetrical firms, possibly not an integer.

Under free entry, gross profit should match the fixed setup cost of production f, i.e.:

$$f = \frac{pq}{\epsilon}$$

implying that the breakeven point of producers is given by:

$$q = \frac{f\epsilon}{p}$$

where f is a model parameter, and ϵ depends on the market share of producers and their perception of how other producers will behave in the market (Cournot or Bertrand behaviour, conjectural variations and so forth). What must be noticed is the absence of a direct link between the scale of firm's output q and the total industry demand.

A standard way of relating perceived demand elasticities to the size of the market is to note that in the first equation, since σ differs from unity, the changes in firm market shares that result from market integration modify the perceived elasticities of demand. Examination of the formula reveals however that this effect is very small unless the firm's market share is significant. In practice, statistical data imply rather low average market shares in industries. If so, the scale of output hardly changes from one simulation to the next; going to the trouble of introducing returns to scale in the model's cost functions is a waste of time. To solve that difficulty, Smith and Venables divided arbitrarily their industries into smaller sub-industries with a low number of firms. This is a valid idea - for household appliances, for example, the number of firms that produce washing machines is a good deal lower than the total number of producers in the industry- but an essentially arbitrary adjustment.

Free entry and quasi-infinitely elastic industry supply

In long term versions of ICMM models, it is customary to assume costless free entry and exit of producers. It is usual to combine this with an assumption of symmetry, which greatly simplifies the specification of Big Nonante Deux and the structure of its solution program; and (again for practical reasons) to let the number of firms be any real number. Jointly, those assumptions imply a crucial property of ICMM models that, as in perfect competition models where constant returns to scale are assumed, industry supply of each category of goods is perfectly elastic at the price defined by the Lerner formula.

The reason is easily set out. Under those assumptions, producers are in a contestable situation in the sense of Baumol, Panzar and Willig (1982). Because entry and exit are costless, any positive rent accruing to members of an industry is wiped out by entry; a loss is eliminated by exit.

The consequence is that ICMM models describe an extremely brutal market behaviour. Market reform wipes out entire industries in response to small changes in demand and supply conditions. This is not inherently wrong. That the distribution of output should be very sensitive in the long run to small differences in competitivity is not unrealistic, but the elimination of sub-marginal production units is slow when their competitive handicap is not large; how long this "long run" would be is a moot point.

Industries are also not homogeneous. Changes that worsen the prospects of a subsector might not affect (or even improve) those of another. Breaking down segmentation in the automobile industry, for example, will squeeze profit margins of European producers, but will very probably improve the prospects of the implants which Toyota, Nissan and other Japanese firms have founded in the UK. This is another reason why the impacts of market reform on industrial sectors might be less brutal than the model predicts. Our view is however that- to the extent that the long run spans a couple of decades at the minimum, the model is not wrong in predicting that the "1992" process will cause revolutionary changes, where industries that seemed permanent features of the industrial landscape of particular countries might, through a prolonged and politically painful process vanish as completely as the coal industry has disappeared in Belgium and the Netherlands.

Utility and the diversity of output

In recent ICMMs, the number of commodities is endogenous. This contrasts with the classical view, expressed in Debreu's Theory of Value for example, that the number of commodities is possibly very large but fixed. If goods were divisible, this would normally imply that the equilibrium problem should be defined over a denumerable number of goods or a continuum. This difficulty is avoided by the assumption that production of the various goods is subject to scale economies. If, for example, getting production of any good under way involves a set up cost, producers will offer consumers at any time a number of goods that is finite. Since it is not in the interest of competitors to produce a good that someone else produces, each producer will have a monopoly for the commodity (commodities) that he sells.[9]

As it would be awkward to assume that utility functions change every time a new product is introduced, we need a more basic utility function that enables consumers to evaluate the satisfactions that any new good will yield. The Dixit Stiglitz (1977) function that is used to represent utility is a CES function where the number of terms corresponds to the number of different goods that firms choose to produce. It implies that consumers attach utility to variety.

Therefore, the extent to which goods are subjectively "different" – as expressed by the values of the elasticities of substitution implied by the Dixit Stiglitz utility functions – is an important factor in assessing the welfare impact of the market integration. Not unreasonably, what consumers gain from an increase in the diversity of goods is larger if goods are highly differentiated (if elasticities of substitution are low) than if they are not (see appendix).

The chief merit of the Dixit Stiglitz specification is its simplicity. A defect is that the substitutability of goods does not depend on the number available. Taking wines as an illustration, consumers would find it impossible to tell wines apart if a thousand varieties existed with a very similar alcohol content, but could distinguish them easily if only a high and a low alcohol variety existed. The elasticity of substitution should thus increase as the number of types rises. The same should be true of the European market as enlargement widens the assortment of goods available to consumers, an effect that the Dixit Stiglitz specification assumes away. Note that this too is a reason to expect that market demand elasticities will change as a result of market reform.

Should demand be consistent with a social utility function?

Our discussion of the ways in which the 300 directives affect the economy suggests that market reform will increase the intensity of competition in many

---

[9]The analytically tractable assumption used by Negishi (1961) in a seminal article on general equilibrium under imperfect competition. In that article, unlike in the more recent literature, the number of goods is exogenous.

ways that cannot be readily translated into changes in the number of competitors in the market. Competition will be enhanced by making goods easier to substitute (changes in norms etc), and by eroding the ever present collusive element of business behaviour (the bank cartel example).

In Burniaux and Waelbroeck (1992), it was assumed that what happened was that goods would become more substitutable, i.e. that substitution elasticities would rise. Had we followed the normal practice in applied general equilibrium models to assume that market demand stems from clearly defined social utility functions- which do not exist except under extremely unrealistic assumptions- this would have implied the absurd assumption that "1992" works by changing utility functions. We decided to assume instead that in a market that is ridden by imperfection and regulation there is no close connection between utility and demand functions; this made it necessary to forsake any calculations of welfare gains. Assuming that an aggregate utility function exists is convenient in many ways, but should not be an obligatory component of "good practices" which are the hallmark of sound modelling research.

Modelling collusion through conjectural variations

In the present paper we have chosen to take the alternative, more orthodox view that perceived demand elasticities change because collusive practices break down as a result of market reform. Here also, we depart from the approach taken in other work.

It has become the tradition in ICMM modelling to assume that interaction between producers takes the form of a non co-operative game of the Bertrand or of Cournot type. Excluding the possibility of cooperation makes sense only if the interaction between agents is not repeated. This is not true of market interaction.[10] The appropriate intellectual framework is repeated games theory where, as implied by the so-called Folk Theorem, an embarrassingly broad variety of forms of cooperation can be sustained by the selfish and rational behaviour of agents.[11]

The threat mechanisms through which collusion can be supported are extraordinarily varied. Humorously, we may list ways of supporting cooperation which range from the murder threats that support Mafia cooperation and tips to newspapermen about insider trading by a leading German trade unionist, to the dynastic alliances that were so important in business in the old days and have not fallen altogether into disuse. Murder, calumny and love have no ready place in general equilibrium models unfortunately, and we must be less inventive. In Big Nonante Deux, collusion is supported by quantity conjectures (see equation (10) in appendix): competitors are deterred from invading markets by

---

[10]It is irrelevant in this context to argue that since the model is a one period model, it must be solved as a non repeated game. What the model provides is a snapshot of the system of threats and behavioural relations that describe behaviour at a point in time.

[11]An excellent overview of the topic is provided in Radner (1986).

threats to raise output if they do, and so triggering a price war.

Structural differences between countries and the distribution of benefits from market unification

A prevalent view is that the unification of the European market posed fewer problems to countries where markets are fairly free and firms large on average than to other members of the Community. Greece, Spain, and Portugal were skilful in exploiting that belief to exchange a large program of economic aid against their support of the single market.

This issue has broad relevance. Can Mexican industry adapt to the North American Free Trade Agreement? Will industry in the many developing countries that have slashed tariffs adapt easily to a more open environment? Many developing countries have argued that they cannot participate in GATT liberalization for banking and insurance, because their firms are too small and unused to the competitive environment of the world market.

This thinking, on the other hand, may be misguided. The shock imposed by market reform will be more severe in countries whose firms are too small but, just as obviously, the payoffs will be greater. One of the model's major goals is to shed light on this issue. This is achieved through the two-fold asymmetry of its structure across countries and regions.

The most pervasive asymmetry stems from the differences between countries in the intensity of competition. The data that we have used suggests that it is in Germany that profit margins are thinnest in the sectors that we have modelled, i.e. by the Lerner rule, i.e. it is in that country that perceived demand elasticities take their highest values.

The other important asymmetry stems from the fact that the "scope for further scale economies" in each country is smaller the higher the average size of the firms. This results from two model features. One is our use of a widely used specification according to which total cost is the sum of a fixed cost, and a variable cost that is proportional to output. The cost savings that result from scale economies therefore fall as output increases. The second relates to our assumption that, through calibration, the firms set-up costs across countries are not strictly proportional to their size. We accept in addition the often expressed view that at any time, the state of technological knowhow sets an upper limit to the scale of output.[12]

2 Data and calibration

Big Nonante Deux is calibrated on 1985 data. These include bilateral trade data built on the basis of the OECD trade data (serie C) and the UN Inter-

---

[12]Pratten (1988) provides empirical engineering estimates of this "minimum efficient size" of firms.

national Trade Statistics Yearbook. Data on outputs and factor contents were collected from national Input-Output tables, the Eurostat Industrial Survey and the Industrial Statistics Yearbook, United Nations, Volume II: Commodity Production Statistics. The number of firms in each industry are calculated by using Herfindahl concentration indices based on the Eurostat Industrial Survey and on national sources for non-EC countries (such as the Census of Manufactures).

An important parameter is the share of fixed costs in total costs, $(1 - \phi_r)$. This indicates the potential for scale economies: i.e. the extent to which average cost decreases when firm size increases.[13] There does exist information showing that average firm size differs substantially across countries, but there is no data on the share of fixed costs in total cost. Different views may be taken on this.

A first "proportional assumption" is that differences in firm size are correlated with product mixes: countries where firms are small on average would be those which are specialized in producing goods where scale economies are not considerable. This would justify assuming that fixed factor shares – and potential economies of scale – are the same for all sectors and countries (25% assumption).

The polar "constant assumption" is to assume that production functions are the same everywhere which implies that the levels of the fixed costs are the same whatever the size of the firms. Under this assumption, fixed costs are calculated from MES (Minimum Efficient Scale) and cost abatements for a given size increase, drawn from the engineering evaluations cited by Pratten (1988). This assumption implies large differences across countries in the fixed cost shares.[14]

In the third "mixed assumption", the central one in the paper, fixed costs are weighted averages of those calculated under the two previous assumptions.

Figures 5 to 8 report fixed factor shares under the three assumptions. In general, the potential for unexploited economies of scale is higher in the UK and the REEC region. For the EC average, the potential for increasing scale is lower in shipbuilding than in the other sectors. In the rest of the world, substantial room for increasing scale exists in the developing countries and for cars in Japan. Although these patterns make sense at a first glance, they are subject to large uncertainties with respect to data.

To represent the special adaptation problems that might confront countries where markets did not work well, we use the extremely bold device of assuming that the purchasing power parity differences in the model base year reflected differences in average markup, and hence differences in the intensity of competition. The chief merit of this assumption is that the ranking that resulted seemed very roughly sensible. The differences were deduced from Purchasing Power Par-

---

[13]It is easily shown that the elasticity of the average cost relative to the firm output is given by $-(1 - \phi)$.

[14]Our calibration method based on the data from Pratten (1988) implies the following world average fixed cost shares: household appliances: 19%; shipbuilding: 18%; iron and steel: 28%. For motor vehicles, the average fixed cost share was assumed equal to 20%.

ity (PPP) data;[15] it was assumed that half of the observed price differentials are related to market distortions, the rest to product differentiation. For the industries under consideration, PPP data for the period 1980-1985 suggest that the US has the most competitive market in the world. In comparison, markets in the EC, the developing countries and Japan would seem to be encumbered by regulations and imperfections that make them less competitive.

A set of initial tariff distortions are taken into account as ad valorem wedges: these involve (i) the EC common external tariffs (from Cawley and Davenport (1988)); (ii) the costs of border formalities[16] within the EC considered as tariff-equivalent (Cawley and Davenport (1988)); (iii) the VAT differentials across countries (see Commission of the European Communities (1988, p.61)).

Given the fixed factor shares and the initial tariffs, the markups and the corresponding perceived elasticities reflect the country-specific price levels; this implies that the model is solved iteratively for the conjectural variations coefficients. [17] Figures 1 to 4 show the levels of the conjectural variations in the benchmark equilibrium. They describe a defensive pattern of behaviour, where producers defend their domestic market by conjectural variations, but do not defend their market shares on export markets.

When fixed factor shares are the same everywhere (the 25% assumption), the base case conjectural variations depend on country-specific price differentials only. They are higher in the UK, the REEC region, and to a lesser extent in Italy, than in France and Germany. The shipbuilding industry is more protected than the other sectors. With the exception of shipbuilding, conjectural variations are higher in the LDCs than in Europe. Under the two other calibration assumptions (the mixed and the constant assumptions), distortions in each country reflect size as well as price differentials : relatively small firms need more non-tariff protection to compensate for their cost disadvantage. Some countries look more protective than others: e.g. the UK (all sectors except shipbuilding), Italy for motor vehicles and France for shipbuilding. Among the EC countries, Germany has the lowest conjectural variations in all four sectors.

---

[15]Eurostat (1987) and Kravis, Heston and Summers (1982).

[16]Border formalities comprise the administrative costs of both exporters and importers; agents' fees and border delays.

[17]We assume that there is only one non-zero conjectural variation on the market for domestic product in each country or, alternatively, that all competitors, whether domestic or foreign, are subject to the same non-zero conjectural variation.

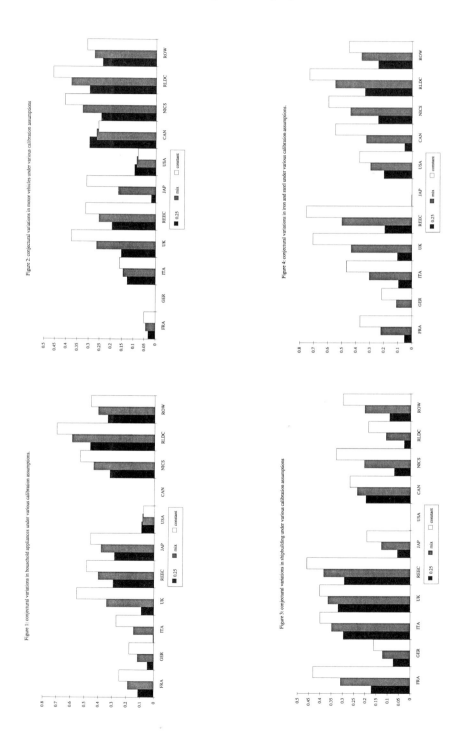

Figure 1: conjectural variations in household appliances under various calibration assumptions.

Figure 2: conjectural variations in motor vehicles under various calibration assumptions

Figure 3: conjectural variations in shipbuilding under various calibration assumptions

Figure 4: conjectural variations in iron and steel under various calibration assumptions.

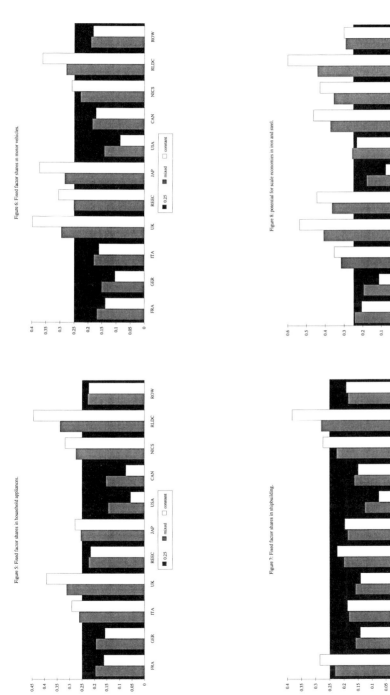

Figure 5: Fixed factor shares in household appliances.

Figure 6: Fixed factor shares in motor vehicles.

Figure 7: Fixed factor shares in shipbuilding.

Figure 8: potential for scale economies in iron and steel.

3 Simulation results

The following sections analyze the effects of implementing the Single Market of 1992. This implies removing a set of (quite low) border barriers of the type considered by traditional trade theory, and implementing a program of market reform that raises the intensity of competition. Border barriers are calibrated in the initial equilibrium for 1985: they involve internal tariffs applied to intra-EC trade and VAT, the rates of which differ across EC members.

3.1 Simulation assumptions

The heart of the 1992 process is market reform. It is assumed that (a) VAT differentials across EC Members are cut by half and (b) that the residual tariffs and other border obstacles to intra-EC trade are suppressed. For the sake of simplicity, barriers that involve real costs and are thus akin to transport costs are treated like ad- valorem wedges. This leads to a slight underestimate of the gains from market unification.

The market structure changes in two ways. First, the perceived elasticities of demand of producers rise as collusion becomes less effective. This effect is modelled via a reduction in conjectural variations to their lowest EC level. Second, producers lose their ability to price discriminate between EC country markets. As explained in the appendix, they determine the total volume of their EC sales as a function of the aggregated perceived demand elasticity on the whole EC market. Here also, conjectural variations are changed : as the market is unified, they are averaged across EC countries.

We have run both medium and long-term simulations. As always, the terms "long run" and "medium run" are to a certain extent conventional, in the sense that, as recent events suggest, the adjustments that the long run version of Big Nonante Deux predicts may begin very swiftly.

In the medium-term, there is no entry or exit of firms. Most firms are unable to reach their new breakeven level of output and sustain losses which they cover in a variety of ways; they may draw down reserves, obtain government support, or persuade their workers to accept low wages to safeguard their jobs.[18] Real wages are sticky. When a shock affects the economy, they move only some way to the market clearing level, so that employment rises or falls. The real wage is a weighted average[19] of a constant real wage [20] and of the market-clearing real wage.

---

[18]The technical device which is used in the specification is to assume that they receive subsidies paid for by lump-sum transfers from consumers. From an economic point of view, other adjustment devices are equivalent to this.

[19]The weight assigned to the equilibrium real wage reflects the extent to which the market is flexible. These weights vary across countries as follows: 0.5 for all EC regions/countries; Japan: 1.0; US: 0.8; Canada: 0.8; NICS: 0.3; RLDCs: 0.2; ROW: 0.6.

[20]Constant in terms of the average consumer price index.

Table 1 Welfare changes from the completion of the Single Market
(medium run solution)

Country	Without wage rigidity	With wage rigidity
FRA	-0.02	1.33
GER	-0.19	-1.22
ITA	0.18	1.50
UK	0.42	0.88
REEC	0.55	2.27
EEC	0.17	0.81

In the long run simulation the labour market clears. The firm losses (or gains) recorded in the medium-term are eliminated by exit (or entry) of firms or varieties. This mechanism is modulated by two assumptions:
(i) The size of firms cannot grow beyond the minimum efficient size identified by Pratten (1988);
(ii) At least one firm survives in each county and industry. This assumption may be taken to mean that firms are not truly symmetric, i.e. that a part of each domestic industry is efficient enough to survive whatever happens. Another interpretation is in terms of the desire of governments to avoid the complete disappearance of particular industries. The tortuous process through which a variety of British governments have kept alive Rover, the remaining national company, illustrates this political behaviour.
In the long run, labour is partly mobile between EC countries and capital is fully mobile through the world.
In what follows, the results presented are based on the "mixed calibration" version, taken as the central case. Failing a mention to the contrary, the figures represent percentage changes with respect to the base case.

3.2   A medium-term view of the Single European Market

Table 1 shows the welfare changes implied by the reference medium-term run. For the whole EC, the welfare improvement is less than 1 per cent: a modest gain indeed, much below those predicted in the Cecchini report. Moreover, it comes out that real wage rigidities account for most of these gains. This point is highlighted by comparing the central case with a counterfactual medium-term scenario in which real wages fully adjust to their market-clearing levels.
In contrast with similar studies, our results point to large disparities in the way EC Members benefit from integration. This of course reflects our "heterogeneous world" approach to the calibration of the model : inter-country

Table 2 Summary outcome of the medium-term scenario

Country	Firm size	Terms of trade	Profit rate	Real wage
FRA	12.2	-2.1	-4.0	0.3
GER	0.3	-3.6	-4.7	-0.2
ITA	18.1	1.0	-8.3	0.2
UK	25.8	5.4	-13.0	0.1
REEC	25.3	4.2	-9.0	0.3
EEC	13.2	1.4	-7.2	0.1

differences, an important and realistic aspect of real economies, do induce large differences in the impacts of policy changes on the various economies. This is a lesson of modelling of general equilibrium under imperfect competition that, we feel, warrants far greater attention than it has received so far in the literature. In the simulations carried out, the REEC region benefits most, while Germany loses in both scenarios.

What causes those results? Table 2 describes some important mechanisms that contribute to those results, which are analysed in the following subsections.

Modifications in producers' perception of the elasticity of demand

Market reform weakens collusion on domestic markets; this raises the perceived elasticities of demand and lowers markups following the Lerner formula. Demand for goods produced by the increasing returns industries rise as a result of the price fall.

Since there is no entry or exit, the average size of firms in the EC increases by 13 per cent only, although increases of more than 20 per cent are reported in the UK and in the REEC region. As the number of producers is fixed and the breakeven points rise sharply, a tendency to oversupply arises, which accounts for the losses reported in Table 2, amounting to 7 percent of turnover on average.

Intra and extra-EC trades, and the terms of trade

The mechanisms that influence the terms of trade in PCMMs also function in ICMMs. In addition, the markup changes induce changes in the terms of trade that are absent from perfect competition models.

Changes in competition on domestic markets affect the market perceptions of both domestic and foreign producers. For instance, the reduced conjectural variation coefficient for French producers of cars on the French market means that national producers as well as German and Japanese ones will perceive the French market as more competitive. Prices of both French and foreign cars will fall. This characteristic of the price reaction functions (20.a), (20.b) and (18.a) of the appendix is consistent with empirical observations by Ginsburgh and Vanhamme (1989), which show that export prices of cars depend more on the level of prices in the importing country than on producer costs.

According to the above mechanism, exporters in "competitive EC countries", i.e. countries that had more competitive markets from the beginning, respond to more open competition in other EC markets by increasing their exports at the cost of a fall in profit margins. This worsens the terms of trade of France and Germany, and improves those of Italy, the UK and the REEC (see Table 2). In Germany, the terms of trade depreciation (3.6 per cent) is not balanced by any gain from the removal of domestic distortions since the country has the most competitive markets in the EC for the increasing returns goods covered by the model. This contributes to the German welfare loss of more than 1 per cent.

Sectoral employment, output and welfare

The results depend on three effects.

The first is the familiar "supply shock" mechanism according to which, if the labour market does not clear, the reduced profit margins that result from the increased competitiveness of markets lower the consumer price index and boost real wages, so that employment rises. This effect accounts for part of the gain in EC welfare.

A second mechanism, that turns out to be a non-negligible offset to the "supply side" boost described above, affects wage claims and unemployment through the impact of the changes in VAT rates on the cost of living. These changes in tax rates are considered as a necessary accompaniment of market unification. If discrepancies in rates remained at today's high levels, consumers would have a strong incentive to use their new freedom to buy wherever VAT rates are low. VAT harmonization increases consumer prices in Germany and the UK.

The third mechanism is mediated through the movement of labour between increasing and constant returns sectors (Table 3). In all EC countries with the exception of Germany, the proportion of increasing returns goods in total output rises. For the EC average, these increases ranges from 10 per cent in household appliances to 19 per cent in shipbuilding. Since imperfectly competitive industries are more labour-intensive, the shift of the pattern of output in favor of increasing-return industries increases employment. This change also influences productivity. Since the marginal productivity of labour exceeds the wage in the imperfectly competitive sector, the countries that experience a shift in favour of increasing returns industries earn an efficiency windfall which boosts their welfare.

Germany, the most competitive country initially, is in fact the loser from the market unification process in the medium term. The mechanism is twofold: first, a loss of competitiveness due to growing pressures to raise wages, as a

Table 3 Changes in output of industries

Country	All sectors	Const. ret. sectors
FRA	1.4	0.9
GER	-1.0	-1.1
ITA	1.5	0.9
UK	0.7	-0.1
REEC	2.0	1.0
EEC	0.8	0.2

result mainly of the VAT harmonization; and, second, the terms-of-trade loss (-3.6 per cent) associated with the changes in mark-ups which result from sharper competition in other EC markets.

Unemployment in Germany increases by 17 per cent; elsewhere in the EC, the reduction in unemployment ranges between 7 per cent in the UK and 30 per cent in the REEC region. The impact on the rest of the world is minimal. Needless to say, these findings depend on the degree to which wage stickiness is effective in the medium term. [21]

3.3 A long-term view of "1992"

Exit and entry of firms, and shifts of industries between countries

The mechanism through which the increasing returns sectors reach equilibrium is quite different in the long and medium term versions of Big Nonante Deux. As in the medium simulation, the greater competitiveness of markets reduces profit margins, raising the breakeven points of producers. In the long term simulation, the number of firms falls through exit until the output of the survivors reaches the breakeven points and losses are wiped out.

As in the medium term simulation, outcomes vary widely across countries. In the integrated EC market, the perceived demand elasticities of producers from different countries do not differ markedly, so that producers have similar breakeven points after the European market is unified. It is in the countries where firms were initially small that breakeven points rise most and that many firms are closed down.

The market shares of eliminated firms/varieties are transferred to the remaining firms/varieties. This will allow most firms to cut their production costs. Where firms are operating at the efficient scale, however, new firms/varieties will proliferate. As a result, welfare changes will differ across countries to the extent

---

[21] The reader will remember that in the model, the real wage is not fully rigid; it adjusts part of the way to the market clearing model.

Table 4 Profit rates (medium term simulation)
and output changes (long term simulation)

Country	Profit rates				Output changes			
	Househ. appl.	Motor vehicles	Ship- build.	Iron Steel	Househ. appl.	Motor Vehicles	Ship- build.	Iron Steel
FRA	-5.2	-3.9	-6.8	-6.1	-6.7	37.0	-34.2	-30.5
GER	-3.0	-4.1	-1.2	-3.5	34.0	24.7	-9.1	-23.4
ITA	-3.8	-8.2	-21.9	-9.2	45.3	-45.8	-68.0	5.4
UK	-7.9	-13.6	-20.3	-11.9	11.0	-54.5	-79.5	17.0
REEC	-13.2	-11.1	-15.5	-7.7	-89.4	-98.1	-91.7	74.7
EEC	-6.0	-6.8	-13.1	-7.4	4.8	-6.0	-60.2	7.1

that firms were initially quite different in size. This process has general equilibrium repercussions on other industries; as labour is mobile, the proliferation of new firms in some industries raises wages, and crowds out labour from the others.

Table 4 links in an interesting way the results of the medium and long terms simulations. As explained, long term equilibrium is attained by weeding out loss making firms, raising the output of the others to the breakeven point. The table compares loss rates in the medium term simulation, and output changes in the long term one.

Unifying the EC market imposes the sharpest strain on the shipbuilding industry: losses are 13.1 per cent of turnover, compared with 7.4 per cent on average in the other increasing-return sectors. Rates of loss also provide informations on country and industry specific comparative advantages. For instance, France reports a loss rates of 3.9 percent in the motor vehicle industry that is less than its average loss rate of 4.7 per cent. Similarly way, Germany has some comparative advantages in shipbuilding and household appliances. Italy seems to be competitive for household appliances. Finally, the REEC region, the region with the least competitive markets according to the calibration, has a comparative advantage in the iron and steel industries. These medium term losses are fairly good predictors of the long run output changes.

Profit rates in the medium term simulation do not tell the whole story, however; the potentials for scale economies also play a significant role (see figures 5 and 6). Germany, for example, derives hardly any benefit from its relatively low loss rate for shipbuilding, because German shipyards are operating at close their maximum size, so that their costs do not respond to the rise in demand. In contrast, the high potential for size increase helps to explain why the REEC region is so successful in developing its iron and steel industry. The inter country movement of labour also matters: in Germany, layoffs in shipbuilding and steel free the labour resources which feed the expansion of the German household appliances and cars industries.

At the EC level, the output of the shipbuilding sector falls dramatically (-60 per cent). Although reporting similar medium-term loss rates, the output of iron and steel increases by 7 per cent, whereas motor vehicle output declines by 6 per cent; the explanation is that the former has a greater potential for scale increases than the latter. As the entry/exit mechanism is so flexible that it takes no account of adjustment costs, there is a strong tendency for output to concentrate in specific countries: household appliances are produced by Italy and Germany, motor vehicle production moves to France and Germany while the REEC region becomes specialized in producing iron and steel.

Not unexpectedly, the long term effect of market unification is specialisation between member countries of the Community. With the exception of shipbuilding, the impact of this structural change on the rest of the world is small. No non-EC country/region suffers perceptible harm.

The shipbuilding case deserves further explanations. The sharp decline in the European shipbuilding industry brings about a worldwide restructuring of that industry, benefiting in particular Third World countries. Almost 80 per cent of shipbuilding demand in the RLDC region had been met by imports, which accounted for a significant share of output in some industrialized countries (33 per cent in France, 47 per cent in Japan). With the collapse of French, German and Italian shipyards, their exports to the RLDC region are redistributed to Japanese exporters and indigenous firms. The latter benefit from a variety of protective devices and have a higher potential of unexploited scale economies than Japanese firms (see Figure 7). The infant shipbuilding industry in the Third World takes off, and achieves economies of scale so successfully that its members are able to confront Japanese competition head-on. A near collapse of the Japanese industry is the result, raising to 40 per cent the share of the RLDC region in world output. These results rely on uncertain assumptions and data, of course. But they deliver the message that in some highly imperfectly competitive industries, market reform in Europe may have a strong impact on firms in the rest of the world.

As a consequence of industry relocations, the EC becomes a net importer of increasing returns goods: intra-EC trade grows by 33 per cent, but imports from non-EC countries rise by 142 per cent. The elimination of non-tariff barriers through the 1992 process works to the advantage of non-EC firms, an outcome which is consistent with the econometric findings of Neven and Roller (1991).

Long-term equilibrium on the labour market

The process of firm relocation implies that increasing-return industries on average migrate from EC Members which were less competitive according with our calibration, such as the UK, Italy and the REEC region, to France and Germany (see Table 4). Since these industries are labour- intensive, this relocation causes French and German equilibrium wages to increase, which triggers a labour migration.

Table 5 Changes in the average size and number of firms
and their effect on the variety index

Country	Number of firms	Firm size	Variety index	Composite cons. price index of IR goods	Average prod. price index of IR goods
FRA	-30.2	63.1	3.5	-1.5	-3.5
GER	-22.3	42.4	4.0	5.5	0.5
ITA	-43.3	50.5	9.7	-5.6	-12.3
UK	-64.7	106.0	12.3	-13.3	-22.3
REEC	-59.3	69.9	9.5	-15.2	-21.3
EEC	-46.9	79.8	7.5	-5.7	-10.4

On the other hand, the employment gains recorded in the medium term vanish over the long run as wages come back to their equilibrium levels. This is the case in the UK, Italy and the REEC region where labour outflows are associated with constant or slightly declining real wages and increasing unemployment. In France, long-term employment is 0.6 per cent above its benchmark level while the real wage increases from its below-equilibrium value in the medium term. The opposite situation prevails in Germany where real wages fall by 1.3 per cent relative to their medium-term levels as a result of declining claims for wage increases as well as of the labour inflow.

Capital mobility

Exits of unprofitable firms cause an outflow of capital from Italy, the UK and the REEC region. Most of this capital goes to France and Germany. However, because the increasing-return sectors is relatively small, capital relocation within the EC accounts for a mere 0.3 per cent of the capacities in the benchmark situation. The proportion of capital leaving Europe is even smaller.

The variety effect

As illustrated in the appendix, a specific feature of the Dixit/Stiglitz demand system is that it relates welfare to the number of products or varieties supplied by each firm. The welfare loss caused by a reduction in the variety of products is the inverse of the variety index[22] given in Table 5.

---

[22]The variety index is the ratio of the composite price calculated at the benchmark producer prices and distortions to the benchmark value of the composite price. Therefore, the variety index reflects the change in the number of firms/varieties on welfare. An increase of the variety index indicates the percentage of their income which consumers would be willing to give up

Table 6 Welfare changes in the medium and long run solutions

Country	Medium run	Long run
FRA	1.33	0.39
GER	-1.22	0.17
ITA	1.50	-0.07
UK	0.88	-0.02
REEC	2.27	0.11
EEC	0.81	0.12

It turns out to be surprisingly large. Indeed, the variety indices increase by 7.5 per cent for the EC as a whole. The impact is particularly large in the countries where the number of firms drops very sharply such as Italy, the UK and the REEC region. It is interesting that the variety index, which is determined by a complex formula that reflects both market shares and changes in the number of differentiated goods sold by all countries, turns out not to be closely correlated with the number of domestic firms.

Welfare changes in the long-term equilibrium

As explained, the exit of firms raises welfare by freeing the resources that were locked up in their fixed costs and by allowing firms to increase their size to the breakeven point. This beneficial impact is in part offset however by the loss in utility which results from the reduction in the number of firms/varieties. Another feature of the long run equilibrium stems from our assumption that the labour market clears in the long run. Part of the medium run increase in welfare was the result of increased employment,[23] caused by the medium-run stickiness of the wage rate. This gain vanishes in the long run solution, where the labour market clears. Both effects contribute to explaining why the welfare gains in the long term solution do not exceed the medium term ones.

Under the mixed assumption, the long term gains from market reform turn out to be negligible at the EC level (+0.1 per cent; see Table 6). Moreover, the countries which gain most from the market integration in the medium term are those which benefit less in the longer run. The explanation is twofold. First, the migrations of labour and capital tend to redistribute the gains from market

---

to be offered the same range of choice as in the base case of the model.

[23] As labour is free to migrate between countries, changes in utility in this model do not necessarily imply corresponding changes in the utility of individual consumers. Correcting the utility measure to eliminate this effect would have implied arbitrary assumptions about the extent to which labour migration is accompanied by migration of the workers' non working spouses and children.

unification, to the benefit of the large countries - France and Germany - which happen to control most of the production of increasing-return goods in the long run. Second, the loss of variety is more severe in those countries where highly imperfect markets had allowed many marginal enterprises to survive.

3.4 Some sensitivity analysis

Sensitivity of the results to the calibration of fixed costs

Table 7 presents results for the two extreme assumptions on fixed cost shares. The more cost structures are differentiated across countries, the more extensive is production relocation. Although this modifies the magnitude of firm relocations, it does not change its direction markedly. Under the 25 per cent assumption, shipbuilding output falls by 16 per cent. The less vulnerable shipyards of France and Germany manage to survive and even increase their market shares. The industrial structure of the EC becomes less specialized than in the mixed assumption scenario. Under the polar fixed cost assumption, in contrast, the relocation of industries is drastic. The European shipbuilding industry is almost completely dismantled, while iron and steel production migrates massively to the REEC region.

Sensitivity of the results to substitution elasticities

There is little empirical evidence about the substitution elasticities between products from various firms, key parameters in the model. In their pioneering work, Smith and Venables (1988), by invoking the Lerner formula, calibrated their values on the basis of observed price-cost margins in the benchmark solution: these ranged between 5 and 40. The basic scenarios were run with elasticity values of 9, at the lower range of the Smith and Venables estimates. As a sensitivity test, we now run the scenarios with elasticities of 20.

The medium term results are quite close to those with elasticities equal to 9. Under the mixed assumption, however, the welfare gain doubles from the medium to the long term run, as reported on the Table 8. Gains are also distributed more evenly across EC members, whereas they were concentrated in France and Germany with the low substitution elasticities. As expected, fewer firms disappear (-40 per cent instead of -47 per cent). However, most of the difference in the results stems from the variety index, which increases by 3 per cent only compared with 7.5 per cent with the lower elasticities. The level of the substitution elasticities reflect a certain weight attributed to variety by consumers. For high elasticity values,[24] this weight falls and the gains from larger scale are no longer compensated by the losses associated with fewer firms/varieties.

---

[24]The elasticity of the aggregate composite price to the number of firms is -0.05 with the elasticity value equal to 20 instead of -0.125 with a value of 9 (see the appendix).

Table 7 Changes in output under alternative calibrations
of fixed costs
(25% assumption (25%) and constant f.c. assumption (Cst.))

Country	CR sectors	Househ. appl.	Motor vehicles	Ship- build.	Iron steel	Total
25%						
FRA	-0.3	0.4	22.6	11.7	0.0	0.5
GER	-0.5	22.7	27.8	5.1	-1.2	0.7
ITA	0.2	35.2	-3.5	-9.2	-1.0	0.2
UK	0.4	15.6	-34.4	-49.3	4.5	-0.2
REEC	1.4	-69.7	-89.7	-22.3	8.6	-0.4
EEC	0.2	4.7	0.9	-15.8	1.7	0.2
Cst						
FRA	0.7	-23.5	26.7	-88.6	-92.8	0.3
GER	0.8	14.0	17.0	-89.5	-93.2	0.0
ITA	1.0	75.9	-35.8	-73.0	-41.0	0.0
UK	0.9	17.6	-6.1	-77.6	29.9	0.9
REEC	-0.1	-86.6	-98.0	-90.1	276.8	1.6
EEC	0.7	3.8	-6.1	-85.8	20.2	0.5

Small, more protected countries (the UK and the REEC region) benefit from scale economies whereas large and less protected countries (France mainly) take advantage of a labour inflow in order to expand increasing return sectors, like the car industry. Thus the choice of substitution elasticities has a significant impact on the long run welfare results.

Remarks on industrial policy in an integrated market

Model simulations imply changes in the pattern of international specialization that seem drastic, in view of the small loss or profit rates that trigger them. For various reasons, those predictions may be excessive. A substantial fraction of the physical and human capital used in various industries is specific, and cannot be transferred readily to other uses. As a result, capitalists will accept a low remuneration rather than close factories. Workers will be willing to accept somewhat lower wages rather than forfeit acquired skills, and face the inconvenience of looking for another job. Government intervention is also likely; using various policy tools (public procurement, subsidies, tax concessions etc.),

Table 8 Welfare changes under
alternative elasticity assumptions

Country	Elasticity = 9	Elasticity = 20
FRA	.39	.34
GER	.17	.10
ITA	-.07	.23
UK	-.02	.40
REEC	.11	.51
EC	.12	.31

politicians will keep firms going.[25]

Cost reductions of this sort might affect the fixed or the variable cost of production. Subsidies to research, to the modernization of installations and the decision of businessmen to accept low profit rates because capital cannot be moved to more profitable uses change fixed costs. Wage givebacks by unions or wage subsidies granted by lowering social security levies affect variable costs.

There are many ways in which fixed and variable costs might ease adjustment, either through the working of market forces or through government intervention. In what follows, it is assumed that government intervention has taken place.

Do the results of the two types of support differ? Tables 9a and 9b compares results from these two types of intervention. In the first, referred to as a production subsidy in Table 9a, firms are subsidized (taxed) to the extent that the industry output decreases (increases).[26] With the second (Table 9b), subsidies are given to firms to keep them into activity whereas taxes have to be paid by new entrants. As the results illustrate, these types of intervention have quite different implications for welfare.

As aggregate output does not change markedly, the production subsidies scheme turns out to be roughly balanced at the EC level, with costs imposed on some countries financed by taxes on others.[27] France and Germany are net contributors, the other EC members are beneficiaries. Under both elasticity assumptions, the EC welfare gain is higher with than without this subsidy/tax, and the additional gains go to the countries/regions which benefit from this support. The subsidies prevent marginal firms in those countries from disappearing, so that their consumers benefit from a greater product variety. On the other

---

[25] Subsidies are strictly controlled under EC law, but government have proved highly inventive in using miscellaneous tricks to grant a moderate amount of assistance.

[26] Subsidies or taxes are calculated by using elasticities of output relative to the unit subsidy the value of which is arbitrarily set equal 5 in the two experiments presented in Table 3.

[27] The Common Agricultural Policy has always worked in this way.

hand, they stimulate scale increases in industries that have large unexploited scale economies (the household appliance industry in Italy; the steel industry in the UK and the REEC region); the number of firms is however unchanged in the EC as a whole.

The subsidy implied by the fixed costs scheme (Table 9b) prevents firms from reaching their breakeven points, checking the increase in their average size (+37 per cent instead of +79 per cent in the long term scenario); this is reasonable, since reducing fixed production costs lowers the gains that can be secured by increasing the scale of output. Interestingly, its impact on welfare depends on the consumers' taste for variety. If substitution elasticities are low (i.e. variety is highly valued), the subsidy actually raises welfare relative to the reference scenario (+0.17 per cent in Table 9a and 0.18 per cent in Table 9b instead of +0.12 per cent in Table 6). This does not happen if substitution elasticities have a value of 20, instead of 9.

That subsidies may be welfare improving is not surprising. The model diverges in two ways from the perfect competition standard on which theorems on the optimality of free trade are based. One is that competition is imperfect; our experiments suggest that this is not what causes the Big92 result that subsidies may be desirable. The other is that the "variety effect", which appears to be the crucial operative mechanism, is an externality from the point of view of buyers. The finding, we think, may have important practical implications, in particular it seems relevant to the hot Uruguay Round debate about whether European governments should be allowed to continue to subsidize national cultural channels, or should allow a free field for competition between suppliers of forms of entertainment.

Table 9a Results with proportional subsidy or tax
applied to production

Country	Welfare	Nb of firms	CR sector	Hous. appl.	Motor vehicl.	Ship-bldg	Iron steel	Total
FRA	-0.0	-36.4	0.1	1.3	7.9	7.6	-1.6	0.4
GER	-0.2	-29.7	0.2	8.2	0.9	9.4	0.2	0.3
ITA	0.2	-46.1	0.5	13.0	-7.9	-18.6	1.7	0.4
UK	0.4	-57.5	0.7	6.9	-13.0	-32.2	10.5	0.5
REEC	0.6	-53.4	0.8	-20.2	-12.0	-24.0	9.1	0.5
EEC	0.2	-46.3	0.5	3.0	-1.7	-13.2	3.6	0.4

Table 9b Results with subsidy or tax
applied to fixed costs

Country	Welfare	Nb of firms	CR sector	Hous. appl.	Motor vehicl.	Ship-bldg	Iron steel	Total
FRA	0.0	-14.3	-0.2	4.4	8.7	14.8	4.5	0.2
GER	-0.2	-11.8	-0.1	9.7	3.1	5.9	2.8	0.2
ITA	0.2	-21.6	0.0	12.4	2.1	-1.2	10.9	0.3
UK	0.5	-28.3	0.0	13.2	7.4	-14.4	24.6	0.4
REEC	0.6	-27.6	0.1	-5.2	1.4	-1.7	17.9	0.4
EEC	0.2	-21.9	0.0	7.2	4.7	-0.3	11.1	0.3

4 Conclusions

From a methodological point of view, the approach departs from similar studies in that it emphasises heterogeneity across countries. This is done in two ways.

First, Big Nonante Deux uses conjectural variation coefficients to represent different degrees of market imperfection. The conjectures reflect collusive practices which expectedly will be discontinued with the implementation of the Single European Market. The conjecture coefficients are calibrated in order to reproduce the price differentials which prevailed across EC members in 1985. In that context, the increase of competitiveness which should result from the removal of NTBs and public procurement practices is represented in our model by both a lowering of the conjectural variations in the more protective countries and a market desegmentation.

Second, countries are further differentiated to the extent that they are entitled with different potentials for additional economies of scale. Here, in the absence of reliable data, the coefficients depend on the calibration assumptions that were used. According to one calibration, fixed cost is the same proportion of total cost in every country/region in the initial period: i.e. the "potential scale economies" are the same everywhere. At the opposite extreme, fixed cost is the same everywhere; the scope for scale economies is thus a good deal larger in the small EEC countries than in the rest of the Community. The basic version of the model used a "mixed calibration" that combines the extreme ones.

As in other models used in this stream of literature, the calibration of Big Nonante Deux involved some heroic assumptions, in particular on the degree of competitivity in various EC countries.[28] Here, nonetheless, are our findings.

The outstanding result is that the study of structural heterogeneity provides a wide variety of novel insights into the policy implications of market reform between countries whose markets are relatively open and free of cumbersome regulations, and others whose markets are quite imperfect. It is usually thought that countries of the second type are the losers of such agreements, and must be compensated for this sacrifice, or provided with generous escape clauses. This is untrue.[29] Analysis of the results provides interesting insights into how this comes about.

The simulation results suggest that gains from the implementation of the Single European Market are quite small.[30] This runs counter the widespread

---

[28] In particular, it would have been desirable to split the "other EEC" group into its Northern and Southern members.

[29] A finding that should not be unexpected, even it runs counter to a widespread belief. Setting aside the fallacious optimum tariff argument and whatever seems to be implicitly accepted by participants to tariff liberalization negotiations, lowering protection likewise does not impose greater losses on high tariff countries than to low tariff ones: on the contrary, the protectionist countries are those that stand to gain most from a move to free trade.

[30] It can be argued that this results from the fact that the model includes only four of the sectors where production may be thought to be subject to scale economies. A more complete model would predict larger welfare gains from market integration, but the results would not

belief that general equilibrium models featuring imperfect competition and increasing returns to scale imply higher estimates of the welfare gains from trade liberalization than general equilibrium models of the traditional type. This is not due to the specification that was chosen; if anything, the model's design stacks the cards in favour of big welfare gains.[31] Imperfect competition and returns to scale do not solve the puzzle that comparisons of the economic performance of countries suggests that the gains from trade liberalization are quite large, whereas the message of economic theory is that they are negligible.[32]

The post-1992 market which Big Nonante Deux describes is a ruthless economic system, where gross profit margins are severely squeezed by market forces and market shares are very vulnerable to the pressure of competitors. Producers are eliminated in droves from this very competitive environment, whether through bankruptcies or through mergers and acquisitions, raising the concentration of industry at the European level.[33] The model describes a post-1992 Europe where entire industries come to be concentrated in one or two countries. Here, features of the model's design do exaggerate such effects.[34] However, relocations of large enterprises across the European area, as they are frequently reported by newspapers since the launching of the EC92 program, suggest that the model is basically correct, although the way medium and long terms are distinguished is doubtless oversimplified. A major goal of the EC92 program was to make markets more open, to do away with a host of obstacles that prevented efficient producers from squeezing out weaker ones and to eliminate host of monopoly rents stemming from special positions in restricted domestic markets. This will promote efficiency, but makes for an economic system where job security is far more limited than in the past, and the shape and very existence of individual producing units much less stable than in the past.[35]

As Big Nonante Deux describes an heterogeneous world, the results it yields point out important redistributional aspects across EC members, even if the gains at the EC level turn to be thin. In that sense; it captures a preoccu-

---

exceed ours by an order of magnitude.

[31] Through the large changes in perceived demand elasticities that are enforced via conjectural variations, and the use of a demand specification which assumes that consumers do not differentiate goods by place of production, i.e. that two French cars are not more substitutable for each other than a French and a Japanese one. On the other hand, it must be stressed that our sectoral coverage does not include all industrial sectors in which further scale economies are achievable.

[32] Krueger (1978) and Balassa (1987).

[33] Providing a justification for the recent strengthening of the antitrust powers of the Commission.

[34] The assumption of symmetry of producers, in particular, which implies that all producers in an industry and country have identical costs of production and become unprofitable together. It is also assumed that (contrary to the message of the Armington assumption) consumers are indifferent to the place of production of goods so that, for example, the elasticity of substitution in France between two French wines is not higher than between a French and a Spanish one.

[35] It is fair to say that the Social Chapter of the Maastricht Treaty is a belated addendum to the single market program rather than a part of the program of European monetary unification.

pation of the promoters of the Single Market, who were concerned over the special problems that the move to an integrated, deregulated market would pose to countries whose markets were encumbered by regulations and market imperfections. The Southern members of the Community used this argument successfully to convince their richer brethren to grant them a large amount of aid in exchange for their support of the EC92 program. The model draws attention to the fairly obvious truth that it is the countries whose markets had been imperfect and overregulated that will derive the greatest benefits from market integration and deregulation, at least in the medium term. They will have to make a larger effort to adapt to the new situation- but the gains that they will derive from market reform will outweigh those which countries with initially more liberal markets will obtain. The picture over the longer run is somewhat mixed and depends on the weight attributed to product diversity. Moreover, part of the medium term gains will be lost, through the movement of capital and labour to the more developed members of the Community which accompanies the relocation of increasing- return industries.

Finally, we have run a variety of simulations to assess the *sensitivity of the results to key parameters*. In general, these reveal a lack of robustness of imperfect competition model results to parameters that we know little about at present. Hopefully, empirical research will fill what is at present a glaring gap in our knowledge of the economy.

Among the variety of results obtained, two seem particularly interesting. First, the share of fixed to total costs is a key parameter. The more production functions are differentiated across countries, the larger the amount of industry relocation which is induced by the market reform.

The second is the high sensitivity of welfare impact to the choice of substitution elasticities between differentiated goods. According to the Dixit-Stiglitz function, utility rises when the number of goods available to consumers increases. Market reform has thus two opposite effects on welfare. It increases it by promoting a fuller use of potential scale economies, but reduces it by narrowing the range of goods available. The second effect can be shown to be stronger when substitution elasticities are low than when they are high. It comes as a striking result that, for the values of the substitution elasticities used in the central case, this effect canceled out much of the efficiency gain brought about by a fuller exploitation of economies of scale, accounting for the low values of the calculated welfare gains. These gains doubled when substitution elasticities of 20 were used instead of the base model values of 9. The distribution of welfare gains across countries also was more even with high than with low elasticities.

5   References

Bilson, J.F. (1980), The rational expectations approach to the consumption function: a multi-country study, *European Economic Review* 13, 273-299.

Balassa, B. (1987), Exports and economic growth: further evidence, *Journal of Development Economics* volume number please, 181-189.

Baumol, W., J. Panzar and R. Willig (1982), *Contestable Markets and the Theory of Industry Structure*, New York: Harcourt Brace Jovanovich.

Burniaux, J.-M., and J. Waelbroeck (1992), Preliminary results of two general equilibrium models with imperfect competition, *Journal of Policy Modelling* 14, 65-92.

Cawley R. and M Davenport (1988), Partial equilibrium calculations of the impact of internal market barriers in the European Community, in *Studies on the Economics of Integration. Research on the "Cost of non-Europe", Basic Findings*, Volume 2, Brussels Commission of the European Communities.

Cecchnini, P. (1988), *1992, The European Challenge: the Benefits of a Single Market*, London: Wildwood House.

Commission of the European Communities (1988), The economics of 1992, *European Economy* 35.

Cox, D., and R. Harris (1985), Trade liberalization and industrial organization: some estimates for Canada, *Journal of Political Economy* 93, 15-145.

Cox, D, and R Harris (1986), A quantitative assessment of the economic impact on Canada of sectoral trade with the United States, *Canadian Journal of Economics* 19, 377-394.

Dixit, A., and J. Stiglitz (1977), Monopolistic competition and optimum product diversity, *American Economic Review* 67, 297-308.

Eurostat (1987), *World Comparisons of Purchasing Power and Real Product for 1980*, New York: United Nations.

Ginsburgh, V. and G. Vanhamme (1989), Price differences in the EC car market: some further results, *Annales d'Economie et de Statistique* 15-16.

Haaland, J. and A. Wooton (1991), Market integration and welfare, CEPR Paper presented at the Third IT 92 Workshop, Kiel, Germany, 1991.

Harris, R. (1984), Applied general equilibrium analysis of small open economies with scale economies and imperfect competition, *American Economic Review* 74, 1016-1032.

Kravis, I., A. Heston and R. Summers (1982), *World Product and Income: International Comparisons of Real Gross Products*, Baltimore: Johns Hopkins University Press.

Krueger, A. (1978), *Foreign Trade Regimes and Economic Development: Liberalization Attempts and Consequences*, Cambridge, Mass : Ballinger for the National Bureau of Economic Research.

Negishi, T. (1961), Monopolistic competition and general equilibrium, *Review of Economic Studies* 28, 196-201.

Neven D. and L. Rller (1991), European integration and trade Flows, *European Economic Review* 35-6, 1295-1310.

Pratten C. (1988), A survey of the economies of scale" in *Studies on the Economics of Integration. Research on the "Cost of non-Europe"*, Basic Findings, Volume 2, Brussels Commission of the European Communities.

Radner, R. (1986), Can bounded rationality resolve the prisoners' dilemma, in A. Mas-Colell and W. Hildenbrand, eds., *Essays in Honour of Grard Debreu*, Amsterdam: North-Holland.

Smith, A., and A. Venables (1988), Completing the internal market in the European Community: some industry simulations, *European Economic Review* 32, 1501-1526.

6   Appendix. Specification of the model

The model has a standard multi-regional, multi-sectoral structure. Countries or regions are denoted by the index r, with $r = 1, ..., R$. The current version of the model involves five EC countries/regions (France, Germany, Italy, the UK and the Rest of the EC members – REEC) and five non-EC regions (Japan, the US, Canada, the NICs[36] and the Rest of the LDCs – RLDC). There are four increasing-return-to-scale sectors, denoted by $i = 1, ..., IS$: household appliances (NACE 345, CITI 3829, ISIC 775); motor vehicles (NACE 35, CITI 3843, ISIC 78-785); shipbuilding (NACE 361, CITI 3841, ISIC 793); iron and steel (NACE 221, CITI 3710, ISIC 67). The output of the residual sector (CS), as well as labour (L) and capital (K), are sold on perfectly competitive markets.

6.1   Consumer behavior

There is one representative consumer in each country or region. His utility is described by a two level system of Constant Elasticity of Substitution (CES) functions. At the first level, the consumer chooses the optimal consumption of each commodity, whereas at the second level commodity demands are allocated between individual countries (in the competitive sector) or firms (in the imperfectly competitive one). Firms in the imperfectly competitive sector in

---

[36] Including Argentina, Brazil, Hong Kong, Israel, South Korea, Philippines, Singapore, South Africa, Taiwan, Thailand and Yugoslavia.

an industry of a given country/region are assumed to be identical. The two-level utility function in each country/region r' (r' is omitted in the following equations) is specified as follows:

$$U = [b_{cs}(\sum_r a_{cs.r}x_{cs.r}^{-\rho_{cs}})^{\rho_g/\rho_{cs}} + \sum_i b_i(\sum_r n_{i.r}a_{i.r}x_{i.r}^{-\rho_i})^{\rho_g/\rho_i}]^{\frac{-1}{\rho_g}} \quad (1)$$

In equation (1), the $x_{cs.r}$ denote consumer demands for the constant-returns commodity. For the increasing-return commodity i, on the other hand, $x_{i.r}$ refers to the demand addressed to each firm, whereas $n_{i.r}$ stands for the number of firms producing the commodity i in country r.[37] The ρ_g, ρ_{cs} and ρ_i parameters are derived from the substitution elasticities between commodities (σ_g for the first level elasticities, σ_{cs} for the second level elasticities for constant-return goods from the r countries or regions, and σ_i for elasticities between products from individual firms from domestic or foreign origins in the i increasing-return industry). The b and a parameters are distribution coefficients at the two levels, respectively.

The utility function (1) is associated with the following price index which is calculated as a CES aggregate of the composite price of the constant-return product (P_{cs}) and of the composite prices of the various increasing-return commodities (P_i):

$$P = [b_{cs}^{\sigma_g} P_{cs}^{1-\sigma_g} + \sum_i b_i^{\sigma_g} P_i^{1-\sigma_g}]^{\frac{1}{1-\sigma_g}} \quad (2a)$$

$$P = [b_{cs}^{\sigma_g}(\sum_r a_{cs.r}^{\sigma_{cs.r}}(p_{cs.r}(1+\tau_{cs.r}))^{1-\sigma_{cs}})^{\frac{1-\sigma_g}{1-\sigma_{cs}}}$$

$$+ \sum_i b_i^{\sigma_g}(\sum_r n_{i.r}a_{i.r}^{\sigma_i}(p_{i.r}(1+\tau_{i.r}))^{1-\sigma_i})^{\frac{1-\sigma_g}{1-\sigma_c}}]^{\frac{1}{1-\sigma_g}} . \quad (2b)$$

In the above expression (2), $p_{cs.r}$ refers to the producer price of the constant-return commodity in region r and $p_{i.r}$ to the producer price of the increasing-return good i; $\tau_{cs.r}$ and $\tau_{i.r}$ stand for ad-valorem taxes or subsidies.

We next derive the demands for the constant-return commodity addressed to each country r ($x_{cs.r}$) and the demands for the increasing-return good i addressed to each individual firm from country r ($x_{i.r}$):

$$x_{cs.r} = a_{cs.r}^{\sigma_{cs}} b_{cs}^{\sigma_g}(p_{cs.r}(1+\tau_{cs.r}))^{-\sigma_{cs}} P_{cs}^{(\sigma_{cs}-\sigma_g)} P^{(\sigma_g-1)}Y, \quad (3a)$$

where P_{cs} is the CES aggregate price index of constant-return commodities from various countries r; Y is the total consumer expenditure and P, the total consumer price index and:

---

[37]This specification does not distinguish between economies of scale and economies of scope. Therefore, $n_{i.r}$ refers equally to the number of firms or varieties in country r.

$$x_{i.r} = a_{i.r}^{\sigma_i} b_i^{\sigma_g} (p_{i.r}(1 + \tau_{i.r}))^{-\sigma_i} P_i^{(\sigma_i - \sigma_g)} P^{(\sigma_g - 1)} Y, \tag{3b}$$

where P_i is the CES aggregate price index of the increasing-return good i and $p_{i.r}$, the price charged by individual firms in each country r (including taxes).

Variety effect in consumer demand

To show how welfare changes as the number of firms is modified, we simplify the demand system, as it is described by equations (1) to (3), by assuming one country and one commodity. The composite price index and the demand adressed to each firm are respectively expressed as follows:

$$P = n^{\frac{1}{1-\sigma}} \alpha^{\frac{\sigma}{1-\sigma}} p$$

and $x = Y/np$ with $Y = PU$.

With σ greater than unity, the composite price index P of the Dixit/Stiglitz utility function increases (decreases) when the number of firms n is reduced (increased). However, since firms are symmetric, entries and exits change their demands proportionnally.

The larger σ, the value of the substitution elasticity between firms products or varieties, the smaller the increase of the composite price P and the reduction of utility U which results from a reduction in the number of firms. As pointed out in discussions of the simulations, this loss is quite significant. The elasticity of the composite price index to the number of firms/varieties is equal to $1/(1-\sigma)$. For a substitution elasticity equal to 9, it means that a 50 per cent reduction of the number of firms implies that the composite price (the welfare) increases (decreases) by 6.2 per cent.

6.2   Firm behavior in increasing return industries

Producers of increasing-return commodities choose their output quantity to maximise profit. Assuming that p is the producer price, the optimal output level x must satisfy the following stationarity condition:

$$p + x\frac{\partial p}{\partial x} - c'(x) = 0, \tag{4}$$

where $\partial p/\partial x$ is the partial derivative of the inverse demand function relative to the firm output x and $c'(x)$ is the marginal cost.

Quantity competition on a segmented market

The stationarity condition (4) can be restated in terms of the perceived elasticity of demand; this leads to equation (5), the well known Lerner pricing rule. On a segmented market, producers optimize their output on each bilateral market rr' by applying condition (4). This means that the sale price of products from country r is different on each country market r' according to the perceived demand elasticity ($\epsilon_{rr'} > 1$) and to the marginal cost in country r (in equation (5), ϕ_r is a constant and pv_r is the price index of variable costs):

$$p_{i.rr'} = \frac{\epsilon_{i.rr'}}{\epsilon_{i.rr'} - 1} \phi_r pv_r \qquad (5)$$

From equation (3b), we derive the demand elasticity perceived by a firm j from country r relative to market r' ($\epsilon_{i.rr'} = \frac{dx_{i.rr'}}{dp(j)_{i.rr'}} \frac{p(j)_{i.rr'}}{x_{i.rr'}}$) as a function of the perceived elasticity of the composite price index of good i in country r' relative to the price paid to the j firm in country r ($\epsilon_{Pi.rr'} = \frac{dP_{ir'}}{dp(j)_{i.rr'}} \frac{p(j)_{i.rr'}}{P_{i.r'}}$):

$$\epsilon_{i.rr'} = \sigma_i - [(s_i - s_g) + (s_g - 1)b_{i.r'}^{\sigma_g}(\frac{P_{i.r'}}{P_{r'}})^{(1-\sigma_g)}]\epsilon_{Pi.rr'} \qquad (6a)$$

$$\epsilon_{i.rr'} = \sigma_i - [(s_i - s_g) + (s_g - 1)s_{i.r'}]\epsilon_{Pi.rr'} \qquad (6b)$$

where $s_{i.r'}$ is the share of the increasing-return commodity i in the total consumer expenditure in country r'.

The next step is to derive the elasticity $\epsilon_{Pi.rr'}$ from the expression of the composite price of the increasing-return good i, as expressed at the right-hand term of equation (2):

$$\epsilon_{Pi.rr'} = p(j)_{i.rr'}^{1-\sigma_i} P_{i.r'}^{\sigma_i-1}[a_{i.rr'}^{\sigma_i}(1 + \tau_{i.rr'})^{\sigma_i-1}$$

$$+(n_{i.r} - 1)a_{i.rr'}^{\sigma_i}(1 + \tau_{i.rr'})^{\sigma_i-1}p(k)_{i.rr'}^{1-\sigma_i}p(j)_{i.rr'}^{\sigma_i-1}(\frac{dp(k)_{i.rr'}}{dp(j)_{i.rr'}} \frac{p(j)_{i.rr'}}{p(k)_{i.rr'}}) \qquad (7)$$

$$+ \sum_{r'' \neq r} n_{i.r''r'}a_{i.r''r'}^{\sigma_i}(1 + \tau_{i.r''r'})^{\sigma_i-1}p_{i.r''r'}^{1-\sigma_i}p(j)_{i.rr'}^{\sigma_i-1}(\frac{dp_{i.r''r'}}{dp(j)_{i.rr'}} \frac{p(j)_{i.rr'}}{p_{i.r''r'}})].$$

The expression between brackets at the end of the second line of the equation (7) represents the perceived reaction of a firm k from country r to a change in the output of the firm j from the same country. It is the price reaction function $R_{i.rr'}^r$ of a firm from country r on market r' and is expressed in terms of the inverse demand functions of both firms. The expression between brackets at the end of the last line of equation (7) is the perceived price reaction $R_{i.r''r'}^r$ of a representative firm from a foreign country r'' to the strategy followed by firm j in country r.

Equation (7) can be rewritten by introducing the market shares.[38] Let us define $s_{i.rr'}$ as the market share of a representative firm from country r in the demand by the country r' for commodity i:

[38]This analytical presentation draws inspiration from a paper by Haaland and Wooton (1991).

$$s_{i.rr'} = \frac{x_{i.rr'} p_{i.rr'} (1 + \tau_{i.rr'})}{X_{i.r'} P_{i.r'}} = a_{i.rr'}^{\sigma_i} p_{i.rr'}^{1-\sigma_i} (1 + \tau_{i.rr'})^{1-\sigma_i} P_{i.r'}^{\sigma_i - 1}. \qquad (8)$$

The reaction function of the aggregate price – see the equation (7) – may be further rewritten as a *weighted average* of the firms price reactions in country r and r'', with $n_{i.r}$ being the number of firms in country r (to which belongs firm j) and $r_{i.r''}$, the number of firms in countries r'':

$$\epsilon_{Pi.rr'} = s_{i.rr'} + (n_{i.r} - 1) s_{i.rr'} R_{i.rr'}^r + \sum_{r'' \neq r} n_{i.r''} s_{i.r''r'} R_{i.r''r'}^r. \qquad (9)$$

The last step is to characterize the expectations of the firm j in country r. We assume that producer j forms *proportional conjectures*: his expectation is that any producer from his own country r or from another country r'' will respond to a one per cent increase of his production by increasing output by γ per cent. Therefore, we have:

$$\frac{dx_{i.\bullet r'}}{x_{i.\bullet r'}} = \gamma_{i.\bullet r'}^r \frac{dx_{i.rr'}}{x_{i.rr'}} \qquad (10)$$

where $\bullet$ stands for the home country r of the firm j as well as foreign countries r''.

For each market r', there is a vector of R conjecture coefficients γ which characterizes the reactions of each country-specific producers to a change of output by a producer from country r, whatever its origin. Therefore, this implies that all producers form the same conjecture about the reaction of a representative producer from a given country. In other words, the reaction of the French producers, for instance, is perceived in the same way by German or Japanese producers.[39] The conjecture (10) is rewritten in terms of the derivatives of firm outputs relative to the price charged by firm j in country r, as follows:

$$\frac{dx_{i.\bullet r'}}{dp(j)_{i.rr'}} \frac{dp(j)_{i.rr'}}{dx_{i.rr'}} = \gamma_{i.\bullet r'}^r \frac{x_{i.\bullet r}}{x_{i.rr'}} \qquad (11)$$

The left-hand term of the equation (11) is calculated by using the demand equation (3b) and yields the following expression:

$$\gamma_{i.\bullet r'} = \frac{-\sigma_i R_{i.\bullet r'}^r + (\sigma_i - \sigma_g) \epsilon_{Pi.rr'} + (\sigma_g - 1) s_{i.r'} \epsilon_{Pi.rr'}}{-\sigma_i + (\sigma_i - \sigma_g) \epsilon_{Pi.rr'} + (\sigma_g - 1) s_{i.r'} \epsilon_{Pi.rr'}} \qquad (12)$$

From (12), we derive equation (13) which expresses the price reaction of any other firm from country $\bullet$ (with $\bullet = 1, ..., R$) as it is perceived by firm j from

---

[39] An alternative and more complicated specification could be to associate a bilateral matrix of conjecture coefficients to each r' market, so that the expectations would be different across producers from different countries.

country r on the market r'. This price reaction depends on the conjecture $\gamma^r_{i.\bullet r'}$ and on the perceived elasticity of the composite price $\epsilon_{Pi.rr'}$ relative to the price $p(j)_{i.rr'}$ charged by firm j:

$$R^r_{i.\bullet r'} = \gamma^r_{i.\bullet r'} + (1 - \gamma^r_{i.\bullet r'})\frac{\sigma_i - S_{i.r'}}{\sigma_i}\epsilon_{Pi.rr'} \tag{13}$$

where:

$$S_{i.r'} = [(1 - s_{i.r'})\sigma_g] + s_{i.r'}$$

Equations (13) and (9) are solved simultaneously for the price reactions $R^r_{i.\bullet r'}$ (for $\bullet = 1, ..., R$), so that the price reactions and the corresponding optimal sales of each firm on market r' depend on the conjecture coefficients, the market shares, the number of firms in each country and the market elasticities:

$$R^r_{i.\bullet r'} = f(\gamma^r_{i.\bullet r'}, s_{i.r'}, s_{i.1r'}, ..., s_{r.Rr'}, n_{i.1}, ..., n_{i.R}, \sigma_i)$$

Once the $R^r_{i.\bullet.r'}$ are known, the perceived aggregate commodity price elasticity $\epsilon_{Pi.rr'}$ (equation (9)) and the perceived demand elasticities $\epsilon_{i.rr'}$ (equation (6)) are calculated.

Equation (13) shows that these price reactions increase when conjectures $\gamma^r_{i.\bullet r'}$ are different from zero. It means that the perceived demand elasticity of a Japanese firm which exports to France, for instance, will depend largely on the perceived price reaction of the French firms. It will fall to the extent that French firms become more competitive which, in turn, is related to the degree of protection from which these firms benefit. On the other hand, any increase of the degree of collusion between French firms - as a result from new protective measures - will induce Japanese exporters to cut their exports to France while their export prices will tend to evolve in line with the French prices.

For didactical purposes, we simplify equations (9) and (13) by assuming that the conjectural variations are the same for all country-specific producers ($\gamma^r_{i.\bullet r'} = \gamma^r_{i.r'}$) so that the expression of perceived demand elasticities can be rewritten in a much simpler way:

$$\epsilon_{i.rr'} = \frac{\sigma_i S_{i.r'}}{S_{i.r'} + (\sigma_i - S_{i.r'})(s_{i.rr'} + (1 - s_{i.rr'})\gamma^r_{i.r'})} \tag{14}$$

Equation (14) shows that the perceived elasticity of demand is lower if producers anticipate a defensive reaction of other producers (associated with a higher value of the conjecture coefficient $\gamma_{i.r'}$), that raises output in response to higher sales by competitors. Such defensive tactics, by lowering the perceived elasticity of demand on a given market, lead competitors to raise their prices and to sell less.

Assuming $\gamma^r_{i.r'} = 0$ leads to the familiar Cournot specification of the perceived demand elasticity. With only one commodity ($S_{i.r'} = 1$), it can be verified that the perceived elasticity is lower the higher the share of the firm from country r in total expenditure:

$$\epsilon_{i.rr'} = \frac{\sigma_i}{1 + (\sigma_i - 1)s_{i.rr'}} \tag{15}$$

The opposite perfectly collusive case involves unitary γ coefficients. Then, the perceived elasticity turns to be equal to $S_{i.r'}$ which derives from the commodity level substitution elasticity, as shown by equation (13). It ranges from unity in the case of a single commodity to the value of the inter-commodity substitution elasticity (σ_g) when the share of commodity i in total expenditure tends to zero.

Quantity competition on an integrated market

On an integrated market, firms maximise their profit by choosing the optimal level of selling as a whole. We first need to define the firm demand on the integrated market, $X_{i.\bar{r}\bar{R}}$ by summing equation (3b) over the countries which are integrated ($\bar{r} = 1, ..., \bar{R}$):

$$X_{i.\bar{r}\bar{R}} = P_{i.\bar{r}\bar{R}} \sum_{\bar{r}'} a_{i.\bar{r}\bar{r}'}^{\sigma_i} b_{i.\bar{r}'}^{\sigma_g} (1 + \tau_{i.\bar{r}\bar{r}'})^{-\sigma_i} P_{i.\bar{r}}^{(\sigma_i - \sigma_g)} P_{\bar{r}'}^{(\sigma_g - 1)} Y_{\bar{r}'} \tag{16}$$

where $P_{i.\bar{r}\bar{R}}$ is the common price that the firm from country $\bar{r}$ charges in the integrated area.

The perceived demand elasticity over the integrated area $\epsilon_{i.\bar{r}\bar{R}}$ is derived from equation (16) and depends on the weighted average of the perceived commodity price elasticities in integrated countries:

$$\epsilon_{i.\bar{r}\bar{R}} = \sigma_i - \sum_{\bar{r}'} \theta_{i.\bar{r}\bar{r}'} \epsilon_{Pi.\bar{r}\bar{r}'}((\sigma_i - \sigma_g) + (\sigma_g - 1)s_{i.\bar{r}'})$$

or

$$\epsilon_{i.\bar{r}\bar{R}} = \sigma_i - \sum_{\bar{r}'} \theta_{i.\bar{r}\bar{r}'} \epsilon_{Pi.\bar{r}\bar{r}'}(\sigma_i - S_{i.\bar{r}'}) \tag{17}$$

with

$$S_{i.\bar{r}'} = \sigma_g - (\sigma_g - 1)s_{i.\bar{r}'}$$

and

$$\theta_{i.\bar{r}\bar{r}'} = \frac{x_{i.\bar{r}\bar{r}'}}{X_{i.\bar{r}\bar{R}}}.$$

In the above expression, $\epsilon_{Pi.\bar{r}\bar{r}'}$ is the perceived reaction of the commodity i price index in country $\bar{r}'$ relative to the price charged by a firm from country $\bar{r}$

which belongs to the integrated area. This elasticity derives from a new equilibrium of reaction functions and is not equivalent to a simple weighted average of the perceived elasticities in the segmented market, as they are specified in the equation (6).

The aggregate commodity price elasticity $\epsilon_{Pi.\bar{r}\bar{r}'}$ can be expressed by using the market shares, as in the equation (9), as a function of:

(i) the price reactions of producers from the same country $\bar{r}(R^{\bar{r}}_{i.\bar{r}\bar{r}'})$;

(ii) the price reactions of producers from foreign countries $\bar{r}''$ which belong also to the integrated market $R^{\bar{r}}_{i.\bar{r}''\bar{r}'}$;

(iii) the price reactions of producers from foreign countries r" outside the integrated area $R^{\bar{r}}_{i.r''\bar{r}'}$:

$$\epsilon_{Pi.\bar{r}\bar{r}'} = s_{i.\bar{r}\bar{r}'} + (n_{i.\bar{r}} - 1)s_{i.\bar{r}\bar{r}'}R^{\bar{r}}_{i.\bar{r}\bar{r}'}$$

$$+ \sum_{\bar{r}''\neq\bar{r}} n_{i.\bar{r}''}s_{i.\bar{r}''\bar{r}'}R^{\bar{r}}_{i.\bar{r}''\bar{r}'} + \sum_{r''} n_{i.r''}s_{i.r''\bar{r}'}R^{\bar{r}}_{i.r''\bar{r}'}. \tag{18a}$$

The aggregate commodity index elasticity perceived by producers from countries r" outside the integrated area $\epsilon_{Pi.r''\bar{r}'}$ is calculated in a similar way on the basis of perceived price reactions by producers from the same country r" $(R^{r''}_{i.r''\bar{r}'})$, the perceived price reactions by producers from other countries which are not integrated $(R^{r''}_{i.r\neq r''\bar{r}'})$ and the perceived price reactions by producers from integrated countries $(R^{r''}_{i.\bar{r}\bar{r}'})$:

$$\epsilon_{Pi.r''\bar{r}'} = s_{i.r''\bar{r}'} + (n_{i.r''} - 1)s_{i.r''\bar{r}'}R^{r''}_{i.r''\bar{r}'}$$

$$+ \sum_{r\neq r''} n_{i.r}s_{i.r\bar{r}'}R^{r''}_{i.rr'} + \sum_{\bar{r}} n_{i.\bar{r}}s_{i.\bar{r}\bar{r}'}R^{r''}_{i.\bar{r}\bar{r}'}. \tag{18b}$$

New conjectures have to be defined within the integrated market. Let $\gamma^{\bar{r}}_{i.\bullet\bar{R}}$ be the expectation of producer j in country $\bar{r}$ which belongs to the integrated market about the reaction of any other producer in the integrated area ($\bullet$ represents the country $\bar{r}$ or any other country $\bar{r}''$ which is part of the integrated area). We make the bold assumption that this conjecture coefficient is calculated as the weighted average of the coefficients for the corresponding market segments. Therefore:

$$\frac{dX_{i.\bullet\bar{R}}}{X_{i.\bullet\bar{R}}} = \gamma^{\bar{r}}_{i.\bullet\bar{R}}\frac{dX_{i.\bar{r}\bar{R}}}{X_{i.\bar{r}\bar{R}}}, \tag{19}$$

with

$$\gamma^{\bar{r}}_{i.\bullet\bar{R}} = \sum_{\bar{r}'} \theta_{i.\bar{r}\bar{r}'}\gamma^{\bar{r}}_{i.\bullet\bar{r}'}$$

for $\bar{\bullet} = 1, ..., \bar{R}$.

Price reaction functions are then derived following a method similar to that outlined in equations (11), (12) and (13). However, we have to distinguish four cases:

(a) the price reaction of a producer from an integrated country $\bar{r}$ as perceived by another producer from that country, given its quantity conjecture $\gamma^{\bar{r}}_{i.\bar{r}\bar{R}}$:

$$R^{\bar{r}}_{i.\bar{r}\bar{R}} = \gamma^{\bar{r}}_{i.\bar{r}\bar{R}} + (1 - \gamma^{\bar{r}}_{i.\bar{r}\bar{R}}) \sum_{\bar{r}'} \theta_{i.\bar{r}\bar{r}'} \epsilon_{Pi.\bar{r}\bar{r}'} \left(\frac{\sigma_i - S_{i.\bar{r}'}}{\sigma_i} \right), \qquad (20a)$$

where $\epsilon_{Pi.\bar{r}\bar{r}'}$ is the $\bar{r}'$ market perceived elasticity of the commodity index to a change of the price of a producer from country $\bar{r}$.

(b) the price reaction of a producer from an integrated country $\bar{r}'' \neq \bar{r}$ as perceived by a producer from the integrated country $\bar{r}$, given its quantity conjecture $\gamma^{\bar{r}}_{i.\bar{r}''\bar{R}}$:

$$R^{\bar{r}}_{i.\bar{r}''\bar{R}} = \gamma^{\bar{r}}_{i.\bar{r}\bar{R}} + \sum_{\bar{r}'} \theta_{i.\bar{r}''\bar{r}'} \epsilon_{Pi.\bar{r}\bar{r}'} \left(\frac{\sigma_i - S_{i.\bar{r}'}}{\sigma_i} \right)$$

$$- \gamma^{\bar{r}}_{i.\bar{r}''\bar{R}} \sum_{\bar{r}'} \theta_{i.\bar{r}\bar{r}'} \epsilon_{Pi.\bar{r}\bar{r}'} \left(\frac{\sigma_i - S_{i.\bar{r}'}}{\sigma_i} \right); \qquad (20b)$$

(c) the price reaction of a producer which does not belong to the integraged area $(r'' \neq \bar{r})$ as perceived by a producer from the integrated country $\bar{r}$, given its quantity conjecture $\gamma^{\bar{r}}_{i.r''\bar{r}'}$:

$$R^{\bar{r}}_{i.r''\bar{r}'} = \gamma^{\bar{r}}_{i.r''\bar{r}'} + \epsilon_{Pi.\bar{r}\bar{r}'} \left(\frac{\sigma_i - S_{i.\bar{r}'}}{\sigma_i} \right)$$

$$- \gamma^{\bar{r}}_{i.r''\bar{r}'} \sum_{\bar{r}'} \theta_{i.\bar{r}\bar{r}'} \epsilon_{Pi.\bar{r}\bar{r}'} \left(\frac{\sigma_i - S_{i.\bar{r}'}}{\sigma_i} \right) \qquad (20c);$$

(d) the price reaction of a producer from an integrated country $\bar{r}$ as perceived by a producer from a non-integrated country $\bar{r}''$, given its quantity conjecture $\gamma^{r''}_{i.\bar{r}\bar{R}}$:

$$R^{r''}_{i.\bar{r}\bar{r}'} = \gamma^{r''}_{i.\bar{r}\bar{R}} + \sum_{\bar{r}'} \theta_{i.\bar{r}\bar{r}'} \epsilon_{Pi.r''\bar{r}'} \left(\frac{\sigma_i - S_{i.\bar{r}'}}{\sigma_i} \right)$$

$$- \gamma^{r''}_{i.\bar{r}\bar{R}} \epsilon_{Pi.r''\bar{r}} \left(\frac{\sigma_i - S_{i.\bar{r}'}}{\sigma_i} \right). \qquad (20d)$$

Table A summarizes how the various equations are used to solve the equilibrium with an integrated market.

Table A Equations used to solve for equilibrium

	$\bar{r}'$ integrated importing countries	r' non-integrated importing countries
$\bar{r}$ integrated exporting countries	price reaction functions (20a,b,c) are used in (18a) in order to calculate one perceived elasticity $\epsilon_{i.\bar{r}\bar{R}}$ (equation (17)) on each integrated market $\bar{r}\bar{R}$	price reaction functions (13) are used in (9) in order to calculate one perceived elasticity $\epsilon_{i.\bar{r}r'}$ (equation (6)) on each segmented market $\bar{r}r'$
r non-integrated exporting countries	price reaction functions (13) and (20d) are used in (18b) in order to calculate one perceived elasticity $\epsilon_{i.r\bar{r}'}$ (equation (6)) on each segmented market $r\bar{r}'$	price reaction functions (13) are used in (9) in order to calculate one perceived elasticity $\epsilon_{i.rr'}$ (equation (6)) on each segmented market rr'

6.3   Production functions

Each increasing-return industry i is described by a two-level production function. At the first level, production requires variable costs proportional to output (ϕ_r) and a fixed amount of fixed cost F_r for each firm/variety (with n_r being the number of firms/varieties). At the second level, variable costs are CES aggregates of labor (Lv) and capital (Kv) whereas fixed costs combine labor (Lf) and capital (Kf) in fixed proportions:

$$\sum_{r'} x_{r.r'} = \phi_r \sum_{r'} x_{r.r'} + n_r F_r$$

$$= [a_{r.Lv} Lv_r^{-\rho_v} + a_{r.Kv} Kv_r^{-\rho_v}]^{-\rho_v} + n_r [a_{r.Lf} F_r + a_{r.Kf} F_r]. \qquad (21)$$

From equation (21), it is easy to verify that the average unit cost is an inversed function of the firm size:

$$\frac{\sum_{r'} p_{rr'} x_{rr'}}{\sum_{r'} x_{rr'}} = \phi_r pv_r + \frac{n_r}{\sum_{r'} x_{rr'}} F_r pf_r \qquad (22)$$

where pv_r is the aggregate price index of variable costs and pf_r, the price index of fixed costs.

5

Completing the European internal market: a general equilibrium evaluation under alternative market structure assumptions[1]

Jean Mercenier

C.R.D.E. and Département de sciences économiques
Université de Montréal

1 Introduction

The European Commission's action for the completion of a single European market before 1993, is generally recognized to involve two complementary pro-competitive components. The first is the removal of all remaining tariffs that restrict intra EEC trade. The second, more drastic (and hypothetical), is the elimination of all forms of visible and invisible non-tariff barriers that give to firms the power to price-discriminate between segmented national markets. As a result, firms would be forced to act on an integrated EEC-wide basis and charge the same price within the Community. The two strategies have been formalized and evaluated for a number of specific sub-industries by Smith and Venables (1988) using a calibrated partial-equilibrium model of trade under

[1] I wish to thank Anton Barten, Camille Bronsard, David Encaoua, Victor Ginsburgh, Fabienne Ilzkovitz, Jacques Robert, Nicolas Schmitt and Randy Wigle for encouragements and discussions at various stages of this research, to Alasdair Smith for kindly providing detailed information on various aspects of the Smith-Venables (1988) methodology and data, to an anonymous referee for careful reading and comments, and to Nathalie Sheehan for her never failing collaboration. I have also benefited from stimulating comments by seminar participants at the Université de Montréal, Université de Paris I and at the University of Western Ontario, and by participants of the European Economic Association Meeting (Cambridge, August 1991), of the IIASA CGE Meeting (Laxenburg, August 1991), of the Second Waterloo CGE Meeting (Waterloo, October 1991) and of the conference on Europe 1992 and Beyond organized in honor of Jean Waelbroeck (Bruxelles, January 1992). None of these bear any responsibility for what follows. Some simulations have been performed on a CRAY at the CEME of the Université Libre de Bruxelles; I am extremely grateful to Simon Erlich for his help on this occasion. Financial support from the European Commission, from the FCAR of the Government of Québec, and from the SSHRC of the Government of Canada is gratefully acknowledged.

imperfect competition, increasing returns to scale and product differentiation. The conclusion they draw from their industry simulation studies is that the welfare gains that may be expected to result from the first strategy are quite mild. In contrast, these may be quite substantial when firms are denied the possibility to exploit their monopoly power on individual national markets.

The aim of this paper is to investigate whether the conclusions of the Smith-Venables partial equilibrium study concerning the no-price-discrimination scenario remain valid when general equilibrium effects are taken into account. Obviously, there are many reasons why this might not be so. Firstly, partial equilibrium neglects the contribution of material components of variable costs: relative price changes in intermediate inputs will affect the firm's ratio of average to variable cost, i.e., the elasticity of scale economies. Also, partial equilibrium assumes constant factor prices. However, if factor prices are to remain unaffected by the emergence of a single European market, then, clearly, there is no reason to make such a big fuss about 1992: the answer is in the assumption. Consistency, therefore, requires that the European Commission's objective be evaluated assuming that more intensive competition for primary factors will result from the policy change. If this is indeed the case, the response of non-competitive firms to market integration could be extremely different from the one reported by Smith and Venables: factor prices influence the potential for scale economies by acting on both variable and fixed costs. Finally, 1992 also means more competition between industries for demand: general equilibrium takes into account the necessary coherence between demands and budget constraints while providing more accurate welfare evaluations than the triangular calculations of partial equilibrium.

The model we use is a static world economy model consisting of six countries/regions: Great-Britain (GB), the Federal Republic of Germany (D), France (Fr), Italy (It), the rest of EEC10 (RE) and the rest of OECD (*ROW*). All countries are fully endogenous and have the same structure. Each country has nine sectors of production (see Table 1) of which four are of the perfect-competitive type. In these sectors, countries are linked by an Armington system implying that commodities are differentiated in demand by their geographical origin. The other five industries operate with increasing returns to scale in non-competitive markets, each firm producing a different good. Final demand decisions are made in each country by a single representative utility-maximizing household. A detailed country- and sector-specific system of price-responsive intermediate demands is specified. All components of demand - final as well as intermediate - recognize differences in products from individual oligopolistic firms in a similar way, à la Dixit-Stiglitz (1977). The model therefore includes ingredients of standard CGE global models [e.g., Gunning, Carrin, Waelbroeck et al (1982), Mercenier and Waelbroeck (1984, 1986), Whalley (1982, 1985, 1986)], of single country models with increasing returns to scale [e.g., Harris (1984), Cox and Harris (1985)] and of trade models with product differentiation at the individual firm level [e.g., Krugman (1979), Smith and Venables (1988)].[2] Note, however, that we do not account for the possibility of firms achieving economies of scope. More importantly, we do not account for the growth effects of 1992 : our focus is on induced reallocations of existing resources, as worldwide factor supplies are assumed fixed. See Baldwin (1989) and Mercenier and Michel (1992) for estimates of the potential dynamic gains from 1992.

Following Smith and Venables (1988), we model "European Integration" as a move from an initial equilibrium with price-discriminated segmented national markets to an equilibrium with firms selling at a unique price on the whole European market. Our evaluations are performed under alternative non-competitive market structure and primary factor mobility assumptions. More specifically, results are reported for the two alternative cases in which firms make their decisions using prices or output, with and without free entry/exit of firms from the industry. In the "short run" (fixed number of firms), capital and labor are assumed perfectly mobile across sectors within national boundaries, while in the "long run" (variable number of firms), intra-EEC mobility of labor and international mobility of capital prevails. The paper also provides systematic comparisons between general equilibrium results and partial equilibrium evaluations of individual sectors.

The paper is organized as follows. In section 2, the structure of the general equilibrium model is presented. Section 3 discusses the assumptions and procedure used for the calibration of the model to the base year data set. Both partial and general equilibrium results are reported in section 4. The paper closes with a brief conclusion.

2 The model

We first define the different commodity sets. Sectors of activity are identified by indices s and t, with S representing the set of all industries so that $s, t = 1,...,S$. S is partitioned into the subset of competitive-constant-returns-to-scale sectors, denoted C, and the subset of non-competitive-increasing-returns-to-scale industries, which we note $\overline{C}$; we have $C \cup \overline{C} = S$. We identify countries by indices i and j, with $i, j = 1,...,W$ and $W = EEC \cup ROW$, where the first subset represents the EEC10, and the last subset represents the OECD countries that do not belong to EEC. In a multi-country multi-sector framework, it is necessary to keep track of the trade flows by their geographical and sectoral origin and destination. We follow the usual practice that identifies the first two indices with, respectively, the country and industry supplying the good, and, when appropriate, the next two with the purchasing country and industry. Thus,

---

[2]See also Nguyen and Wigle (1989) for a global model with imperfect competition and increasing returns to scale. Their model does not include product differentiation at firm level, however, and their modeling of the strategic behavior of firms is somewhat ad hoc.

Table 1 Sectoral disaggregation and industry characteristics

Agriculture and primary products	$\in C$	SITC: 2,3,4
Food, beverages and tobacco	$\in C$	SITC: 1,0
Pharmaceutical products⋆	$\in \overline{C}$	SITC: 54;
		NACE-CLIO: 257
Chemicals other than pharmaceuticals	$\in \overline{C}$	SITC:5-54
Motor vehicles⋆	$\in \overline{C}$	SITC:78;
		NACE-CLIO:350
Office machines⋆	$\in \overline{C}$	SITC: 75;
		NACE-CLIO: 330
Other machines and transport materials	$\in \overline{C}$	SITC:7-78-75
Other manufacturing industry	$\in C$	SITC: 6,8,9
Transport and services	$\in C$	Non-traded

Note: C = competitive; $\overline{C}$ = non-competitive
⋆ sub-industry common with Smith and Venables

a subscript $isjt$ indicates a flow originating in sector s of country i with industry t of country j as recipient. More than once, it will be necessary to aggregate variables with respect to a particular subscript. In order to avoid unnecessary proliferation of symbols, it will be convenient to keep the original notation, but substitute a dot for the subscript on which aggregation has been performed; for instance $c_{.si}$ is an aggregate of c_{jsi} with respect to the first subscript. With these notational conventions, we may proceed to the description of our model.

2.1 Households

It is assumed that domestic final demand decisions in country i are made by a single representative agent. The domestic household values products of competitive industries from different countries as imperfect substitutes (the Armington assumption), while it treats as specific each good produced by individual firms operating in the non-competitive industries. This is represented by a two-level utility function. The first level combines consumption goods ($c_{.si}$) assuming constant expenditure shares (ρ_{si}). The second level determines the optimal composition of the consumption aggregates in terms of geographical origin for competitive industries, or in terms of the individual firm's product for the non-competitive sectors. Assuming symmetry between the n_{js} non-competitive firms operating within country j's industry s, the domestic household's preferences are represented as follows :

$$U_i = \sum_{s \in S} \rho_{si} \ell og(c_{.si}), \sum_{s \in S} \rho_{si} = 1,$$

$$c_{.si} = \left\{ \sum_{j \in W} \delta_{jsi} c_{jsi}^{\frac{\sigma_s - 1}{\sigma_s}} \right\}^{\frac{\sigma_s}{\sigma_s - 1}}, s \in C, \qquad (2.1)$$

$$c_{.si} = \left\{ \sum_{j \in W} n_{js} \delta_{jsi} c_{jsi}^{\frac{\sigma_s - 1}{\sigma_s}} \right\}^{\frac{\sigma_s}{\sigma_s - 1}}, s \in \overline{C},$$

where δ_{jsi} are share parameters and σ_s are substitution elasticities. Observe that when $s \in C$, c_{jsi} denotes the sales of the whole industry s of country j, whereas when $s \in \overline{C}$, it represents the sales of a single firm. Note also that this formulation is sufficiently general to allow for the treatment of non-traded goods; for such goods, $\delta_{jsi} = 0, \forall j \neq i$.

The consumer's total consumption spending at current prices is equal to national income Y_i. This is the sum of labor earnings $(\Sigma_s w_i L_{is})$, and of capital revenues. Capital earnings of national agents include capital rentals at rate r_j and pure profits Π_{js} generated in each country j in proportion Ω_{jsi} to initial claims on domestic and foreign capital stocks : $\Sigma_j \Sigma_s \Omega_{jsi} [r_j K_{js} + \Pi_{js}]$. Note that both primary factors are assumed perfectly mobile across sectors, but immobile internationally.

Final demands c_{jsi} of country i therefore result from maximization of (2.1) subject to the following budget constraint:

$$Y_i = \sum_{j \in W} \sum_{s \in C} p_{js.} c_{jsi} + \sum_{j \in W} \sum_{s \in \overline{C}} p_{jsi} n_{js} c_{jsi}$$
$$= \sum_{s \in S} w_i L_{is} + \sum_{j \in W} \sum_{s \in S} \Omega_{jsi} [r_j K_{js} + \Pi_{js}], \Omega_{jsi} \geq 0, \sum_{i \in W} \Omega_{jsi} = 1,$$

where p denotes prices. Observe that this formulation recognizes the possibility for non-competitive firms to price discriminate between client countries (p_{jsi}) but not for competitive industries ($p_{js.}$).

2.2   Firms

a) Competitive industries

In competitive industries, the representative firm of country i-sector s, operates with constant-returns-to-scale technologies combining capital (K_{is}^v), labor (L_{is}^v) and intermediate inputs (x_{jtis}). Material inputs are introduced in the production function in a similar way as consumption goods are treated in the preferences of households : with an Armington specification for goods produced by competitive industries, with product differentiation at firm level in the imperfectly competitive sectors (Ethier-type specification). Input demands by producer $s \in C$ result from minimization of variable unit cost v_{is} :

$$v_{is}Q_{is} = \sum_{j \in W} \sum_{t \in C} p_{jt}.x_{jtis} + \sum_{j \in W} \sum_{t \in \overline{C}} p_{jti}x_{jtis} + w_i L_{is}^v + r_i K_{is}^v \tag{2.2a}$$

such that :

$$log(Q_{is}) = \alpha_{Lis}log(L_{is}^v) + \alpha_{Kis}log(K_{is}^v) + \sum_{t \in S} \alpha_{tis}log(x_{.tis}),$$

$$x_{.tis} = \left\{ \sum_{j \in W} \beta_{jtis}x_{jtis}^{\frac{\sigma_t - 1}{\sigma_t}} \right\}^{\frac{\sigma_t}{\sigma_t - 1}}, s \in C, \tag{2.2b}$$

$$x_{.tis} = \left\{ \sum_{j \in W} n_{jt}\beta_{jtis}x_{jtis}^{\frac{\sigma_t - 1}{\sigma_t}} \right\}^{\frac{\sigma_t}{\sigma_t - 1}}, s \in \overline{C},$$

where αs and βs are share parameters with

$$\alpha_{Lis} + \alpha_{Kis} + \sum_{t \in S} \alpha_{tis} = 1$$

and $\beta_{jtis} = 0, \forall j \neq i$, if t is non-traded. Observe that although goods enter consumers' preferences and producers' technologies with the same degree of differentiation (substitution elasticities are assumed identical by lack of econometric data), price responsiveness will differ as the βs are sector specific.

Profit maximization implies zero profits and marginal cost pricing in the competitive sectors so that:

$$p_{is.} = v_{is}, s \in C.$$

b) Non-competitive industries

Non-competitive industries have increasing returns to scale in production. We model this by assuming that, in addition to variable costs associated with technological constraints, similar to (2.2), individual firms face fixed primary factor costs. This introduces a wedge between total unit costs V_{is} and marginal costs v_{is}:

$$V_{is} = v_{is} + \frac{\left[w_i L_{is}^F + r_i K_{is}^F\right]}{Q_{is}}, s \in \overline{C},$$

where $Q_{is}, L_{is}^F, K_{is}^F$ denote respectively the individual firm's output, fixed labor and fixed capital.

With initial market segmentation, the non-competitive firm exploits the monopoly power it has on each individual country market. To establish this, each producer is endowed with the full knowledge of preferences (2.1) and technologies (2.2) of its clients. Using this information, he performs a partial equilibrium calculation, assuming that in each country, each individual client's current-price expenditure on the whole industry is unaffected by the firm's own action.[3] On the basis of the resulting perceived demand curves, the firm chooses country specific profit maximizing prices using the Lerner formula:

$$\frac{p_{isj} - v_{is}}{p_{isj}} = \frac{-1}{E_{isj}}, s \in \overline{C}, \tag{2.3}$$

where $E_{isj} < 0$ is the firm's perceived elasticity of demand for market j. E_{isj} depends crucially on whether oligopolistic firms use prices or quantities as decision variables when maximizing profits.

Let us assume first that the control variable is the selling price. E_{isj} will then be the sum of two terms:

$$E_{isj} = \varepsilon_{isj} + \sum_f \lambda_{isj}^f \varepsilon_{isj}^f.$$

The first term measures the direct effect of the firm's action on its own sales, that is, the (perceived) price elasticity of demand. It is straightforward to show that this elasticity is given by the following expression:

$$\varepsilon_{isj} = -\sigma_s + [\sigma_s - 1] \left\{ \frac{c_{isj}}{\left[c_{isj} + \sum_t x_{isjt} \right]} \frac{p_{isj} c_{isj}}{\rho_{sj} Y_j} + \sum_t \left[\frac{x_{isjt}}{\left[c_{isj} + \sum_t x_{isjt} \right]} \frac{p_{isj} x_{isjt}}{\alpha_{sjt} v_{jt} Q_{jt}} \right] \right\},$$

$$\tag{2.4a}$$

which is the sum of the elasticities of each component of country j's aggregate demand with respect to the firm's price, weighted by the relative importance of each sub-demand in the firm's total sale to country j. The second term of E_{isj} accounts for the indirect consequences on its own sales of the reactions the firm expects from each of its competitors f. This indirect effect is the sum over the set of all competitors, of the perceived slope of the competitors' price reaction functions λ_{isj}^f multiplied by the cross-price elasticities of demand ε_{isj}^f, where

$$\lambda_{isj}^f = \frac{\partial log p_{fsj}}{\partial log p_{isj}}, \varepsilon_{isj}^f = \frac{\partial log \left[c_{isj} + \sum_t x_{isjt} \right]}{\partial log p_{fsj}},$$

---

[3] In other words, for a firm producing in country i, sector $s \in \overline{C}$, $\frac{\partial \rho_{sj} Y_j}{\partial a_{isj}} = 0, j = 1, ...W$, $\frac{\partial \alpha_{sjt} v_{jt} Q_{jt}}{\partial a_{isj}} = 0, j = 1, ..., W, t = 1, ..., S$, where a_{isj} represents the firm's action. It is partial in the sense that it does not take into account the true induced income effects (which one can expect to be extremely small).

and the summation runs over the set of all competitors to the firm i under consideration. Cross-elasticities are related to preferences, technologies and market shares in a simple way, so that they can be endogenized. ε_{isj}^f is the sum of the cross-elasticities of each component of country j's aggregate demand with respect to the competitor f's price, weighted by the relative importance of each sub-demand in the firm's total sales to country j:

$$\varepsilon_{isj}^f = [\sigma_s - 1] \left\{ \frac{c_{isj}}{\left[c_{isj} + \sum_t x_{isjt} \right]} \frac{p_{fsj} c_{fsj}}{\rho_{sj} Y_j} + \sum_t \left[\frac{x_{isjt}}{\left[c_{isj} + \sum_t x_{isjt} \right]} \frac{p_{fsj} x_{fsjt}}{\alpha_{sjt} v_{jt} Q_{jt}} \right] \right\},$$

(2.4b)

To determine the conjectures λ_{isj}^f, we shall need some additional assumptions on the perceived reaction functions. These will be detailed in a later section where the calibration of the model to a base year data set is discussed. Observe that with all λ_{isj}^f set to zero, the equilibrium is Bertrand-Nash.

If it is assumed that rather than using prices as decision variables, the noncompetitive firm maximizes profits with respect to quantities supplied on market j, we then have:

$$\frac{1}{E_{isj}} = \tilde{\varepsilon}_{isj} + \sum_f \tilde{\lambda}_{isj}^f \tilde{\varepsilon}_{isj}^f,$$

where the summation runs over the set of the firm's competitors on the j market, and $\tilde{\varepsilon}_{isj}, \tilde{\varepsilon}_{isj}^f$ respectively represent direct elasticities and cross-elasticities of inverse demand functions:

$$\tilde{\varepsilon}_{isj} = \frac{\partial \ell o g p_{isj}}{\partial \ell o g \left[c_{isj} + \sum_t x_{isjt} \right]}, \tilde{\varepsilon}_{isj}^f = \frac{\partial \ell o g p_{isj}}{\partial \ell o g \left[c_{fsj} + \sum_t x_{fsjt} \right]},$$

and $\tilde{\lambda}_{isj}^f$ is the expected output reaction of competitor f consequent to the firm's change in own sales in market j:

$$\tilde{\lambda}_{isj}^f = \frac{\partial \ell o g \left[c_{fsj} + \sum_t x_{fsjt} \right]}{\partial \ell o g \left[c_{isj} + \sum_t x_{isjt} \right]}.$$

Although the computation of the direct and cross-elasticities $\tilde{\varepsilon}_{isj}$ and $\tilde{\varepsilon}_{isj}^f$ is extremely complex because of the distinction made between final and intermediate demands – for each country and non-competitive sector one has to invert the log-linearized aggregate demand system[4] -, they are endogenously determined in the model. However, for the perceived reactions of competitors we

---

[4]It may be shown that for each $s \in \overline{C}$, $i \in W$, $j \in W$, the direct elasticity $\tilde{\varepsilon}_{isj}$ and vector of cross-elasticities $\left(\tilde{\varepsilon}_{isj}^f \right)_{f=1,\ldots,W}$ are the solution of the following system (with $k \in W$):

shall again need some additional assumptions to be detailed in the following section. Observe that a Cournot-Nash equilibrium is obtained when all $\tilde{\lambda}_{isj}^f$ are set to zero.

In the short run, i.e., with a fixed number of producers, the non-competitive firm may experience non-zero pure profits:

$$\Pi_{is} = n_{is}\pi_{is} = \sum_{j\in W} p_{isj} n_{is} \left[c_{isj} + \sum_{t\in S} x_{isjt} \right] - V_{is} n_{is} Q_{is}, s \in \overline{C}.$$

However, free entry and exit in the industry ensure that these profits vanish in the long run.

2.3 General equilibrium

a) Short run: fixed industry structure

In the short run, the industry structure is assumed to remain fixed: there is no entry or exit of firms even though non-zero pure profits may exist in the imperfectly competitive sectors. A short-run Negishi-type imperfectly-competitive equilibrium (see Negishi (1961, 1972) and Arrow and Hahn (1971, chap.6))[5] is a vector of prices (p_{isj}, w_i, r_i) such that:
- n_{is} is fixed;
- supply equals demand on each market:

$$Q_{is} = \sum_{j\in W} \left[c_{isj} + \sum_{t\in S} x_{isjt} \right], s \in S, i \in W,$$

$$L_i^{sup} = \sum_{s\in S} L_{is} = \sum_{s\in C} L_{is}^v + \sum_{s\in \overline{C}} n_{is} \left[L_{is}^v + L_{is}^F \right], i \in W,$$

$$K_i^{sup} = \sum_{s\in S} K_{is} = \sum_{s\in C} K_{is}^v + \sum_{s\in \overline{C}} n_{is} \left[K_{is}^v + K_{is}^F \right], i \in W,$$

where L_i^{sup} and K_i^{sup} represent fixed country specific primary factor endowments;
- profits equal zero in all competitive industries;
- firms in non-competitive industries mark-up prices over marginal costs according to (2.3). The perceived elasticity E_{isj} is evaluated at equilibrium prices

---

$0 = \sum_{k\neq i} n_{ks}\varepsilon_{hsj}^k \bar{\varepsilon}_{ksj}^i + (n_{is}-1)\varepsilon_{hsj}^i \bar{\varepsilon}_{isj}^i - \sigma\bar{\varepsilon}_{hsj}^i + \varepsilon_{hsj}^i \bar{\varepsilon}_{isj}, h = 1,...,W$

$1 = \sum_{k\neq i} n_{ks}\varepsilon_{isj}^k \bar{\varepsilon}_{ksj}^i + (n_{is}-1)\varepsilon_{isj}^i \bar{\varepsilon}_{isj}^i - \sigma\bar{\varepsilon}_{isj} + \varepsilon_{isj}^i \bar{\varepsilon}_{isj}$

where the coefficients ε_{isj}^k are the cross-price elasticities computed from (2.4b).

[5] It should be mentioned, however, that strictly speaking, a Negishi-imperfectly-competitive equilibrium is defined with zero conjectures.

and demands, so that, even though the firm may be mistaken on the true demand curve it faces, for the quantities actually produced, it correctly perceives the prices that will clear the markets.

b) Long run: free entry/exit and international factor mobility

In the long run, the fixed industry structure assumption is relaxed : the equilibrium number of imperfectly competitive firms results from the zero pure profits condition:

$$\pi_{is} = 0, s \in \overline{C}.$$

We consistently assume that in the long run, capital is internationally mobile; at equilibrium, a unique rental price of capital ensures that world supply (assumed exogenous) and demand of capital services balance:

$$\sum_{i \in W} K_i^{sup} = \sum_{i \in W} \sum_{s \in S} K_{is}.$$

We also assume within-EEC labor mobility in the long run, so that firms operating in Europe face a unique wage rate determined by the following balance equation:

$$\sum_{i \in EEC} L_i^{sup} = \sum_{i \in EEC} \sum_{s \in S} L_{is}.$$

3 Calibration

Our base year is 1982; this choice has been made in conformity with the Smith-Venables study. As is standard, the calibration of our CGE model involves three different steps. First, a base year data set is constructed from various standard statistical sources, including bilateral trade flows, separate input-output tables for domestic and imported intrans, disaggregated final demands.[6]

The second step involves choosing some parameter values from secondary econometric evidence. Considerable judgment is usually needed here as one rarely finds econometric studies with identical regional and commodity disaggregation. In the present model, this step involves two groups of parameters. The first concerns the substitution elasticities σ_s. In the Smith-Venables study, these parameters are determined by calibration. Consequently, the values of the trade elasticities depend on the specific market structure assumed to prevail at base year. In some sectors, assuming Cournot rather than Bertrand competition results in a doubling of the computed substitution elasticities–with some

---

[6]Various statistical publications of the EEC(Eurostat Yearly Input-Output Tables, Eurostat National Accounts, Eurostat on Foreign Trade, Eurostat Annual Industrial Survey), of the IMF (International Financial Statistics), of the OECD (Foreign Trade by Commodities).

Table 2 Values of substitution elasticities

	As used in this study	As used by Smith and Venables
Agriculture and primary products	2	
Food, beverages and tobacco	2	
Pharmaceutical products	5	B = 4.7; C = 5.8
Chemicals other than pharmaceuticals	5	
Motor vehicles	10	B = 7.2; C = 13.3
Office machines	10	B = 10.9; C = 32.8
Other machines and transport materials	7	
Other manufacturing industry	4	
Transport and services	2	

Note: B = Bertrand; C = Cournot

computed elasticities reaching as high values as 30–which is somewhat disturbing. In this paper, we adopt a different calibration technique–see below–which avoids dependency of the parameters of the demand systems to market structure assumptions. However, this is achieved at the cost of some compromise on the game-theoretical consistency of the model, as reflected by the exogenous conjectures λ_{isj}^f and $\tilde{\lambda}_{isj}^f$.

The substitution elasticities we adopt are reported in Table 2. For the non-competitive sectors, these have been chosen within the interval provided by the Smith-Venables calibration. Even though the choice has been made on the low side of the range, they give a very price-sensitive representation of the world; in the competitive sectors, the price elasticities have been accordingly chosen somewhat higher than is usually the case in global CGE models. The second group of parameters that we draw from secondary sources are those describing returns to scale and industry concentration. Our main sources have been EEC documents based on the survey by Pratten (1987) and information kindly provided by Alasdair Smith from the Smith-Venables study. Table 3 reports on the ratios of marginal to average unit costs, i.e., the inverse of the scale elasticities, used for calibration. Given the scale parameters, the fixed costs are calculated from:

$$w_i L_{is}^F + r_i K_{is}^F = v_{is} Q_{is} \left[\frac{V_{is}}{v_{is}} - 1 \right], s \in \overline{C}.$$

By lack of reliable data on the composition of fixed costs, we assume that fixed and total costs have the same share of capital and labor inputs. It is worth observing at this stage that the hyperbolic cost function adopted in our study differs from the one used in Smith-Venables (1988, p1507).

The third and final step of our calibration procedure consists in computing the remaining parameters so that the model replicates the base year data as

Table 3 Ratio of marginal to average unit costs
(inverse of scale elasticities)

Pharmaceutical products	.75
Chemicals other than pharmaceuticals	.75
Motor vehicles	.85
Office machines	.85
Other manufacturing and transport materials	.85

an equilibrium. In a model with imperfectly competitive features, the question then arises as to which equilibrium, short run–fixed number of firms and possibly non-zero pure profits–or long-run–free entry/exit ensuring zero-profits–best approximates the real world. This is no easy choice. Clearly, the long term equilibrium is an ideal state that the real world may be thought never to attain. On the other hand, assuming that short-term equilibrium prevails requires additional statistical data if only on economic pure profits and losses, which are bound to be highly speculative in a fairly aggregated world model. It would also require more complex and less transparent calibration procedures (Harris (1984) and Cox and Harris (1985) for instance develop a two-step calibration procedure; in a critical assessment, Wigle (1988) suggests that part of the spectacular results they obtain might be due to this procedure). For these reasons, we assume that the long-run zero-profit equilibrium is a reasonably good approximation of reality in the base year. We therefore have:

$$p_{isj} = V_{is}, s \in \overline{C},$$

which together with the mark-up pricing rule (2.3) uniquely determines the firm's perceived elasticity of demand E_{isj}. However, considerable degrees of freedom subsist as the E_{isj} depend on each competitor's expected reaction function and additional restrictions are needed. We make the following reasonable assumptions on the individual firm's conjectures:

a) all competitors react in the same qualitative way to a change in own price or output;

b) each competitor's reaction is proportional to its share in the relevant market.

From these assumptions, it immediately follows that the conjectures λ_{isj}^f and $\tilde{\lambda}_{isj}^f$ may be written as:

$$\lambda_{isj}^f = \lambda_{isj} SH_{fsj},$$

$$\tilde{\lambda}_{isj}^f = \tilde{\lambda}_{isj} SH_{fsj},$$

where SH_{fsj} is the firm f's share in market j. Therefore, given the values of E_{isj} , the values of λ_{isj} and $\tilde{\lambda}_{isj}$ may be uniquely determined.

4 Market integration

Markets are initially segmented and firms charge different prices on each individual market. Typically, one expects that the firm charges the highest price on the domestic market on which it holds the largest market share; see Mertens and Ginsburgh (1985) for evidence on the automobile industry. If this is indeed the case, when firms are constrained to price-behave on an integrated EEC-wide basis, i.e., to charge a single price within the Community, this will induce a reduction of the price charged by domestic producers on the own market, together with an increase in export prices. The conjecture is that, with fixed industry structure, this will result in lower consumption prices and higher consumer surplus. On the other hand, market integration could reduce short-term industry profits and induce exit of firms, with the consequence that in the long-run, survivors will operate at lower average costs because of initially unexploited economies of scale. Were products homogeneous, this mechanism would unambiguously contribute to increase welfare –as stressed by Harris (1984)–; however, in the present setting where goods are differentiated in consumption as well as in intermediate demands, the rationalization effects may be compensated by the costs of reduced product diversity. Our aim in this paper is to evaluate the sign and magnitude of the welfare changes that may be expected to result from the '1992' integration process. This last mechanism is illustrated in Figure 1 for a single firm.

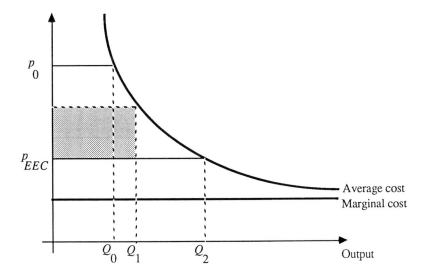

Figure 1

Here, p_0 is the firm's initial average selling price, Q_0 the corresponding zero-profit output. The no-price discrimination constraint forces the firm to reduce its average mark-up over costs. Let p_{EEC} denote the new price and Q_1 the corresponding output level. Even though the firm has moved down along its average cost curve, the price-induced sales expansion is not large enough to prevent it from experiencing short-term negative profits (the shaded area). Long term equilibrium requires that a smaller number of surviving firms operate on a larger scale Q_2 with average costs equal to p_{EEC}. It is easy to imagine how general equilibrium effects may affect this intuitive story. The steepness of the average cost curve will be affected by movements in primary factor prices, whereas changes in relative prices of intermediate goods move both curves up and down which will also affect the average to marginal cost ratio. Furthermore, complex interactions between income and substitution effects on the demand side will determine both the sign and the amplitude of the move from Q_0 to Q_1.

4.1 Design of the experiment

The experiment therefore consists in imposing the following restriction on the pricing rule (2.3):

$$E_{isj} = E_{isEEC}, i \in W, s \in \overline{C}, j \in EEC,$$

where E_{isEEC} is the firm's perceived elasticity of demand computed from the aggregated EEC market.

When firms are assumed to make their decisions in prices, we have :

$$E_{isEEC} = \varepsilon_{isEEC} + \lambda_{isEEC} \sum_f SH_{fsEEC} \varepsilon^f_{isEEC},$$

where SH_{fsEEC} is the share of competitor f in the integrated EEC market. It can easily be shown that the price elasticity of demand on the integrated market is a weighted average of the price elasticities on each individual country market within the Community:

$$\varepsilon_{isEEC} = \frac{\sum\limits_{j \in EEC} \varepsilon_{isj} \left[c_{isj} + \sum\limits_t x_{isjt}\right]}{\sum\limits_{j \in EEC} \left[c_{isj} + \sum\limits_t x_{isjt}\right]}, \varepsilon^f_{isEEC} = \frac{\sum\limits_{j \in EEC} \varepsilon^f_{isj} \left[c_{isj} + \sum\limits_t x_{isjt}\right]}{\sum\limits_{j \in EEC} \left[c_{isj} + \sum\limits_t x_{isjt}\right]},$$

and

$$\lambda_{isEEC} = \frac{\sum\limits_{j \in EEC} \lambda_{isj} \left[c_{isj} + \sum\limits_t x_{isjt}\right]}{\sum\limits_{j \in EEC} \left[c_{isj} + \sum\limits_t x_{isjt}\right]}.$$

In the alternative case, where firms are assumed to use output rather than prices as control variable, we have :

$$\frac{1}{E_{isEEC}} = \tilde{\varepsilon}_{isEEC} + \tilde{\lambda}_{isEEC} \sum_f SH_{fsEEC} \tilde{\varepsilon}^f_{isEEC},$$

where

$$\tilde{\lambda}_{isEEC} = \frac{\sum\limits_{j \in EEC} \tilde{\lambda}_{isj} \left[c_{isj} + \sum\limits_t x_{isjt} \right]}{\sum\limits_{j \in EEC} \left[c_{isj} + \sum\limits_t x_{isjt} \right]},$$

and the elasticities $\tilde{\varepsilon}_{isEEC}$ and $\tilde{\varepsilon}^f_{isEEC}$ are computed from the log-linearized inverse EEC-aggregated demand system.[7]

4.2 Partial equilibrium results

The model, adequately restricted, may be used for partial equilibrium analysis. This should prove a useful exercise for two reasons. Firstly, general equilibrium effects are not easy to disentangle; a systematic partial equilibrium industry investigation will therefore ease our understanding. Secondly, even when operated in partial equilibrium, our model differs from the Smith-Venables framework on more than one important respect: cost functions are not identical and both imperfect market structure assumptions and calibration strategies differ; one therefore wishes to test whether the conclusions reached by the two approaches coincide.

Tables 4a, 4b, 4c and 4d offer a detailed report on our partial equilibrium evaluation of the European market integration. It is readily seen that all sectors share the same qualitative behavior regardless of the type of competition (in quantities or in prices) assumed to prevail. The typical behavior of these industries conforms to our previous conjectures: the integration strategy reduces prices within the EEC. With prices held fixed in other industries, this results in a rightward shift of the industry-wide aggregate demand curve. This "income effect" dominates price substitution effects for all national producers within the industry, so that they experience an increase in the volume of sales, with lower average production costs.[8] The only sector that makes exception to this typical pattern of behavior is the sector for road vehicles. For instance, when competition is in prices, the short run price reduction of French and Italian road vehicles (respectively of -1.6 and -0.9%) is modest compared to those of other competitors (-2.1,-2.7 and -3.7% respectively on British, German and *ROW* cars). As a

---

[7]The systems to be solved are those of footnote 4, after substitution of the EEC-aggregated elasticities $\tilde{\varepsilon}_{isEEC}$ and $\tilde{\varepsilon}^f_{isEEC}$ for ε_{isj} and ε^f_{isj} where appropriate.

[8]Variable unit cost changes result from the fact that a firm's product may serve as intermediate input to an other firm operating in the same industry.

result, French and Italian producers not only experience reduced market shares but also reduced market size, despite expanded demand at the industry level. In the case where firms behave in output rather than in prices, the modest 1.7% short-term price reduction on German road vehicles induces a 3.2% production contraction.[9] In the short run, all firms experience negative profits so that industry concentration increases in the long run as fewer firms survive with lower prices and average costs. The exploitation of potential economies of scale lead to substantial long run welfare gains (measured by consumer surpluses) in all EEC countries, whichever type of competition is assumed. In the short run however, except in very rare cases, producer losses are sufficiently important to outweigh the surpluses consumers obtain from lower prices so that with a fixed number of producers EEC welfare declines. In general, the results prove quite robust to market structure assumptions: the same conclusions hold whether firms are assumed to use prices or quantities as control variables except in the road vehicles sector where the adjustment pattern of national producers is more contrasted.

How do our results compare to those of Smith and Venables (1988) ? A systematic comparison is unfortunately not possible as those authors do not provide any country detail for the industries that are common to both studies. Nevertheless, their EEC-aggregate results, which we reproduced in Table 5, suffice to point to important differences. [10] Most striking, is the almost total absence of aggregate effect they obtain in the Bertrand case. More generally, their results suggest a strong dependency with respect to the type of competition which we do not observe in our model. On the other hand, the welfare gains realized in the Cournot-type scenario are almost not affected by relaxing the fixed-number-of-firms assumptions, whereas in our model, the contrast between short run and long run is quite important in terms of welfare. This can hardly be a surprise : in their model, consumer preferences (the substitution elasticities that measure product differentiation) depend on the specific type of competition assumed to prevail at base year, whereas in our model, these differences in market structure are partially captured at calibration by the λs. However, it is important to observe that, despite these differences, both models have essentially the same behavior.

---

[9]In other words, with this type of competition, negative substitution effects dominate positive "income" effects for German producers. Note that for this sector, qualitative results depend on the type of competition assumed to prevail. Obviously, there is no reason to expect that the relative price changes within an industry induced by the integration experiment should be the same for Bertrand- and Cournot-type competition.

[10]The results in Table 5 are computed by us from Smith and Venables (1988, Table 6, 1520-1521), by subtracting column (3) from (1), (4) from (2), etc. All variables are EEC aggregates.

Table 4a Partial equilibrium effects of integration, assuming competition in prices, without entry or exit

	Country					
	GB	D	Fr	It	RE	ROW
Consumer surplus (% changes)						
Pharmacy	4.6	4.5	4.7	5.0	4.7	0.0
Chemicals	6.7	6.6	6.3	6.8	6.2	0.2
Road vehicules	2.3	2.7	1.9	1.2	2.7	0.0
Office machines	3.6	3.5	3.4	3.5	3.4	0.0
Other transp. mat.	0.7	0.6	0.7	0.8	0.7	0.0
Profits (% of base year cons.)						
Pharmacy	-29.6	-15.2	-15.2	-11.7	-12.1	-0.9
Chemicals	-52.1	-18.6	-23.0	-31.6	-25.6	-3.0
Road vehicles	-2.7	-4.0	-2.7	-1.7	-1.9	-0.1
Office machines	-4.2	-5.2	-5.6	-4.0	-2.5	-0.7
Other transp. mat	-0.7	-0.8	-0.7	-0.7	-0.7	-0.1
Output (% changes)						
Pharmacy	4.4	3.9	5.1	5.6	4.6	0.1
Chemicals	10.4	10.5	8.0	9.0	6.0	-0.3
Road vehicles	0.6	3.8	-1.6	-3.5	5.5	0.4
Office machines	4.3	3.9	6.1	3.5	0.8	0.2
Other transp. mat	0.9	0.7	0.9	1.1	1.1	-0.0
Average cost (% changes)						
Pharmacy	-1.1	-1.0	-1.3	-1.4	-1.2	-0.0
Chemicals	-4.0	-4.3	-2.9	-3.4	-2.2	0.1
Road vehicles	-0.2	-0.7	0.2	0.4	-0.9	-0.1
Office machines	-0.7	-0.6	-1.0	-0.6	-0.2	-0.0
Other transp. mat	-0.3	-0.2	-0.3	-0.3	-0.3	0.0
Variable unit cost (% changes)						
Pharmacy	-0.1	-0.1	-0.1	-0.1	-0.1	-0.0
Chemicals	-2.2	-2.6	-1.4	-1.7	-1.0	-0.0
Road vehicles	-0.1	-0.2	-0.1	-0.1	-0.1	-0.0
Office machines	-0.1	-0.1	-0.1	-0.1	-0.0	-0.0
Other transp. mat.	-0.1	-0.1	-0.1	-0.1	-0.1	-0.0
Prod. prices to EEC (% changes)						
Pharmacy	-4.5	-4.4	-4.7	-5.1	-4.7	-4.2
Chemicals	-7.0	-6.7	-6.3	-6.9	-5.9	-4.3
Road vehicles	-2.1	-2.7	-1.6	-0.9	-2.8	-3.7
Office machines	-3.6	-3.5	-3.9	-3.4	-3.1	-3.3
Other transp. mat	-0.7	-0.6	-0.7	-0.8	-0.7	-0.5
Prod. prices to ROW (% changes)						
Pharmacy	-0.1	-0.1	-0.1	-0.1	-0.1	-0.0
Chemicals	-2.3	-2.7	-1.5	-1.8	-1.1	-0.0
Road vehicles	-0.1	-0.2	-0.1	-0.1	-0.1	-0.0
Office machines	-0.1	-0.1	-0.1	-0.1	-0.0	-0.0
Other transp. mat.	-0.1	-0.1	-0.1	-0.1	-0.1	-0.0

Table 4b Partial equilibrium effects of integration, assuming competition in prices, with entry or exit

	Country					
	GB	D	Fr	It	RE	ROW
Consumer surplus (% changes)						
Pharmacy	4.4	4.3	4.4	4.8	4.4	-0.0
Chemicals	6.4	6.2	6.0	6.5	5.9	0.1
Road vehicules	1.8	2.3	1.4	0.7	2.3	-0.0
Office machines	3.1	3.1	2.9	3.0	2.9	-0.2
Other transp. mat.	0.7	0.6	0.7	0.8	0.7	0.0
Number of firms (% changes)						
Pharmacy	-11.4	-10.9	-12.8	-13.2	-11.5	-0.4
Chemicals	-12.0	-9.2	-13.0	-14.5	-13.8	-0.5
Road vehicles	-9.4	-9.5	-8.5	-5.9	-9.8	-0.1
Office machines	-16.2	-15.7	-15.3	-15.9	-15.1	-1.5
Other transp. mat	-2.9	-2.5	-2.9	-3.2	-2.8	-0.2
Output (% changes)						
Pharmacy	4.1	3.6	4.9	5.5	4.4	0.0
Chemicals	10.0	9.9	7.7	8.8	5.8	-0.3
Road vehicles	-0.3	3.3	-2.7	-4.2	5.3	0.5
Office machines	4.0	3.7	6.7	2.9	0.1	0.1
Other transp. mat	0.9	0.7	0.9	1.1	1.1	-0.0
Average cost (% changes)						
Pharmacy	-3.8	-3.6	-4.3	-4.5	-3.9	-0.1
Chemicals	-6.6	-6.2	-5.8	-6.6	-5.4	-0.1
Road vehicles	-1.5	-2.0	-1.0	-0.3	-2.2	-0.1
Office machines	-3.0	-2.9	-3.2	-2.8	-2.3	-0.2
Other transp. mat	-0.7	-0.6	-0.7	-0.7	-0.7	-0.0
Variable unit cost (% changes)						
Pharmacy	-0.1	-0.1	-0.1	-0.1	-0.1	0.0
Chemicals	-2.1	-2.4	-1.4	-1.7	-1.0	0.0
Road vehicles	-0.1	-0.1	-0.1	-0.1	-0.1	-0.0
Office machines	-0.1	-0.1	-0.1	-0.1	-0.0	0.0
Other transp. mat.	-0.1	-0.1	-0.1	-0.1	-0.1	-0.0
Prod. prices to EEC (% changes)						
Pharmacy	-4.3	-4.1	-4.5	-4.9	-4.4	-3.9
Chemicals	-6.8	-6.4	-6.0	-6.7	-5.7	-4.0
Road vehicles	-1.5	-2.2	-1.0	-0.3	-2.4	-3.5
Office machines	-3.1	-3.0	-3.5	-3.0	-2.6	-2.8
Other transp. mat	-0.7	-0.6	-0.7	-0.8	-0.7	-0.5
Prod. prices to ROW (% changes)						
Pharmacy	-0.0	-0.0	-0.0	-0.0	-0.1	0.0
Chemicals	-2.2	-2.5	-1.4	-1.7	-1.0	0.0
Road vehicles	-0.1	-0.1	-0.1	-0.1	-0.1	0.0
Office machines	0.1	0.1	0.1	0.1	0.1	0.1
Other transp. mat.	-0.1	-0.1	-0.1	-0.1	-0.1	-0.0

Table 4c Partial equilibrium effects of integration, assuming competition in output, without entry or exit

	Country					
	GB	D	Fr	It	RE	ROW
Consumer surplus (% changes)						
Pharmacy	4.4	4.3	4.1	4.4	4.3	0.0
Chemicals	6.3	6.5	5.8	6.4	5.9	0.2
Road vehicules	3.1	2.0	3.3	3.0	3.6	-0.0
Office machines	3.3	3.2	3.2	2.6	3.2	0.0
Other transp. mat.	0.6	0.6	0.7	0.7	0.6	0.0
Profits (% of base year cons.)						
Pharmacy	-28.0	-14.2	-12.9	-10.2	-11.0	-0.8
Chemicals	-48.9	-18.1	-20.7	-29.2	-23.6	-2.8
Road vehicles	-3.6	-4.1	-3.9	-3.1	-2.4	-0.1
Office machines	-3.8	-4.7	-5.0	-3.2	-2.2	-0.6
Other transp. mat	-0.7	-0.8	-0.7	-0.7	-0.6	-0.0
Output (% changes)						
Pharmacy	4.2	3.7	3.5	4.4	4.1	0.2
Chemicals	9.6	11.1	6.3	8.2	5.1	-0.2
Road vehicles	2.4	-3.2	5.7	3.2	31.5	0.1
Office machines	3.7	3.4	5.2	0.1	2.2	0.4
Other transp. mat	0.8	0.8	0.8	0.9	0.7	-0.0
Average cost (% changes)						
Pharmacy	-1.1	-1.0	-0.9	-1.1	-1.1	-0.0
Chemicals	-3.8	-4.4	-2.4	-3.1	-2.0	0.0
Road vehicles	-0.5	0.4	-1.0	-0.7	-3.7	-0.0
Office machines	-0.6	-0.6	-0.8	-0.1	-0.4	-0.1
Other transp. mat	-0.2	-0.2	-0.2	-0.2	-0.2	0.0
Variable unit cost (% changes)						
Pharmacy	-0.1	-0.1	-0.1	-0.1	-0.1	-0.0
Chemicals	-2.1	-2.6	-1.2	-1.6	-1.0	-0.0
Road vehicles	-0.2	-0.1	-0.2	-0.2	-0.2	-0.0
Office machines	-0.1	-0.1	-0.1	-0.1	-0.0	-0.0
Other transp. mat.	-0.1	-0.1	-0.1	-0.1	-0.1	-0.0
Prod. prices to EEC (% changes)						
Pharmacy	-4.3	-4.1	-3.9	-4.4	-4.3	-4.2
Chemicals	-6.6	-6.8	-5.5	-6.4	-5.4	-4.4
Road vehicles	-2.9	-1.7	-3.4	-2.9	-5.8	-3.3
Office machines	-3.2	-3.2	-3.5	-2.4	-3.0	-3.1
Other transp. mat	-0.6	-0.6	-0.7	-0.7	-0.6	-0.5
Prod. prices to ROW (% changes)						
Pharmacy	-0.1	-0.1	-0.1	-0.1	-0.1	-0.0
Chemicals	-2.1	-2.6	-1.3	-1.6	-1.0	-0.0
Road vehicles	-0.2	-0.1	-0.2	-0.2	-0.2	0.0
Office machines	-0.1	-0.1	-0.1	-0.1	-0.0	-0.0
Other transp. mat.	-0.1	-0.1	-0.1	-0.1	-0.1	-0.0

Table 4d Partial equilibrium effects of integration, assuming competition in output, with entry or exit

	Country					
	GB	D	Fr	It	RE	ROW
Consumer surplus (% changes)						
Pharmacy	4.1	4.0	3.8	4.2	4.1	-0.0
Chemicals	6.0	6.2	5.5	6.1	5.6	0.1
Road vehicules	2.5	1.5	2.7	2.3	3.2	-0.0
Office machines	2.8	2.8	2.7	2.1	2.8	-0.1
Other transp. mat.	0.6	0.6	0.6	0.7	0.6	0.0
Number of firms (% changes)						
Pharmacy	-10.6	-10.1	-10.7	-11.2	-10.4	-0.4
Chemicals	-11.2	-8.9	-11.5	-13.3	-12.7	-0.5
Road vehicles	-12.8	-9.6	-12.7	-11.7	-11.9	-0.2
Office machines	-14.8	-14.3	-13.8	-12.3	-13.8	-1.4
Other transp. mat	-2.6	-2.4	-2.7	-2.8	-2.5	-0.1
Output (% changes)						
Pharmacy	3.9	3.5	3.1	4.2	3.9	0.1
Chemicals	9.2	10.5	5.9	7.8	4.8	-0.3
Road vehicles	1.2	-4.0	4.1	2.1	33.9	0.2
Office machines	3.2	3.0	5.3	-0.7	1.8	0.4
Other transp. mat	0.8	0.7	0.8	0.9	0.7	-0.0
Average cost (% changes)						
Pharmacy	-3.6	-3.3	-3.4	-3.8	-3.5	-0.1
Chemicals	-6.2	-6.3	-5.0	-6.1	-4.9	-0.1
Road vehicles	-2.2	-1.0	-2.5	-2.2	-5.3	-0.1
Office machines	-2.7	-2.6	-2.8	-1.8	-2.3	-0.3
Other transp. mat	-0.6	-0.6	-0.6	-0.7	-0.6	-0.0
Variable unit cost (% changes)						
Pharmacy	-0.1	-0.1	-0.1	-0.1	-0.1	0.0
Chemicals	-2.0	-2.5	-1.2	-1.5	-0.9	-0.0
Road vehicles	-0.2	-0.1	-0.1	-0.2	-0.2	0.0
Office machines	-0.1	-0.1	-0.1	-0.1	-0.0	0.0
Other transp. mat.	-0.1	-0.1	-0.1	-0.1	-0.1	0.0
Prod. prices to EEC (% changes)						
Pharmacy	-4.0	-3.9	-3.6	-4.1	-4.0	-4.0
Chemicals	-6.3	-6.5	-5.1	-6.1	-5.1	-4.2
Road vehicles	-2.3	-1.1	-2.7	-2.3	-5.6	-3.0
Office machines	-2.8	-2.8	-3.1	-1.9	-2.6	-2.8
Other transp. mat	-0.6	-0.6	-0.6	-0.7	-0.6	-0.5
Prod. prices to ROW (% changes)						
Pharmacy	-0.1	-0.0	-0.0	-0.1	-0.1	0.0
Chemicals	-2.0	-2.5	-1.2	-1.5	-0.9	0.0
Road vehicles	-0.1	-0.0	-0.1	-0.1	-0.1	0.0
Office machines	0.1	0.1	0.0	0.1	0.1	0.1
Other transp. mat.	-0.1	-0.1	-0.1	-0.1	-0.1	0.0

Table 5 Effect on EC of the European market integration experiment
as evaluated by Smith and Venables (changes in %)

	Bertrand competition		Cournot competition	
	Fixed nb of firms	Variable nb of firms	Fixed nb of firms	Variable nb of firms
Pharmacy				
Output	0.0	0.0	3.0	1.4
Average cost	0.0	0.0	-0.7	-2.0
Welfare	0.0	0.0	0.8	0.9
Road vehicles				
Output	0.0	0.1	7.1	6.5
Average cost	0.0	0.3	-1.2	-1.3
Welfare	0.0	0.0	3.3	3.6
Office machines				
Output	0.0	0.2	16.9	11.5
Average cost	0.0	0.0	-1.7	1.1
Welfare	0.0	0.0	3.0	2.8

4.3   General equilibrium results

We now turn to the general equilibrium evaluation of "Europe 92". The results are reported in Tables 6 and 7a, 7b for the case firms compete in prices
(respectively without and with free entry of firms), and Tables 7c, 7d, when
competition in output is assumed to prevail (respectively without and with entry). Recall that for competitive sectors, average cost = variable unit cost =
producer price; for convenience, we only write the variable unit cost for those
sectors.

It is readily seen that the basic mechanisms highlighted with the partial
equilibrium simulations still hold when general equilibrium effects are taken
into account. We therefore only briefly comment on these results, and leave to
the interested reader the detailed analysis at sector and country specific level.
Forcing firms to act on a single European market results in a significant lowering of prices in the non-competitive industries, with an amplitude that in most
sectors exceeds the one computed for the partial equilibrium case. The resulting more intensive competition for primary factors induces an increase in wages
and rental prices of capital. Consequently, the transmission to the unit cost
in the competitive sectors is of ambiguous sign: primary factor prices increase
whereas material input prices decline. Due to the relatively high price elasticities
adopted in the model, the reallocation of resources induced by the implementation of the Single European Market are quite important in some sectors, in
particular in chemicals and pharmaceutical products. What is most striking

however, is that even though these changes could be looked at as somewhat excessive in some sectors, the consequences on welfare –measured as Hicksian equivalent variations– are relatively mild. Although welfare effects are in all cases unambiguously positive, and systematically larger in the long run than when the industry structure is fixed (approximately two to three larger), these changes never significantly exceed 1%: when competition is in prices, the highest welfare improvement is of 1.08% achieved by Germany in the long run; in the alternative case, where competition in output prevails, the highest improvement is of 1.04% achieved by the British economy. Observe that in contrast with these modest but positive welfare results, the partial equilibrium evaluations with fixed industry structure (Tables 4a, 4c), suggest negative welfare effects. This clearly demonstrates that general equilibrium effects do matter in this case.[11]

These numbers, no doubt, strike as extremely modest compared to what many people in Brussels (and in Washington !) have in mind. They would be even more so if one were somehow to take into account the short term adjustment costs that always accompany large scale structural adjustments. However, it is worth observing that even though the unexploited returns to scale assumed to prevail at base year (as measured by the scale elasticities in Table 3) are most probably somewhat excessive, our welfare estimates could be biased downwards by the fact that, due to a lack of reliable data and to excessive sectoral aggregation imposed by computational tractability, some sub-industries that have been implicitly assumed perfectly competitive, experience fixed costs and increasing returns to scale in the real world. This, for instance, could be the case for some services.

5 Conclusion

The aim of this paper has been to provide a general equilibrium welfare evaluation of the European Commission's action for the completion of a single integrated European market before 1993. In order to do this, we have built a static nine-sector world economy model consisting of six fully endogenous countries/regions in which a subset of industries is recognized to operate under increasing returns to scale and imperfect competition, with price differentiation at the firm level.

In the initial equilibrium, imperfectly competitive firms are assumed to take advantage of the monopoly power conferred to them in each country by national norms, procurement policies and other NTBs, and to price discriminate between client countries. The NTBs, which are impossible to measure, are therefore treated as implicit and inferred from the initial spread of selling prices resulting from specific market structure assumptions. The move towards a single European market is modeled as the elimination of all NTBs, with the resulting

---

[11]I wish to thank an anonymous referee for insisting that this point be highlighted.

Table 6 General equilibrium effects of integration
Aggregate indicators (% changes)

	Country					
	GB	D	Fr	It	RE	ROW
Competition in prices						
Without entry or exit						
Welfare (EV)	0.4	0.5	0.2	0.3	0.2	-0.0
Wage rate	1.0	1.2	0.6	0.6	0.5	0.0
Rental rate of capital	1.0	1.0	0.6	0.8	0.8	-0.0
Cost-of-living index	-0.1	-0.0	-0.1	-0.2	-0.1	-0.0
Terms of trade	0.3	-0.1	0.1	0.5	0.3	-0.6
Competition in prices						
With entry or exit						
Welfare (EV)	1.1	1.1	0.8	1.0	0.8	0.0
Wage rate	0.6	0.6	0.6	0.6	0.6	0.0
Rental rate of capital	0.2	0.2	0.2	0.2	0.2	0.2
Cost-of-living index	-0.6	-0.6	-0.3	-0.5	-0.4	0.1
Terms of trade	-0.1	-0.5	0.2	0.5	0.3	-0.0
Competition in output						
Without entry or exit						
Welfare (EV)	0.5	0.4	0.3	0.4	0.3	-0.0
Wage rate	1.2	0.8	0.9	1.0	1.2	0.0
Rental rate of capital	1.1	0.8	0.8	1.1	1.1	0.0
Cost-of-living index	0.0	-0.2	0.1	-0.1	0.3	-0.0
Terms of trade	0.4	-0.3	0.2	0.7	0.5	-0.6
Competition in output						
With entry or exit						
Welfare (EV)	1.0	1.0	0.7	1.0	0.7	0.0
Wage rate	0.6	0.6	0.6	0.6	0.6	0.0
Rental rate of capital	0.2	0.2	0.2	0.2	0.2	0.2
Cost-of-living index	-0.6	-0.5	-0.3	-0.5	-0.3	0.1
Terms of trade	-0.1	-0.2	0.1	0.4	0.1	-0.1

Table 7a General equilibrium effects of integration, assuming competition in prices, without entry or exit

	Country					
	GB	D	Fr	It	RE	ROW
Profits (% of base year cons.)						
Pharmacy	-21.2	-9.8	-12.4	-9.8	-11.0	-1.5
Chemicals	-47.5	-17.1	-20.8	-29.0	-24.1	-2.2
Road vehicles	-2.3	-3.7	-2.2	-1.3	-1.9	-0.1
Office machines	-3.7	-4.6	-4.5	-3.4	-2.3	-0.6
Other transp. mat	-0.7	-0.8	-0.7	-0.7	-0.8	-0.1
Output (% changes)						
Agriculture	0.5	0.7	0.8	0.1	0.1	0.1
Food and beverages	0.2	0.2	0.4	0.1	-0.1	0.0
Pharmacy	9.4	9.9	7.7	8.1	5.6	-0.3
Chemicals	9.7	9.8	7.3	8.0	4.9	-0.2
Road vehicles	1.8	3.7	-0.3	-1.7	4.1	0.3
Office machines	5.1	4.7	8.5	4.5	-0.3	-0.0
Other transp. mat	1.7	1.5	1.5	1.7	0.6	-0.0
Other manufactures	0.5	0.2	0.2	0.4	0.5	0.0
Services	0.2	0.2	0.1	0.1	-0.2	-0.0
Average cost (% changes)						
Pharmacy	-3.3	-3.4	-2.6	-2.8	-1.9	0.1
Chemicals	-3.2	-3.5	-2.3	-2.5	-1.3	0.0
Road vehicles	-0.4	-0.5	-0.2	-0.0	-0.5	-0.1
Office machines	-0.8	-0.7	-1.6	-0.9	0.1	-0.0
Other transp. mat	-0.3	-0.2	-0.4	-0.5	0.0	-0.0
Variable unit cost (% changes)						
Agriculture	0.1	-0.0	-0.3	0.1	0.3	-0.0
Food and beverages	0.3	0.4	-0.0	0.1	0.3	-0.0
Pharmacy	-1.9	-1.9	-1.3	-1.4	-1.0	-0.0
Chemicals	-1.6	-2.0	-1.0	-1.2	-0.4	-0.0
Road vehicles	-0.3	-0.2	-0.3	-0.5	-0.0	-0.0
Office machines	-0.3	-0.3	-0.6	-0.4	-0.0	-0.0
Other transp. mat.	-0.2	-0.2	-0.3	-0.4	0.0	-0.0
Other manufactures	0.2	0.4	0.1	-0.0	-0.1	-0.0
Services	0.5	0.6	0.3	0.2	0.5	-0.0
Prod. prices to EEC (% changes)						
Pharmacy	-5.8	-5.7	-5.4	-5.8	-5.0	-3.7
Chemicals	-6.0	-5.7	-5.3	-5.8	-4.8	-3.8
Road vehicles	-1.9	-2.3	-1.6	-1.0	-2.4	-3.3
Office machines	-3.4	-3.3	-3.9	-3.4	-2.7	-2.9
Other transp. mat	-0.7	-0.6	-0.8	-1.0	-0.5	-0.5
Prod. prices to ROW (% changes)						
Pharmacy	-2.0	-2.0	-1.3	-1.5	-1.1	-0.0
Chemicals	-1.7	-2.0	-1.0	-1.2	-0.5	-0.0
Road vehicles	-0.3	-0.2	-0.4	-0.5	-0.0	-0.0
Office machines	-0.3	-0.3	-0.6	-0.5	-0.0	-0.0
Other transp. mat.	-0.2	-0.2	-0.3	-0.4	0.0	-0.0

Table 7b General equilibrium effects of integration, assuming competition in prices, with entry or exit and international factor mobility

	Country					
	GB	D	Fr	It	RE	ROW
Number of firms (% changes)						
Pharmacy	-7.7	-6.2	-11.4	-11.5	-10.7	-1.0
Chemicals	-11.1	-7.9	-12.8	-14.2	-13.7	-0.7
Road vehicles	-7.7	-7.8	-8.2	-5.0	-11.9	-0.5
Office machines	-14.3	-13.4	-13.9	-14.7	-16.4	-2.2
Other transp. mat	-2.0	-1.0	-3.0	-3.0	-3.7	-0.4
Output (% changes)						
Agriculture	1.5	1.6	1.4	0.8	0.9	0.1
Food and beverages	1.1	1.0	0.9	0.7	0.5	0.0
Pharmacy	11.7	12.5	8.6	9.8	7.0	-0.6
Chemicals	11.8	12.2	8.2	9.4	6.2	-0.5
Road vehicles	2.9	6.3	-1.8	-2.1	2.9	0.1
Office machines	7.2	7.3	9.4	5.0	-1.7	-0.8
Other transp. mat	3.1	3.4	1.7	2.3	0.6	-0.2
Other manufactures	1.5	1.4	0.6	1.0	0.9	-0.0
Services	1.1	1.2	0.6	0.7	0.2	-0.0
Average cost (% changes)						
Pharmacy	-6.2	-6.0	-5.7	-6.2	-5.2	0.0
Chemicals	-6.8	-6.4	-5.7	-6.6	-5.3	0.1
Road vehicles	-2.2	-2.6	-1.3	-1.0	-2.3	-0.1
Office machines	-3.6	-3.5	-3.8	-3.3	-2.3	-0.2
Other transp. mat	-1.3	-1.2	-1.0	-1.2	-0.7	0.0
Variable unit cost (% changes)						
Agriculture	-0.6	-0.6	-0.7	-0.3	-0.2	0.1
Food and beverages	-0.4	-0.2	-0.3	-0.2	-0.0	0.1
Pharmacy	-2.6	-2.6	-1.6	-1.9	-1.5	0.1
Chemicals	-2.3	-2.7	-1.3	-1.6	-0.9	0.1
Road vehicles	-0.8	-0.8	-0.5	-0.7	-0.2	0.0
Office machines	-0.8	-0.8	-0.8	-0.7	-0.2	0.0
Other transp. mat.	-0.8	-0.8	-0.4	-0.6	-0.1	0.1
Other manufactures	-0.4	-0.2	-0.1	-0.3	-0.3	0.1
Services	-0.1	-0.2	0.0	-0.1	0.2	0.1
Prod. prices to EEC (% changes)						
Pharmacy	-6.7	-6.6	-5.9	-6.6	-5.8	-3.7
Chemicals	-7.0	-6.6	-5.9	-6.6	-5.6	-3.8
Road vehicles	-2.2	-2.8	-1.4	-1.0	-2.4	-3.4
Office machines	-3.8	-3.7	-4.1	-3.5	-2.6	-2.6
Other transp. mat	-1.3	-1.2	-1.0	-1.3	-0.7	-0.5
Prod. prices to ROW (% changes)						
Pharmacy	-2.6	-2.7	-1.6	-1.9	-1.5	0.1
Chemicals	-2.4	-2.7	-1.3	-1.7	-1.0	0.1
Road vehicles	-0.8	-0.7	-0.5	-0.7	-0.2	0.0
Office machines	-0.7	-0.7	-0.6	-0.6	-0.1	0.2
Other transp. mat.	-0.8	-0.8	-0.4	-0.6	-0.1	0.0

Table 7c General equilibrium effects of integration, assuming
competition in output, without entry or exit

	Country					
	GB	D	Fr	It	RE	ROW
Profits (% of base year cons.)						
Pharmacy	-22.4	-8.7	-12.0	-9.5	-11.6	-1.5
Chemicals	-49.8	-17.7	-20.9	-30.1	-25.4	-2.2
Road vehicles	-3.7	-3.5	-4.0	-3.3	-3.1	-0.1
Office machines	-3.3	-3.8	-4.0	-2.7	-2.4	-0.5
Other transp. mat	-0.8	-0.7	-0.8	-0.7	-1.0	-0.1
Output (% changes)						
Agriculture	0.5	0.9	0.7	-0.0	0.0	0.1
Food and beverages	0.2	0.4	0.3	0.0	-0.3	0.0
Pharmacy	9.8	11.5	5.8	7.3	5.2	-0.2
Chemicals	10.0	11.8	6.2	8.0	4.0	-0.1
Road vehicles	4.2	-2.7	6.8	5.2	30.2	-0.0
Office machines	4.6	5.3	8.5	1.4	-2.2	0.2
Other transp. mat	1.7	1.9	1.4	1.7	-0.2	-0.0
Other manufactures	0.5	0.5	0.1	0.3	0.2	0.0
Services	0.2	0.2	0.0	0.1	-0.3	-0.0
Average cost (% changes)						
Pharmacy	-3.3	-4.1	-1.9	-2.4	-1.5	0.0
Chemicals	−3.2	-4.3	-1.8	-2.3	-0.8	0.0
Road vehicles	-0.6	0.2	-1.0	-0.9	-3.0	-0.0
Office machines	-0.7	-1.0	-1.4	-0.3	0.8	-0.0
Other transp. mat	-0.2	-0.5	-0.2	-0.3	0.6	0.0
Variable unit cost (% changes)						
Agriculture	0.2	-0.1	-0.1	0.4	0.6	-0.0
Food and beverages	0.4	0.2	0.2	0.4	0.7	-0.0
Pharmacy	-1.8	-2.3	-1.0	-1.3	-0.8	-0.0
Chemicals	-1.6	-2.4	-0.7	-0.9	-0.2	-0.0
Road vehicles	-0.2	-0.4	-0.2	-0.3	0.4	-0.0
Office machines	-0.2	-0.5	-0.5	-0.3	0.4	-0.0
Other transp. mat.	-0.1	-0.4	-0.1	-0.2	0.4	-0.0
Other manufactures	0.3	0.1	0.3	0.3	0.4	-0.0
Services	0.7	0.3	0.5	0.5	1.0	-0.0
Prod. prices to EEC (% changes)						
Pharmacy	-5.9	-6.2	-4.6	-5.4	-4.8	-4.1
Chemicals	-6.1	-6.6	-4.8	-5.7	-4.5	-4.3
Road vehicles	-3.1	-1.5	-3.4	-3.2	-5.6	-2.9
Office machines	-2.9	-3.2	-3.5	-2.3	-2.2	-2.6
Other transp. mat	-0.6	-0.9	-0.7	-0.8	-0.1	-0.5
Prod. prices to ROW (% changes)						
Pharmacy	-1.9	-2.4	-1.0	-1.3	-0.8	-0.0
Chemicals	-1.6	-2.4	-0.7	-1.0	-0.2	-0.0
Road vehicles	-0.2	-0.4	-0.2	-0.3	0.3	-0.0
Office machines	-0.2	-0.5	-0.5	-0.3	0.3	-0.0
Other transp. mat.	-0.1	-0.4	-0.1	-0.2	0.4	-0.0

Table 7d General equilibrium effects of integration, assuming
competition in output, with entry or exit and international factor mobility

	Country					
	GB	D	Fr	It	RE	ROW
Number of firms (% changes)						
Pharmacy	-7.1	-5.6	-9.4	-9.4	-9.4	-1.0
Chemicals	-10.2	-8.2	-11.0	-12.7	-12.1	-0.6
Road vehicles	-11.4	-7.6	-12.5	-11.1	-13.4	-0.4
Office machines	-11.0	-10.9	-12.4	-9.4	-13.0	-1.9
Other transp. mat	-1.6	-1.7	-2.5	-2.3	-1.9	-0.3
Output (% changes)						
Agriculture	1.4	1.4	1.2	0.7	0.8	0.1
Food and beverages	1.1	0.9	0.8	0.7	0.5	0.0
Pharmacy	10.9	11.8	6.0	8.1	6.5	-0.5
Chemicals	10.9	11.9	6.4	8.7	5.3	-0.4
Road vehicles	4.6	-2.1	5.3	4.8	33.6	-0.2
Office machines	6.1	5.5	8.8	2.0	0.1	-0.2
Other transp. mat	2.9	2.5	1.8	2.5	1.8	-0.2
Other manufactures	1.4	1.0	0.6	1.0	1.0	-0.0
Services	1.1	0.9	0.5	0.8	0.4	-0.0
Average cost (% changes)						
Pharmacy	-5.7	-5.7	-4.5	-5.3	-4.7	-0.0
Chemicals	-6.3	-6.4	-4.8	-5.9	-4.7	0.1
Road vehicles	-2.8	-1.3	-2.8	-2.8	-5.4	0.0
Office machines	-3.0	-2.9	-3.2	-2.2	-2.1	-0.2
Other transp. mat	-1.2	-1.1	-0.9	-1.2	-0.6	0.0
Variable unit cost (% changes)						
Agriculture	-0.5	-0.5	-0.5	-0.2	-0.1	0.1
Food and beverages	-0.3	-0.2	-0.2	-0.1	-0.0	0.1
Pharmacy	-2.4	-2.6	-1.3	-1.7	-1.4	0.1
Chemicals	-2.1	-2.6	-1.0	-1.5	-0.9	0.1
Road vehicles	-0.8	-0.6	-0.4	-0.7	-0.2	0.0
Office machines	-0.8	-0.7	-0.7	-0.7	-0.2	0.0
Other transp. mat.	-0.7	-0.7	-0.4	-0.6	-0.2	0.1
Other manufactures	-0.4	-0.2	-0.0	-0.3	-0.3	0.1
Services	-0.1	-0.1	0.1	-0.0	0.2	0.1
Prod. prices to EEC (% changes)						
Pharmacy	-6.2	-6.2	-4.7	-5.6	-5.2	-3.8
Chemicals	-6.4	-6.6	-5.0	-6.0	-5.0	-4.0
Road vehicles	3.0	-1.4	-3.0	-2.9	-5.7	-2.7
Office machines	-3.1	-3.0	-3.4	-2.3	-2.3	-2.3
Other transp. mat	-1.2	-1.1	-0.9	-1.2	-0.7	-0.5
Prod. prices to ROW (% changes)						
Pharmacy	-2.3	-2.5	-1.3	-1.7	-1.4	0.1
Chemicals	-2.1	-2.6	-1.0	-1.4	-0.8	0.1
Road vehicles	-0.7	-0.6	-0.4	-0.7	-0.2	0.1
Office machines	-0.7	-0.6	-0.6	-0.6	-0.1	0.2
Other transp. mat.	-0.7	-0.6	-0.4	-0.6	-0.1	0.0

possibility for consumers to equalize across-the-border prices through arbitrage and, therefore, the elimination of the possibility for firms to behave as price-discriminating monopolists within the European Community.

Our results indicate that, even though unambiguously positive, the welfare gains that may be expected to result from the 1992 programme are relatively low; certainly much more modest than many people at the European Commission and elsewhere are willing to admit. Depending on the specific market structure assumption made, and on the country one considers, the once and for all rise in welfare that would be achieved ranges between 0.25 and 1.00 percent.

The largest numbers in this range are provided by cases where free entry/exit of firms cum zero long-term pure profits is assumed. In a recent paper, Mercenier and Schmitt (1992) dispute the realism of this assumption. They argue that, because potential firms face sunk costs upon entry (representing, say, flow costs due to investments in research and development, advertising, etc.), the zero-profit condition will not hold in many sectors. If this is indeed the case, the Commission's pro-competitive strategy is less likely to lead to large scale rationalization of production through higher industry concentration. Furthermore, in this free-entry equilibrium with positive pure-profits, there could be scope for existing firms to act more cooperatively among themselves and collectively raise prices in order to capture the rents dissipated by trade liberalization without attracting entry. According to this argument, the welfare gains provided in this paper could be largely overestimated.

There are two other important features in our model that should be questioned. The first is related to the characterization of the interaction among non-competitive firms, that is, the specification of the oligopoly game. Even though it is done in a much more sophisticated way than is usually the case in the applied general equilibrium literature with imperfect competition, our calibration procedure relies on some form of conjectural variations, which are maintained constant during the policy experiments. Although one would be tempted to justify this as a convenient reduced-form representation of an otherwise empirically intractable dynamic game, this is without clear theoretical foundation; see, e.g., Tirole (1989). A second aspect of the model that could be questioned is related to the treatment of the labor market. Indeed, this paper assumes full-employment to prevail at base year. This is certainly not the kind of world European policy makers have in mind. In a subsequent paper, Mercenier (1992) deals with these two issues. Preliminary results indicate that, by neglecting these two features, the present model biases downwards the welfare gains that could result from 1992. In any case, we are indeed very far from the 2.5 to 6 percent estimates provided by the Cecchini Report!

This having been said, it is important to insist on the fact that both this paper and the Cecchini Report only provide estimates of the static gains–those resulting from the reallocation of existing resources only–that may result from the pro-competitive programme. Modest as they are, these gains could indeed turn into much higher numbers if the impact of the policy on growth were taken into account. The analyses by Baldwin (1989) and Mercenier and Michel (1992) suggest that these dynamic gains could indeed be quite significant.

6 References

Arrow, K.J. and F.H. Hahn (1971), *General Competitive Analysis*, Amsterdam: North Holland.

Baldwin, R. (1989), The Growth Effects of 1992, *Economic Policy* 9, 248-281.

Cox, D. and R. Harris (1985), Trade Liberalization and Industrial Organization: Some Estimates for Canada, *Journal of Political Economy* 93,115-145.

Gunning, J., G. Carrin, J. Waelbroeck and associates: J.M. Burnieaux and J. Mercenier (1982), Growth and Trade of Developing Countries: A General Equilibrium Analysis, CEME DP 8210, Université Libre de Bruxelles.

Harris, R. (1984), Applied General Equilibrium Analysis of Small Open Economies with Scale Economies and Imperfect Competition, *American Economic Review* 74, 106-1032.

Krugman, P. (1979), Increasing Returns, Monopolistic Competition and International Trade, *Journal of International Economics* 9, 469-479.

Melo, J. de and D. Roland-Holst (1992), Tariffs and Export Subsidies When Domestic Markets are Oligopolistic, in J. Mercenier and T.N. Srinivasan, eds., *Applied General Equilibrium Analysis and Economic Development*, Ann Arbor: The University of Michigan Press, forthcoming.

Mercenier, J. (1992b), Can '1992' Reduce Unemployment in Europe? On Welfare and Employment Effects of Europe's Move to a Single Market, Discussion Paper 2292, C.R.D.E., Université de Montréal.

Mercenier, J. and P. Michel (1992), A Note on the Growth Effects of 1992, mimeo, Université de Montréal.

Mercenier, J. and N. Schmitt (1992), Sunk Costs, Free-Entry Equilibrium, and Trade Liberalization in Applied General Equilibrium: Implications for 'Europe 1992', Discussion Paper 3992, C.R.D.E., Université de Montréal.

Mercenier, J. and J. Waelbroeck (1984), The Sensitivity of Developing Countries to External Shocks in an Interdependent World, *Journal of Policy Modelling* 6, 209-236.

Mercenier, J. and J. Waelbroeck (1985), The Impact of Protection on Developing Countries: A General Equilibrium Analysis, in K. Jungenfelt and D. Hague, eds., *Structural Adjustment in Developed Open Economies*, MacMillan.

Mercenier, J. and J. Waelbroeck (1986), Effect of a 50% Tariff Cut in the Varuna Model, in T.N. Srinivasan and J. Whalley (eds), *General Equilibrium Trade Policy Modeling*, Cambridge, Mass.: The MIT Press.

Mertens, Y. and V. Ginsburgh (1985), Product Differentiation and Price Discrimination in the European Community: The Case of Automobiles, *Journal of Industrial Economics* 34, 151-166.

Negishi, T. (1961), Monopolistic Competition and General Equilibrium, *Review of Economic Studies* 28, 196-201.

Negishi, T. (1972), *General Equilibrium and International Trade*, Amsterdam: North Holland.

Nguyen, T. and R. Wigle (1989), Trade Liberalization with Imperfect Competition: The Large and Small of It, *European Economic Review*, forthcoming.

Smith, A. and A. Venables (1988), Completing the Internal Market in the European Community, *European Economic Review* 32, 1501-1525.

Tirole, J. (1989), *The Theory of Industrial Orgaization*, Cambridge, Mass.: The MIT Press.

Whalley, J. (1982), An Evaluation of the Tokyo Round Trade Agreement Using General Equilibrium Computational Methods, *Journal of Policy Modelling* 4, 341-361.

Whalley, J. (1985), *Trade Liberalization Among Major World Trading Areas*, Cambridge, Mass.: The MIT Press.

Whalley, J. (1986), Impact of a 50% Tariff Reduction in an Eight-Region Trade Model, in T.N. Srinivasan and J. Whalley (eds), *General Equilibrium Trade Policy Modeling*, Cambridge, Mass.: The MIT Press.

Wigle, R. (1988), General Equilibrium Evaluation of Canada-US. Trade Liberalization in Global Context, *Canadian Journal of Economics* 21, 539-564.

6

Adaptation of Asian countries to policy changes in Western Europe[1]

Helen Hughes

Australian National University

1 Trade between Western Europe and Asia

Most Asian and West European countries have some trade relations. The main Asian trading countries, those of East Asia, however, trade more strongly with North America, Japan and other countries, than with Western Europe. Exports of manufactures from Asia to the United States grew strongly in the long up-swing following the recession of 1981-82. Japan is an important supplier to Asia and opened its market for manufactures as the yen was revalued at the end of the 1980s. East Asian countries also trade with each other and other developing countries. Such trade accounts for 16 percent of their imports and 17 percent of their exports.

Several reasons account for differences in imports from East Asian countries by industrial countries. The United States has been a very open market since the 1950s. Trade rules are more transparent, and explicit and implicit protection measures are lower, in the United States than in Western Europe. Lower transaction costs are incurred than when trading with the several countries of Western Europe. This applies to special arrangements such as the Generalized Scheme of Preferences and the Multifibre Arrangement (MFA) as well as to trade generally. With the exception of exports of sugar, the special arrangements with the African, Pacific and Caribbean states have negligible effects on the trade of even the smallest of Asian countries. For some Asian countries trade with Western Europe is the result of trade diversion. The export of tapioca chips from Thailand is an example. Such trade is subject to arbitrary and sudden interruptions and changes of direction.

---

[1]This paper uses a model developed by the National Centre for Development Studies and the Centre for International Economics by Helen Cabalu, Jytte Laursen, Xinhua Mai, David Pearce and David Vincent. Philippa Dee and Frank Jarrett substantially contributed to the analysis. Tom Frost assembled the data of trade between Western Europe and Asia. I am grateful for the help of all these collabourators but remain responsible for the errors of commission and omission.

Table 1 Asia as destination for industrial country export
1980 and 1990

| | Share of total exports to (%) | | | | Total exports to world (US$ billion) |
| | East Asia[a] | | South Asia[b] | | |
	1980	1990	1980	1990	1990
EC7[c]	5	6	1	1	597
Western Europe[d]	2	3	1	1	1611
Japan	26	24	1	1	289
United States	11	14	1	1	393
Canada	3	4	1	-	132
Total	na	na	na	na	3022

[a] China, Hong Kong, Indonesia, Malaysia, Philippines, Republic of Korea, Singapore, Taiwan, Thailand.
[b] Bangladesh, India, Pakistan, Sri Lanka.
[c] EC7 excluding intra EC7 trade.
[d] Including intra West European trade.
Source: International Economic Data Bank, Australian National University.

Table 2 Asia as source of imports to industrial countries
1980 and 1990

| | Share of total imports from (%) | | | | Total imports from world (US$ billion) |
| | East Asia[a] | | South Asia[b] | | |
	1980	1990	1980	1990	1990
EC7[c]	7	10	1	1	604
Western Europe[d]	3	4	1	1	1667
Japan	22	27	1	1	236
United States	12	19	1	1	516
Canada	3	6	-	-	128
Total	na	na	na	na	3151

[a] China, Hong Kong, Indonesia, Malaysia, Philippines, Republic of Korea, Singapore, Taiwan, Thailand.
[b] Bangladesh, India, Pakistan, Sri Lanka.
[c] EC7 excluding intra EC7 trade.
[d] Including intra West European trade.
Source: International Economic Data Bank, Australian National University.

The Common Agricultural Policy and the European Community's postures in the Uruguay Round have demonstrated how strongly and effectively regional trade arrangements enable vested interests to organise to support protectionist views. It is true that "managed trade", cartelisation and other aspects of "new protection" have been less pervasive than feared in the 1970s, but trade barriers are nevertheless quite considerable. The main burden falls on European consumers, taxpayers who support a large rent-seeking bureaucratic infrastructure, and the unemployed, but trading partners are, of course, also affected.

Basic economic principles suggest that the reduction to internal barriers in goods and service, investment and labour markets in the European Communities and closer relations with other European countries should lead to accelerated growth for Western Europe. This was obviously the source of the impetus toward "Europe 1992" (Cecchini et al. (1988), Baldwin (1989), Greenaway (1991)). The free trade versus protection policy debate in Western Europe will not abate. Export pessimists have, however, suggested that the protectionists will win, and that "Europe 1992" will in no time become "fortress Europe". Some of the studies of 'Europe 1992' have chosen pessimistic assumptions leading to declining trade scenarios.

The competitiveness of East Asian countries is usually taken for granted and analysts such as Anderson (1991) take an upbeat view of the impact of "Europe 1992" on the newly industrialising economies (NIEs) and near NIEs. But other Asian countries are becoming increasingly competitive internationally. The entry of China into exports of manufactures on a large scale drew attention to the almost unlimited supply of low cost, unskilled labour for the export of labour-intensive manufactures, and the thrust toward trade policy improvements in India and the other populous South Asian countries could greatly increase such labour supply. By the end of the 1980s most Asian countries were filling their MFA quotas; a decade earlier China was not a large enough clothing and textile exporter to be an MFA member, and India and the other South Asian countries were not filling their quotas. For trade pessimists, the dangers of a flood of supply of labour-intensive manufactures from Asia has strengthened protectionist views in both exporting and importing countries.

The fundamental error of "export pessimism" (Cline (1982); Streeton (1982)) is, of course, that it ignores the increasing demand for imports in countries with rapidly increasing exports (Ranis (1985)). Trade problems do not lie in the expansion of exports but in the speed with which countries adjust to changing trade patterns. Countries with neutral trade regimes and flexible production structures have proved to be able to adjust quickly to changes in trade patterns.

Europe's trade policies in the 1990s and into the 21st century are going to be of considerable importance to the rest of the world, including Asia, but Asia can do little to affect West European policies. Asian countries, and the rapidly growing countries of East Asia in particular, are fortunately aware that it is their domestic policies that are the key to their own future development, no matter what policies Western Europe adopts. This paper therefore examines how the

Asian countries are likely to adapt to changes in West European policies and to major policy changes within Asia.

2 The Asia General Equilibrium Model

Trade scenarios have traditionally been explored in a comparative static, partial equilibrium framework based on past trends. This gave a very limited perspective of likely trade changes. The development of computable general equilibrium models to which Jean Waelbroeck has made such a major contribution, has greatly enlarged the analytical possibilities for this type of work.

The computable general equilibrium model used here is of the ORANI type (Dixon et al. (1982)). It focuses on real flows of goods and services within and between countries, with emphasis on the response of these flows to policy changes that affect trade.

The model was designed to analyse the likely changes in Asian exports. Particular attention has been paid in the design to Asian countries' exports of labour-intensive commodities, though the other principal sectors and the *rest of the world* have also been included (Cabalu, Laursen, Mai, Pearce and Vincent (1991)).

The model has a comparative static, general equilibrium structure that allows comparisons between two alternative equilibrium positions at some point in the future, one with and one without the trade developments in question. The model results are in percentage changes, measuring the difference between these two positons. The model does not throw any light on the time path taken to move to either of these equilibrium positions. The general equilibrium feature of the model is that it reflects the interdependencies between different actors in economic activity, both within the Asian countries studied in detail, and in the trade flows which occur between these countries and with the *rest of the world*.

2.1 Regional dimensions of the model

In its original version the entities represented in the model were restricted to five *countries* in the Asian region whose economies were modelled in detail and a sixth residual *rest of the world*. The Asian mode provides detail for:

- China

- India

- Other South Asia (Pakistan, Bangladesh, Sri Lanka)

- Near NIEs (Philippines, Malaysia, Indonesia, Thailand)

- NIEs (Republic of Korea, Taiwan, Hong Kong, Singapore).

The *rest of the world* is treated as a trading entity only, importing from, and exporting to, each of the five Asian *countries*.

2.2   Commodity dimensions of the model

Eight commodities and industries are distinguished in each of the economies. These are:

- agriculture

- other primary (forestry, fisheries)

- mining

- processed food

- clothing and textiles

- metal products and machinery

- other manufacturing (including footwear)

- services (includes all other production).

Each industry uses three primary factors of production: labour, capital and land, and a residual fourth category of "other costs".

2.3   Equation groups in the model

The equations of the model are contained in seven groups. These are:

- industry input demands

- commodity supplies

- final demands

- zero pure profit conditions

- market clearing conditions

- trade balances

- miscellaneous equations.

2.4 Industry input demands

Two major assumptions underlie the equations in this group. Subject to a two-level production function, producers in each country are assumed to choose inputs to minimize production costs. The first level of the production function embodies the standard Leontief assumption that there is no substitution among material input categories, nor between them and an aggregate of the primary factors and the residual "other costs" category. The second level uses a constant elasticity of substitution (CES) function to describe substitution between domestic and imported sources of each material input category, and among primary factors. The second level functions implicitly describe import demands not just from other *countries* in the Asian region, but also from the *rest of the world*.

At both levels constant returns to scale are assumed. Recent work suggests that this assumption leads to an underestimation of the negative effects of protective measures if some industries in fact enjoy increasing returns. The positive impact of liberalization may therefore be underestimated by models which assume constant returns.

The effect of assuming elasticities of substitution between material input sources to be constant is that the pairwise substitution elasticities between the domestic and corresponding imported input are the same irrespective of the country supplying the imported input. In the Republic of Korea, for example, the substitution elasticity between domestically produced clothing, textiles and footwear and those imported from China is the same as the substitution elasticity between domestic cloting and textiles and those imported from India. These substitution elasticities are critical in determining the change in trade patterns when policy shocks are imposed on the model. If the price of goods from one source falls relative to the price from other sources then a higher proportion of inputs will be obtained from the cheaper source. The extent of the switch between sources depends on the extent of the shift in relative prices and the values assigned to the substitution elasticities. However, the constant returns to scale assumption implies that if relative prices of goods from the different supplying sources do not change, then demands for goods from each source will move proportionately with output.

In a similar vein, if one primary factor of production becomes cheaper relative to another, then substitution of the cheaper for the dearer factor will mean industries' demands for that factor increase faster than output. If there is no change in relative prices of the primary factors then factor demands will change proportionately with output.

A key assumption is that labour is perfectly mobile among sectors so that changes in the price of labour must be the same for all using industries. However, provisions are made for the prices of capital and land to be industry-specific in each *country*.

2.5 Commodity supplies

Commodity supplies are specific to the sector in which they are produced. Clothing and textile sectors, for example, produce only clothing and textiles. The constant returns to scale assumption means that output of a commodity moves proportionately with the overall input use of the industry in which it is produced. A shift term enables exogenous changes in productivity to be imposed on the commodity supply functions in each country.

2.6 Final demands

The final demand equations describe demands for investment goods and consumption goods classified by country and by source. In addition, demands for a residual domestic category, "other demands" by source are also identified, together with the demands by the *rest of the world* for commodities from each of the Asian *countries*. The investment demands are not disaggregated by using industry. Limited data availability means that the input composition of investment in each *country's* industry is assumed to be that of the economy as a whole.

Producers of investment goods are assumed to minimize costs, subject to constant returns to scale technology. The different material input categories are used in fixed proportions, while substitution is allowed between alternative sources of supply of each input category. Inputs may be sourced domestically, from other Asian *countries* or from the *rest of the world*. If one source of supply becomes cheaper relative to another, then substitution towards that source will occur. The demands for inputs from that source will grow proportionately faster than the growth in total industry investment. With no change in relative prices, the demand for inputs to investment will change in strict proportion to total investment.

Households in each country choose both the mix of commodities for consumption and the country source of those commodities to maximize utility, subject to a budget constraint. Again, potential sources include the *rest of the world*. With no change in the relative prices among sources, the demands by households in a particular *country* for a particular commodity from a particular source are proportional to their demands for that commodity in general, irrespective of its source. However, if relative prices of the goods from each source change, consumers will substitute towards the cheaper source. The degree of substitution is influenced by the extent of the shift in relative prices and the value of the substitution parameter which is assigned to the substitution of goods from different sources.

The commodity mix of household consumption is explained for each country in terms of total consumption expenditure per household and the relative prices between the different commodities consumed. The expenditure pattern depends on the expenditure elasticities of consumption for each commodity and the substitution effects incorporated in own and cross price elasticities of demand for consumer goods in each country.

The residual "other demand" category represents mainly government demands. The model does not explain either the size of these demands or their composition by commodity and source (the latter including the *rest of the world*). The model user can change the size of "other demands" to movements in household consumption expenditure.

Total demand by the *rest of the world* for each commodity from the Asian region is asssumed fixed. The *rest of the world* substitutes between individual *country* sources of each commodity in response to relative prices. If there is no change in relative prices between alternative sources of supply in the Asian region then demands for commodities from each source by the *rest of the world* will remain fixed. In other words, the share of the *rest of the world* market held by each of the five *countries* in the Asian region will stay constant. However, if the prices of, say, China's exports of clothing and textiles of the *rest of the world* fall relative to those from other *countries* in the region, then China will gain an increased share of the *rest of the world* market for clothing and textiles at the expense of other *countries*.

2.7 Zero pure profit conditions

The model assumes perfect competition. This is a fairly common assumption in general equilibrium models. An alternative specification involving imperfect competition usually relies on markup theories of pricing with the markup determined either exogenously or according to some rule. However, work by Harris (1984) indicates that the results of these models are very sensitive to the specification of the pricing behavior of the imperfectly competitive economic units.

Because of the assumption of perfect competition and constant returns to scale, production profits accrue only to factors of production and there are zero pure profits. This is expressed in the model by saying that the revenue per unit of output is fully exhausted by payments to the material and primary factors of production.

In a similar vein, the revenue from producing a unit of capital in each industry in each *country* is fully accounted for the input costs from each source of supply used in producing it. The assumption of zero pure profits in importing means that the domestic selling price of each *country's* imported goods is fully accounted for by the final price at the border, expressed in domestic currency, and any tariff or tariff equivalent of quantitative barriers to imports. The border price of imports in turn equals the export price from the country of origin, plus transport costs. The export price from each *country* equals production costs in that country, less any export subsidies which may be in place.

2.8   Market clearing conditions

For each *country* in the Asia region, demand is set equal to supply for domestically produced commodities and for primary factors, labour, capital and land. The demands for commodities originate from the following sources:

- as inputs into current production in the domestic country and current production in each of the other *countries* in the region;

- as inputs into the production of investment goods, both in the domestic *country* and in the other *countries*;

- consumer demands in both the domestic country and each of the other remaining *countries*;

- 'other demands' both in the domestic country and each of the other remaining *countries*; and

- exports to the *rest of the world*, that is, outside the five economies of the Asian region.

Labour demands are satisfied in each *country* but this does not necessarily impose a full employment assumption. Labour demands may be satisfied with varying degrees of unemployment in the workforce, the degree of unemployment being determined by the price of labour in each country. Similar equivalences between demand and supply are specified for the other two primary factors, capital and land.

2.9   Trade balances

Total import and export volumes are defined both by commodity and in aggregate. Import volumes into each *country* cover imports from all other *countries* from Asia and from the *rest of the world*. Export volumes by each *country* in the region cover exports to the remaining *countries* as well as to the *rest of the world*. Aggregate imports and exports are also defined for each *country* in foreign currency value terms, valued in the currency of the *rest of the world*. The difference between the foreign currency earnings from exports and the foreign currency cost of imports represents the balance of trade for each *country* in Asia.

2.10   Miscellaneous equations

A consumer price index is defined for each *country* as a consumption expenditure weighted sum of the local prices of each of the commodities purchased by its consumers. The commodities are both domestically produced and imported. Since the model does not specify domestic margins and taxes on commodity flows within each *country*, the local prices of goods to consumers within each *country* are the same as for other domestic users, be they producers of current or capital goods or government.

One of the important features allowing flexibility in model use is that real or nominal wages can be fixed exogenously or allowed to vary. When wages are fixed, the choice of fixing them in real or nominal terms is made by setting the degree of indexation of nominal wages to movements in consumer prices. A shift term nevertheless allows quantum changes in the fixed wages.

A number of important national accounts aggregates are defined within the model. For example, real GDP in each *country* is defined from the expenditure side as a weighted sum of real household consumption expenditure, investment expenditure, other demands and real net exports.

The miscellaneous equations also define real rates of return to capital in each industry in each *country*. Provision is then made for these rates to be tied to a single, common economy-wide rate of return in that *country*, or alternatively to vary across industries. The choice of which assumption to adopt is linked to the model user's decision about the degree of capital mobility to allow between industries within a *country*. This issue is returned to shortly. Provision is also made for the economy-wide rates of return to vary across *countries*, or to be held to a common, world level. This decision is linked to the degree of international capital mobility the model user wishes to allow.

Finally, the miscellaneous equations specify an aggregate household consumption function for each *country*. The household demand equations described earlier show how consumers in each *country* allocate a given amount of total consumption spending between commodities and sources, but do not explain how total consumption spending itself is determined. Provision is therefore made for aggregate nominal household spending to vary in strict proportion to a country's nominal GDP. The consumption function needs to be activated, however, and aggregate household consumption spending may instead be held fixed. The choice between options depends on the model user's judgement as to whether the appropriate time frame for the particular simulation is one in which households would have sufficient time to adjust their aggregate spending to induced changes in national income. It is also sometimes convenient for expositional purposes to conduct simulations in which household spending is held fixed. In such cases the macroeconomic effects of the particular experiment in question are channelled through the trade account.

2.11 Closing the model

The model as specified contains many more variables than it has equations to explain them. For a solution to be possible, some variables need to be designated as exogenous. The model user is allowed considerable flexibility in which variables to make exogenous. This adds greatly to the model's usefulness because it means that the user can *close* the model, that is, choose a particular set of exogenous variables, in ways that represent different economic environments or in which policy variables are aimed at different policy targets.

For the experiment reported in the next section, a *short-run* closure was chosen. The main aspect of the closure that gives it a short-run flavor is that capital stocks are held exogenously fixed in each industry in each *country*. This means that although investment spending is occurring, the time horizon is too short for new capital to be installed and operating, or for old capital to be depreciated, in response to increases or decreases in industry profitability. This time horizon must therefore be shorter than the gestation period of new investment, and is typically thought to be about two years. Since real physical capital is not mobile between industries, *a fortiori* it is not mobile between countries.

In closures where industry capital stocks are fixed, industry rates of return must be free to vary across industries in each country. The variation in these rates of return would provide the price signals to which, over a longer time horizon, capital stocks would adjust. In a long run closure, it would be more appropriate to allow capital stocks to vary endogenously, while requiring that industry rates of return be held equal (via capital mobility) to the economy-wide average return.

Another important feature of the closure is that land usage is held exogenously fixed in each industry in each *country*. The assumption that land is immobile between industries is common in both short and long-run environments. But combined with the treatment of capital, the assumption means that labour is the only primary factor mobile between industries in the short term. Reallocation of labour between industries becomes one of the critical mechanisms by which economies can respond to external shocks in the short term.

Real wages are held fixed in each country in real terms. This means that not just the allocation of labour, but also the total amount of labour employed, responds to changes in industry demands in the face of external shocks. Of course, where the results suggest that aggregate employment increases, the model is assuming that there are unemployed workers who would be willing to join the workforce at the going wage to satisfy the additional demand. Whether this assumption is reasonable depends in part on the extent of the projected increase in labour demand, but none of the simulation results in the next section suggest employment changes of sufficiently draconian size to call the assumption into serious question.

Aggregate household consumption spending, investment spending and "other" (mainly government) spending are also held fixed in each *country* in real terms. With domestic absorption fixed, the macroeconomic effects of the trade development scenarios are felt through the trade accounts of each *country*. This reflects in part a deliberate strategy to set the *trade* implications of the various scenarios, in their starkest relief. Were domestic absorption in each country to respond to changes in domestic income, then the trade account results in the next section would tend to be more moderate – a fall in export sales in the face of adverse circumstances, for example, does not need to be as great if the burden of industry contraction can be shared through a fall in domestic sales.

The set of bilateral exchange rates between each of the *countries* and the *rest of the world* are held fixed as a numeraire for the model system. This is simply because the model is a typical general equilibrium model that can be solved for *relative* prices, but cannot determine the overall *level* of prices. This aspect of the closure is not important in itself, because the allocation of commodities and factors in models such as this is invariant to which price set is chosen as numeraire – any other set would have done as well. The choice of numeraire does, however, have implications for the way some of the price variables are interpreted.

One of the most important prices for an open economy is the real exchange rate, which in general can vary either because domestic prices change relative to foreign prices, or because the nominal exchange rate changes. Choosing the set of nominal exchange rates as numeraire simply means that in this model, changes in the *real* exchange rate for a *country* are fully reflected in the reported changes in domestic relative to foreign prices. Since prices in the *rest of the world* are also held exogenously fixed as part of the model closure, it is possible to take an index of domestic prices for a *country*, such as the consumer price index, and interpret it as showing changes in the real exchange rate between that *country* and the *rest of the world*.

Other aspects of the model closure follow from the nature of the model experiments. For example, import tariffs and export subsidies are held exogenously fixed because they are not used as (endogenous) instruments to achieve a particular (exogenous) policy target in any of the experiments in question. Transport costs are also treated as exogenous.

2.12   The data base and values of behavioral parameters

The data requirements of the model are of two types – estimates of behavioral parameters such as substitution elasticities and expenditure elasticities, and estimates of the shares of individual industry cost items in total costs and sales categories in total sales. The behavioral parameters would be required in any sensible economic model but the share coefficients are required because the equations of this model have been linearized.

The data base from which cost and sales shares are calculated was constructed from two main sources. The first consists of a set of input-output tables for Asian countries, which describe the cost and sales patterns for individual industries in each country. The second source is information on trade flows from the International Economic Data Bank at the Australian National University (IEDB). It allows the individual country data bases to be linked by each country's trade pattern. An input-output table for each *country* was constructed by aggregating the tables for each of its countries. In the process, the eight sector breakdown of commodities and industries described earlier was largely dictated via the need to convert country input-output tables with diverse commodity coverage into a common industry/commodity set. Each of the country input-output tables was then expressed on a 1985 base in US dollars. The country tables were finally aggregated to form a *country* table after adjusting for intra-regional trade flows. Finally, the import flows in each *country* input-output table were split across the sources using the trade flow data base in the IEDB.

Empirical estimates are few for a number of parameters used in the model. These parameter settings had to be based on judgement. Their values are described in detail in Cabalu, Laursen, Mai, Pearson, Vincent (1991).

Both the share coefficients and the behavioral parameters are inevitably subject to uncertainty but in particular model experiments the results will typically be more sensitive to some than to others. The important task is to understand which are the critical parameters or share coefficients for the particular use to which the model is being put. Sensitivity analysis can then be conducted on these values if required.

2.13 Understanding the model

The model is used to examine the impact on the Asian economies of possible developments in the world trade environment related to changes in Western Europe and within Asia. The actual response will depend in part on the ability of Asia to maintain or increase its penetration of industrial country markets (Panoutsopoulos (1990)).

One reason for continued growth is the likelihood that the industrial countries can continue to absorb growing quantities of exports from industrial countries. The penetration to date has been low partly for this reason and the industrial countries' demand is unlikely to be nearly as inelastic as the export pessimists predict. There is not much point in modelling a positive impact of 'Europe 1992' on world trade because there is a general agreement that Asian countries would be well situated to take advantage of such growth. But many Asian economies are likely to adapt flexibly even to unfavourable changes that follow from policy changes in Western Europe.

The model highlights some of the ways in which they can adapt. It takes the toughest possible stance on the growth of export markets by assuming that total demand by the *rest of the world* for exports of each commodity from Asia is fixed. This is a worst case scenario that takes the export pessimists at their word. Growth of the market in industrial countries is ruled out. All that the countries of the region can do in this market is fight for market share.

So how might the Asian economies adapt? This depends on international features of their economies and on the way that the separate countries of the region interact through trade. The model implicitly incorporates two main sources of flexibility – one on the demand side and one on the supply side.

There is no doubt that a high degree of trade exposure can make sectors within an economy particularly susceptible to external shocks. Somewhat paradoxically, trade exposure can also help to insulate that economy as a whole from the adverse effects of such shocks. An expansion of China's exports of clothing and textiles is likely to impact adversely on clothing and textile sectors in other countries. But as these sectors contract, they will release resources, particularly labour and material inputs, which are then available for other sectors. Whether other sectors will absorb the resources, and thereby prevent an overall decline in employment and income, depends on whether those sectors can easily generate additional sales. This is more likely if they face relatively elastic demand for their output.

The vast body of trade literature concludes that sectors which are subject to international competition face more elastic demands than those which are not. This is built into the model through the choice of values for the behavioral parameters. Consuming households, for example, substitute between alternative sources of a single commodity more easily than they do between different commodities. This ensures that a domestic producer selling on the domestic market in competition with imports of the same commodity will see a more elastic demand than a producer who is the sole source of domestic supply. One way in which sectors can generate increased sales is by replacing imports.

Another way is by exporting. Export demands also tend to be price elastic because the exports are generally competing in foreign markets with alternative sources of supply of the same commodity.

Thus sectors which might wish to use the resources released by declining sectors elsewhere in the economy are more able to generate the required sales if they are trade exposed. This is the precise sense in which the model shows how trading nations can trade their way out of trouble.

The ability of sectors to absorb resources may nevertheless be limited on the supply side. In the short-run environment of these experiments, labour is the primary factor of production which is mobile between sectors. The ability of sectors to absorb additional labour is limited if they are inherently intensive in the use of other primary factors that are fixed in the short run – capital or land. Intensive use of fixed factors limits flexibility on the supply side.

Some international trade developments may impact adversely on all sectors of an economy. In this case a country is less likely to be able to insulate itself by reallocating resources between sectors. What it may be able to do, however, is to maintain its level of sales by taking a larger market share from other *countries* in the region.

Table 3 summarizes the critical features of the model's data base. The summary measures give a picture of the demand elasticities faced by the individual *country* industries, and a measure of their short-run supply elasticity.

The first two columns summarize the trade exposure of each industry in each *country*. The first column gives, for each commodity, the share of imports from all sources, both Asia and the *rest of the world*, in apparent consumption in

Table 3 Indicators of demand and supply responsiveness in the Asia model

Country/Industry	Import share in apparent consumption (%)	Export share in total sales (%)	Supply elasticity
NIES			
Agriculture	10.00	0.71	0.56
Other primary	25.28	20.41	0.76
Minerals	92.22	1.75	1.75
Processed food	10.62	8.49	6.78
Clothing and textiles	7.76	15.39	3.38
Metal products and machinery	36.73	22.96	2.18
Other manufactures	26.46	33.51	2.34
Services	3.60	16.58	1.14
Near NIES			
Agriculture	61.65	4.62	0.33
Other primary	3.51	12.80	0.25
Minerals	38.05	50.26	0.07
Processed food	58.92	12.15	1.26
Clothing and textiles	13.77	18.07	1.12
Metal products and machinery	69.65	29.86	1.06
Other manufactures	39.82	24.86	0.41
Services	1.44	5.71	0.70
Other South Asia			
Agriculture	5.08	3.64	0.31
Other primary	0.95	2.39	0.26
Minerals	62.63	18.95	0.83
Processed food	14.04	2.40	2.15
Clothing and textiles	14.06	26.25	1.07
Metal products and machinery	64.90	1.67	0.70
Other manufactures	40.50	8.00	0.99
Services	0.75	1.52	0.30
India			
Agriculture	0.18	1.32	0.65
Other primary	0.36	5.10	0.54
Minerals	38.15	2.81	1.06
Processed food	5.15	9.34	3.87
Clothing and textiles	1.15	11.22	1.94
Metal products and machinery	3.90	3.98	1.81
Other manufactures	9.98	6.08	1.91
Services	0.19	1.71	0.86
China			
Agriculture	2.50	1.38	0.99
Other primary	1.84	0.99	0.86
Minerals	0.92	6.47	0.48
Processed food	1.90	3.85	0.52
Clothing and textiles	6.21	10.01	0.52
Metal products and machinery	8.40	3.85	0.75
Other manufactures	5.34	4.48	0.45
Services	1.15	2.56	1.15

that *country*. The second column gives, for each industry, the share of exports in total sales.

The most striking feature of these numbers is the relatively high degree of trade exposure of industries in the NIE and near NIE countries, and the relatively low trade exposure of industries in China and India. The Other South Asian region lies somewhere in between.

The low trade shares for China and India in part reflect their size. For China they also reflect policies which until the mid-1970s were designed to make China completely self-sufficient. The low trade shares for India reflect the distortions arising from its import substitution policies. The industries in these countries do not face particularly elastic demands for their products. They tend to be limited by the size of the domestic market and are less able than industries in other *countries* to generate additional sales in the short term. The model thus tends to show that India and China have less flexible economies than the NIEs and near NIEs.

The third column of Table 3 shows the short-run partial supply elasticities for each of the industries in each of the *countries*. The model data base does not contain these elasticities in explicit form. The short-run partial elasticities that apply when the model is given a short-run closure can nevertheless be calculated from the data base. Since primary factors as a group are used in strict proportion to output, the ability of industries to expand output depends on their ability to absorb additional amounts of the variable primary factors. Thus the short-run supply elasticities are functions of the elasticity of substitution between fixed and variable primary factors, the share of variable factors in value added, and the share of value added in total output.

Most of the supply elasticities are around a value of unity. Few of the elasticities are particularly high, mainly because the elasticity of substitution between primary factors has been given a relatively low short-run value of 0.5.

One or two of the supply elasticities are worth noting. The supply elasticity of the mining industry in the near NIE group is particularly low because this is a relatively capital-intensive activity. Although the sector is very trade exposed and could achieve additional sales if it could increase output, it is unlikely to contribute to the flexibility of the near NIE country group in the short-run because its ability to produce additional output is severely limited. Elsewhere, the supply elasticity of the processed food sector varies quite markedly across countries because of variations in the labour intensity of this activity across *countries*.

Generally, industries in the NIEs and India tend to have higher short-run supply elasticities than industries in other *countries*, particularly in the large manufacturing and service sectors. In the case of the NIEs it is clear that the elasticities are higher because this group of countries developed its manufacturing sector on generally labour-intensive lines in accordance with an idea of where its long-term comparative advantage lay. The same feature also contributes to the short-term flexibility of the NIEs and to their ability to adapt to external shocks.

Generally, therefore, the trade-exposed economies have features to allow them to adapt to external shocks. How they perform in comparison with economies that are more insulated, and therefore less vulnerable, can only be judged by looking more closely at the model results.

3   Trade Scenarios

The model was used to conduct the following four experiments which are indicative of the types of shocks likely to affect the region's exports.

The first two shocks originate in the world economy.

(A) A 10 per cent fall in the demand by the *rest of the world* for all commodities from the Asian region resulting from a "fortress Europe".

(B) A 10 per cent decline in the demand by the *rest of the world* for clothing and textiles from the Asian region. If reforms in Eastern Europe lead to an expansion of labour-intensive manufactures sales to Western Europe to encourage greater economic and political unity, some of the supplies currently originating in Asia may be replaced.

The second two shocks originate in policy changes within Asia.

(C) A 10 per cent productivity improvement in China's clothing and textile sector. This could be brought about by further economic reforms which would be likely to be implemented first in those parts of the Chinese economy engaged in trade. China's clothing and textile sector is the most export-oriented of its eight sectors in the model.

(D) Productivity improvement in India's clothing and textile sector. This scenario is perhaps more speculative, given the slow pace of liberalization in India to date. The Indian economy is of sufficient size, however, for improvements in its performance to have a noticeable impact on the other economies in the region.

3.1   Experiment A: Recession in the rest of the world

The impact of a "fortress Europe" outcome of "Europe 1992" has been modelled by a 10 per cent decline in demand by the *rest of the world* for each of the eight commodities from the Asia region. To begin to understand the impact on sectoral output in the region it is useful to look at the proportion of each industry's output that is currently sold to the *rest of the world*. This determines the magnitude of the fall in demand for each sector's output in the first instance.

The initial shares of each industry's output that are sold to the *rest of the world* have been calculated from the model's data base (Table 4). In all but the

Table 4 Sectoral shares of output sold to the *rest of the world* (%)

Sector	China	India	Other S. Asia	Near NIEs	NIEs
Agriculture	-	-	2.1	3.1	-
Other primary industry	-	4.8	1.6	4.5	19.3
Mining	-	-	18.7	30.9	-
Processed food	-	6.8	2.0	8.5	-
Clothing and textiles	8.6	11.0	24.6	16.8	6.4
Metal products and machinery	2.9	3.4	1.0	27.2	12.7
Other manufacturing	2.7	5.5	6.7	21.7	27.4
Services	2.0	1.7	1.3	5.0	8.0

NIEs, the clothing and textile sectors are relatively dependent on sales to the *rest of the world*. In the NIEs and near NIEs, the metal products and machinery and other manufacturing sectors are more dependent than in the other countries on trade, following the switch of these countries' industries into products such as machine tools and consumer electronics. In the near NIE group and the Other South Asian countries, the mining sectors are also dependent on sales to the *rest of the world*.

The results of Experiment A are reported in Table 5. The model's projected impact of the trade decline on sectoral outputs shows that for the most part, the largest declines in sectoral output occur in industries for which the decline in demand by the *rest of the world* comprises a significant portion of total demand. This is particularly noticeable among the clothing and textile sectors of the region.

Among sectors facing similar declines in demand, output falls further, and prices decline by less, when supply is relatively price responsive. The near NIE mining sector's output is small, despite its relatively high exposure to the *rest of the world*, because it is capital intensive and its supply is particularly unresponsive to prices. Rather than contracting output, this sector maintains output but experiences a profit squeeze on its fixed capital. The profit squeeze is the counterpart, on the cost side, to the relatively large price fall for its output.

The trade decline in the *rest of the world* does not have adverse effects on all industries in the region. Some are able to expand. The metal products and machinery industries in China, India and Other South Asia are not directly dependent on sales to the *rest of the world*. These industries nevertheless face downward pressure on the price of their output because they are a relatively close substitute in the markets of the region for metal products and machinery

Table 5 Effects of a 10% decline in export demand
by the *rest of the world* (in % changes)

	China	India	Other S. Asia	Near NIEs	NIEs
Effects on outputs					
Agriculture	0.41	0.06	-0.05	0.11	0.31
Other primary industry	-0.08	-0.54	-0.23	-0.30	-1.54
Mining	0.24	1.31	-0.75	-0.08	0.97
Processed food	-0.14	-0.27	0.03	-0.12	0.48
Clothing and textiles	-0.71	-1.27	-1.91	-1.31	-1.46
Metal products and machinery	0.06	0.11	0.39	-0.59	-0.21
Other manufacturing	-0.13	-0.46	-0.15	-0.37	-2.22
Services	-0.20	-0.20	-0.09	-0.44	-0.83
Effects on prices					
Agriculture	-2.49	-3.81	-2.72	-3.13	-1.50
Other primary industry	-3.07	-5.04	-3.46	-4.93	-5.41
Mining	-2.61	-2.33	-2.62	-4.93	-2.66
Processed food	-2.37	-4.04	-2.57	-3.45	-2.38
Clothing and textiles	-5.24	-4.91	-5.39	-5.07	-3.91
Metal products and machinery	-2.92	-3.64	-1.23	-2.97	-2.84
Other manufacturing	-3.33	-3.63	-2.25	-4.23	-3.89
Services	-3.23	-4.22	-2.68	-4.10	-4.22
Effects on employment					
Agriculture	0.70	0.12	-0.17	0.38	1.28
Other primary industry	-0.15	-1.13	-0.83	-1.22	-3.36
Mining	0.66	2.72	-2.67	-0.91	1.56
Processed food	0.69	-0.56	0.11	-0.44	0.91
Clothing and textiles	-3.03	-2.64	-6.82	-3.44	-2.34
Metal products and machinery	0.17	0.23	1.39	-1.85	-0.42
Other manufacturing	-0.53	-0.97	-0.55	-1.83	-4.38
Services	-0.38	-0.42	-0.32	-1.07	-1.58
Macroeconomic effects[a]					
Consumer price index	-3.0	-4.0	-2.6	-3.7	-3.4
Real GDP	0.2	-0.1	-0.1	-0.4	-0.7
Aggregate employment	0.1	-0.3	-0.5	-1.0	-1.9
Export volume	-2.1	-6.2	-8.6	-6.7	-6.2
Import volume	-4.2	-4.3	-2.3	-1.5	-3.3
Trade balance	-12699	-896	-307	-1487	-3133

[a] All results are expressed in percentage changes, except for the balance of trade which is expressed as absolute changes in millions of 1985 US dollars.

from the NIEs and near NIEs; the prices of these products fall because of the decline in demand from the *rest of the world*. The industries in China, India and Other South Asia are able to counter this pressure, however, because their input costs, particularly material and nominal wage costs, also fall as other industries contract in their home countries. For these industries, the cost declines outweigh the decline in output prices and they are able to expand.

Some industries are more adversely affected than their direct exposure to the trade decline in the *rest of the world* would indicate. The clothing and textile sector in the NIEs is not as dependent on the *rest of the world* as other textile sectors in the region. Nevertheless, its output falls by about as much. Costs do not decline by as much as those in the other textile sectors of the region, so that they lose market shares within the region.

The projected results for sectoral employment follow directly from the projected impact on sectoral output.

Real GDP and employment fall throughout Asia, except in China. Most of the sectors in China that are dependent on exports to the *rest of the world* are still relatively small. The sectors that are able to pick up resources and expand in the *rest of the world* represent a large proportion of the total economy; agriculture expands to replace imports. Because of the particular sectoral mix of impacts in China, overall activity expands. In volume terms the trade balance improves. This is a direct reflection of the expansion in real GDP. In foreign currency value terms, however, China's trade balance deteriorates. Although the volume of imports shrinks by more than the volume of exports, the prices of China's exports to the rest of Asia fall by more than the prices of its imports. In value terms the fall in exports exceeds the fall in imports.

Elsewhere in the region the trade decline brings declines in real GDP and employment, along with deteriorations in the trade account in both volume and value terms.

In summary, a 10 per cent decline in the *rest of the world's* demand for each of the eight commodities in the region is estimated to have the following effects:

- a decline in the total volume of trade in the region – both import and export volumes decline in all five *countries*;

- decreases in output and employment in the sectors that are most dependent on the *rest of the world* as a destination for their output;

- a mix of decreases and increases in output and employment in the other sectors, depending on whether the induced declines in their output prices are matched by induced declines in input costs; and

- an overall decline in real GDP and employment in all economies of the region except China. China appears as an exception here not because of any peculiarities in its economy, but because some of the sectors in a position to gain from the trade decline are large.

The overall message from these results is that while a trade decline may have predictable impacts on the region in macroeconomic terms, the mechanisms of adjustment for particular sectors may be rather subtle. Even sectors with apparently similar characteristics may face different prospects, depending on the balance of induced changes in their output prices and input costs.

3.2 Experiment B: Increased exports of clothing and textiles from Eastern Europe

As a result of recent political developments in Eastern Europe there is the possibility that its trade with Western Europe and hence with the *rest of the world* in the model will increase. Given its pattern of endowments and the structure of its input costs, this trade is likely to include relatively labour-intensive manufactures. This raises the prospect of substitution by the *rest of the world* against exports from Asia, especially if exports from Eastern Europe are encouraged for political as well as economic reasons. The possibility has been modelled by a 10 per cent decline in the *rest of the world's* demand for clothing and textiles from Asia.

A 10 per cent decline in clothing and textile demand by the *rest of the world* means that the Asian countries face increased competition. The output, employment and price effects of this experiment are shown in Table 6. In China, each sector is affected in much the same way as the corresponding sectors in the other *countries* of the region, although the effects tend to be smaller because China's textile sector is less dependent on sales to the *rest of the world*.

At the macroeconomic level, the effects of Eastern Europe's increased exports on *countries* other than China are indicated in Table 6. In China itself, the contraction of the clothing and textile sector, a relatively small sector in China, is more than outweighed by the expansion of other, larger sectors. An interesting feature is that the same is not true for India, a country with similarly low trade exposure. Part of the reason is that some of China's non-textile sectors, particularly agriculture, are more supply elastic than India's.

In summary, an expansion in clothing and textile exports from Eastern Europe would have the following effects:

- a decline in clothing and textile output and employment in all five Asian *countries*;

- increases in output and employment in most other sectors;

- only in China is the expansion of non-textile sectors sufficient to offset the decline in textiles and lead to an overall increase in real GDP and aggregate employment. This is largely because of the relatively small size of its textile sector and the relatively large size and supply responsiveness of its agricultural sector;

Table 6 Effects of a 10% decline in clothing and textile
demand by the *rest of the world* (in % changes)

Sector	China	India	Other S. Asia	Near NIEs	NIEs
Effects on outputs					
Agriculture	0.13	0.00	-0.00	0.01	-0.00
Other primary industry	0.09	0.06	0.02	0.01	-0.02
Mining	0.21	0.39	0.13	0.02	0.17
Processed food	0.09	0.16	0.12	0.02	0.03
Clothing and textiles	-0.68	-1.41	-1.81	-1.55	-1.75
Metal products and machinery	0.13	0.14	0.12	0.04	0.07
Other manufacturing	0.11	0.07	0.09	0.01	-0.04
Services	0.05	0.00	-0.01	-0.02	-0.04
Effects on prices					
Agriculture	-0.75	-0.93	-0.65	-0.34	-0.19
Other primary industry	-0.80	-0.85	-0.58	-0.34	-0.34
Mining	-0.52	-0.46	-0.11	-0.08	-0.19
Processed food	-0.60	-0.87	-0.61	-0.33	-0.24
Clothing and textiles	-3.12	-2.00	-3.39	-2.58	-1.19
Metal products and machinery	-0.57	-0.74	-0.25	-0.16	-0.19
Other manufacturing	-0.57	-0.72	-0.37	-0.24	-0.27
Services	-0.80	-0.91	-0.62	-0.37	-0.35
Effects on employment					
Agriculture	0.22	0.01	-0.00	0.04	-0.02
Other primary industry	0.16	0.13	0.08	0.05	-0.04
Mining	0.57	0.81	0.47	0.21	0.27
Processed food	0.44	0.33	0.42	0.08	0.06
Clothing and textiles	-2.89	-2.94	-6.47	-4.06	-2.82
Metal products and machinery	0.36	0.28	0.41	0.13	0.14
Other manufacturing	0.43	0.14	0.31	0.07	-0.09
Services	0.10	0.00	-0.02	-0.04	-0.08
Macroeconomic effects[a]					
Consumer price index	-1.0	-1.0	-0.7	-0.4	-0.3
Real GDP	0.1	-0.0	-0.0	-0.1	-0.1
Aggregate employment	0.1	-0.1	-0.2	-0.1	-0.2
Export volume	-0.5	-1.1	-2.9	-0.5	-0.5
Import volume	-1.6	-0.9	-0.7	-0.1	-0.2
Trade balance	-3841	-188	-140	-30	-272

[a] All results are expressed in percentage changes, except for the balance of trade which is expressed as absolute changes in millions of 1985 US dollars.

- elsewhere in the region, aggregate employment and real GDP decline; and

- the volume of trade declines and trade balances deteriorate in foreign currency value terms throughout the region.

This experiment confirms that supply responsiveness can help countries to adapt to external shocks. In China, the agricultural sector is not itself hit by adverse developments and is able to expand by using resources released by other sectors.

3.3 Experiment C: A 10 per cent productivity improvement in China's clothing and textile sector

As a result of productivity improvement, China's clothing and textile sector *could* produce 10 per cent more output while using the same inputs. The sector does not expand output by the full 10 per cent, however, because expansion starts to put downward pressure on clothing and textile prices in China. Because some of the additional output is exported, there is also downward pressure on the prices of China's clothing and textiles in the rest of the region. Results of the experiment are given in Table 7. The sectoral output results show that China's clothing and textile output expands by only 3.27 per cent. The commodity price results show that even this modest increase produces a significant fall in clothing and textile prices in China.

Because of the productivity improvement, China's clothing and textile sector can achieve a 3 per cent increase in output while using fewer inputs. It releases labour and material inputs for use by other sectors. If the other sectors, particularly the trade-exposed sectors, can achieve even a small reduction in costs to improve their competitiveness, they would be able to expand sales by exporting and replacing imports, and prevent an overall fall in employment.

Real wages in China are assumed to be rigid, as they are in other *countries*, so the required improvement in competitiveness of the non-textile sectors cannot come about through a fall in real wages. But the price reduction for clothing and textiles is passed directly on to the other consumer price index. It is also passed on to using industries in China, causing small reductions in their costs and further, indirect reductions in the general level of prices. Even though real wages are fixed, the overall level of China's prices and nominal wage costs can fall relative to prices and wage costs in the rest of the region. This provides the improvement in competitiveness whereby the non-textile sectors in China can expand. The prices of non-textile commodities also fall in China, but by less than the fall in textile prices.

The expansions are larger for those non-textile sectors that are trade exposed and have relatively elastic supplies. The metal products and machinery sector and the other manufacturing sector face a relatively high degree of import competition, by China's standards, and also export a small but significant proportion of their output. China's mining sector also exports, and is not very

Table 7 Effects of a 10% productivity improvement
in China's textiles and clothing (in % changes)

Sector	China	India	Other S. Asia	Near NIEs	NIEs
Effects on outputs					
Agriculture	1.15	-0.01	-0.00	-0.00	-0.07
Other primary industry	0.88	0.09	0.02	-0.00	0.01
Mining	1.84	0.92	0.32	0.06	0.80
Processed food	0.85	0.31	0.24	0.10	0.19
Clothing and textiles	3.27	-2.69	-3.65	-3.24	-7.15
Metal products and machinery	1.14	0.29	0.29	0.05	0.33
Other manufacturing	1.04	0.09	0.15	0.01	-0.13
Services	0.53	-0.02	-0.02	-0.10	-0.18
Effects on prices					
Agriculture	-6.36	-2.34	-1.78	-1.44	-1.17
Other primary industry	-6.74	-2.24	-1.72	-1.45	-1.63
Mining	-4.36	-1.20	-0.38	-0.50	-1.05
Processed food	-4.96	-2.22	-1.67	-1.29	-1.36
Clothing and textiles	-28.30	-4.37	-7.39	-6.22	-5.61
Metal products and machinery	-4.72	-1.90	-0.79	-0.76	-1.02
Other manufacturing	-4.54	-1.85	-1.15	-1.06	-1.38
Services	-6.72	-2.31	-1.73	-1.47	-1.81
Effects on employment					
Agriculture	1.95	-0.02	-0.01	-0.01	-0.31
Other primary industry	1.59	0.18	0.07	-0.01	0.03
Mining	5.05	1.93	1.16	0.64	1.29
Processed food	4.06	0.65	0.86	0.35	0.36
Clothing and textiles	-26.93	-5.59	-13.02	-8.52	-11.51
Metal products and machinery	3.26	0.59	1.02	0.15	0.66
Other manufacturing	4.11	0.19	0.55	0.06	-0.26
Services	1.02	-0.04	-0.08	-0.23	-0.34
Macroeconomic effects[a]					
Consumer price index	-8.2	-2.4	-1.9	1.5	-1.8
Real GDP	2.2	-0.0	0.1	-0.1	-0.3
Aggregate employment	1.1	-0.1	-0.4	-0.3	-0.9
Export volume	12.1	-2.7	-5.7	1.5	-1.9
Import volume	-15.1	-2.1	-1.3	-0.3	-0.8
Trade balance	10126	-456	-273	501	-1063

[a] All results are expressed in percentage changes, except for the balance of trade which is expressed as absolute changes in millions of 1985 US dollars.

capital intensive. The agricultural sector faces a small amount of foreign competition on both import and export markets, and can expand its supply relatively
easily.

For the rest of the countries in the region, the most important impact of the
productivity improvement in China's clothing and textile sector is the fall in
demand for their own output. This competition is felt in their sales to China,
on their own home market and in third markets. But even for the most successful
exporters of textiles, the home market is the most important market and the
output response of these countries' textile sectors is largely explained by the
intensity of the competition from China in this market and the resulting decline
in demand for their own products.

The NIEs' clothing and textile sector is the most adversely affected. Total
imports account for about 7 per cent of their apparent consumption of clothing
and textiles. A close examination of the model's data base also shows that they
receive more than 40 per cent of these imports from China, mainly because of the
amount of China's trade that is channelled through Hong Kong. The reduction
in the price of China's textiles in world markets would be felt most strongly
by countries such as the Republic of Korea. At the other extreme, imports
of clothing and textiles account for about 4 per cent of apparent consumption
in India, while China supplies only about 8 per cent of those imports. The
reduction in demand felt by India's textile sector is not very great.

The size of the contraction in the textile sectors outside of China is not
just a function of the fall in demand they face, but also a function of the price
responsiveness of their own supply. The short-run supply elasticity is higher
for the NIEs' textiles than for India's. Supply considerations therefore tend to
reinforce the demand effects on output, although they moderate the effects on
prices. The NIEs' clothing and textiles face the largest contraction, while India's
faces the least. Despite this, the decline in textile prices in the two countries is
about the same.

The response of the non-textile sectors outside of China depends on the
improvement in competitiveness they enjoy as a result of falling prices and wage
costs. They all experience broadly similar reductions in their cost structure. The
pattern of output responses across these sectors and countries reflects the price
responsiveness of their supply and demand. For example, processed food in India
and Other South Asia are able to expand more than most other sectors because
their supply is relatively price responsive. The decline in price and cost structure
is equivalent to a real depreciation, explaining the movement of resources out
of the largely non-traded service sectors in some countries. None of the non-
textile, trade-oriented sectors outside of China receive the same improvement in
competitiveness that China's non-textile sectors receive. None expands to the
same extent as in China.

The sectoral employment effects follow directly from the effects on sectoral
output. In the absence of productivity improvements, sectoral employment
moves in the same direction as sectoral output, but by a greater amount. This

is because labour is the primary factor of production that is variable in the short-run and primary factors as a group are required in strict proportion to output in each *country* industry.

As expected, China's real GDP is larger than it would be otherwise, following the improvement in the productivity of its clothing and textile sector. Because of that productivity improvement, however, aggregate employment does not need to rise by as much as real GDP. With real domestic absorption assumed to be fixed, the improvement in real GDP is expressed as an improvement in the trade account. The aggregate volume of exports rises and the aggregate volume of imports falls. This is consistent with China's improvement in competitiveness *vis-à-vis* the *rest of the world* (as indicated by results for China's consumer price index) being significantly better than that achieved by other countries in Asia. The changes in export and import volumes also translate into an improvement in China's trade balance in foreign currency value terms.

The macroeconomic results indicate that the least-exposed countries elsewhere in the region suffer relatively little from the expansion of China's exports. In India the decline in real GDP and aggregate employment is slight. Total export volumes decline as India's textile sector contracts. Aggregate import volumes also contract because India's industries succeed in replacing imports, particularly those from the *rest of the world*, following their own small improvement in competitiveness. Exports fall by more than imports, however, and the trade balance compensates in foreign currency value terms.

The Other South Asian and near NIE countries face slightly greater contractions than India in real GDP and employment. The main reason is that their trade exposure is correspondingly greater. In both countries export volumes contract by more than import volumes, but the export contraction in the near NIE block is very much smaller than in Other South Asian countries. Textile exports represent a smaller proportion of the total export bundle in near NIE than in Other South Asia. The fall in near NIE's textile exports is not offset by increased exports of other products because near NIEs lose competiveness relative to the other *countries* of the region. Nevertheless, the overall impact on export volumes is smaller in the near NIE group than in Other South Asia. The reason that the near NIE group's trade balance actually improves in foreign currency value terms is that the group starts from a position of substantial deficit. Although the *percentage* change in the value of imports is smaller than the *percentage* change in the value of exports, the initial value to which it applies is very much larger.

The reductions in real GDP and employment are greatest in the NIEs, although the reductions in export and import volumes are not substantially worse than for the near NIE group. Most of the non-textile, trade-oriented sectors in the NIEs are able to adapt as well, if not better, than those in the near NIE countries. The external shock in question happens to have hit the textile sector which is not only trade exposed and therefore vulnerable to competition, but is also one of the most price responsive sectors on the supply side. Its output contracts by more than any other sector in Asia.

In summary, a 10 per cent productivity improvement in China's clothing and textiles sector is estimated to have the following effects:

- an increase in real GDP and employment in China but decreases in the other four *countries*;

- an increase in China's export volume but decreases elsewhere;

- a decrease in import volumes for all five *countries* in the region; and

- an improvement in China's trade balance but decreases for India, Other South Asia and the Asian NIEs.

The general conclusion is that China would benefit from a 10 per cent productivity improvement in its clothing and textile sector but other countries, in the absence of appropriate policy action, would not.

To put the magnitude of their losses in perspective, consider that 10 per cent of China's clothing and textile sector equals almost all of Other South Asia's, roughly 50 per cent of the near NIEs' and 25 per cent of India's or the NIEs'. An alarmist with a partial equilibrium perspective might, indeed, be tempted to suppose that an expansion of China's exports would wipe out labour-intensive manufactures elsewhere in the region.

3.4 Experiment D: Comparison between China and India

China and India are large countries in terms of population – 1114 million and 833 million respectively in 1989. Given the margins of error involved in such measurements, their GDP per capita, US$350 and US$340 in 1990, is very similar (World Bank 1992).

The productive capacity of the two economies also has similarities, but there are also major differences. Both countries are still predominantly agricultural. In 1965 both countries had about 80 per cent of the population living in the countryside. In India this is now thought to have fallen to about 30 per cent and in China to 50 per cent, but differences in definition of "urban" make this a dubious statistic. What has clearly happened is that off-farm rural production increased in both countries as rural productivity rose with policy reforms from the early 1970s in India and from 1979 in China (with the return, in effect, of private enterprise in farming).

India has a strong private industrial sector with a very considerable potential for increasing productivity if trade and other liberalization were to take place. The public sector is inefficient, but small when compared to China's State enterprise productivity, which improved a little in the early 1980s, but appeared to fall again in the second half of the 1980s. Township, village and small cooperative/private enterprises grew rapidly in the 1980s, but while private returns to managers and workers have clearly risen, the social returns to these enterprises are more dubious. The principal source of rising efficiency in the 1980s has been "informal" investments for export by Hong Kong and Taiwanese entrepreneurs in township, village and cooperative/private enterprises. These employ some 5 million workers, mainly in Southeastern China, but outside the Special Economic Zones, which supply less than 2 per cent of China's exports.

Both India and China have inadequate infrastructures, though India's is better than China's.

India has managed its macro policy quite well since the 1960s, but it is still highly protectionist and has no foreign investment 'informal' export sector to match China's.

This experiment considers the impact of a 10 per cent productivity improvement in India's clothing and textile sector. Results are given in Table 8. As before, this means that the Indian clothing and textile sector would produce 10 per cent more output, using the same inputs. While the Chinese clothing and textile sector's actual output increase was about 3 per cent under these circumstances, India's clothing and textile sector's expansion is limited to less than 1 per cent. The supply elasticity of the Indian sector is noticeably greater than in China, so it is not supply constraints that are limiting the output expansion. Instead it is because the Indian sector is relatively less trade exposed than the Chinese sector. Because of its greater dependence on the domestic market it faces a much smaller aggregate demand elasticity. Output expansion is limited by the excessive downward pressure on prices that expansion would cause.

With output expansion limited to less than 1 per cent, the Indian clothing and textile sector releases proportionately more resources than the Chinese sector did. Some of India's non-textile sectors are therefore able to expand. Processed food and mining are supply responsive and trade exposed so they are particularly well placed to take advantage of resources released by clothing and textiles. The general effect of the productivity improvement on India's industries is the same as it was in China – all are able to expand. In India's case, the sector in which the productivity improvement occurs is not able to take much advantage of the improvement so the benefits are spread by the movement of greater labour and material inputs to other sectors.

Outside of India the sectoral output, price and employment effects are similar to the impact of an expansion in any competitor's textile output. Clothing and textiles in all other *countries* contract, while most non-textile sectors are able to gain from the resources that are released. The size of the adjustments are smaller than with a productivity improvement in China, simply because a 1 per cent expansion in India's textile output is a much smaller addition to the total market than a 3 per cent increase in China's clothing and textile output.

In macroeconomic terms the expansion of all India's industries leads to an improvement in real GDP. labour is released from clothing and textiles into other sectors whose absorptive capacity is limited because they are less labour intensive, so aggregate employment acutally contracts. In Other South Asia,

Table 8 Effects of a 10% productivity improvement
in India's textiles and clothing (in % changes)

Sector	China	India	Other S. Asia	Near NIEs	NIEs
Effects on outputs					
Agriculture	0.06	0.03	-0.00	-0.00	-0.00
Other primary industry	0.03	0.47	-0.03	-0.03	-0.18
Mining	0.10	2.21	0.10	0.02	0.19
Processed food	0.03	1.04	0.01	-0.10	0.01
Clothing and textiles	-0.28	0.93	-0.76	-0.59	-0.73
Metal products					
and machinery	0.06	0.83	0.07	0.02	0.04
Other manufacturing	0.04	0.50	0.04	0.00	-0.11
Services	0.00	0.05	-0.01	-0.04	-0.08
Effects on prices					
Agriculture	-0.49	-5.15	-0.52	-0.52	-0.23
Other primary industry	-0.53	-4.51	-0.62	-0.63	-0.63
Mining	-0.37	-2.50	-0.12	-0.11	-0.25
Processed food	-0.44	-4.76	-0.53	-0.63	-0.31
Clothing and textiles	-1.46	-12.01	-1.67	-1.30	-0.73
Metal products					
and machinery	-0.41	-4.03	-0.26	-0.26	-0.27
Other manufacturing	-0.44	-3.89	-0.35	-0.36	-0.36
Services	-0.54	-5.00	-0.51	-0.52	-0.47
Effects on employment					
Agriculture	6.09	0.06	-0.01	-0.00	-0.01
Other primary industry	0.05	0.97	-0.09	-0.10	-0.39
Mining	0.28	4.61	0.34	0.27	0.30
Processed food	0.16	2.17	0.04	-0.35	0.02
Clothing and textiles	-1.18	-18.90	-2.71	-1.55	-1.17
Metal products					
and machinery	0.16	1.72	0.27	0.05	-0.09
Other manufacturing	0.14	1.03	0.14	-0.00	-0.21
Services	0.00	0.11	-0.03	-0.09	-0.16
Macroeconomic effects[a]					
Consumer price index	-0.6	-5.4	-0.5	-0.6	-0.4
Real GDP	0.0	0.9	-0.0	-0.1	-0.1
Aggregate employment	0.0	-0.2	-0.1	-0.1	-0.2
Export volume	-0.4	9.2	-1.4	-0.7	-0.5
Import volume	-0.9	-4.9	-0.3	-0.1	-0.3
Trade balance	-2366	-974	-62	8	-296

[a] All results are expressed in percentage changes, except for the balance of trade which is expressed as absolute changes in millions of 1985 US dollars.

the near NIEs' and the NIEs' contraction of clothing and textiles is not offset by expansion elsewhere and real GDP and employment fall. In China, as before, the expansion of agriculture is more than sufficient to offset the contraction in clothing and textiles so that real GDP and employment expand slightly. In India and China the increases in real GDP are matched by improvements in net export volumes although in both cases the balance of trade deteriorates in foreign currency value terms. Elsewhere real net exports fall as real GDP falls, but in the near NIE group there is a small improvement in the trade balance in value terms.

In summary, a 10 per cent improvement in the productivity of India's clothing and textile sector has the following effects:

- a small increase in India's output of clothing and textiles, with decreases elsewhere;

- increases in output in most non-textile sectors throughout the region; and

- an increase in real GDP though not in aggregate employment in India, with decreases in both real GDP and aggregate employment elsewhere.

The main differences betwen the effects of clothing and textile productivity improvements in India and China occur within those *countries*. The current Indian clothing and textile sector is less able to take advantage of its productivity improvement. While its home market is better insulated from import competition, the industry is more restricted by the resulting low elasticity of demand in that market and does not have the same opportunity as the clothing and textile sector in China to expand sales by replacing imports.

Correspondingly more of the benefits of the productivity improvement in terms of resources saved are passed on to other sectors in India.

Elsewhere in the region, India's textile productivity improvement causes less adjustment than China's textile productivity improvement, mainly because India's sector is considerably smaller. The patterns and mechanisms of adjustment, however, are similar.

4 Conclusions

The Asian economies were treated in groups to make the analysis manageable, but within each group, and of course, within India and China, there is a large range of experience.

4.1 The NIEs

The NIEs are clearly strong and flexible economies. Changes in Europe are not likely to have a major impact on their growth because they will be able to work their way around problems. Hong Kong and Singapore have adopted macro stability combined with neutral trade policies. Hong Kong has had almost no goverment regulations, confining government to policy determination and the supply of public goods and housing. Singapore has intervened slightly more in the economy, but where market trends ran counter to government intervention, market signals were allowed to prevail. Singapore is moving toward further liberalization of the economy in preparation to catching up with industrial economies in productivity and living standards. The prospective absorption of Hong Kong into China in 1997 is, however, leading to a hollowing out of the skill base as uncertainty with regard to China's policy grows.

Taiwan and the Republic of Korea also based their success on attaining macroeconomic stability in the late 1950s and early 1960s respectively, but they were unable to get rid of high protection, repressed financial systems and other forms of intervention in the economy because of the vested interests of entrepreneurs and bureaucrats. A high level of government intervention has thus been essential to make exports possible. This has led to rent seeking. Exports have been achieved, but at very considerable cost in terms of living standards. Domestic and US pressures are now urging both countries to liberalize their economies. Taiwan is ahead of Korea in opening up its economy and improving living standards. It is likely to find changes in world trade trends easier to handle than Korea.

4.2 The near NIEs

The model runs suggest that the combination of a rich resource base with stable macroeconomic policies and relatively modest protection makes Indonesia, Malaysia and Thailand even stronger and more flexible than the NIEs. Opportunities in the primary sectors would be likely to balance limited world markets for manufactures. The Philippines, however, despite a very similar resource endowment to that of Thailand, has performed badly because of poor macroeconomic and highly protectionist policies. No change of policies and hence of performance seems likely.

4.3 China

China is the only centrally planned economy that has to date succeeded in creating a major export sector. A number of policy measures, including the establishment of special economic zones, substantial devaluation (though not to equilibrium exchange rates), foreign exchange retention schemes and fiscal incentives for foreign investors were adopted to this end, but none were successful.

The bulk of export growth has come from labour-intensive goods produced by overseas Chinese entrepreneurs (mainly from Hong Kong and Taiwan) who have "informally" invested in township, village and cooperative/private enterprises to avoid government regulations. Much of the inspection, packaging and finishing of these products is undertaken in Hong Kong, on which China's exports are highly dependent. Provided that the Chinese government continues to close its eyes to the informality of these activities, China will be able to increase its exports. The model reflects the flexibility of this sector and of private enterprise in agriculture. The weakness of macroeconomic policies, the failure to unify domestic prices and the continuing importance of the inefficient state sector, could, however, make further growth difficult if reform does not continue and if Hong Kong becomes closed in.

4.4 India

India is still a highly protected economy with a considerable public sector and pervasive and complex regulations. Exporting has been facilitated by offsets to protection, but the value of such offsets to exporters is limited and total exports have remained low in comparison to China. The economy accordingly continues to be strangled by balance of payments constraints. India will have to increase exports to maintain the strenghtening of growth achieved in the 1980s, and this will require a substantial reduction of protection. The model reflects the present rigidity of the economy.

4.5 Other Asia

Pakistan has followed similar policies to India, with somewhat less public planning and somewhat better growth and export results. Less stable macroeconomic policies and very high protection have led to a considerable bias against agriculture and exports in Bangladesh. Sri Lanka's policy reforms came late (in 1979) and have been limited in scope. Political upheaval has made for further difficulties.

With the exception of Hong Kong and Singapore, the Asian countries could improve their policy framework considerably to deal with difficulties arising out of negative developments in Europe. Paradoxically, pessimistic global scenarios could even have positive effects by accelerating the pace of policy change, but policy changes would be costlier.

4.6 Regional Trade

Regional trade in East Asia is growing strongly because the NIEs are importing raw materials from the near NIEs and low cost labour-intensive industrial goods from China. ASEAN, the most successful of developing country regional arrangements, has largely remained a political pressure group with little economic content. It has not moved to customs union, let alone common market arrangements. Its member countries are young in political terms and very disparate. They are aware of the high costs and low benefits created by developing country regional arrangements. The Asia Pacific Economic Cooperation Group (APEC) recognizes that the East Asian countries' economic success has resulted from the openness of the multilateral trading framework and has put its weight behind the Uruguay negotiations. The importance of trade with the United States is likely to prevent the creation of a regional arrangement. Most of the East Asian countries prefer close political ties to the United States to those with Japan. Regional relations within South Asia and between Southeast and Northeast Asia have a long way to go before becoming effective. The APEC initiative is expected to become more formal under the nurture of regional politicans, bureaucrats, the consultants who feed the process and other international agencies which thrive on it, but the scope for a formal trade "bloc" (in contrast to initiatives in the western hemisphere) remains tenuous (Hughes (1991)). The emphasis is likely to continue to be on domestic and multilateral policies within and outside regional trading arrangements.

5   References

Anderson, K. (1991), Europe 1992 and the Western Pacific economies, *The Economic Journal* 101, 1-14.

Baldwin, R. (1989), On the growth effects of 1991, *Economic Policy* 9, 247-281.

Begg, D. et al. (1990), *Monitoring Integration: The Impact of Eastern Europe*, London: Centre for Economic Policy Research.

Cecchini, P. et al. (1988), *The European Challenge 1992: The Benefits of a Single Market*, Aldershot: Wildwood House.

Cabalu, H., Laursen, J., Mai, Y., Pearce, D. and Vincent, D. (1991), The Asia Model, Working Paper No.91/14, National Centre for Development Studies, Australian National University, Canberra.

Cline, W. (1982), Can the East Asian model of development be generalized?, *World Development* 10, 81-90.

Dixon, P., Parmenter, B., Sutton, J. and Vincent, D. (1982), *ORANI: A Multisectoral Model of the Australian Economy*, Amsterdam: North Holland.

Greeneway, D. (1991), Implications of the EC92 Program for Outside Countries, New York: United Nations.

Harris, R.G. (1984), *Trade, Industrial Policy and Canadian Manufacturing*, Toronto: Ontario Economic Council.

Hughes, H. (1991), Does APEC make sense?, *ASEAN Economic Bulletin* 8, 125-136.

Panoutsopoulos, V. (1990), The supply determinants of the developing countries' penetration of the United States market for manufactures, PhD thesis, National Centre for Development Studies, Canberra.

Ranis, G. (1985), Can the East Asian model of development be generalized: a comment, *World Development* 4, 543-545.

Streeton, P. (1982), A cool look at "outward looking" strategies for development, *The World Economy* 5, 159-170.

World Bank (1992), *World Development Report 1992*, New York: Oxford University Press.

7

Determinants of the Anti-dumping and Countervailing Duty Decisions of the European Communities[1]

P.K.M. Tharakan

University of Antwerp

J. Waelbroeck

University of Brussels

1 Introduction

The Commission of The European Communities (EC) is an important user of anti-dumping and countervailing duty (AD/CVD) measures[2]. The political economy aspects of the AD/CVD decisions of the EC have been subjected to detailed analysis by the present authors in recent studies (Tharakan (1991a)), Tharakan and Waelbroeck (1992)). In this paper we sum up the salient elements of the above-mentioned studies and thus provide for the first time a complete picture of the determinants of the AD/CVD decisons of the EC.

The AD/CVD actions of the main trading nations have attracted considerable attention in recent years. This is because of the fear that the antidumping mechanism is being transformed into a selective trade restricting device. Indeed the terminology used in defining "dumping" in Article VI of the GATT, the subsequent antidumping code and the corresponding regulations of the contracting

---

[1]Some officials of the Commission of the European Communities and lawyers with antidumping case experience have been of considerable help in formulating some of the hypotheses tested in this study. They prefer to remain anonymous and are not of course responsible for the inferences we have drawn from our empirical findings. André Sapir's comments on the first part of this paper (which was presented at the Conference) and those of an anonymous referee are gratefully acknowledged.

[2]According to one estimate (Montagnon and Kellaway (1990)), during 1980-1988, the leading users of antidumping measures initiated 1665 cases. For a recent critical review of EC's antidumping policy, see GATT (1991), Volume I, especially pages 17-19.

parties for defining "dumping" and "injury" is vague enough to lend itself to elastic interpretation and hence, misuse.

The AD/CVD proceedings initiated in the EC might lead, after due investigation, to: (a) a rejection of the claim, (b) imposition of anti-dumping or countervailing duty or (c) the acceptance of the undertakings given by the exporters. Imposition of duties requires that both dumping and consequent material injury to the EC industry have been found. Separate investigations are carried out by the Commission of the European Communities to verify whether dumping and injury have taken place. If an affirmative finding is made on both counts, the EC still have the option of terminating the proceedings without imposing the duties but by accepting an undertaking. Such undertakings are agreements between the Commission of the European Communities and exporters (importers) of allegedly dumped merchandise whereby the latter agree to revise their prices or cease exports to the extent that the Commission is satisfied that either the dumping margin or the injurious effects of the dumping are eliminated.

In the present study, first we report the results of our investigation on the determinants of the EC's dumping/no dumping and injury/no injury decisions. Subsequently the results of the analysis concerning the determinants of the EC's choice between the acceptance of undertakings and the imposition of definitive duties are presented. Both exercises were carried out within the framework of the theory of the political economy of trade policy decisions. This theory emphasizes the role played by the interdependence between economic problems, political forces and institutions in reaching trade policy decisions. Its central tenet is that there is a market for protection. Those who demand protection are motivated by the expected additional gains from it. Those who have the power to supply protection might be induced to do so or refrain from granting protection for various reasons such as pressure group influence, hopes of gaining votes, fear of international retaliation, etc. As clarified in the ensuing sections, the empirical exercise reported in section 2 is based on a particular variant of the political economy approach while the one on section 3 relies on a more general version of it.

2 The Determinants of the Dumping and Injury Decisions of the EC

2.1 Dumping and Injury decisions: A brief description

The EC's procedures concerning dumping determination involve four standard steps: the determination of the "normal value" of the product under investigation, the determination of its export price, the adjustments necessary to ensure comparability, and the calculation of the dumping margin as the difference between the two. The criteria used in this part of the investigation is, by and large "technical" and less overtly "political". But some of the technical criteria codified in the dumping determination regulations of the EC make the exporters from non-market economies particulary vulnerable to "affirmative finding", for reasons well-documented by different authors (see for example Jacobs (1989), Tharakan (1991b), Vermulst (1987)). This vulnerability stems essentially from the freedom which the GATT regime permits in such proceedings. This consists mainly in the option (often exercised) permitted to the investigating authorities to ignore the nominal prices or costs in the non-market economies and base the normal value estimates on the prices or costs of a producer of the like product in an "analogue" market economy. If the market economy analogue chosen for this purpose happens to be highly protected, at a higher level of economic development than the country of the defendant or the industry characterised by an important degree of concentration, the constructed value is apt to be high and an "affirmative finding" likely. In the vast majority of the relevant cases in the EC, the analogue country proposed by the complainants was accepted by the Commission[3].

The injury determination procedure of the EC, unlike the dumping determination, is more susceptible to political influences. First of all, the disentangling of the various causes of injury to domestic industry and ascribing to dumping that part of injury which it could have triggered is a complicated task. Some of the indicators such as the "margin of price undercutting" which is increasingly being used by the EC in injury tests, have no sound economic foundation. The EC uses a "lesser duty rule" according to which the level of antidumping duty is limited to the amount required to eliminate the injury to the Community industry where this is less than the margin of dumping[4]. But in practice this shifts the emphasis - and the pressure - from the dumping to the injury investigation[5]. Finally, within the EC regulations, there is no possibility for the disclosure of confidential information collected by the Commission to the parties involved. This means that the investigating authorities are the only ones with access to the complete file and this is particularly disadvantageous to the defendants who have no easy access to the data that could refute or verify the claims of injury to domestic industry in the importing country.

2.2 Hypotheses, specification and variables

The hypotheses, specification and the selection of a number of the variables in the econometric exercise in this part of the study were inspired by an interesting model of the political economy of administered protection presented by Finger, Hall and Nelson (1982)[6]. Essential to the FHN model is the distinction

---

[3]See for example, the annex to Vandoren (1986).
[4]See Article 13(3) of Council Regulations (EEC) 2423/88.
[5]See Jacobs (1989).
[6]Hereafter referred to as the FHN model or study, André Sapir raised the point whether a framework of analysis used for analysing the American experience is necessarily applicable to Europe. Both the U.S. and the EC anti-dumping regulations are GATT consistent. A careful

between the political and technical tracks of protection. In the former, political influences are brought to bear directly on individual trade disputes. Technical track decisions such as AD/CVD determinations are made administratively. The technical track helps the government to shift the blame by pointing out to the losing side that no other decision was possible according to the rules. The FHN model includes both political and technical variables in the regressions concerning dumping and injury determinations, but expects that the technical variables will perform better in the former, while the political variables will predominate in the latter.

The dependent variables in our analysis of the EC are the case decisions (affirmative or negative) in the dumping (D/N_D) and injury (I/N_I) proceedings. In the logit regression analysis used, the dependent variable takes the value of 1 for the anti-dumping cases in which affirmative finding was made and O where the complaint was rejected. A similar 1, O specification of the dependent variable was made in injury/no injury decisions. An affirmative finding in the former case means that the EC found the defendant to have been "dumping"[7]; in the latter, injury to the European industry was found "to be caused by such dumping". The regressions cover every case decided during the period 1980-1987 by the European Communities: 280 observations of dumping/no dumping decisions and 296 observations for injury/no injury decisions. The identification of the relevant political and technical track variables was based on a detailed study of the functioning of the EC's AD/CVD mechanism.

The political track variables, which can be divided into international political influences and domestic political influences, include the proportion of the EC exports which are imported by the country of the defendant (X) and a dichotomous variable which identifies cases brought against the Third World countries (TW). The variable X tests the hypothesis that high dependence of the EC on the export markets of the defendant could act as a restraining influence in dumping finding. Hence the expected sign of the coefficient is negative. We have left the expectation concerning the sign of the coefficient of TW open because in spite of the claims of some of the Third World countries, the spokesmen of the Commission vehemently protest their special and constructive treatment of the exporters from the developing countries. The domestic political influence

---

comparison of the two sets of regulations and practices show a very high degree of similarity. There are certain important differences too which are noted above and, in more detail, in Tharakan and Waelbroeck (1992). Where such differences are specific, they are sought to be taken into account in the selection of the explanatory variables (for e.g., inclusion of the centrally planned economies variable and omission of the administrative reorganisation threat variable). Where the differences pertain to the degree of the likely influence of the political economy variables or the differences in the characteristics of the two economies, we expect them to lead to differences in the signs of the coefficients or the degree of the level of significance. This is explained in some detail in Tharakan and Waelbroeck (1992).

[7]According to Article VI of GATT, dumping takes place when the export price is less than "normal value". In practice, the "normal value" is considered to be the price at which the product is sold in the defendant's country or more often, determined on the basis of a "constructed price".

variables reflect the impact of industry concentration, case- and industry size on the findings in dumping cases. Since protection is a public-good for producers, concentration should reduce the temptation for free riding, and have a positive sign in the regressions. But this expectation has rarely been confirmed by empirical work (see Magee, Brock and Young (1989, pp. 87-91)). We have sought to combine the elements of concentration and cohesion by developing a dichotomous variable (CON) which identifies the cases initiated by associations of industries in which 25% or more of the output is produced by 5 firms. A positive sign is expected for CON. The other domestic political influence variables are the case size (SIZE) and industry size variables, the latter represented by the number of people employed (JOB) and the value added (VA). The case size is represented by the value of the imports (at NIMEXE 6 digit level) of the product concerned from the defendant's country. The bigger the size of the case, the higher would be the pressure for an affirmative finding. For all three variables (SIZE, JOB, VA) a positive correlation is expected.

The first group of technical variables are comparative cost indicators, designed to identify any protective bias of the AD/CVD mechanism, in favor of producers who suffer from a comparative disadvantage in international trade. The capital intensity variable (KL) is expected to yield a negative sign since on Heckscher-Ohlin grounds, the highly developed EC might be expected to have a comparative advantage in capital intensive industries. The human capital intensity variable, represented by the average wages and salaries per worker (WAGE), should on neo-factor proportions grounds have a negative sign. But high human capital intensity and the consequent "economic rent" in the form of above average wages is also a characteristic of strategic industries. So if the EC tends to protect industries with high human capital intensity on "strategic trade policy" grounds, WAGE variable will yield a positive sign[8]. As to the sign of the scale economies (SCALE), prediction is difficult due to the following reasons: the EC has a large domestic market but it is not yet effectively integrated. Consequently, it is doubtful that firms have succeeded in effectively exploiting the potentialities for scale economies. CPE is a dichotomous variable which identifies cases in which the defendant is from a centrally planned economy. It is classified as a technical variable because the "affirmative finding bias" they face is, as clarified above, due to the technical criteria codified in the dumping regulations and not due to international political considerations. The final technical variable consists of the number of different products (at NIMEXE 6 digit level) covered by the case (TEC). The lawyers consulted point out that a precise definition of the product makes the first line of defence usually used

---

[8]André Sapir has drawn our attention to the fact that economies of scale are more relevant to the strategic trade policies than human capital. While accepting the importance of economies of scale in this context, we would like to point out that the higher than average wages are also considered to be a characteristic of industries with "rent". Our formulation seeks to verify whether such 'rent yielding industries' are sought to be protected by the EC by the AD/CVD mechanism.

by the defendants, i.e. the product concerned is not a "like product"[9] difficult to sustain in both dumping and injury determinations, thus increasing the likelihood of affirmative finding. And a precise definition of the product usually implies a larger number of products (for example, a NIMEXE 6 digit level). Consequently we expect a positive sign for the TEC variable.

The specification for the regressions for injury contain the same set of variables as in the dumping regressions with two exceptions. The Third World dummy and the centrally planned economies dummy are not relevant when we consider injury determination, which deals with the effects of alleged dumping in the EC market.

The complete specifications used were:

$$D/N_D = f(X, TW, CON, SIZE, JOB, VA, KL, WAGE, SCALE, CPE, TEC) \quad (1)$$

$$I/N_I = f(X, CON, SIZE, JOB, VA, KL, WAGE, SCALE, TEC) \quad (2)$$

Estimation of equations (1) and (2) necessitated the compilation of a database built on case by case basis and consisting of more than 2500 observations[10]

2.3   Regression results

The above specifications are single equation models of the type generally seen in the analysis of the political economy of trade policy decisions. No problem of simultaneity arises with respect to the equations estimated. Each equation explains a different endogenous variable. No forgotten feedback comes to mind where one of the independent variables would be influenced to a meaningful extent by antidumping or injury determinations.

As the results of the logit regressions reported in table-1 show, the only political track variable which yielded a significant result in the dumping regressions in the Third-World dummy. It has a negative sign, thus lending credence to the EC's claims that it is in fact being lenient towards the developing country exporters.

Unlike the political track variables, the technical track variables perform well in the dumping-regressions. Four out of five such variables are significant. The capital intensity has yielded the expected negative sign, thus suggesting that fewer affirmative findings are made in capital intensive industries. But this is not the case for the human capital intensive industries if we consider wages and salaries as a proxy for the neo-factor proportions determinant of comparative advantage. The coefficient is significant and positive. This could mean that EC

---

[9]As required by EEC 1988, Article 2(12) of Council Regulations (EEC) 2423/88.

[10]For details concerning the measurement of the variables used, see appendix A.

Table 1 Logit analysis of influences of AD/CVD decisions and injury
determinations by the European Community

Hypotheses and variables	AD/CVD Decisions		Injury Determinations	
	Hypoth. sign (A)	Regression results (B)	Hypoth. sign (C)	Regression results (D)
Political track hypotheses				
International political influences				
Proportion of exports	-	0.0019	-	0.0039
to the country		(0.0180)		(0.0404)
Against a developing	?	-1.0250*	?	
country		(-1.8247)		
Domestic political influences:				
Industry concentration	+	0.2279	+	1.0174*
		(0.3784)		(1.9561)
Case size	+	-0.0014	+	0.0010
		(-0.4190)		(0.2102)
Industry size:				
Employment	+	-0.3587	+	-0.5439*
		(-1.2406)		(-2.8144)
Value added	+	0.0699	+	0.2429*
		(0.6307)		(3.4995)
Technical track hypotheses				
Comparative costs:				
Capital intensity	-	-0.1736*	-	-0.1089*
		(-1.8898)		(-2.0981)
Average wage	?	0.3391*	?	0.0004
		(1.8398)		(0.0033)
Scale economies	?	0.0625	?	-0.0125
		(1.1595)		(-0.4133)
Against a centrally	+	1.8088*	?	
planned economy		(2.4663)		
Technical precision:				
Number of products	+	0.9357*	+	0.3388*
		(2.6443)		(1.9877)
Constant		-0.2067		3.2142*
		(-0.1263)		(2.8328)
Proportion of affirmative				
decisions sucessfully predicted		89%		86%
Number of observations		280		296

might be influenced by the 'rent shifting approach' suggested by the strategic trade policy models; or it could just reflect attempts to protect the human capital intensive industries which the Commission considers to be important for Europe's industrial future. The dummy representing the centrally planned economies yielded a highly significant coefficient and has the expected positive sign. This is clearly a confirmation of the claim advanced in knowledgeable legal circles that some of the technical criteria codified in the AD/CVD regulations of the EC make the defendants from the centrally planned economies particularly vulnerable to affirmative findings. The technical precision variable yielded a positive sign and is significant, suggesting that the precise identification of the product increases the probability of affirmative findings.

A number of political track variables have come alive in injury regressions. The domestic political influences are the relevant ones. Industry concentration is clearly significant and has the expected positive sign. The European associations of some of the highly concentrated industries have been very active in preparing the AD/CVD cases initiated by them or their members[11]. The defendants can hardly match them especially on injury determinations in which the variables are related to the EC market conditions. This is made worse by the strict confidentiality rule which keeps the defendants largely in the dark about the data on the injury to the EC industry[12]. Case-size is not a significant determinant of injury decisions. But the industry size variables - value added and employment - are. Value added yields the expected positive sign. The employment variable yields a negative sign that is unexpected, as one would expect that industries with a large labor force will have significant political clout and will succeed in obtaining more protection. One reason for this anomaly could be be that industries with large labor force have managed to obtain selective protection through even more forceful devices such as VERS including the Multifibre Arrangement (MFA). This takes out of the regression the extreme observations which could account for the unexpected result.

Unlike the political track variables, the technical track variables fared poorly. An exception is the capital intensity variable which yielded the expected sign and is clearly significant. The number of products has yielded the hypothesized positive sign and is significant[13].

---

[11]Some well-known examples of such associations are CEFIC (Chemicals), EUROFER (steel), EUROMETAUX (non-ferrous metals) and EACEM (electronics).

[12]An interesting illustration of this point came up in connection with the audio-cassette case concerning Japanese exporters. According to the lawyers defending the Japanese exporters, the commission calculated the market share figures used in the injury findings by including the output of Japanese affiliates producing *inside Europe*, but the Commission denies this. See Gardner (1991).

[13]Examination of simple correlation between independent variables for the two "tracks" (political and technical) showed that "across the track multicollinearity" is high in the cases of scale economies and value added. The dropping of these two variables changes very little in the performance of the other independent variables and nothing in the general pattern of results in the dumping regressions. In the injury regressions also no important changes take place when the scale economy variable is dropped. But the dropping of the highly significant

We carried out likelihood ratio (LR) tests for both the dumping and injury regressions to verify the strength of the political and technical track variables[14]. When only the political variables are used in the dumping regressions, the likelihood ratio obtained is 28.1822 which is significant at 0.01 confidence level. This means the null hypothesis that there is no difference between the complete specification and the constrained specification containing only the political variables can be confidently rejected for dumping. But when the constrained dumping specification contains only the technical variables, the resulting LR is 7.0634 which is not significant even at 0.20 level. This shows that the technical variables are clearly the dominant ones in the dumping regressions.

The LR ratio for the injury regressions containing only the political variables is 23.406; when only the technical variables are retained it is 22.720. Both are significant at 0.01 confidence level showing the importance of both categories of variables in the injury determination. But the LR ratio for the injury specification containing only the political variables is somewhat higher, suggesting a slight dominance of such variables in injury determination.

3 The Determinants of the E.C.'s Decisions on Antidumping Undertakings

3.1 Undertakings: A brief description

According to Article 10, paragraph 1 of the Council Regulation (EEC 2423/88), "where during the course of an investigation, undertakings are offered which the Commission, after consultation considers acceptable, the investigation may be terminated without the imposition of provisional or definitive duties". Such undertakings are agreements between the Commission of the European Communities and exporters of allegedly dumped merchandise whereby the latter agree to revise their prices or cease exports to the extent the Commission is satisfied that either the dumping margin or the injurious effects of the dumping are eliminated.

Undertakings play a very important role in the termination of AD/CVD cases in the European Communities. More than 70% of the affirmative decisions reached during the period covered by this study were terminated with the acceptance of undertakings. This high frequency of anti-dumping undertakings in the E.C. is probably due to the exporters finding the arrangement profitable[15]

---

value added variable from the injury regressions cause the employment variable to lose its significance. But the employment variable still retains its negative sign and no important across-the-track changes take place.

[14]Where L_1 is the value of the likelihood functions for the unconstrained model and L_0 the value when the constraints are imposed, the likelihood ratio is computed as $LR = 2(L_1 - L_0)$. The LR statistic thus obtained is distributed asymptotically as a chi-squared variable with degrees of freedom equal to the number of constraints.

[15]Price increases as distinct from the payment of anti-dumping duties mean that the ex-

while the Commission considers it a less harmful way to end the proceedings. To the extent the EC's decision to accept an offer of undertaking clearly bestows a 'benefit' on the exporter, compared to what would have been otherwise the case, the reasons behind the choice between the two options (undertakings and definitive duties) are of importance. Yet here it is where the EC's antidumping practice is the least transparent. The Commission has stated that the Community is impartial in its stance on the acceptance of undertakings as an alternative to the imposition of duties (Commission of the European Communities 1983, p. 4). But in practice, the Commission and ultimately the Council have considerable discretionary powers in this matter. So the recourse to undertakings which is made in settling the majority of cases where 'affirmative decisions' are reached is governed by a set of rules which are not publicly known.

3.2 Hypotheses, specifications and variables

Information gathered mainly from the following three sources was used in formulating the explanatory hypotheses:

(a) The reasons given in the case decisions for refusing to accept the undertakings;

(b) the explanations provided by the practitioners, i.e. lawyers with antidumping case experience and administrators of the Commission of the European Communities, and;

(c) elements of the currently available stock of the theory of the political economy of protection to the extent they are applicable to the question under consideration here.

The objective of the analysis is to determine the influence of the explanatory variables formulated on the basis of the information gathered from the above mentioned sources, on the likelihood of an undertaking being accepted (or rejected) in terminating anti-dumping cases in the European Communities. This is of course a different objective than that of the exercise presented in section 2 and hence, the dependent variable and most of the explanatory variables used are different. In the logit regression analysis used here, the dependent variable takes the value of 1 for the anti-dumping cases terminated by the acceptance of undertakings and 0 where definitive duties were imposed. The sample contained 249 observations covering all the cases pertaining to the two categories of decisions during the period covered by the study.

EC sources claim that a major factor which influences the decision to accept or reject an offer of undertaking is the facility or lack of it in monitoring that agreement. Any undertaking related to a case involving an exporter and

---

porters can pocket the difference instead of paying it into the coffers of the governments of the importing countries.

one product is of course normally easier to monitor than that involving many products and many exporters. In the latter case the Commission could feel that the risk of circumvention is likely to increase and might be reluctant to accept the proferred undertaking. To test this hypothesis we have introduced a variable (MON1) representing the number of products (at NIMEXE 6 digit level) and exporting companies (MON2) involved in that case. Confirmation of the hypothesis would lead to negative signs for the coefficients of the two variables.

Lawyers for the defense in anti-dumping cases strongly feel that undertakings on behalf of exporters from countries running persistent trade surpluses against the European Communities are difficult to negotiate. In political economy terms, the 'rent transfer' implicit in the undertakings could be expected to be available only for exporters from countries which 'behave' by not accumulating trade surpluses by what are perceived to be unfair means. How persistent the bilateral trade deficit of the EC has to be for the exporters from the country concerned to evoke the Commission's (or Council's) displeasure, is a matter of conjecture. We have used three alternative versions of the variable, each implying a diminishing time horizon. TENSE1 represents the cases where the EC had bilateral trade deficit with the country of the exporter during each one of the 5 years preceding the case decision; TENSE2 denotes the cases where such bilateral trade deficit occurred in at least three out of the preceding five years; and TENSE3 indicates where there was bilateral trade deficit in the year preceding the case decision. A negative sign to the coefficient would suggest the confirmation of the hypothesis.

The fear of retaliation could be an element influencing the decisions of the EC not only in cases of dumping and injury but also on undertakings. As in the case of the regressions reported in table-1, in the regressions for undertakings also we have used a variable representing the fear of retaliation which consists of the proportion of EC exports directed to the country of the defendant in the anti-dumping case. If the fear of retaliation induces the EC to accept undertakings, this variable (RETAL) would yield a positive sign.

The dummy variable representing the developing countries enters the specification of the regressions to verify whether once dumping and injury were found, the EC prefers to make use of price undertakings in terminating the cases involving the Third World countries, as suggested by the GATT[16]. Two variants of this variable were used: The first variant (TW1) makes use of a very broad definition of the Third World in the political-economic sense[17]; the second (TW2)

---

[16]Article 13 of Appendix 11 to the 'Agreement on Implementation of Article VI of the General Agreement on Tariffs and Trade' requires that 'possibilities of constructive remedies provided for by this code shall be explored before applying anti-dumping duties' where developing countries are involved. The main 'constructive remedy' provided for by the above-mentioned Agreement (in Article 7) is the mechanism of price-undertakings.

[17]As in the regressions concerning dumping and injury, the Third World countries TW1 include also Yugoslavia and the Oil exporting countries (Saudi Arabia, Libya and Kuwait) which in spite of their high income per capita levels have low gross-manufacturing output per person. This definition corresponds to that of the variable TW used in the dumping and

includes only the NICs[18]. Such a distinction was made in the present regression in view of the importance of this "soft option" of the EC, for the defendants from the developing world.

Just as in the regressions pertaining to dumping and injury we have attempted to verify whether lobbying by the defendants has an impact on the pattern of decisions, we have included a variable (CON) representing the degree of concentration and cohesion in the regressions for the undertakings also[19]. The reason is that according to practising lawyers, the complainants are wary about the possibility of their competitors using the windfall gains from the undertakings to develop better varieties of the product to gain a greater market share later in Europe or in third markets, and hence are likely to lobby against the EC accepting such agreements. For reasons explained in section 1, such lobbying has greater possibility of success where the industries concerned are characterised by concentration and cohesion.

Given the concern of the EC to foster high technology industries, the question can be of course raised whether the Commission is inclined to deny the 'soft option' of undertakings in the anti-dumping cases involving high technology industries. The EC sources deny the prevalence of any such policy, but the lawyers with anti-dumping case-experience do not rule out the possibility of such a tendency. A recent study commissioned by the EC (Eurostat 1989) has identified at a very disaggregative level, products which are considered to be high technology intensive. Using this detailed classification, we have developed a dummy (HITEC) which is introduced in all cases involving high technology products.

The lawyers who plead for Japanese firms in anti-dumping cases claim that in recent years it has become very difficult to get the Commission to accept the undertakings offered by their clients. They believe that this approach reflects a trade policy change of relatively recent origin. They suggest that the Commission's attitude towards Japan perceptibly hardened from 1985 on. In fact 1985 was the year in which major cases against Japanese exporters, such as Komatsu, Brother, Canon, Silver Seiko, Tokyo Electric, Tawa Sankiden etc, led to the imposition of high definitive anti-dumping duties. The Commission officials stoutly deny any bias against exporters from any country. To determine whether being a Japanese company adversely affected from 1985 (but not before) the exporters' chances of ending anti-dumping cases in the EC with undertakings, we have used two variables: J84 and J85. For the first variable, the dummy comes alive in all the cases involving Japanese firms from the beginning

---

injury regressions.

[18]Exporters from the following countries which are considered as NICS (TW2) in this study were involved in antidumping cases in the sample used: Argentina, Brazil, Hong Kong, Mexico, Singapore, South Korea, Taiwan and Yugoslavia.

[19]CON takes the value of 1 in cases where the complainant is a professional association of an industry in which at least 25% of the European production is concentrated in the hands of 5 firms. A negative sign is expected for CON.

of 1980 till the end of 1984; for the second variable it comes alive in all such cases from the beginning of 1985 to the end of 1987. If the hypothesis suggested by the practising lawyers is correct, the coefficient attached to J85 should yield a negative sign while the one attached to J84 will not.

The complete specifications used were:

$$U/N_U = f(MON1, MON2, TENSE1, X, TW1, CON, HITEC, J84, J85)$$
$$(3)$$

$$U/N_U = f(MON1, MON2, TENSE1, X, TW2, CON, HITEC, J84, J85)$$
$$(4)$$

$$U/N_U = f(MON1, MON2, TENSE2, X, TW1, CON, HITEC, J84, J85)$$
$$(5)$$

$$U/N_U = f(MON1, MON2, TENSE2, TW2, CON, HITEC, J84, J85) \quad (6)$$

$$U/N_U = f(MON1, MON2, TENSE3, TW1, CON, HITEC, J84, J85) \quad (7)$$

$$U/N_U = f(MON1, MON2, TENSE3, TW2, CON, HITEC, J84, J85) \quad (8)$$

In the above equations, the symbol U/N_U represent the dichotomous dependent variable, undertakings granted/undertakings denied. All the other symbols are explained in the text.

3.3 Regression results

The results of the logit analysis of the influence of the above-described variables on the choice of the European Communities between the acceptance of undertakings and the imposition of definitive duties are reported in Table 2.

The variable representing the number of products (MON1) has systematically yielded a negative sign suggesting that the greater the number of products involved in a case, the lesser are the chances of it being concluded by an undertaking. But the coefficient is not statistically significant. On the other hand, the variable representing the number of firms (MON2) has the expected negative sign and is significant in all regressions except one. These results go some way

Table 2 Logit analysis of influences on the antidumping undertaking decisions of the European Community 1980-1987

Hypotheses and variables	Hypoth. sign	1	2	3	4	5	6
Constant	-	3.11*	3.09*	3.59*	3.58*	3.31*	3.34*
		(6.64)	(6.59)	(6.49)	(6.46)	(6.35)	(6.37)
Nb of products involved (MON1)	-	-0.13	-0.14	-0.12	-0.13	-0.12	-0.13
		(-1.35)	(-1.46)	(-1.29)	(-1.42)	(-1.26)	(-1.36)
Nb of firms involved (MON2)	-	-0.24*	-0.24*	-0.27*	-0.26*	-0.26*	-0.26*
		(-1.96)	(-1.92)	(-2.10)	(-2.05)	(-2.10)	(-2.05)
Persistence of bilateral trade deficit for EC for 5 years (TENSE1)	-	-0.73*	-0.73*				
		(-2.07)	(-2.06)				
Bilateral trade deficit for at least 3 out of 5 years (TENSE2)	-			-1.09*	-1.09*		
				(-2.56)	(-2.57)		
Bilateral trade deficit for EC in the preceding year (TENSE3)	-					-0.72*	-0.78*
						(-1.82)	(-1.96)
Proportion of EC exports to the country (X)	+	-0.20*	-0.19*	-0.21*	-0.20*	-0.22*	-0.20*
		(-2.28)	(-2.17)	(-2.55)	(-2.44)	(-2.61)	(-2.50)
The country concerned is a Third World nation (incl. the NICs) (TW1)	?	-0.93*		-1.13*		-1.02*	
		(-2.28)		(-2.74)		(-2.53)	
The country concerned is a NIC (TW2)	?		-0.82*		-1.08*		-1.01*
			(-1.90)		(-2.48)		(-2.36)
Complainant is a profesional assoc.in ind.where 5 firms acccount for at least25% of output (CON)	-	-0.90*	-0.96*	-0.82*	-0.89*	-0.89*	-0.94*
		(-2.35)	(-2.50)	(-2.14)	(-2.32)	(-2.32)	(-2.48)
The product is considered by EC as high technology (HITEC)	?	0.89	0.94	0.83	0.88	0.86	0.92
		(1.30)	(1.38)	(1.20)	(1.29)	(1.26)	(1.34)
Pre-1985 cases in which defendent is Jap. firm (J84)	+	1.60	1.64	1.51	1.54	1.45	1.48
		(1.42)	(1.45)	(1.34)	(1.38)	(1.29)	(1.32)
1985 cases in which defendent is Jap. firm (J85)	-	-2.55*	-2.54*	-2.49*	-2.49*	-2.57*	-2.56*
		(-2.59)	(-2.56)	(-2.55)	(-2.53)	(-2.63)	(-2.60)
Percentage of undertakings succssf.predicted		80.3	79.1	80.7	80.3	79.9	78.7
Number of observations		249	249	249	249	249	249

Note: An * indicates that the coefficient is significantly different from 0 at the 95% level.

in confirming the concern of the Commission with the facility for monitoring as a consideration for the acceptance of anti-dumping undertakings. All three variants (TENSE1, TENSE2 and TENSE3) of the trade tension variables have yielded, with one marginal exception, highly significant coefficients and have negative signs. While all three variants make a good performance, TENSE2 representing the bilateral trade deficit of the EC for at least 3 out of the 5 years, could be said to have a slight edge in terms of the size of the coefficient and the t values. In any case, it is difficult to avoid the conclusion that short term bilateral trade deficits which in principle should have nothing to do with the Communities' choice, in this instance have influenced the EC's decision to deny the 'softer option' to individual exporters from the countries concerned. But on the other hand the fear of retaliation does not deter the EC from refusing undertakings. As the result of the RETAL variable shows, exporters from countries which absorb a high proportion of exports have in fact clearly had difficulties in having AD/CVD cases terminated with undertakings.

The variables representing the Third World countries have yielded interesting results. Recall that the results of the dumping regressions showed that the EC is being lenient towards the developing countries in the case-decisions concerned. The present regressions show the other side of the coin. The coefficient of the variable TW1 (which stands for the Third World countries in the broad sense of the term) has a negative sign and is highly significant. So contrary to GATT's 'constructive remedy' advice, the Third World countries have clearly had difficulties in obtaining the softer option once 'dumping' is found. When we use the TW2 variant (which includes only the NICs), the negative sign persists and the coefficients remain significant, except in one case. Apparently at present the NICs are at the receiving end of this tough posture of the EC, but other developing countries when they graduate to NICs might possibly find that undertakings are difficult to obtain. In general the EC seems to be following a 'carrot and stick' policy as far as the Third World is concerned. Considerate for dumping decisions but, once dumping is found, difficult in granting undertakings.

As would be recalled, the lobbying variable yielded a negative and significant result in the injury regressions. In the present regressions, the lobbying effect variable (LOB) has systematically yielded a negative sign and is highly significant in all cases. In other words, in the EC industries with a high degree of concentration and cohesion, the Commission not only has a tendency to find 'injury' due to dumping but is also prone to refuse the offer of undertakings made by the defendants. But there is no evidence that the EC is systematically refusing anti-dumping undertakings in cases involving high technology products. The HITEC variable has, in all regressions yielded a positive sign, although it is not significant in any of them. The variable representing the pre-1985 cases in which the defendant was a Japanese firm (J84) has yielded a positive sign in all the regressions, although the coefficient is not significant. But the picture changes drastically if we take into consideration such cases since 1985

(J85). The sign of the coefficient is negative and it is highly significant in all the regressions. The opinion advanced by knowledgeable legal circles that the Japanese defendants face considerable difficulties in recent years to have their offer of undertakings accepted by the EC is clearly vindicated.

4 Conclusions

The present study provides the results of a comprehensive, econometric analysis of the determinants of the European Communities' decisions concerning dumping, injury and undertakings. Elements of the theory of the political economy of protection, information gathered from case decisions and discussions with experienced practitioners were used to develop the specifications which were tested in the econometric exercise. The results yield a number of insights, the most important of which are the following.

EC's dumping decisions are mainly influenced by technical track variables while its injury decisions clearly show the influence of political track considerations also. Consequently it is the injury determination system of the EC which is more vulnerable to constructive criticism and possibly more amenable to improvement. Given the apparent influence of the domestic political track variables on injury determination in the EC, the critics of the system would be well-advised to press for the abolition of the strict confidentiality rule and the use of more technically sophisticated and economically relevant injury determination methods. This is all the more important because of the strong evidence we have found that the EC industries with high concentration and cohesion are systematically getting their way in injury findings. The last mentioned finding also raises the question of a potential conflict between the anti-dumping policy and the competition policy of the EC.

The criteria by which the 'softer option' of anti-dumping undertakings are made available or denied to exporters were not well-known till now. Yet such undertakings accounted for more than 70% of the AD/CVD cases terminated by the EC during 1980-1987. The results reported in this study throw new light on this matter. For example, although the Commission's claim that the facility for monitoring is an important consideration in its decisions concerning undertakings is correct, it is also true that the prevalence of bilateral trade deficits even during short term periods have led to undertakings being denied to exporters from such countries. There is no evidence that the Commission is following a policy of refusing undertakings in cases involving high technology products, but there is evidence that since 1985 the Japanese firms involved in anti-dumping cases clearly face a special disadvantage in obtaining acceptance of undertakings by the EC.

Interestingly, some common threads running through the two sets of results reported here provide us with a more complete understanding of the EC's AD/CVD policy. For example, now we know that in dumping decisions the EC is lenient towards defendants from Third World countries, but once dumping is found, they will have a lot of difficulty in obtaining undertakings. We also know that that the tough component of this policy is directed towards the exporters from the NICs. The fear of retaliation has no impact on EC's decisions concerning dumping and injury and does not at all stop it from refusing undertakings to exporters from important trading partners. Further it emerges that the EC industries with high concentration and cohesion are not only successful in winning injury decisions but also seem to be effective in having undertakings denied to their foreign competitors found to the dumping.

All these findings could be of use in improving the anti-dumping and countervailing policy of the EC and making it more in accordance with the guiding principles of the GATT.

5   References

Commission of the European Communities (1983 to 1989) *Annual Reports of the Commission of the European Communities on the Community's Anti-dumping and Antisubsidy Activities*, Brussels.

C.E. (1987), Règlement (CEE) No. 2273/87 du Conseil du 15 juin 1987 remplaçant les annexes du règlement (CEE) No. 3420/83 relatif aux régimes d'importation des produits originaires des pays à commerce d'Etat non libéré au niveau communautaire, *Journal Officiel des Communautés Européennes*, L217/1-3, 6 août 1987.

Council regulations (EEC) No.: 2423/88 (1988) on protection against dumped or subsidized imports from countries not members of the European Economic Community, *Official Journal of the European Communities*, L 209/1, 2.8.1988, 1-17.

Commission of the European Communities, *Official Journal* C and L series, various issues during the period 1980-1987.

Commission of the European Communities (1989), Horizontal Mergers and Competition Policy in the European Community, *European Economy* 40.

Eurostat, *External Trade, Analytical Tables - NIMEXE - Exports*, various years.

Eurostat, *Structure and Activity of Industry: Annual Inquiry - Main Results* (1983/84 to 1987/88).

Eurostat, 1989, *Statistical analysis of extra-EUR 12 trade in hi-tech products*.

Finger, J.M., H. K. Hall and D. R. Nelson (1982), The political economy of administered protection, *The American Economic Review* 72, 452-466.

Gardner, D. (1991), EC antidumping ruling against Saudi group reversed by court, *Financial Times*, June 28.

GATT (1991), *Trade Policy Review: European Communities*, Vol. I, Geneva.

IMF (1982), *Direction of Trade Statistics: Yearbook*, Washington D.C.

IMF (1988), *Direction of Trade Statistics: Yearbook*, Washington D.C.

Jacobs, F. (1989), Antidumping procedures with regards to imports from Eastern Europe, in M. Maresceau, ed., *The Political and Legal Framework of Trade Relations Between the European Community and Eastern Europe*, Doordrecht: Kluwer.

Magee, S.P., W. A. Brock and L. Young (1989), *Black Hole Tariffs and Endogenous Policy Theory: Political Economy in General Equilibrium*, Cambridge: Cambridge University Press.

Montagnon, P. and L. Kellaway (1990), The predators and investors, *Financial Times*, April 9.

Tharakan, P.K.M. (1991a), The political economy and anti-dumping undertakings in the European Communities, *European Economic Review* 35, 1341-1359.

Tharakan, P.K.M. (1991b), East European State-trading countries and anti-dumping undertakings, in: P.K.M. Tharakan, ed., *Policy Implications of Anti-dumping Measures*, Amsterdam: North Holland.

Tharakan, P.K.M. and J. Waelbroeck (1992), Anti-dumping and countervailing duty decisions in the EC and in the U.S.: an experiment in comparative political economy, *European Economic Review*, forthcoming.

Vandoren, P. (1986), EEC anti-dumping enforcement against imports from state-trading countries, Commission of the European Communities, mimeo.

Vermulst, E. A. (1987), *Anti-dumping Law and Practice in the United States and European Communities*, Amsterdam: North-Holland.

6   Appendix A

The information on case decisions which was used to build the dichotomous dependent variable for the dumping, injury and undertakings regressions is from the Commission of the European Communities (1983 to 1989). Proportion of EC exports to the country of the defendants (X) was calculated by using the trade figures from EUROSTAT: *External Trade, Analytical Tables-NIMEXE-Exports* for the relevant years. In identifying the Third World countries (TW1), a very broad definition of the Third World in the political economic sense was used, including Yugoslavia and the Oil Exporting countries (Saudi Arabia, Libya and Kuwait) which in spite of their high income per capita levels, have low gross manufacturing output per person. Argentina, Brazil, Hong Kong, Mexico, Singapore, South Korea, Taiwan and Yugoslavia were considered a NICs for the purpose of this study. The concentration variable (CON) was built on the basis of information collected from the following sources: whether the complainant is a professional association or not was ascertained from the relevant issues of the EC, *Official Journal*; whether in the industry (NACE 3 digit level) concerned, 5 firms accounted for at least 25% of the output in the EC was ascertained from the Commission of the European Communities (1989, p.41). In a limited number of cases in which the relevant data were not available from the above source, reliance was placed on the information provided by the Federation of Metalworking Industries (FABRIMETAL). The case size (SIZE) was estimated as follows. The NIMEXE number of the products involved in each one of the cases was identified from the relevant issues of the EC *Official Journal*. Import value figures at NIMEXE six digit level were then collected from EUROSTAT: *External Trade, Analytical Table-NIMEXE-Imports* for the relevant years. For the number of people employed (JOB) the data on the number of persons employed excluding homeworkers were used. Value added (VA) is the gross value added at factor costs. Capital intensity variable (KL) was calculated by using the flow concept introduced by Lary (1968). Average wage was calculated by using the data on gross wages and salaries paid, excluding remunerations to homeworkers on the payroll. The scale economies variables (SCALE) was quantified as value added per unit (firm). The data necessary for calculating the above-mentioned variables (JOB, VA, KL, WAGE and SCALE) were collected from EUROSTAT (1983/84 to 1987/88). Note that for the years from 1980 to 1985, the EC total is taken as the total of the figures pertaining to the "Big Four", i.e. Germany, France, Italy and the U.K. For the years from 1986 on, the data pertaining to Spain is also included with those of the other four countries. The information necessary for constructing the dummy representing the Centrally Planned Economies (CPE) was gathered from CE (1987). The number of products involved (MON1, TEC) was obtained from the relevant issues of the *Official Journal*. The dummy variable used for MON2 takes the value of 1 when more than 1 exporter is involved and 0 otherwise. The three alternative variables (TENSE1, TENSE2 and TENSE3) used to quantify the trade tension hypotheses were developed on the basis of the information gathered from IMF (1982,1988) except in the case of Taiwan for which the data were collected from EUROSTAT: *External Trade-NIMEXE-Imports*. Information necessary for constructing the HITEC variable was obtained from EUROSTAT (1989) which lists, at SITC 5 digit level, the products which are considered technology intensive. The correspondence between SITC 5 digit and NIMEXE 6 digit was made on the basis of the information given in the *Official Journal*, serie L, 368, 29.12.1986. For the construction of J84 and J85, see section 3.2.

8

The Logic of EC Commercial and Industrial Policy Revisited in 1992[1]

Alexis Jacquemin

Université Catholique de Louvain and EC Commission

André Sapir

Université Libre de Bruxelles, EC Commission and CEPR

1 Introduction

During the past three decades, Jean Waelbroeck has much contributed to analyzing the construction of the European Community (EC). In the 1960s and 1970s, his work on the EC was mostly concerned with positive issues, often attempting to measure the progress of integration and quantifying its impact on trade flows. In the 1980s, as Jean became one of Europe's wise men, he added policy recommendations to his fine research work.

At the 1982 CEPS Annual Conference, three years before the publication by the EC Commission of the White Paper on Completing the Internal Market, he presented a contribution entitled "The Logic of EC Commercial and Industrial Policy Making". The paper, published in 1984, reviewed the theoretical arguments relevant to the Community's economic policy-making and drew conclusions on a crucial question of the day: "What should the EC do?"

Ten years later, his conclusions are more relevant than ever. Three of them may be underlined.

First, the main contribution which the Community can make to Europe's economic dynamism "is to eliminate obstacles to trade between members". Waelbroeck added, however, that "[p]rospects for rapid progress in this direction are poor. Would an à la carte approach...make it possible for the more free-trading Community members to move forward...?" (Waelbroeck (1984), p. 122). Since then the White Paper was adopted in 1985 and the Community is

---

[1]The authors are grateful to Herbert Glejser and an anonymous referee for helpful comments.

well on its way to completing the internal market by the end of 1992, but one may wonder what triggered this process.

A second conclusion is that "Community economic policies should reflect a vision of Europe's role in the world trade system. It is an illusion to believe that the EC could be protectionist against third countries yet be engaged in free trade internally" (Waelbroeck (1984), p. 122). Since then, it has been confirmed that the distinction between "internal" and "external" competition is in fact more and more blurred given the trans-continental nature of direct investments and the importance of intra-firm trade, the increasing mixing up of final products, and the continuous process of relocation of activities all over the world.

A third message is that, although trade theory in general justifies a liberal policy stance, two important qualifications to this principle must be recognized. Firstly, "a country (e.g. the EC) can do better by using its economic power than it could under free trade", but as Waelbroeck was quick to recognize, "this puts it at risk of retaliation". Secondly, "as a result of externalities and economies of scale, clever planning can lead to better results than market forces" (Waelbroeck (1984), p. 122). The current discussions on a European industrial policy are largely based on the latter argument.

The purpose of this paper is to extend Waelbroeck's analysis in the light of developments that have occurred during the past ten years. The remainder is divided in three parts. Section 2 reviews the progress towards the completion of the internal market. Section 3 examines the relationship between internal and external competition in Europe. Section 4 looks at the role of strategic trade and industrial policies . Section 5 concludes.

2   Progress Towards the Completion of the Internal Market

From its origin until the recent Maastricht Summit, the European integration project has been viewed with scepticism by many "specialists" and journalists. Despite being proven wrong as each stage of integration developed, the scepticism was carried forward stage to stage. As stated by Keohane and Hoffmann (1989), in the years immediately prior to the signing of the Single European Act, in February 1986, few observers anticipated anything but stagnation or even decay of European integration. "In his sceptical analysis of European decision-making during the 1970s, published in 1983, Paul Taylor stressed the limits imposed by states on European integration, arguing that 'the challenges to sovereignty were successfully resisted and the central institutions failed to obtain the qualities of supranationalism.' His academic analysis echoed the cover of *The Economist* on March 20, 1982, showing a tombstone with the words, 'EEC Born March 25th, 1957, moribund March 25th, 1982, *capax imperii nisi imperasset.*' (It seemed capable of power until it tried to wield it)."

Why has reality since 1985 contrasted so sharply with these predictions? When the European Community (EC) launched the 1992 programme in the mid-1980s, it had been faced with a decade of mounting macroeconomic problems. By that time, the growth of production in the EC was lagging well behind that of the United States and Japan, while unemployment stood at nearly 12 percent. Simultaneously, Europe faced industrial challenges by competitors at both ends of the "technological spectrum". In mature sectors, characterised by relatively standardised production technologies, the newly industrialised economies (NIEs), had become strong competitors to European producers. In high-tech sectors, dominated by oligopolistic corporations that can take advantage of scale economies and learning by doing, European firms were falling behind enterprises from Japan and the United States.

Most observers pointed towards the same diagnosis of the European malaise (often referred to as "Eurosclerosis"): the existence of market rigidities responsible for the sluggish response of European economies to the shocks of the world economy (see, for instance, Lawrence and Schultze (1987)). Also, to the extent that industrial sectors are subject to economies of scale, the fragmentation of the European market by domestic protectionist measures was viewed as having undermined European competitiveness (for econometric evidence on the impact of trade barriers and scale economies on European competitiveness, see Jacquemin and Sapir (1988)).

In 1985, the programme for the completion of the internal market was conceived as an antidote to these problems. It embodied the two elements which Jean Monet had judged essential for the progress of European integration: a deadline and an institutional framework. The Commission presented the White Paper listing its 279 proposals for the completion of the internal market. The Council also passed the Single European Act, which, by instituting qualified majority voting (instead of unanimity) for the White Paper directives, has provided the institutional framework more conducive to bargaining and compromises between Member States. And the "magic date" of 1992 was set as the deadline for completing the single European market.

Since then, the process of European integration has advanced at a rapid pace. By the Summer of 1987, the Commission has already presented 170 proposals listed in the White Paper, of which more than 70 were adopted by the Council. By November 1991, the Commission had formulated all the 279 proposals set out in the White Paper, 217 of which had been approved by the Council. Decisions had been taken in all fields of economic activity. In a number of areas, all the measures set out in the White Paper were already entirely completed.

The main measures already adopted cover the following domains:
- public procurement;
- technical harmonisation;
- capital movements;
- financial services;

- free circulation of professionally qualified persons;
- right of residence;
- company law and statute for a European company;
- company taxation;
- transport;
- industrial and intellectual property;
- audiovisual;
- telecommunications;
- abolition of border controls.

Despite impressive progress by the Commission and the Council, two problems remain for completing the internal market. The first concerns the implementation by the Member States of the directives adopted by the Council. On average, more than 70% of the adopted directives requiring national implementation measures have been instituted in the Community. But there are wide differences between the Member States. Italy trails far behind the pack with only half of the directives transformed into national law, while Denmark has consistently been the best performer with over 90%. The enforcement of EC regulations is to be achieved with the help of sanctions and court actions. The second problem involves areas where the Council has faced difficulties in reaching agreement. The principal area of disagreement has been the harmonisation of indirect tax - which, unlike most internal market measures, requires unanimity. But the general consensus is that the key elements of the internal market programme will be implemented, on time, by January 1993. As the *Financial Times* has recently noted: "One fundamental point is clear. The unexpected achievement of the single market formula in capturing the imagination of businesses, politicians and ordinary people around the Continent has helped imbue the overall goal of European integration with a new driving frorce". (December 18, 1991).

3 Internal and External Competition

Theoretical and empirical research suggest that import competition within European markets imposes a major constraint on domestic firms' price-cost margins. The program for the completion of the EC's internal market by 1992 is largely based on the effects expected from a reinforcement of such a constraint. The 1992 program requires the removal of barriers still affecting intra-EC trade, and hence the strengthening of European competition. According to the European Commission's assessment of the economic effects of this liberalisation, the overall result will be a significant welfare gain. Given these expectations, the combination of internal and external liberalisation may be a superior policy to internal liberalisation alone if external liberalisation also exerts an appreciable competitive impact.

Two recent studies shed light on this question.

The first one (Neven and Röller, (1991)) examines, on the basis of a sample of some twenty-five industrial sectors (two-digit classification), the extent to which trade is affected by the Community's non-tariff barriers. The conclusion is that on average Community trade is affected by these barriers but that trade with the rest of the world is as much, if not more, affected. This conclusion applies especially in sectors like textiles and cars, in which trade is subject to Article 115 of the Treaty of Rome. In such cases, barriers to intra-EC trade have been erected in order to limit extra-EC imports. The removal of non-tariff barriers in the Community should therefore lead to increased integration within the world economy, provided that it is not accompanied by increased protectionism against the outside world.

The second study, (Jacquemin and Sapir (1991a)) shows that the degree of competitive discipline imposed by imports varies not only according to the characteristics of the industry in question, but also according to the origin of the imports. On the basis of a sample of about 100 industrial sectors (three-digit classification), the analysis made for the four major member countries concludes that, on average, extra-Community imports have a greater competitive impact that intra-Community imports.

Various factors may explain this difference:

> intra-Community trade is concerned more with differentiated goods (intra-industrial trade), with the result that many imported goods exert only slight competitive pressure since they correspond to relatively segmented markets and are imperfect substitutes for domestic products;

> intra-Community import operations are frequently more dependent on the decisions of national producers, particularly where those producers are integrated downstream towards the distribution sector and sell manufactured goods abroad through their own distribution networks; or again where there are mutual representation agreements with their foreign competitors aimed at ensuring control of the sale of products imported into their respective countries;

> intra-Community trade frequently takes place between subsidiaries and divisions of a group which is established in different Community countries. Increased intra-group trade of this type is part and parcel of a strategy of internationalising production which does not reflect any pressure on monopoly power, but instead implies a reinforcement of the oligopolistic nature of the European market.

If we accept that competition has the effect of maximising the efficiency of a single integrated market, it is clear that the opening-up of the Community area to the rest of the world would increase the potential gains that the Cecchini studies attribute to the liberalisation of intra-Community trade alone.

Competition policy is one of the most important guarantees for the internal and external liberalisation of the Common Market. It is by no means certain that, post-1992, economic agents will accept the operation of competition. As experience following the lowering of tariff barriers has shown, the EC authorities may well be confronted with growing private and public strategies that seek to diminish or distort competition. The EC authorities must then ensure implementation of "credible rules" that are directly applicable to all, including third-country companies. The competition rules of the Treaty of Rome are already applicable to both public and private restrictions of competition and, in both cases, have been tightened.

Concerning public restrictions, an example relevant for the external impact of 1992 is the increased transparency of state aid policy, required by the Commission and, when necessary, the recovery of aids granted illegally.

Concerning private restrictions, a central regulation about mergers and acquisitions was adopted in December 1989. This regulation sets up EC controls over Community-wide, cross-border operations, and there is a mandatory prior notification of the planned mergers of this kind. One characteristic is also crucial for the external impact of 1992: for assessing whether a merger is or is not compatible with the Common Market, the only basis is its impact on effective competition, at the exclusion of cost savings or other offsetting efficiencies. This absence of an "efficiency defense" in the text of the regulation reduces sharply the dangers of mixing competition policy with industrial policy (see Jacquemin (1990)).

Ambiguity remains over the interactions between EC trade and competition policy. Compared to the rule-based competition policy (probably the most impersonal and the least discriminatory means of social control of an economy), trade policy allows much more discretionary power. According to Article 113 of the Treaty of Rome, "the common commercial policy shall be based on uniform principles", but the trade rules do not exclude the adoption by the Council of Ministers of anticompetitive protectionist measures. In fact, maintaining intra-EC competition is a much more accepted goal than safeguarding competition from outside.

More specifically, the pressures for not disrupting economic transactions between member states could lead to a difficult choice between the erosion of intra-EC free trade and the erosion of free trade with the rest of the world. One unhappy implication is that in several domains, not only trade and competition policy follow different roads, but also interact in a perverse way. While a free trade policy is part of competition policy, the use of instruments such as antidumping duties and voluntary export restraints not only affects extra-EC trade but, through a feedback effect, mitigates competition within the EC. Some authors (for example, Patrick Messerlin (1989)) argues that in fact European antidumping (allowed by Article VI of GATT) actions have a pro-cartel and pro-merger propensity. Such actions increase the capacity to cartelise for firms unable to collude without some kind of public support; they also induce EC firms to merge with foreign firms operating in EC markets to the extent that EC-owned foreign exporters are more immune to antidumping measures.

At a time of globalisation of business strategies, the solution is not simply to improve antidumping criteria and procedures, but also to develop international cooperative agreements between antitrust authorites, intended to achieve consensus concerning principles and implementation of a world competition policy. Progress is on the way through multilateral discussions (OECD, UNCTC), but also EC bilateral negotiations (with U.S. Federal Trade Commission and Department of Justice; Japanese MITI and Fair Trade Commission).

4   Strategic Trade Policy and Industrial Policy

The view that a large country can do better by using its economic power than it could under free trade is well known in the case of competitive markets, and has found some new thoretical justification in the so-called "strategic trade theory".

In the case of competitive markets, economic theory teaches that unilateral free trade is apt to produce a Pareto-optimal situation. However, this is true only of a "small" country, that is a country whose international transactions have no impact on international prices. Where, by contrast, a country is sufficiently large to be able to influence world prices, it will generally benefit from eschewing free trade and imposing an optimum import or export tax. However, the ensuing improvement in welfare for the large country is usually gained at the expense of its trading partners. The use of an optimum commercial tax is therefore a zero-sum game. Of course, the final outcome of this game will depend on the strategies of the different players. The country which imposes an optimum tax will obtain an improvement in welfare if its trading partners remain passive. If, however, they take retaliatory measures, all the countries involved could suffer a loss in welfare compared with the free trade situation. In that event, the optimum solution is cooperation aimed at ensuring free trade.

The European Community, with its market of 320 million consumers, is clearly a "large country". As such, the trade barriers it maintains could be desirable from the viewpoint of its collective welfare. It could even be argued that a reinforcement of some of those barriers would provide an optimum solution. Such a policy would, however, be undesirable. A substantial proportion of Community imports of certain traditional products (particularly clothing) comes from developing countries which do not possess the economic strength to resist the import barriers imposed by the large industrialized countries. Those barriers therefore entail a transfer of income from the poor to the rich countries that runs counter to a better distribution of world income.

Where the international trade context is one of markets under imperfect competition, other arguments are used in favor of strategic trade policies. In their seminal paper, Brander and Spencer (1983) define strategic trade policy as an intervention that changes the strategic interaction in an imperfectly competitive industry and thereby the equilibrium outcome.

A number of empirical studies have attempted to shed light on the consequences, for collective welfare, of the removal of the various types of tariff and non-tariff barriers affecting the external opening-up of the Community. These studies provide a good indication of the main implications; while, owing to their partial nature and sensitivity to hypotheses chosen, they can scarcely provide general quantitative estimates, certain lessons can be learnt from them. The following three sectors will be used as illustrations: a traditional sector (namely textiles and clothing), a major mature industry (cars) and a growth industry (aircraft).

Among the traditional sectors, the *textile and clothing industry* has long been an area of dispute industrialized and developing countries. This industry, which is highly labor-intensive (particularly in the clothing sector), plays a key role in the industrialization process which the developing countries are undergoing. It accounts for a quarter of their revenue from exports of manufactured products. At the same time, this industry continues to have appreciable importance in the industrialized countries, particularly as an employer of low-skilled labor in certain regions. For that reason, the textile and clothing industry is heavily protected in the Community and in the other industrialized countries. Community producers are protected from foreign competition by the common external tariff (which, on average, is 7% for textiles and 13% for clothing). In addition, imports from many developing countries are strictly limited by the quantitative restrictions laid down by the Multifibre Arrangement (MFA).

Many studies have examined the impact of tariff and non-tariff barriers in the textile and clothing sector. The paper by Trela and Whalley (1989) is particularly useful in that it presents a general equilibrium model for assessing the impact of the dismantling of such barriers. The main finding of this work is that the abolition of customs duties and the Multifibre Arrangement would bring about an improvement in the welfare of both the developing and industrialized countries. The increase in welfare would amount to US$8 billion (at 1986 prices) for the developing countries and to US$3.5 billion for the Community.

The improvement in welfare in the Community is, of course, an overall consequence which conceals two opposing effects: on the one hand, a loss for producers and, on the other, a gain for consumers. An OECD study (1985) shows that the adjustment may be severe because the job losses would be concentrated in regions already hard hit by unemployment. However, part of the large gains for consumers could be channelled towards promoting the reallocation of the workers affected to more productive jobs.

The *car industry* is a sector for which many quantitative studies have been carried out based on one or other imperfect competition model. This industry is protected against extra-Community competition, both by the common external tariff (approximately 10%) and the use of Article 115 of the Treaty of Rome, which has preserved the effectiveness of certain national quotas in a number of countries. An article by Laussel and others (1988) is particularly revealing of the main factors involved in the search for an optimum commercial policy in this field.

Using a Cournot-type model, they examine the rivalry between European and Japanese companies on the Community's national markets on the basis of the assumption that European and Japanese cars are differentiated between each other but are perfect substitutes within each group. On the basis of a Community welfare function correctly defined as the sum of consumers' surplus, the profits earned by European firms on each market and the income of the Community authorities, they compare the effectiveness of various European policies. Their main conclusions are as follows:

1. Quotas are generally found to be ineffective, except in promoting collusion between Japanese producers. This is confirmed by many previous studies, according to which such quotas, even where they benefit European producers, are prejudicial to overall Community welfare (Venables and Smith (1986)).

2. Rival commercial policies pursued by European countries generally lead to a deterioration in collective welfare.

3. A small increase in the current common external tariff is in general favorable to collective welfare, although the gains are remarkably low owing to the relatively low level of rents (or surpluses) accruing to the Community authorities.

4. The best policy is to replace quotas with Community subsidies, particularly if this is combined with an increase in the common external tariff. This stems partly from the acquisition of monopoly rents of foreign producers and partly from a fall in European companies' costs, which may lead to prices closer to true marginal costs. Even in the event of a major shift in sales in favor of Japanese producers, the additional gain by European consumers would be much greater than the profit reduction suffered by Community firms.

Even though this type of exercise fails to answer important questions, it goes to the heart of the problem. It shows that strategic policies are in fact capable of generating gains in national welfare.

The study made by Winters (1988), which examines in more general terms the policies that may replace Article 115, broadly confirms the above findings. The simple abolition of national quotas would substantially increase Community welfare. Their replacement by a Community quota (which would be the sum of existing national quotas for a given product), although less favorable, especially for those countries which had hitherto been without quotas, would at least be an improvement on national quotas. A system of uncoordinated and possibly rival national subsidies is also an inferior policy to Community action.

With regard to the growth sector, the *aircraft industry* is clearly one of the fields in which strategic action is frequently taken to modify interactions between producers and hence equilibria. One basic objective is to cause a shift in profits from foreign to national firms (Brander and Spencer (1985)). Other objectives include the wish to modify international competitive conditions by means of entry support policies. In this connection, Dixit and Kyle (1985) classified the possible equilibria where a government decides to cover all or part of the substantial sunk costs which must be borne by a company wishing to enter an international high-tech market which is more or less monopolized. Under certain conditions, they show that such action may simultaneously increase national and global welfare.

They cite, by way of illustration, the case of Airbus. By challenging the dominant position enjoyed by Boeing, which controlled up to 80% of the market in passenger aircraft and which benefited from enormous defence contracts, the Airbus economic interest grouping has seen its world market share increase from 11% in 1985 to more than 30% today. The result is an intensification of international competition which, despite distortions created by strategic action, is likely to produce a net gain in world welfare.

The Baldwin and Flam (1989) study goes further since it simulates quantitatively the effects of these strategic policies on the basis of a partial equilibrium model calibrated for the case of short-haul aircraft with 30 to 40 seats. This market, which is relatively well defined, comprises three producers: a Brazilian (Embraer), a Canadian (de Havilland) and a Swedish producer (Saab-Scania). This industry is characterized by a homogenous and durable product, major static and dynamic economies of scale, a high level of R&D expenditure and initial investment and marginal costs which diminish substantially as a result of the learning process. Policies likely to affect capacity and production choices therefore have appreciable effects on costs and profits and on the distribution of the latter and welfare between countries. Each firm is assumed to choose the (constant) capacity which maximizes its profits, given world demand, the capacity of competitors and its technology. In addition, two of the three governments in question seem to have used strategic commercial policies, namely restrictions on access to their domestic markets (Canada) and export subsidies (Brazil).

On the basis of their simulations of the effects of an absence of strategic commercial policies, the authors reach two conclusions: these policies have actually transferred profits from foreign firms to the domestic firm; and world welfare has not been reduced for all that. The action taken has increased welfare by cutting average marginal costs and/or by increasing competition. Similar results have been obtained for other growth sectors (for example, 16KRAM chips; see Baldwin and Krugman (1987)).

The conclusion from these studies should not be one of general encouragement given to strategic commercial policies. It is rather a question of recognizing that, given the possibility of achieving gains in national (and, occasionally, even international) welfare through such policies, it is inevitable that the public authorities, which are already inclined to adopt them as a result of the activities of pressure groups, will increasingly have recourse to strategic policies if the current drift in the international environment towards the formation of economic blocs and the adoption of non-cooperative attitudes continues.

The previous discussion confirms the conclusion drawn by Meade, nearly 40 years ago, at the end of his *magnum opus* on international economic policy. "A liberal economic order in the modern world is not...a negative act of mere laissez-faire. It requires a considerable development of international, if not supranational, economic organization." (Meade (1955), p. 572). The role of institutions and policies is all the more essential in today's world, where the international trade context is increasingly one of markets under imperfect competition. In this case, the Pareto-optimal solution frequently requires the exchange of information, negotiation or coordination, which, to be effective, may require public intervention.

This may then lead us back to traditional recommendations favorable to free trade. But this return to sources is no longer based on the result obtained by the "invisible hand", according to which the pursuit of individual interest alone produces the greatest benefit to society as a whole. It is based, instead, on the need to avoid, through deliberate policies, a process of unilateral strategies and counter-strategies leading to ruinous trade wars.

Hence the crucial role which the Community institutions and such international bodies as GATT are required to play in devising codes of conduct and consultation, monitoring and cooperation mechanisms which are credible, workable, verifiable and stable. They also play an important part in limiting the perverse effects of asymmetries which exist between countries and which are based on such diverse factors as development level, size, type of government or quality of information.

The need to reinforce the rules of conduct governing international trade is particularly important for the developing countries, since their relative weakness makes them vulnerable to action by the large industrialized countries.

This leads us to consider the connections between trade policy and industrial policy. According to Richard Caves (1987), most problems imputed to trade policy really call for industrial policy corrections, "a conclusion of many years' discussions that plays to the new-founded interest in policies focused directly upon distortions in the domestic market of open economies" (p.70). Discussions of industrial policy have emphasised the role of market failures, two of them having been identified in the quotation from Jean Waelbroeck, i.e. "externalities" and "economies of scale". More generally, economic analysis has identified serious weaknesses in market mechanisms. Even where there is "perfect" competition, the general assumption about the effectiveness of market forces no longer holds true and has given way to well-recognised exceptions which often have a crucial impact on our economies:
- external effects between activities (pollution), between markets (networking economies) and between geographical areas (transport);
- "public goods" which the producer cannot appropriate for his exclusive use and for which private production is insufficient (training of human resources,

scientific research);
- incomplete information and asymmetry in the information available to market participants.

These situations call for more information, coordination and stimulus - functions which the price system alone cannot provide.

The instruments needed go beyond competition policy and are clearly set out, in the European context, in the 1990 Communication by the EC Commission to the Council of Ministers on "Industrial Policy in an Open and Competitive Environment". They include the establishment of trans-European networks, the promotion of cooperation in R&D and the introduction of large-scale educational programmes. Furthermore, a limited number of new activities relating to the Community's technological base are characterised by the simultaneous presence of imperfect conditions of competition (extensive economies of scale and learning, resulting in competitive advantage, high costs of entry, etc.). A Community support policy may be warranted here provided it is conceived in terms of world competition.

Such support requires:
- a precise diagnosis of the needs not met by existing market conditions;
- a real commitment on the part of those concerned, mainly business;
- a Community system for monitoring, at the highest level, the use to which the support is put.

One important dimension is that the objective laid down in Article 130f of the Treaty of Rome, namely "to strengthen the scientific and technological basis of European industry and to encourage it to become more competitive at international level", encompasses more than just Community firms. The presence of multinational firms moving in from outside the Community to become an integral part of the European industrial fabric and contributing to its revitalisation is also in the Community's interest. Making the Community, rather than other locations, more attractive to direct foreign investment, particularly in the field of research and technology, is becoming an important element of our competitiveness. However, this implies that foreign firms must be subject to the Community legislative framework that ensures a level playing field, including the need for economic and social cohesion. By the same token, when foreign firms seek to participate in large-scale European projects, the best response is not to exclude them but to determine the most suitable form of involvement, with an eye to securing free competition at world level. Such free competition would also mean that European firms must be given the opportunity to participate in similar large-scale projects outside the Community. This would have many repercussions and would in turn boost the Community's competitiveness.

Under this approach the Community would send out a two-fold message. First, it should avoid stating a determination to give systematic support to its "strategic industries" in order to conserve their strictly European character. Internally, this would be unrealistic; externally, it would conjure up anew the image of "Fortress Europe".

Table 1 Intra-regional trade in Europe, America and East Asia
(intra-regional exports as a percentage of total exports)

	1982	1990
Europe		
EC	54	61
EC and EFTA	64	70
America		
US and Canada	30	34
Asia		
ASEAN	20	20
ASEAN and rest of East Asia	40	44

Second, as an alternative, it should make clear that European industry is perfectly capable of competing at world level provided there is effective competition, and signal its determination to maintain effective competition by concerted action.

5   Conclusion

As we have seen, several events have occurred in Europe since 1985 which can explain why the scepticism regarding the progress of integration displayed by Jean Waelbroeck and many others in the early 1980s has not materialised. In addition, the achievement of the overall goal of European integration has become even more credible with the agreements on monetary and political union reached at the December 1991 Maastricht Summit.

On the other hand, Jean's view on commercial and industrial policy are today more valid than ever. But their concrete relevance will depend upon the various possible scenarios and choices regarding international economic relations which will confront the Community after 1992.

The process of European integration, together with regional tendencies in America and in Asia, has created a sentiment of fragmentation of the trading system into three blocs (see Table 1 which shows clearly that regional trade is far more important in Europe than in either America or Asia[2]). This situation could either reinforce or weaken the existing multilateral trading system. The two scenarios are possible and correspond to a distinction between what we have described elsewhere as "natural integration" and "strategic integration" (Jacquemin and Sapir (1991b)).

The former situation involves "natural" trading partners geographically close

---

[2]Sources: *Financial Times* 3.2.1992 and GATT

to one another, which adopt a liberal trade policy vis-à-vis third countries. European integration fits perfectly well this description, except for the agricultural sector. As Robert Lawrence has recently indicated, "[o]pen regional blocs can actually promote and facilitate external liberalisation... The postwar experience with the EC is heartening." (1991, p.26).

Strategic integration, on the other hand, refers to a situation where member countries pursue a common trade policy at the expense of third countries. Obviously, natural integration could lead to strategic integration. If the three blocs decide to play a noncooperative game, natural integration could, indeed, be used as a leverage fo strategic cooperation.

The first choice that confronts Europe is to know, on the one hand, which of the cooperative or noncooperative scenarios is more likely, and on the other, what its interest is. As we have already stressed, the possibility of heightened tensions leading to conflictual relations among economic blocs and a drift of the international system cannot be excluded. The view put forward here is that such a prospect is harmful for the world in general and Europe in particular. In order to avoid this prospect, Europe should use all its influence in favor of the cooperative scenario.

Assuming this scenario prevails, the next step, regarding the identification of the actors of the cooperation, raises a delicate problem. The principal alternative is cooperation on world scale versus cooperation between either industrial or developing countries. If the second alternative is adopted, it would probably imply cooperation within the triangle EC-USA-Japan.

In the commercial field, multilateral liberalisation on a world scale is generally considered most attractive. It offers the advantage of enabling a better international specialisation thanks to various possible trade-offs. In addition, multilateralism encourages the improvement of political relations by allowing for the diffusion of commercial tensions which, within a narrow bilateral framework, could degenerate into sharp conflicts. Nonetheless, multilateral trade liberalisation also carries problems. One of its main problems concerns "free riders". This issue arises mainly in the context of certain developing countries which are perceived as enjoying the rights of the multilateral system without respecting its obligations. Clearly, the reinforcement, or even the survival of GATT as a pillar of international trade requires the integration of these countries in the multilateral system. The failure or success of the Uruguay Round depends on the capacity of both industrial and developing countries to exchange mutually advantageous concessions. A failure would have grave consequences, not only in the commercial field. It would lead to an increasing disequilibrium in the distribution of wealth at the expense of the vast majority of the world's population and could strengthen centrifugal socio-political factors.

Whatever the outcome of the Uruguay Round, it will likely be necessary to reinforce the cooperation among industrial countries which operate within a "strategic environment". Concerning the EC, the USA and Japan, it is clear, indeed, that the actions of each bloc deliberately influence (and are influenced by) the actions of its partners. It is important, however, that such cooperation among these giants does not turn into a cartel at the expense of other, smaller nations. It should therefore be ensured that this cooperation will be open to all countries, just as GATT codes can be signed by all GATT members. In other words, the cooperation among a limited number of powerful countries should not lead to the exclusion of weak nations, but, rather, should help reinforce international cooperation.

Finally, cooperation should extend beyond trade policy. In view of the increasing globalization of corporate strategies, the time has come to recognize the need for international cooperation in the field of competition policy.

6 References

Baldwin, R. and H. Flam (1990), "Strategic trade policies in the market for 30-40 seat commuter aircraft," *Weltwirtschaftliches Archiv* 125, 484-500.

Baldwin, R. and P.R. Krugman (1987), "Industrial and international competition in wide-bodied jet aircraft," mimeo.

Brander, J.A. and B.J. Spencer (1985), "Export subsidies and international market share rivalry," *Journal of International Economics* 18, 83-100.

Caves, R. (1987), "Industrial policy and trade policy: the connections," in H. Kierzkowski, ed., *Protection and Competition in International Trade*, Basil Blackwell, Oxford.

Dixit, A. and A.S. Kyle (1985), "The use of protection and subsidies for entry promotion and deterrence", *American Economic Review* 75, 139-152.

Jacquemin, A. (1982), "Imperfect market structure and international trade," *Kyklos* 35, 75-93.

Jacquemin, A. (1990), "Horizontal concentration and European merger policy", *European Economic Review* 34, 539-550.

Jacquemin, A. and A. Sapir (1988), "European integration or world integration?", *Weltwirtschaftliches Archiv* 123, 127-139.

Jacquemin, A. and A. Sapir (1991a), "Competition and imports in the European market," in L.A. Winters and A. Venables, eds., *European Integration: Trade and Industry*, Cambridge: Cambridge University Press, 82-91.

Jacquemin A. and A. Sapir (1991b), "Europe post-1992: internal and external liberalization," *American Economic Review* 81, 166-170.

Keohane, R. and S. Hoffmann (1989), "European integration and neofunctional theory: community politics and institutional change," paper presented at the Florence Workshop on the Dynamics of European Integration, September 1989.

Laussel, D., C. Montet and A. Peguin-Feissolle (1988), "Optimal trade policy under oligopoly," *European Economic Review* 32, 1547-1565.

Lawrence, R.Z. (1991), "Emerging regional arrangements: building blocks or stumbling blocks", in R.O'Brien, ed., *Amex Bank Review Prize Essays*, Oxford: Oxford University Press, 23-35.

Lawrence, R.Z. and C.L. Schultze (1987), "Barriers to European growth: overview" in R.Z. Lawrence and C.L. Schultze (eds.), *Barriers to European growth*, Washigton, D.C: The Brookings Institution. Reprinted in A. Jacquemin and A. Sapir, eds., (1989), *The European Internal Market*, Oxford: Oxford University Press, 251-297.

Meade, J. (1955), *The Theory of International Economic Policy, Volume two: Trade and Welfare*, Oxford: Oxford University Press.

Messerlin, P. (1989), "Antidumping regulations or protrust law? The EC chemical cases," World Bank, mimeo.

Neven, D.J. and L-H. Röller (1991), "European integration and trade flows," *European Economic Review*, 35, 1295-1309.

OECD(1985), *The Costs and Benefits of Protection*, Paris.

Trela, I. and J. Whalley (1989), "Unravelling the threads of the MFA," *Seminar Paper 448*, Stockholm, Institute for International Economic Studies.

Venables, A.J. and A. Smith (1986), "Trade and industrial policy under imperfect competition," *Economic Policy*, 1, 622-672.

Waelbroeck, J. (1984), "The logic of EC commercial and industrial policy making," in A. Jacquemin, ed., *European Industry: Public Policy and Corporate Strategy*, Oxford: Clarendon Press.

Winters, L.A. (1988), "Completing the European internal market," *European Economic Review* 32, 1477-1499.

9

The Bush Initiative, the MERCOSUL and Latin American Integration: a View from Parallel 22°53'43"S[1]

Renato G. Flôres Jr

FGV and UFRJ, Rio de Janeiro

1 Introduction

On June 27th, 1990, President George Bush, in a speech at the White House, launched a "global American trade region proposal": the Bush initiative. After the Canada-US agreement, and while negotiating a similar one with Mexico, the United States had turned back to their South American neighbours. Was it out of concern with the outcomes in the world trade system? Or a way to counterpose a "Fortress America" to "Fortress Europe"?

Irrespective of its motivation, the act did not fall in the void; two lines of action followed in Latin America the President's proposal. Some countries, as Venezuela and Chile, speeded up their bilateral talks with the US in order to implement closer ties with the northern cousin. In the south, on the other hand, Brazil, Uruguay, Paraguay and Argentina accelerated the creation of something more than a free trade area, actually a union close to the spirit of Europe 92 called the MERCOSUL. Less than one year after the White House speech, an umbrella treaty was signed on March 26th, 1991, between the four countries.

Latin American integration is no new issue at all. As documented in various studies - CEPAL(1959), Urquidi(1960) and Silva(1990) to cite a few - many have been the attempts toward it and one interesting question is why they have failed. Cynics say that in all cases poverty was united with misery and so the result was nought. Stalwart anti-Americans put the blame always on the US, invoking examples as the sad diplomatic history of the Central American Common Market. Truth probably lies deeper, and has more shades.

---

[1]Financial support from CNPq, grant No.402158/91.1, is acknowledged. Thanks are due to Winston Fritsch, Joao Bosco M. Machado and Carlos Rodriguez; Cristhiane de Oliveira Castro and Murilo R. Alambert Rodrigues were invaluable research assistants. Comments by Helen Hughes, Jean Mercenier, Jean Waelbroeck and an anonymous referee obliged me to sharpen the arguments in the previous versions. I remain solely responsible for the findings and conclusions.

Though aware that history may repeat itself once again, this paper looks at some issues raised by these recent events. The perspective is basically from a regional, Latin American standpoint. As the subject is quite broad, the focus is mainly on the trade aspects (specially manufactures) of the possible unions.

Econometric support is given - as well as possible - to all the arguments, since many of the discussions about the integration till now have had a more qualitative character[2]. The preliminary stage of the analysis makes for the use of techniques closer to those frequently found in the young Waelbroeck (1962, 1964 and 1967, for instance), in spite that some flavour of the ideas in the mature Waelbroeck (1987), Burniaux and Waelbroeck (1991) is tentatively added[3]. It is also hoped that this will constitute groundwork for numerical partial and general equilibrium modelling exercises.

The structure of the paper is as follows. In section 2 a few considerations on the macroeconomics involved are made. Though rather general, this section sets an essential background for evaluating the integration possibilities. Basic macroeconomic issues are actually crucial for ambitious developments as those envisaged in the MERCOSUL. The core of the paper is section 3, where trade complementarities and impacts are evaluated through different techniques. Section 4 briefly contrasts the path led by the Bush initiative with other strategic alliances. Based on the previous analyses, Section 5 explores some trade strategies with a view on the main consequences for the trade and industrial policies of the countries discussed. One of its main points is that US partnership should be dealt with separately.

The overall conclusion of the paper is that Latin American integration is beneficial more from a behavioural and political viewpoint rather than a quantitative one. It may be an important incentive for creating an enabling environment for stabilization and growth in the region, though its actual trade impacts will be in the average moderate. A final section elaborates this in more detail.

2   A Latin American monetary system?

Macroeconomic instability was pervasive among LA[4] economies during the eighties. This is well reflected not only in the inflation rates but also in the wild exchange rate fluctuations.

Taking Brazil and Argentina as an example, either the US$/austral and US$/cruzeiro rates or the austral/cruzeiro rates have varied in a way more than enough to inhibit any steadier, non-speculative transaction between both

---

[2]See, for instance, the papers and documents issued by FUNCEX (Fundação Centro de Estudos de Comércio Exterior, Rio de Janeiro), INTAL (Instituto para la Integración de America Latina, Buenos Aires), the essays in Velloso (1990) and the papers of a recent seminar at the Development Centre, OECD, Paris, November, 1991.

[3]The reader is certainly aware of the wide gap between the flavour of a (honest) table wine and that of a *grand cru classé*.

[4]From now on, LA = Latin America or Latin American.

Table 1 Exchange rate volatility Argentina and Brasil
(quarterly data)

	US$/cruzeiro (1983-I to 1990-IV	austral/cruzeiro 1983-I to 1988-IV
μ	.576	.522
σ	.534	.297
max	2.725	1.897

Source: IMF, International Financial Statistics, various issues.

countries. Table 1 shows some volatility measures for these series.[5] The speed of quarterly change in the US$/cruzeiro rate, from 83/II to 90/IV, has averaged 57.6% with a standard deviation of 53.4%. It is not necessary to believe in a Mundell-Fleming setting to conclude that an environment with these values is quite far from stabilization.

The trade accounts suffered accordingly as many of the attempted adjustment policies have applied indiscriminate imports restrictions, lowering even further the level of regional transactions. An immediate positive consequence of the Bush initiative has been the growing awareness of LA governments that regional trade liberalisation may be compatible with an external adjustment program.

In the MERCOSUL case this is not merely desirable: it is a must. For a dramatic illustration it suffices to consider the competitiveness factor, used in many trade equations (see Khan and Knight (1985)'s famous "IMF model" and also an earlier discussion on the "competitive edge" by Waelbroeck (1967)):

$$C = (p_m/p)e(1 + t)$$

where p_m is the price of imports in the foreign currency, e is the exchange rate, p is the domestic prices level and t is the ad-valorem tariff; imports varying inversely with C.

The tariff reduction schedule set between Argentina and Brasil in the MERCOSUL treaty stipulates that all tariffs will be zeroed on January, the 1st, 1995. Assuming a linear yearly tariff reduction until then, this scheme can be combined with the volatility figures in Table 1, so that relative decreases in C can be computed (supposing $dln(p_m/p)$ to be zero). The results can be quite frightening for some domestic producers in both sides, who risk being swept by significant price falls. Table 2a shows the twelve main Brazilian imports[6]

---

[5]The rows give the mean (μ), the standard deviation (σ) and the maximum value (max) of the relative increases of the exchange rate during the period.

[6]By chapters of the Nomenclatura Brasileira de Mercadorias - NBM. NBM has 98 chapters which can be easily mapped into "chapters" (two digits level) of the SITC, United Nations.

Table 2a Brazilian main imports from Argentina, 1989-1990

	% of total imports	Tariff (%)
Meat	3.23	18.57
Fish	2.87	23.35
Dairy products	2.97	32.35
Vegetables and roots	4.91	17.12
Fruit	5.96	31.22
Grain		
Cereals	5.03	20.74
Processed	15.17	28.75
Various vegetable inputs		
for dyes, gums, etc.	18.06	23.48
Fats and oils (animal		
and vegetal)	2.56	19.49
Organic compounds	3.30	24.32
Air transport material	7.09	36.56
Electric machines	3.12	63.57

Source: Secretaria da Receita Federal/CIEF.

from Argentina, during 1989-90, while Table 2b gives the corresponding dC/C reductions if the 52.2% austral/cruzeiro oscillation operates against Brasil.

However, much more is at stake. A serious credibility problem, in all the instances described by Persson (1987), affects present day macroeconomic strategies in many LA countries[7]. As pointed out by Dornbusch (1990), this generates an unfortunate spillover: adjustment *per se* - if by any chance attained - is no guarantee that growth will follow suit. An external measure of confidence, translated, for instance, in new forms of direct investment in non-speculative sectors[8], can be an important help. This need of an exogenous push is a point that will come over in the next section.

The setting of common targets, as the creation of a Latin American Monetary System (LAMS) in the fashion of the early European Monetary System (EMS), will also sooner or later be required. However, it will only be feasible - as happened in the European case - with much weaker inflationary pressures.

---

[7] A main cause for the present state of things has certainly been the manifold orthodox and heterodox anti-inflationary recipes tried in Brasil and Argentina during the past few years

[8] Perhaps it is worth reminding that even for one of the nowadays model LA economies as Mexico the credibility issue is not exactly solved; to quote *The Economist*, Dec. 14th 1991: "If there is one thing that keeps economists there awake at night, it is the knowledge that about 75% of the inflow of capital is going into easily liquidated portfolio investment, not into new factories;... One thing is certain about this money: it is hot. If there were a shock of confidence, the inflow could quickly go into reverse."

Table 2b Changes in the competitive edge
(Values of dC/C for the commodities in Table 2a (%))

	Minimum	Average	Maximum
First year	-55.9	-57.6	-61.9
Up to January 95	-66.8	-78.7	-91.1

Official commitment to coordination and control is probably more important here than in the other experiences. In spite of a favourable mood, the too general level of the present official statements does not give much evidence yet on the ability to solve the many concrete problems related to this.

Moreover, a financial institution will have to anchor the system, as the Bundesbank did (and still does) for the EMS. This raises interesting questions, whose answers depend on the regional scope of the integration. If the Bush initiative is taken fully, the Federal Reserve has no match for this role and, in a longer view, would have to face it. Objections will perhaps be found more inside than outside the U.S. At the MERCOSUL scale, Brasil, Argentina and even Uruguay, the financially more stable of the three, may have different arguments for housing a Southern Cone Central Bank, but actually, at present, neither qualifies for the task.

3   The impact on trade

The evaluation of trade impacts needs some preliminary characterization studies, many of which still lack for the LA economies. Therefore, a broad view of the trade profile of some South American countries is first presented here. Partial evaluations based on traditional approaches to analyse trade flows matrices then follow. Deeper considerations of economies of scale, factor intensities and technology close the section.

3.1   A geographical exercise

Some basic trade patterns within LA can be revealed even at an aggregation level somewhat higher than ideal[9]. Of course, the patterns discerned depend also on the questions posed. Attention was centred on two of the many possible

---

[9]In all the ensuing analyses use has been made of trade flow matrices compiled by ALADI for 1980 and 1985. The twelve commodity groups plus a "others" category roughly correspond to one-digit or aggregations of two-digit SITC codes. It is somewhat unfortunate that the latest year is 1985, as this was an imports contraction year for most countries studied.

ones: What are the prospects for strengthening the position of the union as an exporter? What are the prospects of a more intense common trade?

Table 3a shows the specialization and intra-industry indexes for five countries: Argentina, Brasil, Chile, Uruguay and Venezuela. The formulae for the indexes are described in section 1 of the Appendix.

Analysis of the figures in Table 3a shows a reasonable complementarity in the export specialization patterns of the five countries. At the aggregation level used, with the exception of chemicals, for each sector there is a country with a high value for the index (for instance, a value higher than 1.8). Brasil is specialized in the more advanced sectors while Uruguay and Argentina present a more traditional profile. The high figure in the first row is due to Venezuela's oil exports.

The intra-industry indexes have been computed for the global value of exports and imports of each country and may serve as preliminary signals of trade creation or scale economies possibilities. It is interesting to see that Brasil, Argentina and Chile show a high intra-industry trade in fuels and ores, while the very low values for Venezuela and Uruguay account for their respective positions as exporter and importer. Metals manufactures, for Chile, Venezuela and Argentina, and machines, for Brasil and Uruguay, might be sectors where trade creation or production specialization can take place (all with values higher than 70). Transport equipment and wood and paper, involving Argentina with Brasil and Uruguay, respectively, may be other candidates.

Correlations between imports and exports vectors, and between the exports and imports vectors among themselves appear in Table 3b (only values above .45 are displayed). High correlations between imports or exports may signal toward a greater power in the international markets, and between an export and an import vector may indicate trade creation prospects. The last ones occur mainly with Venezuela as an exporter and are due to the country's fuel exports. The only (weak) evidence of complementarity regards Venezuelan imports and Brazilian exports. These two countries, together with Uruguay and Argentina have an imports vector similar to Chile's. With the exception of Venezuela, the other four countries have a similar external profile.

3.2 Trade flows analysis

Two methods of analysis were used: a) Armington (1969)'s equation for the percentage change in the demand for specified imports from a given country, in value terms; b) Verdoorn and Schwartz (1972)'s "share approach". An outline of the techniques is given in section 2 of the Appendix; Tables 4a and 4b show the results. In order to improve the interpretation, in Table 4c, the shares of each country in the others' imports are shown.

Armington effects (Table 4a) for Brasil reflect in general the low share its

Table 3a Specialization and intra-industry trade indexes
for five South American countries, 1985

	Chile	Venezuela	Argentina	Brasil	Uruguay
Specialization index (exports)[a]					
Fuels, ores and minerals	-	3.67	-	-	-
Food and live animals	-	-	2.11	-	2.50
Textiles	-	-	-	1.32	3.98
Leather industry	-	-	3.39	-	1.61
Wood and paper	3.81	-	-	-	1.04
Mineral manufactures					
(non-metallic)	-	-	-	1.95	1.20
Chemicals	-	-	1.00	1.48	1.16
Metals	4.06	-	-	1.07	-
Machines	-	-	-	2.02	-
Transport equipment	-	-	-	1.83	-
Arms and ammunition	-	-	-	2.17	-
Precious materials	5.16	-	-	-	5.64
Others	-	-	-	1.87	2.35
Intra-industry trade (Balassa)					
Fuels, ores and minerals	91	5	93	71	9
Food and live animals	39	28	7	23	26
Textiles	22	1	36	15	20
Leather industry	53	11	2	14	17
Wood and paper	33	13	69	30	71
Mineral manufactures					
(non-metallic)	10	31	51	53	85
Chemicals	41	24	60	98	53
Metals	96	71	78	27	35
Machines	2	2	41	91	92
Transport equipment	17	3	89	61	47
Arms and ammunition	8	1	13	81	10
Precious materials	1	87	15	64	5
Others	8	7	25	42	39

[a]Only values higher than 1 are shown.
Source: BID-INTAL: El Comercio Latino-Americano, 1988.

Table 3b Exports-imports correlation coefficients, 1985

		Importer	Importer		
		Chile	Venezuela	Brasil	Uruguay
Exporter	Venezuela	.47		.90	.81
	Brasil	-	.45		-
Exports only					
	Brasil	.63	-		.63
	Argentina	.50	-	.95	.75
Imports only					
	Chile		.77	.79	.85
	Brasil	.79	-		.94
	Argentina	.94	.83	.61	.73

Source: BID-INTAL: El Comercio Latino-Americano, 1988.

neighbours have in its total imports and exports[10]. If the 19.9% increase in total imports from the MERCOSUL is applied on the 2.13% they represent of total Brazilian imports, a final value of only 2.55% is obtained. However, in the cases of Uruguay and Paraguay, the impacts (again for total imports) rise to 88.95% and 81.19%, respectively, the MERCOSUL share in the global imports of these countries. To better frame these percentages, in 1985, Brazilian imports from the MERCOSUL were of US$ 699.8m while Uruguayan and Paraguayan imports amounted to US$ 746m and US$ 696m, respectively. The same applies to the exports: keeping in the MERCOSUL case, multiplying the impacts for Uruguay, Argentina and Paraguay by their shares in Brazilian exports results in an increase from 3.7% to 4.4% in total exports to the MERCOSUL. The introduction of Chile and Venezuela does not alter much the impacts picture but improves the absolute figures. Brazilian exports, for instance, which to the MERCOSUL were US$ 990m in 1985, in the enlarged region amounted to US$ 1,523m.

The Verdoorn and Schwartz figures (Table 4b) give a sharper idea of global integration effects. For the total flow the results are roughly around 10%, what amounts to say that the integration would be responsible for the assumed growth -- exactly 10%. Sectoral estimates point out the absence of interchange or the rather small flows in many situations.

The aggregate level of the analyses and their partial approach certainly hide

---

[10]The values in Table 4a are for a substitution elasticity $\sigma = 3$. The results are a linear function of the price reduction, that is why the 10% figure was used. See section 2 in the Appendix.

Table 4a Trade impacts Armington effects[a] (in %)

	Brasil	Argentina	Uruguay	Paraguay	Chile	Venezuela
MERCOSUL						
Total imports						
from union	19.9	19.8	19.0	18.9	-	-
from others	-0.1	-0.2	-1.0	-1.2	-	-
Chemicals						
from union	19.2	16.7	12.8	4.8	-	-
from others	-0.8	-3.3	-7.2	-15.2	-	-
Textiles						
from union	12.7	12.3	8.7	14.0	-	-
from others	-7.3	-7.8	-11.3	-6.0	-	-
Fuels, ores						
and minerals						
from union	19.8	19.3	19.2	9.9	-	-
from others	-0.2	-0.7	-0.8	-10.1	-	-
Transp. equipm.						
from union	19.1	17.4	0.5	7.4	-	-
from others	-0.9	-2.6	-19.5	-12.6	-	-
MERCOSUL plus Chile						
and Venezuela						
Total imports						
from union	19.9	19.8	19.0	18.8	19.2	19.8
from others	-0.1	-0.2	-1.1	-1.2	-0.8	-0.2
Chemicals						
from union	19.0	16.6	12.7	4.8	17.1	19.0
from others	-1.0	-3.4	-7.4	-15.3	-2.9	-1.0
Textiles						
from union	12.7	12.2	8.0	14.0	15.6	19.4
from others	-7.3	-7.8	-12.0	-6.1	-4.5	-0.6
Fuels, ores						
and minerals						
from union	19.0	19.3	19.1	9.9	11.4	20.0
from others	-1.0	-0.7	-0.9	-10.1	-8.6	-0.0
Trans.equipm.						
from union	19.1	16.7	0.5	7.4	15.5	17.3
from others	-0.9	-3.3	-19.5	-12.6	-4.5	-2.7

[a] Assuming a 10% price reduction among the specified customs union members.

Table 4b Trade impacts Verdoorn and Schwartz effects[a] (in %)

From	Brasil	Argentina	Uruguay	Paraguay
Total flow				
to Brasil	-	10.0	11.2	11.7
Argentina	8.5	-	10.5	10.6
Uruguay	8.7	10.4	-	10.4
Paraguay	11.7	10.2	10.1	-
Chemicals				
to Brasil	-	10.0	12.5	11.4
Argentina	0.9	-	11.1	12.3
Uruguay	1.5	10.6	-	10.0
Paraguay	6.2	8.9	8.7	-
Textiles				
to Brasil	-	10.2	10.9	9.0
Argentina	9.9	-	11.9	7.3
Uruguay	11.2	11.1	-	8.0
Paraguay	neg	neg	neg	-
Fuels, ores and minerals				
to Brasil	-	0.7	ng	ng
Argentina	neg	-	10.2	ng
Uruguay	neg	1.1	-	ng
Paraguay	neg	2.7	ng	-
Transp. equipm.				
to Brasil	-	7.2	10.0	ng
Argentina	9.6	-	12.2	ng
Uruguay	20.6	9.1	-	ng
Paraguay	17.1	6.7	10.9	-

[a] neg = negative value; ng = negligible or no flows in the direction.

Table 4c Import shares (in % of total imports)

	Brasil	Argentina	Uruguay	Paraguay	Chile	Venezuela
Total imports						
from MERC	2.1	6.3	74.7	68.3	44.9	14.6
from MERC, Chile						
and Venezuela	3.5	7.2	78.8	69.3	74.1	15.9
Chemicals						
from MERC	3.9	16.6	35.8	76.1	12.5	4.6
from MERC, Chile						
and Venezuela	5.1	17.1	36.7	76.2	14.6	4.9
Textiles						
from MERC	36.4	38.7	56.6	30.0	21.8	2.8
from MERC, Chile						
and Venezuela	36.7	38.9	59.8	30.3	22.2	2.9
Fuels, ores						
and minerals						
from MERC	1.0	3.6	4.0	50.4	0.6	0.0
from MERC, Chile						
and Venezuela	5.1	3.6	4.5	50.4	43.1	0.0
Transp. equipm.						
from MERC	4.5	13.1	97.5	63.0	22.5	13.4
from MERC, Chile						
and Venezuela	4.5	16.5	97.5	63.0	22.5	13.5

some special opportunities, the findings being a preliminary indication. The hypotheses in the simulations, neglecting not only other country's price variations but also dynamic internal effects caused by the association, make for a short run character of all figures presented.

3.3 Technology, economies of scale and the factor content of the trade balance

The few studies on economies of scale in LA have been rather local and lack a common methodological approach. Patten (1991) highlights some interesting points, but does not bring out much data not already found in Cline (1984). As a broad conclusion, scale in LA is smaller than in developed economies. Scale gains are likely to have been fully attained in traditional manufacturing sectors such as shoes and leather and textiles and clothing, where LA countries are competitive. In the more advanced sectors, the smaller MES (minimum efficient scale) can be explained by a more restricted supply of specialized inputs, lowering the global wage costs on one hand but limiting the scale possibilities on the other. The lower value therefore reflects a certain technological backwardness.

Though a deeper analysis is needed, it follows that, apparently, scale gains from the integration will not be remarkable, at the aggregate sector levels of this study. Even for a non traditional sector as transport equipment, which accounts for a large share of Brasil's manufactures exports to other LA countries, a freer trade area would not be a decisive factor for global scale gains. They may nevertheless take place in subsectors where significant intra-industry trade is present: a considerable portion of the transport equipment trade flow between Brasil and Argentina (see Tables 2 and 3) is related to aerial transportation components where a production line complementarity exists between industries in both countries. Similar cases may perhaps be found in subsectors of iron and steel, involving Chile, Argentina and Brasil, and machines, between Brasil and Uruguay.

Scale gains can also be achieved by unifying the marketing and distribution efforts in export markets, a weak point in LA exports to developed countries. The correlations in Table 3b provide a positive indication of this possibility.

The problems of scale are thus strongly intertwined with the technology issue and the question *whether the internal market dynamics generated by the integration will be able to change the technological state of the art* is worth posing.

MERCOSUL countries, in comparison with other trading nations, belong to the group whose technological intensity of imports is high while that of exports is low[11]. Nevertheless, in spite of all problems, the exports pattern of the main MERCOSUL members - and most specially Brasil - has been progressively moving towards the more advanced sectors. A factors content regression of net exports, in the lines of Branson and Monoyios (1977), tried with 1980 data for Brasil (see section 3 of the Appendix), provides already some evidence on the changing pattern of Brazilian exports. The estimated coefficients were: skilled labour:.102, capital inputs: .403 and labour: -.005; their signs show the diminishing importance of labour intensive net exports.

The growth and development needs of the Southern Cone, allied with the previous arguments on where scale gains can be achieved, signal to a strategic target of increasing their manufactures export penetration in the developed blocks. This is also in accordance with the need of a higher productivity in the domestic manufactures sector to successfully counteract the contraction measures unavoidable in a macroeconomic stabilization path[12]. In this context, foreign direct investment (FDI) comes over as a key issue.

A discussion of how to attract FDI to the new customs unions and of its more profitable forms is outside the scope of this paper. An analysis of the multinational firms role in the Brazilian economy during the seventies - a role significantly responsible for the above regression findings - may perhaps suggest some constructive ideas.

---

[11]The same is true of Canada and Spain, and a low technological content of exports is not necessarily a deterrent to prosperity (see, for instance, Fritsch and Franco (1988)).
[12]See section 2.

Table 5a Foreign direct investment in Brasil, 1986-1990
Registered investment by origin[a]
(in US$ billion)

	USA	Japan	EC	ALADI
1986				
1st sem.	5.4	2.1	6.0	0.1
2nd sem.	5.4	2.2	6.4	0.1
1987				
1st sem.	5.3	2.2	6.8	0.1
2nd sem.	5.6	2.4	7.4	0.1
1988				
1st sem.	5.8	2.4	7.1	0.1
2nd sem.	6.3	2.5	7.3	0.1
1989				
1st sem.	6.5	2.6	7.2	0.1
2nd sem.	7.1	2.6	7.8	0.1
1990				
1st sem.	7.1	2.7	8.0	0.1
2nd sem.	7.1	2.6	7.8	0.1

[a] At the end of the period, not including reinvestment.
Source: Banco Central do Brasil.

4 The other partners

The points in section 3 entitle asking a further question: given the set of all possible regional associations, is the path led by the Bush initiative, or the MERCOSUL itself, really the best one?

If FDI is accepted as an important engine to LA growth the answer falls short from the affirmative. Table 5a shows the amount of registered FDI in Brasil, by origin, during the period 1986-1990. Contrary to the more pessimistic views, total amounts have at least not decreased. While participation of LA countries is almost non-existent, the position of Japan and the EC is far from negligible, the last one being consistently higher than that of the US. This fact is reinforced by the results of Table 5b, on the 40 biggest foreign groups in Brasil: European presence accounts for 64.1% of total assets and 64.6% of total revenues. The establishment of closer links with these two areas seems mandatory and, at least for Brasil, is a natural follow up to its recent foreign policy, of which diversification of the international partnerships has been an important feature, Ricupero (1989).

If the scope of transactions is broadened and services are comprised, a recent

Table 5b The 40 biggest foreign groups
operating in Brasil, by origin
(balance sheet values in US$billion at the end of 1990)

	Number of groups	Net assets	Net receipts
Europe			
EC	19	4.60	26.64
Germany	8	2.05	7.74
France	5	1.10	9.55
UK	2	0.90	5.28
Italy	2	0.30	2.22
Benelux	2	0.25	1.85
Switzerland	4	0.55	2.57
Finland	1	0.06	0.17
Americas			
US	14	2.42	14.65
Argentina	1	0.38	1.02
Africa			
South Africa	1	0.12	0.41

Source: Gazeta Mercantil.

study, EC(1990), has shown that there is considerable advantage in strengthening trade in services links between Brasil and the EC in various key sectors as telecommunications and construction and engineering. Considering air transport, associations with other regions can also be interesting, as the Southern African countries with Brasil and Australia with Argentina.

Not only in relation to specific nations there may be attractive partnerships. A unified, stronger presence in interest collusions like the Cairns Group for agriculture, and a common negotiating line in forums like the GATT represent a concrete advantage. In both instances, given the internal diversity of the Latin American "continent", a Southern Cone union makes more sense than a larger, more ambitious association.

5 Trade strategies: a broad view

Orthodox free traders usually get much worried about the possibility that countries joining trade blocks will be more protectionist toward those outside than they were before. However, as "what matters is not so much free trade as its role in letting the market do its destructive work", (Waelbroeck (1991)), the main question here should be *whether the envisaged regional associations will benefit the existing market distortions in LA and/or create new cocoons for negative trade diversion effects in the Vinerian sense.*

An answer at this point of time is not an easy job; many indeterminacies plague the road of any conceived integration. A basic assurance can be found in the way the existing treaties bind their signataries to openness. Articles 1, 4 and 5c) of the Assunción Treaty, which sets the guidelines for the creation of the MERCOSUL, are close in spirit and form, though much less detailed, to their counterparts, i.e. Articles 9 to 37, in the Treaty of Rome (which established in 1957 the European Community).

If the above point reinforces the need of a clear and binding trade policy for an LA block, it does not necessarily deny that such a policy should be a twofold process, with one strategy for integration itself, and another one for the negotiations of the whole block with the rest of the world, the US in particular.

In the first case, notwithstanding the varied (though in general limited) scope of the sectoral impacts and the difficulties caused by the country differences and Brasil's disproportionate size, liberalisation should happen at a fast pace anyhow. This seems in time with the rapid changes in LA and even potential problems as those pointed out in section 2 should not be taken as an irremovable argument against it.

If integration comprises the US, size factors - in all possible aspects - become more dramatic, implying that liberalisation should proceed at a slower speed.

Brasil has a trade *contentieux* with the US to be streamlined before engaging in a closer association, with due regard being paid first to the protectionist attitudes on both sides. These are correlated with the degree of competitiveness and technological development in the different sectors of the economy.

MERCOSUL (or Brazilian) tradeable sectors with the US, can thus be classified into:

a) those which are competitive in one region but do not suffer protectionist pressures in the other,

b) those competitive in one region but protected and/or backwards in the other.

Agreements should first aim at total liberalisation of trade in the (a) sectors. As regards (b), things are not so simple. Latin American (b)-sectors exports are mainly traditional manufacturing ones[13] as steel and industrial chemistry, where the US has lost competitiveness. In the North American side, most (b)-sectors are advanced technology ones, some of them also found with a certain degree of regional competitiveness in LA countries, but shielded by protective barriers and unable to face the impact of US imports.

Latin Americans want unrestricted market access for their (b)-sectors exports and transfer of technology for the ones they lag behind. The US face heavy lobbying from their backwards (b)-sectors and want market access for their exports, safeguarded by patent and property rights. The common divisor

---

[13] Not all of them necessarily labour intensive (see the end of section 3).

is by no means evident as strategic trade policy arguments, à la Brander and Spencer (1981), can produce different conclusions, depending on the development project envisaged.

It is in this dilemma that the Bush initiative can help significantly, irrespective of the pace of negotiations between LA and the US. A joint investment effort in which the American region as a whole could be considered as a field for the location of new multinational investment could contribute for easing up the tensions between the two Americas.

The same policy should apply to the other trading partners, but, to avoid a backwards bilateralism, under the GATT's multilateral regime. This means especially an as-strict-as-possible application, by the LA block, of the most favoured nation principle.

6 Conclusions

The sustaining of a free trade area, as an initial step for ambitious integration plans, supposes a degree of macroeconomic coordination which is still too far in the region. At the current levels of instability, even the tariff reduction schedules can bring about disastrous consequences. Also, in the near future, a monetary system operating as the EMS in its early stages is perhaps a too far fetched expectation. However, the attempt at a coordinated monetary policy and at a global regional stabilization is a very positive attitude, and the integration programme can act as a powerful motivation for it.

In the case of the classic trade creation and diversion effects, it seems that, in overall terms, for an association like the MERCOSUL short run impacts will be rather timid for Brasil, somewhat less so for Argentina, and even less for Uruguay and Paraguay. An enlargement of the group, encompassing for instance Chile and Venezuela would enhance the exports spectrum of the union, while improving its bargaining power in the international community. Trade creation effects, due to the complementary characteristics of these two countries *vis-a-vis* Brasil and Argentina, especially, would also be improved. Integration with the US is advocated as a second stage in the process.

Further explorations of trade impacts need a more disaggregate study and may produce interesting results in manufactures sectors where a reasonable degree of actual intra-industry trade is present. At the level used in this paper, part of the intra-industry intensity is probably sheer Heckscher-Ohlin trade. A sort of gains of scope, more than of scale, seems to be the most likely outcome of the integration dynamics anyway. Significant scale gains apparently require a technological change that the integration *per se* might be unable to produce.

Summing up, merits appear to be at first more related to the political rather than the economic side. Within this framework, engagement of Chile may perhaps be easier than that of Venezuela, as the latter one has strong links with its partners in the Andean Pact (Pacto Andino). This is not necessarily a shortcoming: Venezuela could be a natural way to bring in its Andean associates of which Peru is (at the least) geographically important. However, reminding that in reality there is more than one south America, this further step seems unlikely in the near future. And so, the Bush initiative.

The initiative could be of help if a common investment location policy could be designed for the American region as a whole. Given that this is being already aimed at in the Canada+US+Mexico agreement, it is doubtful if further area enlargements would meet a favourable reaction in the US.

Finally, integration should not be an excuse for closing the doors to the outside. By all means, and independently of the regional links established, other partners like Japan and the EC should not be forgotten in a development strategy where foreign direct investment is a must.

7 References

Armington, P.S. (1969), A theory of demand for products distinguished by place of production, *IMF Staff Papers* 16, 159-178.

Balassa, B. (1967), *Trade Liberalisation Among Industrial Countries*, New York: McGraw Hill.

Brander, J.A. and B.J. Spencer (1981), Tariffs and the extraction of foreign monopoly rents under potential entry, *Canadian Journal of Economics* 14, 371-389.

Branson, W.H. and N. Monoyios (1977), Factor inputs in US trade, *Journal of International Economics* 7, 111-132.

Burniaux, J.M. and J. Waelbroeck (1991), Preliminary results of two experimental models of general equilibrium with imperfect competition, Discussion Paper 9106, CEME, Université Libre de Bruxelles.

CEPAL (1959), *The Latin American Common Market*, New York: United Nations.

Cline, W.R. (1984), Latin America's stake in econonomic integration, in E. Conesa, ed., *Terms of Trade and the Optimum Tariff in Latin America*, Washington, D.C.: Institute for Latin American Integration and Inter-American Development Bank.

Dornbusch, R. (1990), Da estabilizaçao ao crescimento, *Revista Brasileira de Economia* 44, 102-115.

EC (1990), Brazil+EC trade in services: measurements, Issues and perspectives, Final project report, Commission of the European Communities, DG XII.

Fritsch, W. and G.H.B. Franco (1988), *Foreign Direct Investment and Industrialization in Brazil*, OECD Development Centre.

Khan, M.S. and M.D. Knight (1985), Fund-supported adjustment programs and economic growth, Occasional Paper 41, Washington, D.C.: IMF.

Persson, T. (1988), Credibility of macroeconomic policy: an introduction and a broad survey, *European Economic Review* 32, 519-541.

Pratten, C.F. (1991), Economies of scale and Latin American exports *and* Appendix E: Estimates for economies of scale in industries, in H. Schwartz, ed., *Supply and Marketing Constraints in Latin American Manufacturing Exports*, Washington, D.C.:Inter-American Development.

Ricupero, R. (1989), Comércio exterior brasileiro: competitividade e perspectivas, in G. Fonseca Jr. and V.C. Leao, orgs., *Temas de política Externa Brasileira*, Brasilia: Instituto de Pesquisa de Relaçoes Internacionais-IPRI e Editora Atica.

Silva, C.J. da (1990) Antecedentes históricos do processo de integraçao latino-americana: ALALC, MCCA, Pacto Andino, in V.M.P. Seitenfus e L.A. De Boni, coord., *Temas de Integraçao Latino-Americana*, Petrópolis: Vozes.

Stern, R. and K.E. Maskus (1981), Determinants of the structure of US foreign trade, *Journal of International Economics* 11, 207-224.

Urquidi, V. (1960), Trajectoria del Mercado Común Latinoamericano, Mexico: Centro de Estudios Monetarios Latinoamericanos.

Velloso, J.P. dos R. (1991), ed., *O Brasil e o plano Bush: oportunidades e riscos numa futura integraçao das Américas*, Sao Paulo: Nobel.

Verdoorn, P.J. and A.N.R. Schwartz (1972), Two alternative estimates of the effects of EEC and EFTA on the pattern of trade,*European Economic Review* 3, 291-336.

Waelbroeck, J. (1962), La demande extérieure et l'évolution des exportations belges, *Cahiers Economiques de Bruxelles* 15, 397-412.

Waelbroeck, J. (1964), Le commerce de la Communauté Européenne avec les pays tiers, in *Intégration Européenne et Réalité Economique*, Bruges: De Tempel.

Waelbroeck, J. (1967), On the structure of international trade interdependence, *Cahiers Economiques de Bruxelles* 36, 495-511.

Waelbroeck, J. (1987), International trade in services: comment, in O. Giarini, ed., *The Emerging Services Economy*, Oxford: Pergamon Press.

Waelbroeck, J. (1991), A thousand years of European economic history: twelve secrets for the High Road, Conference presented at an OECD seminar.

8 Appendix: Methodological Considerations

8.1 Specialization and intra-industry indexes

Calling X_j^i country i exports in sector j and X^i total country i exports, export specialization within a group of countries is defined as:

$$(X_j^i/X^i) \cdot (X_j/X)^{-1}, \tag{1}$$

where X_j is total sector j exports in the group of countries considered and X is, accordingly, total exports.

Intra-industry trade in sector i, for country j, is measured by the Balassa formula, Balassa (1967):

$$(1- \mid X_j^i - M_j^i \mid /(X_j^i + M_j^i)) \times 100, \tag{2}$$

where M_j^i is country i imports of sector j goods while X_j^i refers to exports, both values being now global.

8.2 Derivation of the trade impacts

Let $[X_{ij}]$ be a trade flows matrix where each entry gives the amount of country i imports of a given manufacturing sector that comes from country j. Let $[P_{ij}]$ be the corresponding import price matrix. The well-known Armington (1969) model gives the variation in the value of imports from country j', $d(lnX_{ij'}P_{ij'})$, as a function of three variations: an income variation, the variation in all P_{ij} prices - $j \neq j'$, i fixed - and the variation in the price indexes (over all import origins) of other manufactures. The results assume constant elasticities of substitution between competing imports, i.e., from different countries but in the same sector, and a CES function aggregating all X_{ij} imports for each country i.

Supposing no income variations and negligible cross elasticities of demand (for conveniently defined manufactures groups), Armington's formula (14) simplifies to (where S_{ij} is the share of country j in the total value of imports, σ is the substitution elasticity, and η, the price elasticity):

$$d(lnX_{ij'}P_{ij'}) = -[(\sigma - 1) - S_{ij'}(\sigma - \eta)]d(lnP_{ij'}) + \sum_{j \neq j'} [S_{ij}(\sigma - \eta)]d(lnP_{ij}) \tag{3}$$

By further supposing that (equal) price variations took place only between the members of the integration at stake (for instance, the MERCOSUL), the above equation for j' such a member becomes:

$$
\begin{aligned}
d(lnX_{ij'}P_{ij'}) &= -(\sigma - 1)d(lnP_{ij'}) + \sum_{mercosul} (\sigma - \eta)S_{ij}d(lnP_{ij}) \\
&= -d(lnP_{ij'})[(\sigma - 1) - (\sigma - \eta)S_{mercosul}] \\
&= -d(lnP_{ij'})[\sigma(1 - S_{mercosul}) + (\eta - 1)]
\end{aligned} \tag{4}
$$

If j' is a country outside the integration, it is easy to see that the effect is:

$$
d(lnX_{ij'}P_{ij'}) = \sum_{mercosul} (\sigma - \eta)S_{ij}d(lnP_{ij}) = d(lnP_{ij})(\sigma - \eta)S_{mercosul} \tag{5}
$$

From the above formulae one sees that the higher the share of the union in the country imports the smaller will be the relative impact in the imports from the union and, consequently, the higher will be that in the imports from non-members.

A value of 1 (one) was used for η and σ was set equal to 2 and 3. A unitary price elasticity is a traditional guess in the literature further justified by the aggregation level used, with "sectors" embodying intermediate as well as final consumption goods. Moreover, in the case of Brasil, previous econometric work on (aggregate) imports equations showed that the hypothesis of a unitary price elasticity could not be rejected.

In the Armington approach the elasticity of substitution between competing imports and the related domestic product is the same, the latter being one of the "imports". Estimates, for each sector, of the fraction due to the domestic production are needed. This was done for the case of total imports; in the other sectors the share relative to total imports was used. Consequently, for them, the results are an underestimate of the true value for a union country, and the reverse for a non-union country.

An extension of Armington's ideas, which bypasses the above problem, is the so-called analytical approach by Verdoorn and Schwartz (1972). In the same paper, a formulation of the famous "share approach" is suitable for our purposes.

Considering two periods, 0 and t, let the values at time t divided by the base values, of the following variables, be denoted as:

- F_{ij} the trade flow (total or sectoral) from country i to country j;

- M_j country j imports and

- B_i country i exports.

Verdoorn and Schwartz (1972) write the flow increase as the sum of two parts, $F_{ij} = E_{ij} + Y_{ij}$, where Y_{ij} is the natural increase (or the *anti-monde* evolution) and E_{ij} the one due to the integration. Calling $D_{ij} = E_{ij}/Y_{ij}$, the relative integration effect, they arrived at the following formula:

$$D_{ij} = \frac{A_{ij} - 1}{1 - \frac{\beta_{ij} + \mu_{ij} - 2\beta_{ij}\mu_{ij}}{2 - \beta_{ij} - \mu_{ij}} A_{ij}} \tag{6}$$

where

$$A_{ij} = \frac{F_{ij}}{\frac{1-\beta_{ij}}{2-\beta_{ij}-\mu_{ij}} M_j + \frac{1-\mu_{ij}}{2-\beta_{ij}-\mu_{ij}} B_i} \tag{7}$$

and β_{ij} and μ_{ij} are, respectively, the shares of the trade flow in the base period in country i exports and country j imports.

Negative values can be produced for the integration effect if A_{ij} is smaller than one. Noticing that A_{ij} is the growth in the flow divided by a weighted average between M_j and B_i, this can happen if, for instance, the flow increases less than these two values or if more weight is given to a value higher than F_{ij}.

For the simulations it was supposed that, for each pair of MERCOSUL countries, exports and imports would grow at the historical rates observed during 1980-85[14] and a 10% increase was used for the bilateral flows.

8.3 The factors content regression

Cross section studies on the impact of factor inputs on net exports originated with the so-called "Leontief paradox". The Branson and Monoyios (1977) and the Stern and Maskus (1981) regressions were tried for Brasil, with data from the 1980 input output set of matrices at their deepest disaggregation. This means that 104 commodities were used (oil was excluded). Explanatory variables were: skilled labour - constructed in a way similar to the one in Branson and Monoyios (1977), labour and capital. Heteroscedasticity corrections (by the total demand vector) greatly improve the results, which present a consistent set of signs: positive for skilled labour and capital, and negative for labour. The F-test is significant at less than 1% and $R^2 = 21\%$. However, the significance of the three main coefficients cannot be considered good: it is around 30%.

---

[14]Actually, for imports, a ratio of 1 was supposed, as imports decreased for all the four countries during the period considered.

10

Designing Gradual Transition to Market Economies

Irma Adelman and Peter Berck

University of California, Berkeley

Dusan Vujovic

University of Belgrade

1 Introduction

The dilemma of transition from socialist to market economies consists of overcoming not only the ideological barriers to transition but also the real dislocations involved. On the one hand, an abrupt transition is desirable in order to achieve a consistent set of prices, incomes, and resource allocations; on the other, it is feared that such a transition may result in economic chaos in the short run, since the resource allocation, income distribution and price solution of the current system may be very far from those of a market-allocation and market-price system.

Discussions of system-reform in Eastern Europe were scant at the time the paper was first written (July of (1990))[1]. By now, however, the literature on reform in Eastern Europe has exploded. Reform issues discussed in the literature include: stabilization (Commander (1992), Edwards (1992), and Lipton and Sachs (1990)), structural adjustment (Bourguignon and Morrisson (1992), Coricelli and de Redenza Rocha (1991), and Morrison (1992)), privatization and its financing (Danji and Milanovic (1991), Felix, (1991), Harberger (1992), Hinds and Pohl (1991), Laffont and Tirole (1990), Sachs (1992) and Tirole (1990)), institutional reform (Krueger (1992), Galal (1991), Newbery (1992), Willig (1992)) and reform sequencing (Blanchard (1990), Csaba (1991), Commander (1992), Edwards (1992), and Newbery (1991)).

Our discussion of reform centers solely on institutional reform. The key questions with respect to institutional reform can be grouped under five dif-

---

[1]This paper was first presented at the World Congress of the Econometric Society, in Barcelona, Spain, August 23-9, 1990.

ferent headings: (1) reform scope (partial versus complete reform); (2) reform intensity (big bang versus gradual reform); (3) sequencing of reforms (stabilization precedes or accompanies liberalization); (4) resolution of potential conflicts between liberalization, macroeconomic stabilization, and structural change; and (5) performance criteria for reform (inflation, deficit reduction, government and public sector size, economic growth, international competitiveness, distributive impact).

The new orthodoxy on economic reform stresses complete and immediate reform (For expositions of the new orthodoxy see Balassa (1990), Edwards (1992), Harberger (1992), International Monetary Fund (1986), Krueger (1992), Lipton and Sachs (1990), Sachs (1992) and Walters (1992)). Its implementation entails stabilization, trade and price liberalization, business deregulation and privatization, and reduction in the size of government and increases in its efficiency. The standard ingredients of stabilization packages include tight demand policies, wage controls, deficit reduction and real depreciation. The standard ingredients of liberalization include changes in trade regimes, deregulation of interest rates, investment and credit allocation mechanisms, privatization of public enterprises, reforms of the fiscal system, and sectoral reforms. The new orthodoxy recommends that, in terms of sequencing, structural reforms should be preceded by macroeconomic austerity stabilization programs and that, in terms of intensity of implementation, shock therapy should be favored over gradualism.

The credibility of the new paradigm is buttressed by the fact that state-led development has suffered strong blows in both Latin America and in the formerly socialist countries in Eastern Europe. Nevertheless, there is a great deal of debate on the prescriptions of the new orthodoxy. Some of the controversy centers on how specific measures work out in practice (e.g. Is devaluation contractionary or expansionary in the short and long run? Why does inflation persist despite cuts in monetary growth?). A more serious debate started recently concerning the impact of orthodox economic-reform packages on economic growth and distributive justice. Based on ample evidence from different countries Dornbush (1991) argues that the transition to medium and long term growth following stabilization programs is quite slow. In particular, investment activity tends to lag seriously behind adjustment and liberalization (Solimano (1992a)). And the social costs of adjustment have been high (Bourguignon and Morrisson (1992)). As a result, arguments for a more moderate approach to reform are being voiced.

The advocates of a gradual approach to reform claim that protracted macroeconomic austerity leads to contraction in both current and future output through a prolonged reduction in capital formation (Bruno (1992), Dornbush (1991), Coricelli and de Redenza Rocha (1990), Serven and Solimano (1992a and 1992b), and Solimano (1992a and 1992b). Rapid liberalization may generate further destabilizing effects. For example, trade liberalization may lead to lower tariffs and budgetary problems; devaluation may lead to inflation and expectations of further inflation may lead to capital flight; interest rate reform may slow investment; and wage restraint may lead to recessionary expectations. Politically, it is also argued that disappointment with the economic performance of most East European economies following shock therapies invites backlash. The resulting "...rise in economic insecurity makes the politics of transition very complicated, bringing the shadow of a slide back to authoritarianism and/or populism quite real" (Solimano (1992b)). The gradualist approach makes a clear distinction between the need for shock treatment in stabilization and gradualism in structural reforms (Bruno (1992)).

Proponents of the new orthodoxy downplay the adverse effects of macro restraint on growth and emphasize the positive effects of liberalization on the productivity of investment and the overall efficiency of the economy. They insist on changes in policy regimes (as opposed to changes in instruments) and on shock therapy and rapid liberalization (Sargent (1982)). Politically, they contend that gradualism will lead to a backlash since the East European citizenry views gradualism as an indication of a lack of commitment to transition to a market economy.

Experience with reform is on the side of gradualism. Quick market-based reforms were tried in both some Latin American countries and in some East European ones. Although the starting positions of Latin American countries were quite different in many respects, their economies responded similarly to rapid price and trade liberalization (Bourguignon and Morrisson (1992), Dornbush (1991), and Serven and Solimano (1992b)). In Chile, Mexico and Bolivia quick market-based reforms in the 1970s and the 1980s indicated that stabilizing inflation took much longer than anticipated (7 years in Mexico and Chile) and involved considerable costs in lower levels of economic activity and real wages, while the transition to sustainable growth following stabilization was much more difficult than expected and took 5 to 6 years.

Similar studies for a group of East European countries (Hungary, Poland, Czechoslovakia, Bulgaria and Romania) are based on a much shorter time period (1990-1992) and encompass countries with a great variety in initial conditions (Solimano (1992b)). Restrictive demand policies and wage controls were a common feature of reform. Generally, the East European countries responded with a much greater contraction in economic activity than the Latin American countries. There are three possible explanations for the greater severity of the impact on East European countres: (a) stabilization triggered demand contraction with a Keynesian impact on output (Berg and Sachs (1992)); (b) the reform was accompanied by adverse supply and organizational shocks caused by the rapid dismantling of central planning domestic supply networks, institutional uncertainties with respect to property rights, and worker and managerial incentive systems, and tight credit policies; and (c) external shocks associated with the disintegration of the CMEA trading block and with rapid trade liberalization.

By contrast, China and South Korea were cases of gradual economic reform. Unlike Eastern Europe, China (Lu and Weimer (1992) and World Bank (1990)) started from controlled macroeconomic conditions and conducted the reforms within the framework of the old socialist system. China avoided large macroeconomic dislocations during the transition process, though some inflation did develop, and its rate of economic growth during the transition has averaged 8.5% a year.

Korea is also a case of successful gradualism. In implementing its Second Five Year Plan (1964-68), South Korea started with rapid economic stabilization, as a prelude to increased investment and gradual trade liberalization (Adelman (1967)). Inflation was brought under control within a year, the rate of economic growth increased tenfold and unskilled wages tripled. Market based reforms to reduce monopolies and diminish the role of government were undertaken by the government only in the mid to late seventies. Nevertheless, the government has continued to play a significant role in the economy (Amsden (1989)). Over the reform period, poverty decreased substantially, despite an increase in inequality during the 1980s, and average growth rates of GNP have continued at a double digit level.

The present paper offers a theory of reform design which combines the major advantages of quick transition with the advantages of gradual reform. The design proceeds in two steps. In the first step, the market is introduced and all allocations and targets in the socialist economy are replaced by their subsidy-and-tax price equivalents. The resulting market solution exactly reproduces the existing socialist solution in incomes, profits, and production, consumption and trade decisions. This step combines the advantages of an abrupt institutional transition– immediate price and trade liberalization– with the advantages of complete gradualism– zero immediate economic descriptions to the economy and society. This step is equivalent to replacing standards with taxes or subsidies in the environmental literature (Baumol and Oates (1988)) and quotas with tariffs in the trade literature (Bhagwati (1965)).

In the second step, the subsidy-and-tax equivalents associated with a target profile of the economy are calculated and a gradual, but internally consistent, approach to these target-subsidies and taxes is devised. This two step procedure makes the institutional transition abrupt, but shields the participants from immediate consequences of reform for some period of time. It thus allows time for consumers and producers to adjust to the institutions of markets, while not sacrificing the internal consistency of reforms. Institutional reform is not merely a matter of changes in the rules of the game; it also requires adjustment in behavior patterns and in thinking by economic actors. While the former can occur abruptly, the latter requires time. Our procedure allows for this.

Our concept of gradualism differs from the usual. In usual parlance, gradualism is associated with piece-meal reform. This leads to inconsistencies in incentives and generates confusion, so that the transition is fraught with uncertainty and accompanied by very little learning. By contrast, in our approach, the simultaneous reduction of all socialist-equivalent subsidies and taxes makes the transition orderly and internally consistent. Note also that our procedure allows the government to settle upon a desired profile of incomes and quantities at the end of the transition process. The market equilibrium at the end of the transition is not necessarily a zero subsidy, zero tariff equilibrium. Our procedure thus allows for some guidance of the economy, but through prices and markets rather than through targets and allocations. These are the primary guidance procedures currently used in market economies.

The feasibility of our approach depends upon the government's ability to precommit to a believable trajectory of changes in taxes and subsidies. The capacity to precommit varies among East European countries. In some, the state is still "hard", and continues to have authority and the ability to precommit. In others, there has been a loss of legitimacy, vacillation, and an increase in nationalist and ideological conflicts which precludes believable precommitment.

The two-step procedure is illustrated through a computable general equilibrium model. In a socialist economy with incomplete and distorted markets and quantitative restrictions (Yugoslavia), we calculate the price equivalents of the distortions. We then design viable transitional policy regimes by applying the corresponding taxes and subsidies to an equivalent neoclassical, unrestricted, computable general equilibrium model and phazing them out gradually. The choice of Yugoslavia for illustrative purposes may be somewhat unfortunate, in view of recent events which have torn the country apart. But our work was never intended as a policy prescription for Yugoslavia *per se*. Yugoslavia has already undergone a gradual, though still incomplete transition. Its reform history is long, collective enterprises and markets are well established, and most quantitative and price restrictions are of the "soft" variety.

In the next section we present the theory underlying the reform design. In section three, the existing distortions are evaluated in a set of "rent SAMs" arising from import quotas and from domestic price and quantity controls. In section four, we discuss the implications of these distortions for the desirability of reform. In section five, the subsidy cum tax price equivalents are calculated and the model is tested with different institutional reforms in factor markets. The final sections discuss some potential pitfalls in the transition, and why our model understates the real world difficulties of reform.

2 A theoretical statement of our approach to reform

An idealized socialist system consists of M classes of agents, called institutions. Agents within a class receive the same government subsidies, own the same quota rights, and face the same prices. Thus all opportunities for trade within an institution are exhausted by the socialist price system.

Institutions interact by buying and selling goods and factors of production at the socialist prices p_c. These prices are not necessarily market clearing prices, so the inter-institution transfers are limited by quotas, q. The distortions of prices and quantities from their market values cause rents to accrue to institutions. Socialism has rules that determine the distribution of these rents, as well as the distribution of ordinary profits. Thus any change in prices leads to a change in incomes and therefore in demand. Because the socialist rules may lead to negative profits for some operating enterprises, socialist governments make lump sum payments as well as levy more ordinary taxes.

In this section we shall show that the socialist allocation can be reproduced with one set of commodity taxes for each commodity/institution and a lump sum subsidy for each institution. The result is a generalization to a whole economy of the equivalence of tariffs and quotas in the trade literature (Bhagwati (1965)) or the equivalence of taxes and standards (Baumol and Oates (1988)) in the environmental literature. It shares the limitations of equivalence theorems in these literatures.

Although a tariff and a quota can induce the same market outcome, e.g. level of imports, a quota confers a rent upon the owner of the quota. For instance, U.S. voluntary import quotas for automobiles, textiles and steel were estimated to increase foreign profits by $ 14 billion annually. An equivalent tariff would not have this effect (Tarr (1989, p. 2)). Bhagwati and Srinivasan (1976) and Krueger (1974) carry the argument a step further and argue that the potential existence of rents (or tariff revenues) induces agents to work to obtain these rents for themselves (rent seeking) wasting resources in the process (directly unproductive activities). In the environmental literature, firms prefer equally restrictive standards (quotas) to taxes because the taxes not only induce a cutback in pollution but also transfer money from the firm to the government.

Abstracting from rent seeking, a quota is equivalent to a tax plus a lump sum transfer. Lump sum taxes are difficult to envision in a capitalist system. In the environmental literature, lump sum taxes can be avoided by taxing to a standard: the regulated firm is forgiven its tax liability on the first q units of pollution and taxed only on the remainder. More generally, in public finance, infeasibility of lump sum taxation leads to only second best allocations being feasible (Diamond and Mirrlees, 1971): without lump sum taxes, there may not exist a tax that exactly duplicates all the effects of a quota.Under socialism, the effects of quotas can be reproduced exactly since lump-sum taxes and subsidies are ubiquitous in socialist economies.

Taxes and quotas also have divergent effects when there is uncertainty. Consider a tariff, constant across years, set to give the same imports as a quota in a base year. In any year but the base, differences in demand and supply induced by a host of variables (like OPEC) will cause the realized effect of the tariff to be different from the quota level (Krueger (1974)). This is formally the same as an uncertainty argument in a two-period world: decisions are made in period one and the consequences, seen as random from period one, are accepted in period two. Weitzman's prices versus quantities argument is carried out in this setting and he finds (Weitzman (1974)) that the two instruments are not equivalent. If getting the quantity right is very important (like getting medicine to a disaster area) one should use quotas. If getting costs right (in the sense that price equals marginal cost) is important, then one should use prices (taxes). Finally, taxes and quotas are not equivalent when there is monopoly power (Bhagwati (1978)). In short, the substitution of subsidies and taxes for mixed quotas and price controls gives exactly equivalent outcomes only in a certain, static, competitive, non-rent-seeking environment.

The Price-Quota Equivalence Theorem

The equilibrium allocation of any mixed system of price and quantity controls can be replicated as the equilibrium of a price system with institution-specific commodity-taxes and lump-sum subsidies. We prove this proposition by considering each of the institutions in turn and devising a tax and subsidy system that results in the institution making the same choices that it made under socialism. The general method of the demonstration is to write a Lagrangian expression for the institution's choice problem and show that quota constraints on that choice are the same as unrestricted choices made with respect to a modified price system. Once it can be shown that no institution changes its choices, it is obvious that the sums of the institutional choices are the same as well.

In our abstract socialist economy, there are n goods, which include final goods, factors of production, goods traded in the clearing-currency area, and goods traded in the convertible-currency area. Each institution is represented by a unique integer i. The net quantity demanded in the initial state (socialism) by the i-th consuming institution is the n -vector $x_{0i} = (x_{01i}, ...x_{0ni})$. Netputs of producing sectors are (n-vectors) y^i. Quotas are (n-vectors) q^i, prices are p^i, etc. Prices are row vectors while quantities are column vectors, so they are always conformable for multiplication. When there is no danger of confusion, we will omit the institution-specific superscripts

The socialist case we consider is that there is a price vector p_c (not necessarily the market price, p_m) and a quota vector q for each institution. We find the tax vector t, and subsidy vector s that give the same x (or y) as the socialist system. We shall refer to this system of t and s as the market-equivalent-of-socialist-subsidies or the MESS tax system. In the following section, we estimate the MESS taxes empirically by taking distortions one at a time.

Consumers: Each type of consumer chooses goods, x, to maximize utility, $U(x)$, subject to a budget constraint and quantity rationing constraint. The formal problem is

$$V = \max U(x) \text{ s.t. } m = p_c x \text{ and } x \leq q$$

Some elements of q may be very large, which is to say there is no binding constraint on how much of that good can be bought. Under the usual assumptions about utility, one can use the Kuhn Tucker theorem to find the solution to this constrained problem. The solution can be found by finding the saddle point $(x^*, \lambda^*, \gamma^*)$ of the Lagrangian,

$$L_0(x, \lambda, \gamma) = U(x) + \gamma(m - p_c x) + \lambda(q - x)$$

To convert this to a problem with just a budget constraint, notice that (x^*, γ^*) is also a saddle point of

$$L_1(x, \gamma) = U(x) + \gamma[m + (\lambda^*/\gamma^*)q - (p_c + \lambda^*/\gamma^* x]$$

(Proof: When $x = x^*$, $\lambda^*/\gamma^*(q - x^*) = 0$, so minimizing L_1 or L_0 on γ give the same answer; when $\gamma = \gamma^*$, maximizing L_1 and L_0 obviously give the same answer for x). Since (x^*, γ^*) is a saddle point, x^* also solves the problem

$$W = maxU(x)s.t.m + (\lambda^*/\gamma^*)q = (p_c + \lambda^*/\gamma^*)x$$

Thus problem "V" and problem "W" have the same solutions for given p,m, and q. Moreover (by complementary slackness) the value of the lump sum subsidy, s, exactly equals the value of the commodity taxes, $s = (\lambda^*/\gamma^*)q = (\lambda^*/\gamma^*)x$

Since λ^* depends on p_c, q and m, the demand curves from "W" and "V" are not the same. Put differently, there is a tax structure, (λ^*/γ^*), and subsidy structure, $(\lambda^*/\gamma^*)q$ that will reproduce the quota-based demand, x_0, but it will not reproduce the quota-based demand curve.

Firms: Each firm's problem is to maximize profits, p, at prices p_c, using netputs y. Negative values of elements of y indicate inputs, positive values outputs. Netputs are differentiated by being untraded, traded in the clearing zone, or traded in the hard-currency zone.There are potentially separate quotas for each. The firm's problem is max $p_c y$ s.t. $y \in T$ and $y \geq q$, where T is the production technology, assumed neoclassical, and q is the production-quota. We assume that there exists a feasible y and that in the socialist allocation the firm was operating on its production function. As with the consumers, let λ^* be the shadow prices of the quotas. The firm's decisions can be decentralized by having it face prices $p_x + \lambda^*$ and receive lump sum transfer $s = \lambda^* q$. Since the firm hires the same factors with the taxes as it did with the quotas, its payments to factors are identical. Since profits (sum of rents and quasi rents) are unchanged, its payments to other institutions are unchanged. And, by construction, it produces the same output.

Trade: International trade is just the opportunity to transform one product into another at a fixed ratio given by international prices. We take all quotas as accruing to firms other than the trade firm (no voluntary import quotas); so quotas in international trade are formally quotas on the internationally-traded inputs of ordinary firms and consuming institutions. When p_c is not the same as the world price (it differs by a tariff), the capitalist analogue of p is p_c plus the same tariff.

Aggregate: By construction, each class of firms and each class of consumer makes the same material choices under the modified the price system it made in the price and quota system. Thus the price-only allocation is feasible. It is supported by prices $p_c + \lambda^{i*}/\gamma^{i*}$ for consuming institutions and $p_c + \lambda^{i*}$ for producing institutions. These prices are indexed from the old socialist prices p_c. The natural choice for numeraire is the trade institution; nontradables have prices derived from tradeable prices in the manner of Little and Mirrlees. Consumer j would face taxes $t^j = \lambda^{1*} - \lambda^{j*}\gamma^{i*}$ and producer i would face taxes $t^i = \lambda^{1*} - \lambda^{i*}$. Clearly, (p, t, s) are an equilibrium price, tax, and subsidy (vector) triplet.

By construction the lump sum subsidies are exactly exhausted by the firm (consumer) specific commodity taxes. Thus this system has the same government budget as the previous system.

In the event of a government miscalculation or a change in circumstances (such as a change in international prices), the new equilibrium system would continue to be feasible: prices would simply adjust to clear markets. The system would not however, maintain quantities at the old levels.

In the case where the law of one price holds under socialism, the taxes are ordinary commodity taxes or tariffs. That is, the taxes/subsidies drive a wedge between consumption (even intermediate consumption) and production prices, but all buyers face the same price. Given that the lump sum distributions are done once and for all, when the system is converted to capitalism, the lump-sum taxes are then not available to affect income distribution. The resulting tax structure is of the type discussed in Diamond and Mirrlees (1971). If the socialist economy had used its price and quantity constraints to maximize social welfare, then the tax structure after conversion would consist of the optimal commodity taxes. Since optimal commodity taxes are characterized by productive efficiency, and the socialist system taxes intermediates, we know that the implied commodity taxes are not optimal. How far they are from optimal is an empirical question.

3 Quantifying the MESS system of taxes and subsidies

The reformed planning systems,[2] which have come to dominate most East European economies since the 1960s, use both quantity and price instruments to manage semi-or-fully decentralized economies. In principle, quantity and price controls can lead to the following outcomes: supliers are on their supply curves while consumers are rationed; or suppliers are off their supply curve while consumers buy as large a quantity as they want at the rationed price. In each of these cases, prices can be either above or below market-clearing prices and quantities can be either larger or smaller than their free-market equilibrium.

Positive consumer scarcity rents (CSR) arise whenever the demand price is greater than the effective market price. CSR cannot be negative, since consumers cannot be driven away from their demand curves. In the notation of the theory of the preceding section, the CSR are equal to $(\lambda^*/\gamma^*)q$. Producer rents (PR) exist whenever the effective market price differs from the supply price. This can hapen under pure price controls, pure quantity rationing and combinations of the two. Producer rents can be either positive (PPR) or negative (NPR). In the notation of the previous section, the producer rents equal λ^*q. In reality, numerous factors in socialist economies cause an underestimation of production costs and supply prices. The nominal supply curve is then below the true-cost supply curve and consumer subsidies are larger.

The most frequent case observed in socialist economies combines all the distortions described above: (a) controlled prices at levels below nominal supply prices; (b) quantity rationing at levels above normal supply responses for given controlled prices, causing nominal operational losses in public enterprises; (c) additional subsidies granted through unrealistic determination of production costs, causing real operational losses; and (d) rent-seeking behavior (including an underground economy), aimed at capturing scarcity rents.

The accounting flows measured in non-market economies capture only the rectangles circumscribed by the observed market price and the observed quantity sold. Price or quantity controls give rise to hidden flows represented by the consumer scarcity rents and the producer rents in figures 1-3. These hidden flows must be added to the flows captured by existing statistics in order to obtain a representation of the actual values of transactions taking place in the economy. These "true" transaction values are given by the sum of market flows, consumer scarcity rents, and producer rents.

A partial equilibrium evaluation of these rents will not suffice. We therefore proceed to estimate the distortions that must be replaced by the MESS tax system in two steps: First, we estimate the direct price-equivalents of the quantity and price controls arising from a particular type of distortion in each

---

[2]This section is abstracted from Adelman, Berck, and Vujovic (1990). The interested reader is referred to that paper for greater detail.

sector of the economy. Second, we use information contained in a Social Accounting Matrix (SAM) to evaluate the direct and indirect rents received by
each activity and to distribute these rents to factors, enterprises, households
and government; and between current consumption, investment and the public
deficit. This yields the incidence of rents as well as the incidence of taxes and
subsidies that must be reproduced by the MESS tax system.

The estimation of rents and their allocation among activities and institutions
is performed for Yugoslavia as of 1987, using the base SAM of table 1. The major types of distortions in socialist countries originate from import controls (or,
in some socialist countries but not in Yugoslavia, export targets); domestic price
controls; or from a combination of domestic price and quantity controls. Each
distortion gives rise to a set of interconnected flows that can be portrayed in a
"rent/MESS SAM" due to that particular distortion. The rent/MESS SAMs
indicate the changes in the values of the flows arising from specific distortions.
As evident from the theory presented in the previous section, the rent SAMs
also indicate the tax/subsidies and lump-sum transfers that must be added to
the base-SAM economy to induce the same static behavior and economic outcome for all institutions and sectors as under the existing non-market (quantity
and/or price control) distortion. The procedures, data and sources used to derive the rent SAMs are discussed in detail in Adelman, Berck and Vujovic (1991)
and the interested reader is referred to that paper for a full description of the
methodology. Here, we present only an abbreviated discussion.

Import Quotas

When import restrictions are present, the supply price, which is the price reflected in the base SAM, is below the demand price. This gives rise to consumer
rents from imports.

Figure 1 shows the case of import quantity rationing. The horizontal supply
curve is the world price and the demand curve is that of the importing industry.
A tariff of $p_d - p_s$ is the equivalent of the quota; rents are $(p_d - p_s)Q$ which is
equal to $Q_{sj}(\lambda^{j*})$.

Our major source of information for import quotas was a detailed analysis
of restricted imports produced by the Yugoslav government, using the six-digit
Brussels commodity classification (see Adelman, Berck and Vujovic (1991) for
greater detail). For each commodity, we estimated how binding the quotas were
by comparing imports in 1987 whith imports in 1979-81, a period of liberal
import restriction with a roughly similar level of gross output. Once sectoral
import quantity restrictions were quantified, the import-price equivalent of these
restrictions was estimated using the elasticity of import demand derived from
regression analysis based on time series and information on the point of intersection of the demand curve with the supply quantity. Our estimates indicate that
the rent equivalent of quotas ranged from 10% to 66% of the value of sectoral
imports. Rents for convertible-currency-area imports averaged 25.9% and from

clearing-area imports 23.8%.

The rent flows arising from import quotas, which must be replaced by the MESS tax system, are presented in the SAM of table 2. This SAM was obtained by applying the price-equivalents of the import-quantity controls computed for each sector to the import quantities to calculate the changes in value of the flows due to import-rationing. We start the computation of adjusted flows by focussing on the import components of the activity-rows of the base SAM. The changes in the activity-rows of the "import-rent SAM" of table 2 reflect the difference between the demand price and the supply price of imports applied to the base quantity of imports. This total sectoral rent is then allocated to intermediate and final demand deliveries in proportion to import shares in total supply on the domestic market. Since exports are entirely domestic goods they are not repriced in the activity rows intersecting the "Rest-of-the-World" columns of the SAM.

The rents in the activity rows cascade down through the SAM. Since they imply changes in the "true" intermediate and investment costs they affect value added and its components. Wandering down the rows of the SAM, wages in Yugoslavia are set with respect to an average consumption bundle and adjusted to keep pace with the value of that bundle. To reflect this fact, we added to the wages of each labor skill the increased value of the re-priced import component of their consumption bundle.

We assumed that profits absorb the net effects of the re-pricing of intermediates, investment and wages. Investment in most socialist economies, once approved by state or regional governments, carries with it rights to obtain priority access to rationed imported investment goods. We therefore allocated the increased value of re-priced imported investment goods by sector of destination and imported inventories to each sector's capital row of this SAM. Note that the sum of all entries in the capital-row of the import-rent SAM of table 2 is equal to the change in value of total investment. This implies that, except for investment, the re-pricing of imports merely leads to transfers among enterprises, and does not lead to any additional rents elsewhere in the system.

Households get net positive rents from imports consisting of their consumption rents. In our SAM, government gets no consumption rents from imports, since it consumes only non-tradable, non-productive services. There is therefore no change in the value of government consumption and no effect on the government deficit.

The "Rest-of-the-World" row, which contains sectoral imports, does not carry any rents even though it is imports that give rise to rents throughout the rest of the system. Since imports are already valued at world prices in domestic currency in the base SAM, and since we assume that their suply is perfectly elastic and that there are no changes in the exchange rate, the entries for imports in the base SAM already reflect the full payment for imports to the rest of the world.

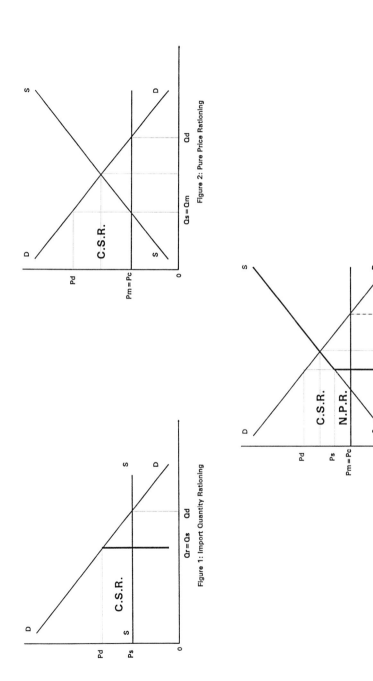

Figure 1: Import Quantity Rationing

Figure 2: Pure Price Rationing

Figure 3: Price and Quantity Rationing

Table 1 Base 1987 SAM

Columns AGRI – LABSK

	AGRI	ENER	IRON	META	CHEM	TEXT	FOOD	OTIN	CNST	TRAN	OPSE	NPSE	LABHS	LABSK
AGRI	2899	13	5	8	156	278	3518	320	34	155	183	240	0	0
ENER	347	3609	716	352	483	168	100	300	166	832	598	315	0	0
IRON	5	31	2363	1764	64	21	15	94	211	37	95	96	0	0
META	122	222	205	4565	171	95	123	236	437	589	607	844	0	0
CHEM	432	122	108	483	2994	642	265	690	74	126	160	700	0	0
TEXT	40	19	23	252	77	2695	30	139	39	204	154	221	0	0
FOOD	747	0	0	1	52	220	2202	5	0	161	971	290	0	0
OTIN	63	44	130	360	202	77	129	1050	1309	173	251	258	0	0
CNST	36	44	12	141	24	12	14	52	1691	129	108	351	0	0
TRAN	323	24	321	822	403	187	243	460	951	1210	720	369	0	0
OPSE	274	303	578	638	379	222	170	260	311	957	597	545	0	0
NPSE	41	39	17	169	82	58	65	42	86	275	222	283	0	0
LABHS	420	71	39	248	76	58	70	62	126	383	163	2478	0	0
LABSK	356	179	97	649	101	161	120	157	459	998	716	1622	0	0
LABUN	3113	481	279	1957	524	1521	707	1033	1477	3264	2565	3245	0	0
CAP	1333	1885	666	2390	1063	1280	1299	879	558	2959	1495	1754	0	0
ENT	0	0	0	0	0	0	0	0	0	0	0	0	0	0
RHHL	0	0	0	0	0	0	0	0	0	0	0	0	140	317
MHHL	0	0	0	0	0	0	0	0	0	0	0	0	874	1688
UHHL	0	0	0	0	0	0	0	0	0	0	0	0	2066	2259
GOVIN	208	280	65	588	159	316	192	240	355	1032	561	614	1112	1340
GOVMX	57	70	85	452	229	85	30	54	18	0	5	38	0	0
GOVSL	124	1154	0	1022	379	532	711	337	0	0	1334	0	0	0
INVSAV	0	0	0	0	0	0	0	0	0	0	0	0	0	0
ROWCL	89	851	290	466	387	109	19	91	0	33	56	0	0	0
ROWCV	524	664	381	2627	1422	380	251	328	0	206	1334	-924	0	0
TOTAL	11551	10064	6378	19986	9426	9094	10332	6917	8264	13723	11637	14263	4193	5614

Columns LABUN – TOTAL

	LABUN	CAP	ENT	RHHL	MHHL	UHHL	GOVIN	GOVMX	GOVSL	INVSAV	ROWCL	ROWCV	TOTAL
AGRI	0	0	0	545	1247	756	0	43	18	837	60	235	11551
ENER	0	0	0	85	376	1009	0	38	31	693	65	254	10064
IRON	0	0	0	0	460	0	0	411	166	5693	156	608	6378
META	0	0	0	108	196	1144	0	193	126	7131	209	816	19986
CHEM	0	0	0	48	694	453	0	166	56	1231	233	907	9426
TEXT	0	0	0	220	1087	1871	0	126	137	817	80	312	9094
FOOD	0	0	0	82	261	2941	0	0	0	977	145	566	10332
OTIN	0	0	0	3	13	832	0	0	0	817	410	444	6917
CNST	0	0	0	315	1283	344	0	0	0	5043	0	1634	8264
TRAN	0	0	0	193	976	2962	0	0	6	1079	410	1363	13723
OPSE	0	0	0	76	337	3101	0	0	1	413	350	0	11637
NPSE	0	0	0	0	0	904	11608	0	0	0	0	0	14263
LABHS	0	0	0	0	0	0	0	0	0	0	0	0	4193
LABSK	0	0	0	0	0	0	0	0	0	0	0	0	5614
LABUN	0	0	0	0	0	0	0	0	0	0	0	0	20166
CAP	0	0	0	0	0	0	0	0	0	0	0	0	16904
ENT	0	16904	0	0	0	0	0	0	0	0	0	0	6311
RHHL	1456	256	6311	0	315	0	107	0	0	0	2	369	10593
MHHL	4781	290	0	0	193	0	1231	0	0	0	1	245	9109
UHHL	9526	111	0	0	76	0	5302	0	0	0	2	431	19707
GOVIN	4403	0	0	0	0	0	0	0	0	0	-48	-1129	21514
GOVMX	0	0	0	0	0	0	0	0	0	0	0	0	1177
GOVSL	0	0	0	0	0	0	0	0	0	4186	0	0	4373
INVSAV	0	0	0	10593	1993	3156	110	0	0	0	93	-924	18889
ROWCL	0	0	0	0	0	0	0	0	0	0	0	0	2390
ROWCV	0	0	0	0	785	188	3194	504	0	0	0	0	8117
TOTAL	20166	16904	6311	10593	9109	19707	21514	1177	4373	18889	2390	8117	

Sectoral acronym=AGRI=agriculture; ENER=energy; IRON=iron and steel; META=metals and metal based industries; CHEM=chemicals; TEXT=textiles; FOOD=food and beverages; OTIN=other manufacturing industries; CNST=construction; TRAN=transportation and communications; OPSE=other productive services; NPSE=non-productive services.

LABHS=High-skilled labor; LABSK=Skilled labor; LABUN=Unskilled labor; CAP=Capital; ENT=Enterprises; RHHL=Rural household; MHHL=Mixed household; UHHL=Urban household; GOVIN=Government income; GOVMX=Import and export taxes/subsidies; GOVSL=Sale tax; INVSAV=Investment/savings; ROWCL=Rest of the world, clearing; ROWCV=Rest of the world, convertible.

Table 2 SAM of import quota rent/tax-subsidy flows

	AGRI	ENER	IRON	META	CHEM	TEXT	FOOD	OTIN	CNST	TRAN	OPSE	NPSE	LABHS	LABSK
AGRI	41	180	0	19	24	4	8	5	0	2	3	3	0	0
ENER	17	1	36	30	1	0	0	20	8	42	30	16	0	0
IRON	0	1	40	234	9	0	0	2	4	1	2	2	0	0
META	6	11	10	27	165	5	6	12	22	30	31	43	0	0
CHEM	24	7	6	10	3	35	0	38	2	7	9	38	0	0
TEXT	2	1	1	0	1	106	15	5	2	8	6	9	0	0
FOOD	10	0	2	6	3	1	29	17	21	2	13	4	0	0
OTIN	1	1	2	6	0	1	2	2	5	3	4	4	0	0
CNST	1	0	8	4	2	3	1	4	4	0	0	0	0	0
TRAN	2	0	1	9	5	1	0	0	0	6	4	2	0	0
OPSE	4	4	2	0	5	1	1	1	2	14	9	8	0	0
NPSE	0	1	4	4	0	0	2	1	7	0	0	0	0	0
LABHS	7	3	0	10	1	1	1	16	23	6	3	39	0	0
LABSK	6	8	0	31	2	1	1	0	0	16	11	26	0	0
LABUN	49	0	0	0	8	24	11	0	0	52	41	52	0	0
CAP	-35	270	-20	490	226	113	0	-28	-103	-129	-22	-246	0	0
ENT	0	0	0	0	0	0	0	0	0	0	0	0	0	0
RHHL	0	0	0	0	0	0	0	0	0	0	0	0	4	5
MHHL	0	0	0	0	0	0	0	0	0	0	0	0	17	23
UHHL	0	0	0	0	0	0	0	0	0	0	0	0	46	61
GOVIN	0	0	0	0	0	0	0	0	0	0	0	0	0	0
GOVMX	0	0	0	0	0	0	0	0	0	0	0	0	0	0
GOVSL	0	0	0	0	0	0	0	0	0	0	0	0	0	0
INVSAV	0	0	0	0	0	0	0	0	0	0	0	0	0	0
ROWCL	0	0	0	0	0	0	0	0	0	0	0	0	0	0
ROWCV	0	0	0	0	0	0	0	0	0	0	0	0	0	0
TOTAL	133	486	92	875	452	307	130	96	-0	60	142	0	67	89

	LABUN	CAP	ENT	RHHL	MHHL	UHHL	GOVIN	GOVMX	GOVSL	INVSAV	ROWCL	ROWCV	TOTAL
AGRI	0	0	0	4	3	8	0	0	0	12	0	0	133
ENER	0	0	0	0	19	51	0	0	0	3	0	0	486
IRON	0	0	0	0	0	0	0	0	0	10	0	0	92
META	0	0	0	6	24	59	0	0	0	365	0	0	875
CHEM	0	0	0	3	11	25	0	0	0	40	0	0	452
TEXT	0	0	0	3	27	74	0	0	0	48	0	0	307
FOOD	0	0	0	1	14	39	0	0	0	13	0	0	130
OTIN	0	0	0	0	4	13	0	0	0	13	0	0	96
CNST	0	0	0	2	0	0	0	0	0	0	0	0	0
TRAN	0	0	0	3	7	15	0	0	0	6	0	0	60
OPSE	0	0	0	5	14	44	0	0	0	6	0	0	142
NPSE	0	0	0	0	0	0	0	0	0	0	0	0	0
LABHS	0	0	0	0	0	0	0	0	0	0	0	0	67
LABSK	0	0	0	0	0	0	0	0	0	0	0	0	89
LABUN	0	0	0	18	82	220	0	0	0	0	0	0	320
CAP	0	0	0	0	0	0	0	0	0	516	0	0	516
ENT	0	0	0	0	0	0	0	0	0	0	0	0	0
RHHL	18	0	0	0	0	0	0	0	0	0	0	0	27
MHHL	82	0	0	0	0	0	0	0	0	0	0	0	122
UHHL	220	0	0	0	0	0	0	0	0	0	0	0	327
GOVIN	0	0	0	0	0	0	0	0	0	0	0	0	0
GOVMX	0	0	0	0	0	0	0	0	0	0	0	0	0
GOVSL	0	0	0	0	0	0	0	0	0	0	0	0	0
INVSAV	0	516	0	0	0	0	0	0	0	0	0	0	516
ROWCL	0	0	0	0	0	0	0	0	0	0	0	0	0
ROWCV	0	0	0	0	0	0	0	0	0	0	0	0	0
TOTAL	320	516	0	27	122	327	0	0	0	516	0	0	0

For acronyms see footnote to Table 1.

The rents arising from import controls are in line with semi-industrial countries: they are 1.9% of GDP at factor costs. Unskilled workers capture about one third of the total import rents and two thirds of consumption rents. Nevertheless, imputing import rents increases apparent inequality slightly. Import rents augment rural household incomes by 1%; mixed, urban-rural, household-incomes by 1.3%; and urban household incomes by 1.6%. The existence of the import-control system hides penalties on enterprises in consumer-goods sectors (agriculture, food, other industries, construction, transport, and all services) and iron. It grants hidden favors to priority sectors – energy, metals, chemicals and textiles. The hidden penalties range from 1.5% of profits in "other productive services" to 18.5% in construction. The hidden favors are more concentrated, ranging from 8.8% in textiles to 21.3% in chemicals.

Domestic Price Controls with Full Quantity Adjustment

Price controls have been declining in most socialist countries. However, some controls continue to exist. Price liberalization for some "basic" intermediates and consumer goods has tended to be continually postponed. And inflation has led to the imposition of new types of price controls through price formation and indexation rules.

Price controls with full quantity adjustment are illustrated in figure 2. The demand curve DD is the sum of the demands from final and intermediate use. The supply curve, SS, is marginal cost of the producer. The observed price, p_m is the controlled price p_c. The consuming sectors are "rationed" to quantity Q_s because that is all that is produced. They are assumed to divide it among themselves efficiently. The consuming sectors are assumed to not use up any significant resources in acquiring Q_s, so they earn consumer scarcity rents CSR in amount $(p_d - p_c)Q_s$. Consumers' (exact) share of those rents are $Q_{si}(\lambda^{i*}/\gamma^{i*})$ and producers' shares are $Q_{sj}(\lambda^{j*})$ where $Q_s = Q_{si} + Q_{sj}$. These are the rents that must be replaced by the MESS tax-cum-subsidy system.

The effect of price controls on individual sectors was estimated from recent sectoral studies or from product-price comparisons for representative samples of commodities in a sector comparing domestic prices with"landed-world-prices" (see Adelman, Berck and Vujovic, (1991) for details). Individual product-price distortions were aggregated to the sectoral level using production weights. Our estimates of sectoral rents stemming from price controls ranged from 10% to 25% and averaged 11.7% of gross output.

The economy-wide rent flows arising from domestic price controls in Yugoslavia as of 1987 are given in table 3. We start by re-pricing the total value of flows in the activity-rows of the base SAM at their landed-world-market-equivalent price. We then distribute the change in the value of total transactions among sectors and institutions in proportion to the corresponding cell entries in the total flows excluding exports of the base SAM of table 1. Exports (and imports) were not re-priced, since, in the base SAM, they are already valued at world prices in domestic currency.[3] We end up with changes in the values of expenditures on intermediates, households and government consumption, and inventories and investment in each sector.

The changes in the activity rows, in turn, lead to changes in the value added rows. Since wages in Yugoslavia have been indexed, we added the increased cost of the new consumption bundle to the wages of each labor skill. Similarly, we re-priced the cost of inventories and investment goods by sector of destination, using the investment matrix. The increased cost of investment and inventories is allocated to the capital account of each sector since, in socialist economies, once investment is approved by the state, firms are allowed to retain the necessary funds within enterprises. We assumed that profits absorb the effects on each sector of the re-pricing of all of these flows. They are, therefore, calculated as residuals and entered into the capital-row of the SAM.

We complete the circular flow of rents arising from the re-pricing of domestic flows by first crediting the savings-investment account with an amount equal to the total change in the value of investment goods. Enterprises are then credited with the balance from the profit and loss account in the capital-row of the SAM. The sum of producer rents arising from domestic activities includes changes in the cost of government consumption expenditures (on a nontradable). Changes in the cost of government consumption are not directly compensated by equivalent changes in taxes on value added or commodities. Increased cost of government consumption, however, does not generate a decline in government savings. This is so because enterprises in Yugoslavia and other socialist countries "transfer" their balances, after provision for investment, to government, crediting them to the state if positive and submitting them for financing by the government if negative.We reflect this in the SAM by having the enterprise-account credit the government-income account with the difference between total enterprise profits and losses and the change in investment. This difference, of course, equals the increased cost of government consumption. Thus, this entire process leads to a "rent SAM" that is balanced, and to a balanced government-income account(i.e. no change in the government deficit).

Numerically, the SAM of table 3 indicates that the "soft" price controls in the domestic economy lead to hidden flows to consumers: on the average, household incomes would be 7.8% higher than at the controlled market prices reflected in the base SAM. However, inequality would also be somewhat higher. At world market prices, the ratio of urban to rural incomes would be 3.5% higher and the ratio of high-skilled wages to unskilled wages would be 2% higher than with existing, controlled, prices. Existing price controls nominally imposed to generate more equality in actuality thus serve to mask some inequality. Under domestic price controls investment appears to be underpriced by about 7.2%.

---

[3]This assumes that the repricing of domestic goods was done at the existing nominal exchange rate and with unchanged sectoral real trade balances.

Table 3 SAM of domestic price controls rent/tax-subsidy flows

	AGRI	ENER	IRON	META	CHEM	TEXT	FOOD	OTIN	CNST	TRAN	OPSE	NPSE	LABHS	LABSK
AGRI	322	504	1	1	17	31	391	36	4	17	20	27	0	0
ENER	49	7	101	54	68	24	23	55	23	118	85	45	0	0
IRON	1	101	511	382	14	5	0	20	46	8	21	21	0	0
META	1	511	382	68	0	91	38	98	10	18	23	0	0	0
CHEM	61	15	15	68	424	20	198	0	0	15	87	99	0	0
TEXT	67	0	0	0	5	0	0	8	0	19	16	26	0	0
FOOD	0	0	0	0	4	2	24	45	0	119	71	53	0	0
OTIN	0	0	2	21	39	18	36	55	254	204	127	36	0	0
CNST	5	7	31	80	81	47	16	10	93	68	55	116	0	0
TRAN	32	2	123	136	20	9	24	5	66	31	13	70	0	0
OPSE	58	65	4	42	8	5	36	13	17	82	59	203	0	0
NPSE	10	10	8	20	43	13	16	85	38	268	211	133	0	0
LABHS	34	6	23	53	434	125	58	10	121	177	324	266	0	0
LABSK	29	15	343	161	−389	83	−430	474	177	1324	2461	0	16	34
LABUN	256	39		−1019									98	182
CAP	117	693	343	−1019	434	−389	83	−430	474	177	1324	2461	231	245
ENT	0	0	0	0	0	0	0	0	0	0	0	0	0	0
RHHL	0	0	0	0	0	0	0	0	0	0	0	0	0	0
MHHL	0	0	0	0	0	0	0	0	0	0	0	0	0	0
UHHL	0	0	0	0	0	0	0	0	0	0	0	0	0	0
GOVIN	0	0	0	0	0	0	0	0	0	0	0	0	0	0
GOVMX	0	0	0	0	0	0	0	0	0	0	0	0	0	0
GOVSL	0	0	0	0	0	0	0	0	0	0	0	0	0	0
INVSAV	0	0	0	0	0	0	0	0	0	0	0	0	0	0
ROWCL	0	0	0	0	0	0	0	0	0	0	0	0	0	0
ROWCV	0	0	0	0	0	0	0	0	0	0	0	0	0	0
TOTAL	1042	1366	1166	131	619	1711	2894	0	1156	1143	2112	3556	344	461

	LABUN	CAP	ENT	RHHL	MHHL	UHHL	GOVIN	GOVMX	GOVSL	INVSAV	ROWCL	ROWCV	TOTAL
AGRI	0	0	0	0	21	59	0	0	0	93	0	0	1042
ENER	0	0	0	12	53	143	0	0	0	9	0	0	1366
IRON	0	0	0	0	0	0	0	0	0	128	0	0	1166
META	0	0	0	7	28	64	0	0	0	103	0	0	1163
CHEM	0	0	0	0	0	0	0	0	0	88	0	0	0
TEXT	0	0	0	20	98	264	0	0	0	0	0	0	887
FOOD	0	0	0	0	2	5	2894	0	0	0	0	0	0
OTIN	0	0	0	31	126	290	0	0	0	757	0	0	1156
CNST	0	0	0	41	208	660	0	0	0	106	0	0	1143
TRAN	0	0	0	19	84	225	0	0	0	88	0	0	2112
OPSE	0	0	0	0	0	0	0	0	0	0	0	0	3556
NPSE	0	0	0	0	0	0	0	0	0	0	0	0	344
LABHS	0	0	0	0	0	0	0	0	0	0	0	0	461
LABSK	0	0	0	0	0	0	0	0	0	0	0	0	1656
LABUN	0	0	0	81	339	1236	0	0	0	0	0	0	4266
CAP	0	2894	0	0	0	0	0	0	0	1372	0	0	2894
ENT	0	0	0	0	0	0	2894	0	0	0	0	0	131
RHHL	0	0	0	0	0	0	0	0	0	0	0	0	619
MHHL	0	0	0	0	0	0	0	0	0	0	0	0	1711
UHHL	0	0	0	0	0	0	0	0	0	0	0	0	2894
GOVIN	0	0	2894	0	0	0	0	0	0	0	0	0	0
GOVMX	0	0	0	0	0	0	0	0	0	0	0	0	0
GOVSL	0	0	0	0	0	0	0	0	0	0	0	0	1372
INVSAV	0	1372	0	0	0	0	0	0	0	0	0	0	0
ROWCL	0	0	0	0	0	0	0	0	0	0	0	0	0
ROWCV	0	0	0	0	0	0	0	0	0	0	0	0	0
TOTAL	1656	4266	2894	131	619	1711	2894	0	0	1372	0	0	

For acronyms see footnote to Table 1.

At world prices, GDP at factor costs would be 12.9% higher and GDP at market prices would be 11.2% higher than under controlled domestic price.

Domestic Price Controls with Constrained Supply Adjustment

Three types of quantity constraints accompany price controls in most socialist economies: the government sets hard quantity constraints; "self imposed" quantity constraints are negotiated betwen producers and either the government or some parastatal institutions; controls on investment and frequent price-control changes give rise to constraints on quantity adjustment.

The case of domestic price controls with constrained supply adjustment is portrayed in figure 3. Price is set at p_c, but the industry is forced to achieve an output target (quota) of Q_s. Consumers receive scarcity rents of $Q_s(p_d - p_c)$ or $Q_{si}(\lambda^{i*}/\gamma^{i*})$, the shadow values calculated from using Q_s as a quota on consumption, while producers lose negative producer rents $(p_s - p_c)Q_s$ or $Q_{sj}(\lambda^{j*})$, the shadow value calculated from using Q_s as a production target. This is reflected by a lump sum transfer to producers in the MESS system.

There is no direct way of estimating the negative producer rents arising from constrained supply in the presence of price controls. However, indirect estimates can be obtained. Sectors with quantity constraints combined with price controls are characterized by the persistent coexistence of three features: (1) persistent use of social capital in sectors (projects) which, over long periods, cannot yield rates of return greater or equal to the opportunity cost of capital; (2) exercise of political pressure by the government to prevent enterprises (sectors) making losses from going out of business and force them to continue producing; and (3) provision of continual subsidies. We therefore use these features to signal the existence of negative producer rents arising from the combination of (mostly soft) quantity and price controls.

We take the rate of interest on Yugoslav foreign loans in 1987 (10.3%) to be the opportunity cost of public capital. For sectors with rates of return on capital below the opportunity cost of capital, the negative producer rents are computed by applying the difference between the two rates to the value of the base-period capital stock. The sectoral rates of return are computed at prices including rents from import-quotas and domestic price controls, and with respect to a re-priced capital stock that reflects investment rents. The results of this calculation indicate the existence of sizeable negative producer rents in agriculture, other industries, and transportation, and very low negative producer rents in iron and steel.

Table 4 traces the negative producer rent flows throughout the SAM. We reconstruct the flow of negative producer rents by first entering the positive corrections to the rate of return on capital for sectors in which the opportunity cost of capital is higher than the rate of return in the sector. That is, we assume that the negative producer rents are fully reflected in the corrections to the imputed value of capital services in each sector.

Table 4 SAM of negative producer rent flows
(billion 1987 dinars)

| | ACTIVITIES | | | | LAB | CAP | ENT | HOUSE | GOVIN | INV | ROW | TOTAL |
	AGRI	IRON	OTIN	TRAN	OR			HOLDS		SAV		
ACTIVITIES	0	0	0	0	0	0	0	0	0	0	0	0
LABOR	0	0	0	0	0	0	0	0	0	0	0	0
CAP	928	66	551	680	0	0	0	0	0	0	0	2225
ENT	-316	-7	-369	-170	0	2225	0	0	0	0	0	1364
HOUSEHOLDS	0	0	0	0	0	0	0	0	0	0	0	0
GOVIN	-612	-59	-182	-510	0	0	682	0	0	-682	0	-682
INVSAV	0	0	0	0	0	0	682	0	-682	0	0	0
ROW	0	0	0	0	0	0	0	0	0	0	0	0
TOTAL	0	0	0	0	0	2225	1364	0	-682	0	0	0

For acronyms see footnote to Table 1.

The negative producer rents are then split between enterprises and government in each sector, in proportion to the manner in which the government favors each sector. In agriculture, for example, government bears 70% of the opportunity loss, while in iron and steel it bears 90% of the loss. By contrast, in "other industries"—a sector that the government discriminates against— enterprises bear two thirds of the opportunity loss. On the average, enterprises directly bear only 35% of the negative producer rents. The government absorbs the rest in the form of low interest loans, "selective credits" from the national bank, interest forgiveness, grants from a "reserve fund" established by legally mandated reserve-deposits from all enterprises, and by merging profitable with unprofitable enterprises and banks.

However, in absorbing the estimated 2/3 of the negative producer rents, government is partially acting merely as an intermediary for redistribution between well-off and worse-off companies. We estimate that only roughly 50% of negative producer rents assigned to the government in activity columns was ultimately borne by the government. This estimate is based on Central Bank data concerning the relative size of capital subsidies extended through soft agriculture-related loans and other "selective credit" instruments, as well as on data about Central Bank assumptions of "foreign exchange losses". For the remaining 50%, the government is effectively compensated by "well-off" enterprises as reflected in the entry in the cell at the intersection of the government-income row and enterprise column. This entry indicates a redistribution among enterprises in different sectors.

Effect of Controls: The Rent-MESS System

Table 5 presents the SAM incorporating all the rent (MESS tax) adjustments arising from import quotas, domestic price adjustments, and combined price-quantity controls. For brevity, we refer to this SAM as the "revealed-MESS-SAM". Comparison of the revealed-MESS-SAM of table 5 with the original SAM of table 1 indicates the following.

First, the accounting or tax adjustments required to account for distortions are pervasive. The only unadjusted transactions are the entries in the "rest-of-the-world" columns and rows, since they are already valued in the domestic-currency-equivalent of world prices. (Of course, in a behavioral model these entries would also change since the price/tax adjustments for distortions imply changes in the real exchange rate.)

Second, for Yugoslavia as of 1987, these adjustments were not out of line with what would be found in a typical semi-industrial non-socialist country.

Third, there is a large dispersion in the distribution of rents (taxes) among actors.

Table 5 SAM with base flows corrected for cumulative rents/MESS flows

	AGRI	ENER	IRON	META	CHEM	TEXT	FOOD	OTIN	CNST	TRAN	OPSE	NPSE	LABHS	LABSK
AGRI	3262	15	5	9	175	313	3959	361	39	174	206	270	0	0
ENER	413	4253	853	455	576	200	191	465	198	992	713	376	0	0
IRON	7	38	2915	2176	79	26	19	116	260	46	118	119	0	0
META	128	234	215	4799	179	99	130	248	459	619	638	888	0	0
CHEM	517	146	129	578	3582	768	318	826	88	151	191	837	0	0
TEXT	41	19	24	262	80	2800	31	144	40	212	160	230	0	0
FOOD	824	0	0	2	58	242	2428	6	0	178	1071	320	0	0
OTIN	64	45	132	366	205	78	131	1067	1330	176	255	262	0	0
CNST	41	50	14	163	27	14	16	60	1944	148	124	404	0	0
TRAN	356	26	354	906	444	206	268	507	1049	1335	794	407	0	0
OPSE	336	372	710	783	465	273	208	319	381	1174	733	669	0	0
NPSE	51	49	22	211	103	47	81	52	83	343	277	353	0	0
LABHS	461	78	43	272	83	63	76	68	139	420	179	2720	0	0
LABSK	391	196	106	713	111	176	132	172	505	1096	786	1781	0	0
LABUN	3418	528	306	2149	575	1670	776	1134	1622	3583	2817	3563	0	0
CAP	2343	2848	1055	1861	1722	1003	1383	971	928	3687	2797	3969	0	0
ENT	-316	0	-7	0	0	0	0	-369	0	-170	0	0	0	0
RHHL	0	0	0	0	0	0	0	0	0	0	0	0	159	356
MHHL	0	0	0	0	0	0	0	0	0	0	0	0	989	1893
UHHL	0	0	0	0	0	0	0	0	0	0	0	0	2343	2575
GOVIN	-405	280	5	588	159	316	192	58	355	522	561	614	1112	1340
GOVMX	57	70	85	452	229	85	30	54	0	0	5	0	0	0
GOVSL	124	1154	0	1022	379	532	711	337	0	0	76	38	0	0
INVSAV	0	0	0	0	0	0	0	0	0	0	0	0	0	0
ROWCL	89	851	290	466	387	109	19	91	0	33	56	0	0	0
ROWCV	524	664	381	2627	1422	380	251	328	0	206	1334	0	0	0
TOTAL	12726	11916	7636	20860	11041	9401	11350	7013	9420	14926	13891	17819	4603	6164

	LABUN	CAP	ENT	RHHL	MHHL	UHHL	GOVIN	GOVMX	GOVSL	INVSAV	ROWCL	ROWCV	TOTAL
AGRI	0	0	0	546	1270	823	0	43	18	942	60	235	12726
ENER	0	0	0	101	448	1203	0	38	45	78	65	254	11916
IRON	0	0	0	0	0	0	0	193	31	732	156	608	7636
META	0	0	0	114	484	1203	0	411	30	7486	509	1987	20860
CHEM	0	0	0	58	235	542	0	166	12	874	209	816	11041
TEXT	0	0	0	154	721	1945	0	126	9	1260	233	907	9401
FOOD	0	0	0	243	1199	3244	0	56	9	1078	80	312	11350
OTIN	0	0	0	83	265	845	0	137	31	830	145	566	7013
CNST	0	0	0	3	15	40	0	0	0	5800	114	444	9420
TRAN	0	0	0	347	1416	3268	0	0	0	1191	419	1634	14926
OPSE	0	0	0	237	1197	3806	0	6	1	506	350	1363	13891
NPSE	0	0	0	95	421	1129	14502	0	0	0	0	0	17819
LABHS	0	0	0	0	0	0	0	0	0	0	0	0	4603
LABSK	0	0	0	0	0	0	0	0	0	0	0	0	6164
LABUN	0	0	0	0	0	0	0	0	0	0	0	0	22142
CAP	0	0	0	0	0	0	0	0	0	0	0	0	24567
ENT	0	22023	0	0	0	0	0	0	0	0	0	0	21162
RHHL	1555	256	0	0	0	0	107	0	0	0	2	369	2804
MHHL	5202	290	0	0	0	0	1231	0	0	0	1	245	9850
UHHL	10982	111	0	0	0	0	5302	0	0	0	2	431	21746
GOVIN	4403	0	9887	37	188	504	0	0	4186	0	-48	-1129	23726
GOVMX	0	0	0	0	0	0	110	0	0	0	0	0	1177
GOVSL	0	0	0	0	0	0	0	0	0	0	0	0	4373
INVSAV	0	1888	11275	785	1993	3194	2474	0	0	0	93	-924	20777
ROWCL	0	0	0	0	0	0	0	0	0	0	0	0	2390
ROWCV	0	0	0	0	0	0	0	0	0	0	0	0	8117
TOTAL	22142	24567	21162	2804	9850	21746	23726	1177	4373	20777	2390	8117	

For acronyms see footnote to Table 1.

Fourth, Yugoslavia as of 1987 does not appear to be a case of haphazard or conflicting distortions. The distortions arising from trade restrictions and those arising from domestic controls seem to reinforce, rather than cancel, each other. Furthermore, the incidence of rents accurately reflects the conscious choice of instruments to achieve stated social policy objectives. It reflects a policy of support of "modern" industries through provision of subsidized inputs. It also reflects a policy to provide basic goods and services at prices that place them within reach of most households. (This, of course, is not to say that the distortions are optimally chosen nor do we imply that the policy of using distorted prices to foster social policy is a good one. Indeed, we argue quite the opposite.)

Fifth, the pattern of indirect support of "modern" industries through subsidizing input industries seems to have been overdone. The average rents accruing to "basic input" industries are more than twice as high as those accruing to the industries whose modernization the subsidies are intended to support. A policy of correct output prices for basic industries coupled with production-subsidies to "modern" industries is more efficient, in the sense of requiring less rents.

Sixth, on the "basic needs" side, the rents to consumers are of the order of 12% of the consumption basket.[4] The cost of achieving these price reductions via explicit and implicit subsidies appears to be much larger than the decreases in consumer prices it accomplishes. If measured in forgone gross profits, the cost is 2.4 times larger than the benefits acquired through cheaper consumer goods; and total rents are more than 5.5 times bigger than consumer rents. Even the pure fiscal costs alone have a benefit-cost ratio that is smaller than unity (.85). A policy of pricing consumer goods and services corectly and then using lump sum subsidies to households is fiscally more efficient.

Seventh, subsidies through investment in fixed assets are the main mechanism for subsidizing production. This imparts an investment bias to the economy. Overall, the net subsidies to activities through intermediates are negative. Net subsidies through intermediates are calculated as gross subsidies received by the activity, via smaller cost of intermediate inputs, minus gross subsidies paid by the activity, via smaller prices on its final good sales. For all goods and services, net subsidies are about -10% of GDP while subsidies through investment are +2.5%. There are significant and systematic intersectoral variations, however.

Eighth, since profit rates bear the brunt of the distortions, the apparent

---

[4]The calculated consumer rents underestimate rents from underpriced non-productive services. Housing, as a part of non-productive services, includes only the value of current service and maintenance of existing housing stock. It does not reflect the equivalent of "owner-occupied" imputed rent. We did not attempt to correct for the omission of "owner-occupied rent" since it does not appear in the official statistics. We thus greatly underestimate the subsidies accruing to consumers, given that market clearing apartment rents in Yugoslavia are 10 to 15 times bigger than controlled rents on socially owned apartments.

rates of return are very unreliable indicators of true profitability. The ratio of rents to base flows is the largest in the capital-row of the revealed-MESS-SAM and the dispersion in the ratio of rents to base flows is also the biggest, varying from +126% of profits to -22%.

Ninth, unlike the case for a typical semi-industrial country, the major distortions in Yugoslavia are due to domestic controls. Import controls account for only 13% of total rents, 2% of 1987 GDP at factor costs, 6.1% of total price distortions and 14.2% of distortions in rates of return to capital. By contrast, domestic price controls account for 87% of total rents, 13% of base GDP at factor costs, 41% of total distortions in prices and 96% in distortions in rates of return to capital.

Tenth, the existence of distortions complicates the formulation of economic policy. Explicit subsidies portray only a small part of the picture. Relative subsidies through rents are different from relative overt subsidies, so that it is easy to over or under-subsidize a particular sector or institution.

Eleventh, the macro aggregates are all bigger with prices that reflect the existing major distortions. Adjusted gross output and GDP at market prices are 13.7% larger than in the 1987 base. Adjusted consumption is 16% above the base and household incomes are 9% greater. Trade represents a smaller share of GDP than in the base. There is a significant change in the functional distribution of income, with the share of capital income being 7% higher than in the base and the share of labor income 2% lower. There are also major changes in the government accounts; government expenditures are 14.8% higher at corrected prices and government savings are 22% less. At adjusted prices, the domestic price level, using domestic absorption, is 12.6% higher and the real exchange rate is correspondingly overvalued.

4   How strong is the static case for reform?

Our analysis of the distortions to measured flows in the previous section reveals several, partially hidden, biases that are induced by the existing distortions. The overall impact of the distortions is an "anti-production" and "over-investment" bias within enterprises. The net effect of price and quantity controls on inputs and outputs is a decrease in enterprise profits (negative net intermediate rents over all enterprises and sectors). This decrease is partially recouped by positive net subsidies to investment. The net effect is to encourage the familiar build-up of excess capacity and capacity under-utilization in enterprises in socialist countries. This anti-production bias is over and above the bias which low wage incentives and rent-seeking on the job impart to labor productivity. Thus, the general import of the distortions introduced by the soft controls is to bias the system towards low factor productivity.

On the average, enterprises gain through subsidies to inputs while losing through the subsidies which they, in turn, must grant buyers of their products to quality for these input subsidies. This policy of "subsidy through intermediates" offers incentives to enterprises to use technology that is intermediate-input intensive. This feature of socialist production is a familiar finding in international comparisons between socialist and non-socialist semi-industrial countries. The succession of reforms of socialist systems has been aimed at increasing total factor productivity and reducing input-output ratios. Our analysis suggests that these features of socialist economies are built into the price and quantity control system they use.

Parallel to these distortion-induced biases to productivity, we found biases in incentive systems that favor or penalize types of enterprises and types of activity. We found a mild pro-export bias in Yugoslavia as of 1987. Even though at corrected prices the average Yugoslav enterprise loses 2.6% per unit of exports, it loses even more (5.6%) by producing for the domestic market. We also found a pro-consumption bias to controls (the net rate of production subsidy is -2.7% for consumption and -6.3% for the other production for the domestic market). On the production side, "modern" industries are the only ones in which distortions introduce a positive bias to produce. "Basic" industries and services all have negative production incentives.

On the distribution side, the hidden distortions favor capital over labor. (Of course, capital is regarded, both ideologically and in fiscal practice, as social capital). The hidden distortions also serve to mask some inequalities among groups of consuming households (skilled vs unskilled and urban vs rural). These results make the apparent differences in distributional performance among socialist and semi-market developing countries smaller than they appear to be on the basis of official statistics.

Thus, the net effect of the current system of controls is to introduce biases into the economy. Some of these biases are intentional, and some are the unintentional byproducts of controls. The pro-investment, pro-modern industry, pro-consumer goods production biases of policy are intentional. The anti total-factor productivity biases are unintended consequences of the pattern of distortions introduced by the price and quantity controls. So are the encouragement of wasteful, resource-using, production technologies that promote heavy use of intermediates, and unnecessary build-up of capacity coupled with substantial capacity underutilization.

How distorted is the Yugoslav economy when all is said and done? No economy is ideal. All economies have some open and hidden wastes, misguided regulations, and inappropriate biases or inefficient use of instruments. And institutions in all economies have inherent distributional and activity-promoting biases. Is the Yugoslav cup half empty or half full? On the half full side, there is a surprising coherence to the pattern of hidden incentives. At first (and even second) blush, the system of rents from various sources appears so complex to economists used to being able to employ market prices plus tax systems to trace the incidence and biases imparted by policy that any coherence in the resulting pattern, efficient or not, appropriate or not, is surprising. Economic institutions in Yugoslavia appear to have adapted over the years to the presence of "soft" price and quantity controls in the system. Different interest groups have managed to voice their concern when "undersubsidized" and conceal "excess profits" arising from oversubsidization. By the same token opposing interest groups, appear to have been effective in preventing large departures from the existing constellation of "controls" in order to preserve their present distribution of overt and covert benefits.

On the half empty side, this "generalized bargaining system" has been very time consuming and has often failed to converge. Our analysis of distortions also suggests that the biases imparted by the system of hidden rents promote significant productivity losses and wasteful resource use, and hence lead to lower ultimate living standards than would be possible with the overt use of prices and tax instruments. Moreover, at several places in section 3 we pointed out that, even in its own terms, the system of indirect support of certain activities and sectors is fiscally inefficient.

When all is said and done, we estimated that the totality of flow-rents at existing quantities in Yugoslavia as of 1987 was only of the order of 13-15%. But how much resource waste do these consumer-and-producer-rent rectangles promote? We now turn to an analysis that permits us to answer this question.

5 The modelling of reforms and experiment results

Our experiments with reform were performed with a computable general equilibrium (CGE) model of Yugoslavia as of 1987. This model was adapted from a set of computable general equilibrium models of Yugoslavia that reflected the special features of socialist trade and self-management (Vujovic and Labus (1990), and Adelman, Vujovic, Berck and Labus, (1990)). For the current experiments with reform we made these models more neoclassical. We suppressed the distinction between convertible and clearing-currency (CMEA)trade. In reality, CMEA clearing-trade lists have been abolished and prices for trade among CMEA countries are set in hard currency at world prices. There is therefore no loss in generality in treating all trade as convertible-currency trade. We also made wage distribution rules more neoclassical, removing the specific wage setting rules in force in that model and replacing them with marginal productivity rules. The demand side of the labor market was already neoclassical in the model from which we started. We used a fixed exchange rate closure in foreign trade and either a fixed-wage or a full-employment closure in the labor market. This made the model a standard CGE with the usual features: two level CES production functions with three labor skills and sector specific capital but mobile labor; linear expenditure systems for consumption by each of three classes of households (rural, urban and mixed rural-urban); Armington import functions and constant elasticity of transformation domestic and export supply functions; and market-clearing prices for commodities. There was only one nontradeable sector, "non-productive services". This sector is also the only one consumed by government. The exchange rate was used as numeraire.

The CGE-base for comparison was a base with tariffs and subsidies imposed on the initial SAM of table 1, the "market-price-SAM" in actual 1987 prices, to make it equivalent to the revealed-MESS-SAM of table 5 that incorporates existing consumer and producer rents. The SAM used for the base-CGE replaces consumer and producer rents with sets of commodity-taxes or subsidies and import-tariffs on activities; and a set of consumer and producer lump-sum transfers for institutions. The new tax instruments include "quota-tariffs" on imports and domestic-commodity taxes; investment subsidies, production subsidies, and subsidies compensating for negative producer rents to enterprises; and consumption subsidies to consumers. Of these, the subsidies compensating for negative producer rents and the consumption subsidies are lump-sum. The investment subsidies in fixed assets are ad-valorem, computed through the investment matrix, on exogenously specified investment by sector of destination. The production subsidies were ad valorem, and were computed on both current use of intermediate inputs and net changes in inventories. The net balance of these transfers is absorbed by government savings. One can think of this step as "revealing the MESS". The solution of the base CGE reproduces the real activities and real income flows underlying the revealed-MESS-SAM of table 5, just as the theory indicated it would. It thus generates a SAM that is identical to table 5. This is the departure point for the experiments with reform.

There is some question whether, psychologically, the participants in the economy actually perceive the SAM of table 5 or whether they have the "money illusion" of the SAM of table 1. We believe that perceptions are split between the two tables, and that herein lies one of the socio-psychological difficulties of the transition process. We believe that consumers and producers in socialist economies perceive the incomes of table 5 and the lower prices of table 1, forgetting or suppressing the rent-seeking activities, barter, and grey-market transactions that accompany the SAM of table 1. They thus have an inconsistent picture of their reality. Part of the transition process involves making the economic actors aware of the SAM of table 5, by revealing the correct prices underlying the SAM of table 1, so that their perceptions become internally consistent.

The experiments with transition reported below represent two kinds of reform processes: reductions in taxes and subsidies, on the one hand, and changes in the institutional rules underlying factor and commodity markets, on the other. Reductions in taxes and subsidies are necessary to convert a third-best equilibrium into a second-best one. We calculate two steps in the tax reform process– a 50% cut in all taxes and subsidies imposed to transform the table-1 SAM into the table-5 SAM, and the full abolition of all of these taxes (100% cut). When tariffs, taxes, and subsidies are completely removed, the (exogenously set) exchange rate is devalued to the value calculated for the "true" exchange rate by comparing the revealed-MESS-SAM and the original SAM. The devaluation is set at half this amount for the 50% tax/subsidy reductions. This part of the reform process can be thought of as "undoing the MESS

For each of these tax-cum-subsidy-reduction steps we model cumulative reforms in commodity and factor market institutions. The first stage of reform consists of neoclassical clearing of commodity markets with no capital markets i.e. capital remaining sector specific. The second stage consists of freeing capital markets as well. This stage is modelled by allowing capital stock to move between sectors in the short run so as to equalize rates of return. The reallocation of capital is decided within the general equilibrium framework of the model.

Each of these institutional regimes is considered with two different types of labor markets. In the first labor market, worker pressures and unions are strong enough to maintain nominal wages but firing and hiring of workers is possible. In the second labor market, firms are able to set wages, but there is a target employment level at the macro-economic level (in most of our experiments the target employment level is full-employment).

Each stage of reform is also calculated with or without some increases in factor productivity. Increases in labor productivity are likely for either of two reasons: the fear of firing combined with the possibility of real wage improvements under the first type of labor market regime or the fear of decline in both nominal and real wages under the second type. Increases in capital productivity are likely to result from the liberalization of the trade regime, with the availability of freer imports of intermediates and upgrading of machinery. The productivity improvements assumed in the experiments are mild, averaging 4.5% for capital and 1.7% for labor.

Table 6 summarizes some of the sectoral results while table 7 presents the macroeconomic results of reform. We focus mostly on the full MESS reduction, 100% cut, results. The 50% cut results are similar in character, but less dramatic in effect. Reducing taxes and subsidies is a deflationary process. This means that the tax reform is always good for exports and usually for the trade balance.[5] The general deflation extends to the consumer price index but food prices rise relative to the consumer price index. The reforms are therefore always good for the rural sector. Depending on the labor market regime, nominal wages remain either constant or fall, but the real wages of the employed always rise. Nevertheless, unless the commodity market reforms are accompanied by capital market reforms, urban real incomes and real consumption decline.

---

[5]The exceptions to this are in the commodity plus capital market experiments with fixed nominal wages and 50% and 100% tax/subsidy reductions and the commodity plus capital market experiments with flexible nominal wages and 100% tax/subsidy reduction. The trade balances in these experiments are, respectively, 96.7%, 92.4% and 72% of base.

Table 6 Main reform experiments
Real sectoral data (base = 100)

	Base Values	Commodity markets reform				Capital markets reform			
		Fixed wages 50%	100%	F.employment 50%	100%	Fixed wages 50%	100%	F.employment 50%	100%
Employment									
AGRI	1009.6	96.6	93.6	97.8	95.7	100.3	99.9	101.5	102.0
ENER	155.2	99.7	100.3	101.7	103.7	102.6	104.9	103.7	106.9
IRON	132.3	102.8	108.4	106.8	115.6	103.3	107.4	105.2	111.0
META	763.0	98.1	96.5	100.2	100.2	101.0	101.5	102.5	104.3
CHEM	187.1	100.8	103.1	104.0	108.8	103.9	107.6	105.8	111.2
TEXT	547.4	96.2	92.6	98.4	96.5	100.3	99.6	102.5	103.5
FOOD	246.4	95.5	91.8	97.1	94.5	101.8	102.7	103.7	106.0
OTIN	424.8	94.0	89.2	96.0	92.5	99.5	98.5	101.3	101.6
CNST	691.9	100.1	100.4	100.6	101.3	101.0	101.9	101.5	102.7
TRAN	1141.5	98.0	96.3	99.8	99.5	102.1	103.3	103.8	106.4
OPSE	674.1	101.1	102.8	102.8	106.0	104.6	108.8	106.4	112.2
NPSE	1071.1	100.0	100.0	100.0	100.0	110.3	117.8	110.4	117.7
TOTAL	7044.4	98.6	97.7	100.0	100.0	103.8	106.5	105.0	108.6
By skill									
High skilled	520.4	99.3	98.7	100.0	100.0	106.8	111.6	105.0	108.6
Skilled	1053.1	99.0	98.5	100.0	100.0	104.4	107.6	105.0	108.6
Unskilled	5470.9	98.5	97.3	100.0	100.0	103.1	105.2	105.0	108.6
Capital stock									
AGRI	22745.6	100.0	100.0	100.0	100.0	100.6	95.4	97.6	95.0
ENER	24628.2	100.0	100.0	100.0	100.0	104.7	103.3	102.6	104.5
IRON	10241.4	100.0	100.0	100.0	100.0	103.9	103.1	101.8	104.4
META	14432.5	100.0	100.0	100.0	100.0	101.3	97.0	98.6	97.2
CHEM	9631.1	100.0	100.0	100.0	100.0	104.2	102.8	101.8	103.6
TEXT	6668.9	100.0	100.0	100.0	100.0	99.8	94.0	96.8	93.5
FOOD	8551.4	100.0	100.0	100.0	100.0	101.4	96.9	98.4	96.5
OTIN	9425.8	100.0	100.0	100.0	100.0	99.8	94.1	97.1	94.2
CNST	7792.4	100.0	100.0	100.0	100.0	103.0	100.1	100.0	99.8
TRAN	35797.5	100.0	100.0	100.0	100.0	101.6	97.5	98.7	97.2
OPSE	15753.5	100.0	100.0	100.0	100.0	104.1	102.6	100.9	102.0
NPSE	13711.5	100.0	100.0	100.0	100.0	113.7	117.7	110.6	117.7
TOTAL	179379.7	100.0	100.0	100.0	100.0	103.0	100.0	100.2	100.0
Production									
AGRI	10757.8	97.8	95.9	98.7	97.2	99.3	98.2	100.0	97.8
ENER	7324.2	99.9	100.1	100.5	101.0	101.9	103.7	102.7	103.2
IRON	5622.9	101.0	102.9	102.4	105.3	101.7	104.7	102.8	103.7
META	15418.3	98.9	98.1	100.1	100.1	99.7	99.4	100.6	98.7
CHEM	7008.0	100.3	101.2	101.6	103.4	102.2	104.7	103.3	103.7
TEXT	7987.4	98.7	95.7	99.1	98.0	98.9	97.2	99.9	96.8
FOOD	9321.2	98.1	96.6	98.8	97.7	99.8	99.2	100.4	98.9
OTIN	6107.6	97.2	94.8	98.1	96.4	98.1	96.2	98.9	95.7
CNST	8264.0	100.1	100.3	100.5	101.1	100.8	101.5	101.1	101.1
TRAN	13484.3	98.9	97.9	99.9	99.7	100.5	100.7	101.4	100.2
OPSE	10166.5	100.7	102.0	102.0	104.1	103.5	106.9	104.7	106.3
NPSE	14224.7	100.0	100.0	100.0	100.0	110.3	117.8	110.4	115.1
TOTAL	115686.9	99.2	98.7	100.1	100.2	101.7	103.0	102.5	102.2

For acronyms see footnote to Table 1.

Table 6 (cont.) Main reform experiments
Real sectoral data (base = 100)

	Base	Commodity markets reform				Capital markets reform			
	Values	Fixed wages		F.employment		Fixed wages		F.employment	
		50%	100%	50%	100%	50%	100%	50%	100%
Net exports									
AGRI	-317.6	98.2	99.1	92.2	89.5	103.2	107.9	100.1	110.5
ENER	-1196.1	98.8	98.1	98.5	97.7	101.8	103.1	101.8	103.2
IRON	93.9	130.9	173.8	156.7	215.7	119.2	162.3	137.3	148.8
META	-596.4	97.5	93.5	76.5	58.9	110.4	115.5	98.0	125.2
CHEM	-784.6	94.7	88.7	89.9	80.7	101.1	98.8	98.3	100.7
TEXT	650.8	98.0	94.5	106.0	108.2	94.5	87.7	99.4	84.4
FOOD	122.7	90.7	79.8	107.6	108.1	81.0	61.5	90.6	53.8
OTIN	291.4	96.7	94.7	106.2	110.2	89.7	82.2	95.6	78.2
CNST	557.4	101.4	103.1	103.6	106.8	101.3	103.0	102.7	102.0
TRAN	1814.3	100.7	101.8	104.3	107.8	100.6	101.4	102.8	99.8
OPSE	322.4	132.9	169.3	158.2	210.5	122.6	153.7	137.5	142.4
NPSE	0.0	0.0	0.0	0.0	0.0	0.0	0.0	0.0	0.0
TOTAL	958.3	120.7	143.8	169.6	224.5	91.3	94.9	120.6	72.9
Relative prices[a]									
AGRI	100.0	104.4	111.8	103.8	110.4	112.9	127.5	112.3	124.6
ENER	100.0	95.1	93.2	98.0	98.0	102.4	104.5	103.0	101.2
IRON	100.0	97.2	96.0	98.7	98.3	104.0	106.2	104.1	103.1
META	100.0	102.4	108.0	103.6	109.8	110.0	121.5	110.3	118.0
CHEM	100.0	97.2	96.8	99.0	99.6	104.3	108.2	104.9	104.6
TEXT	100.0	101.1	105.0	101.0	104.4	109.5	120.2	109.0	116.9
FOOD	100.0	101.4	105.3	101.0	104.4	110.2	121.2	109.6	118.2
OTIN	100.0	107.3	118.7	107.5	118.8	117.4	138.2	116.9	134.4
CNST	100.0	98.0	98.8	97.1	97.1	105.5	111.6	104.5	109.2
TRAN	100.0	100.8	104.9	99.7	102.9	109.0	119.5	108.1	116.9
OPSE	100.0	95.0	92.6	94.7	92.0	102.0	103.9	101.5	101.3
NPSE	100.0	100.0	100.0	100.0	100.0	100.0	100.0	100.0	100.0
TOTAL	100.0	100.0	102.7	100.3	103.1	107.8	116.2	107.5	113.1

[a]Traded vs nontraded.
For acronyms see footnote to Table 1.

Table 7a Institutional reform in commodity and factor markets
Reform of all commodity markets
Real aggregate results (base = 100)

	Base	Fixed nominal wages Tax/subs reduction			Fixed employement Tax/subs reduction		
		50%	100%	100%+e	50%	100%	100%+e
GDP							
Total GDP	62856	99.3	98.7	101.6	99.8	99.6	102.7
Consumption	42201	98.6	97.3	100.6	98.4	97.0	100.3
Investment	19697	99.6	99.3	99.6	99.4	98.9	99.1
Exports	11465	101.2	103.0	106.4	104.0	107.7	112.3
Imports	-10507	99.4	99.3	99.8	98.0	97.0	97.2
Labor markets							
Nominal wages	1.000	100.0	100.0	100.0	93.1	89.0	87.0
Employemnt[a]	7044	98.6	97.7	97.1	100.0	100.0	100.0
Real wages	1.000	103.2	107.9	112.2	101.1	104.3	107.8
Prices							
GDP deflator	1.000	97.8	93.8	89.3	92.7	85.9	80.4
CPI	1.000	96.9	92.7	89.2	92.1	85.3	80.7
Food prices	1.000	99.4	97.2	93.5	94.1	88.9	84.0
Exchange rate	1.000	106.1	112.6	112.6	106.1	112.6	112.6
Disposable income							
Rural	2230	99.7	100.6	103.8	100.3	101.8	105.4
Mixed	8602	97.8	96.1	99.1	97.5	95.6	98.7
Urban	21018	97.0	94.0	96.8	96.7	93.5	96.3
Household consumption[b]							
Rural	1981	100.2	101.8	105.0	100.5	102.4	105.9
Mixed	7670	98.3	97.3	100.4	97.9	96.8	99.8
Urban	18048	97.1	94.1	96.9	96.8	93.6	96.5
Government							
Expenditure	14502	100.5	100.7	104.7	100.4	100.6	102.2
Savings	2474	91.7	80.7	79.1	87.3	74.4	71.8

[a] In thousand of employed persons.
[b] Including own consumption.

Table 7b Institutional reform in commodity and factor markets
Reform of commodity and capital markets
Real aggregate results (base = 100)

	Base	Fixed nominal wages Tax/subs reduction			Fixed employement Tax/subs reduction		
		50%	100%	100%+e	50%	100%	100%+e
GDP							
Total GDP	62856	102.8	104.8	106.3	103.3	105.7	108.6
Consumption	42201	104.6	107.4	108.7	104.8	107.7	109.8
Investment	19697	99.5	99.1	99.3	99.4	98.8	98.7
Exports	11465	101.3	103.2	106.2	103.1	106.4	113.3
Imports	-10507	102.2	103.9	103.3	101.5	102.6	100.9
Labor markets							
Nominal wages	1.000	100.0	100.0	100.0	96.1	93.4	85.8
Employemnt[a]	7044	103.8	106.5	103.7	105.0	108.6	108.6
Real wages	1.000	101.5	105.0	109.6	100.6	103.4	105.1
Prices							
GDP deflator	1.000	97.6	93.3	89.1	94.6	88.2	78.9
CPI	1.000	98.5	95.2	91.2	95.6	90.3	81.6
Food prices	1.000	101.8	101.5	96.9	98.7	94.3	86.4
Exchange rate	1.000	106.1	112.6	112.6	106.1	112.6	112.6
Disposable income							
Rural	2230	102.0	104.5	106.5	102.7	105.7	109.3
Mixed	8602	101.0	101.5	103.2	101.4	102.2	104.1
Urban	21018	100.3	99.3	100.9	100.6	100.0	101.8
Household consumption[b]							
Rural	1981	102.8	106.2	108.1	103.2	104.6	110.0
Mixed	7670	101.5	102.8	104.4	101.8	102.4	105.2
Urban	18048	100.3	99.5	101.0	100.7	100.8	101.9
Government							
Expenditure	14502	111.7	119.9	120.5	111.6	119.7	122.0
Savings	2474	96.4	87.6	84.7	93.9	83.5	76.5

[a] In thousand of employed persons.
[b] Including own consumption.

Table 7c Institutional reform in commodity and factor markets
Deaprtures from the initial design of the
gradual transition to market economy
Real aggregate results (base = 100)

	Base	Biased reduction in Tax/subs	Wage push inflation spiral 1	2	3	4	Increased cons. from gvmnt
GDP							
Total GDP	62856	99.3	99.3	99.1	98.9	98.7	100.1
Consumption	42201	98.8	98.6	98.7	98.7	98.8	99.9
Investment	19697	99.8	99.6	99.7	99.8	99.9	99.5
Exports	11465	100.2	101.2	100.3	99.3	98.3	101.9
Imports	-10507	99.4	99.4	100.0	100.5	101.1	100.3
Labor markets							
Nominal wages	1.000	100.0	100.0	102.5	107.2	114.2	98.4
Employemnt[a]	7044	98.6	98.6	98.2	97.7	97.3	100.0
Real wages	1.000	101.3	103.2	103.9	104.7	105.4	101.9
Prices							
GDP deflator	1.000	100.0	97.8	99.7	103.6	109.8	96.6
CPI	1.000	98.7	96.9	98.7	102.4	108.3	96.5
Food prices	1.000	100.3	99.4	101.3	105.3	111.5	99.0
Exchange rate	1.000	104.0	106.1	106.1	108.1	112.3	106.1
Disposable income							
Rural	2230	98.7	99.7	99.5	99.3	99.1	100.8
Mixed	8602	97.7	97.8	97.9	98.0	98.1	100.5
Urban	21018	97.6	97.0	97.1	97.2	97.3	99.6
Household consumption[b]							
Rural	1981	99.0	100.2	100.1	100.0	100.0	101.0
Mixed	7670	98.0	98.3	98.4	98.6	98.7	100.6
Urban	18048	97.6	97.1	97.2	97.3	97.4	99.6
Government							
Expenditure	14502	100.6	100.5	100.5	100.5	100.5	99.8
Savings	2474	97.8	91.7	93.4	95.1	96.8	88.1

[a] In thousand of employed persons.
[b] Including own consumption.

The static effects of the reforms are not dramatic. Commodity market reforms unaccompanied by the establishment of capital markets lead to slight declines in real GDP, consumption, urban and mixed household disposable incomes and consumption unless accompanied by improvements in efficiency. Improvements come mostly from the liberalization of capital markets and from efficiency gains.

The reform scenario with the most adjustment pain is that of commodity reform without capital markets and with fixed nominal wages. In the three experiments reflecting this scenario we have up to 2.9% additional unemployment[6], drops in urban real disposable incomes and consumption of up to 6%, and about six sectors with declining employment. In the experiment reflecting complete removal of MESS taxes and subsidies, shifts in the structure of relative prices range from -7.4% (other productive services) to +18.7% (other industry). Government savings decline by about 20%. Since government savings include interest payments to banks, this decline indicates a sharp increase in the traditionally defined government deficit. This is the scenario that both the population and the government of socialist countries fear. Of course, in our gradual approach we reach it only in the second step.

The brunt of the transition cost is borne by non-wage income recipients and, ultimately, household consumption. This reflects cuts in lump-sum transfers and affects urban households most heavily. Their real income is almost 6% lower at the end of the transition process. There is an export boom due to devaluation reinforced by a significant (6.2%) net domestic deflation caused by the removal of MESS taxes/subsidies. The growth of exports partially compensates for the decline of all other components of GDP. The trade surplus improves more than 40% contributing to an improved external position of the country. The proportionate reduction in MESS taxes/subsidies changes relative prices which, in turn, drive changes in sectoral production and sectoral composition of trade. The production of wage goods falls and the production of heavy industry and services goes up. Given the fixed nominal wages and fixed capital stock by sector, sectoral employment bears the brunt of induced changes in sectoral production. The dislocations in the labor force are substantial: 240 thousand or 3.4% of the employed lose their jobs; of these 80 thousand find jobs in expanding sectors. But this is the most disruptive reform scenario. However, it is noteworthy that, even in this worst-case scenario, the nightmare of governments and East European populations — the economy falling apart — does not materialize.

The flexible wage scenario suggests a rather good tradeoff between wages and unemployment. In this scenario, real wages are lower (by between 2 and 3 percentage points) than in the fixed wage case, but they are still above the base and there is no new unemployment. In addition, the foreign trade balance

---

[6]Base unemployment in Yugoslavia, excluding workers temporarily employed abroad, was about 13% of the labor force in 1987. Total unemployment under this scenario is thus 15.9%.

is considerably better (70% better than in the reform with fixed nominal wages and 2.25 times better than the base) thus assuaging fears that liberalizing trade will endanger the country's external position. However, the government deficit is somewhat larger and mixed and urban households are faced with somewhat lower (0.5%) real incomes and consumption. The dislocations in the labor force are considerably smaller than with the fixed wage scenario: 113 thousand people or 1.6% of the employed must change jobs from contracting to expanding sectors. The pattern of relative price changes and the pattern of expanding and contracting sectors is very similar to that of the fixed nominal wage scenario.

The introduction of capital markets generates a substantial relative improvement over the base, especially when efficiency gains are added. In macroeconomic terms, the transition looks virtually painless, except for a slight deterioration in trade balance over the base. But our model overstates the immediate gains to be expected from the introduction of a capital market, since it is based on a degree of capital reallocation among sectors which can only be accomplished over a period of time, say two or three years. The capital stock in six sectors declines, with the largest decline being 6% (textiles and other industries). The largest expansion of capital stock (17.7%) is recorded in non-productive services, a sector with a small capital stock (see table 6 for details).

The impact of capital markets can be gauged by comparing equivalent labor market scenarios with and without capital markets. With fixed nominal wages, the introduction of capital markets makes the largest difference: GDP is 6.1% higher, employment is larger by 8.8%, and household incomes and consumption are about 5% above the comparable scenario without the capital market. The losses in urban household real incomes are virtually wiped out by the introduction of capital markets.

The "best" scenario involves gains in factor efficiency. These were assumed to be rather small, (for details see table 8 below) and represent orders of magnitude that might be expected realistically to occur annually, once institutional reforms are carried out. These productivity gains cannot be expected to occur in the absence of the sorts of reforms in factor and commodity markets that are represented in our experiments, although it is probably not necessary to go to the 100% reduction in taxes and subsidies to achieve them. The achievement of gains in productivity has been the major, rather elusive, aim of past partial reforms introduced in most socialist economies. It is also the main driving force behind the desire for sweeping reforms of the socialist economies of Eastern Europe.

Table 8 Efficiency increases (in %)

| | Overall | Capital | Labor | | |
			High Skilled	Skilled	Unskilled
AGRI	1.0	0.0	1.0	0.0	0.0
ENER	0.0	5.0	1.0	0.0	0.0
IRON	0.0	10.0	2.0	3.0	3.0
META	0.0	5.0	2.0	2.0	2.0
CHEM	1.0	10.0	2.0	2.0	2.0
TEXT	1.0	3.0	3.0	1.0	1.0
FOOD	0.0	5.0	3.0	1.0	1.0
OTIN	0.0	2.0	2.0	1.0	1.0
CNST	0.0	0.0	2.0	3.0	3.0
TRAN	0.0	5.0	2.0	1.0	1.0
OPSE	0.0	4.0	2.0	3.0	3.0
NPSE	0.0	4.0	2.0	3.0	3.0
TOTAL	0.2	4.3	1.9	2.0	1.6

For acronyms see footnote to Table 1.

With productivity gains which average 4.3% for capital and 1.7% for labor, and a .2% gain in overall efficiency, the reform does not produce economic contraction under any of our institutional scenarios. Efficiency gains contribute most to improved macroeconomic performance when the institutional setup approaches the neoclassical ideal, adding 4.7 percentage points to GDP. They contribute least to GDP when capital markets function but labor markets are rigid (1.5%). Exports react most and investment reacts least to efficiency gains. Across all experiments, higher efficiency benefits all consumer groups, especially rural households.

Our results thus suggest that a less painful transition from socialism to capitalism than is feared by East Europeans in the throes of reform is possible. They also indicate that the static gains from reform are rather limited. Furthermore, they are once-and-for-all gains. The major gains from reform are dynamic, and reside in the continuing increases in factor productivity which they make possible. Their achievement requires effort, commitment to reform, and government credibility. In the meantime, many things can go wrong. We explore a few, alas not unlikely, scenarios for sabotaging the reform effort.

6   Ways in which the reform can go wrong

Our model results substantially understate the difficulties of reform for many reasons. On the modeling side, we have not incorporated asset and monetary effects that are likely to contribute to inflation. We have also not modelled imperfect information, expectations and uncertainty. Nor have we depicted socio-political opposition to reform or lags in adjustment.

Our results assume that the actors in the system know their production functions. It is not clear that they do. What they know are the input-output relationships with existing, distorted, prices and quotas and under existing institutional constraints on the use of labor.

Our results also assume that management objectives shift smoothly from those pursued under socialism to profit maximization. In reality, this shift is one that needs to be learned. Currently, socialist managers are engaged in optimizing net rents. This implies maximizing rationed inputs, investment allocations, credit and foreign exchange allotments, and direct subsidies while minimizing output targets. They are skilled negotiators with the government and with other enterprises, and have built up a personal network of relationships and reciprocal claims that enables them to carry out these negotiations successfully. In the existing institutional environment,their technical and managerial skills, even if they were originally trained as engineers and economists, have fallen into disuse. At best, one can identify some top managers who would be good managers of public enterprises in a market environment. Very few among them would make good managers in a corporate private enterprise sector. Although a lot of socialist managers have become increasingly aware that the present rent-seeking system is not macroeconomically viable, what they see as the alternative is even less attractive to them personally. It makes some of their personal capital (access to the network), management skills, and management structure within their enterprises obsolete, and depreciates their effectiveness and comparative advantage. They have every personal incentive to oppose the transition. They can mobilize the support of politicians and bureaucrats who, directly or indirectly, appointed them to their present posts, as well as the support of workers who feel threatened by the uncertainties of the reform. By contrast, unlike top managers, technocrats at intermediate levels have every incentive to support a transition to market systems. Their skills have been greatly depreciated by the current system and, they have also been severely underpaid, even relative to other workers.

Substantial opposition to reform is also likely to come from some currently employed workers. The transition is likely to be opposed by those employed workers who do not expect labor markets and market competition to provide them with jobs or with better career opportunities. Presently, employees enjoy a low but certain cash income, relatively large fringe benefits, and complete job security. The present system suits best well-established, settled, middle-aged, skilled workers who either have second jobs (moonlighting or private agriculture) or enjoy rent-seeking privileges in their social sector job. It is, therefore, likely that the opposition of middle-aged and older workers will be more pronounced, reflecting their smaller taste for risk, and their awareness of their lower ability to compete in the labor market or to start an independent small business. By contrast, the young are likely to favor the reform and competition for jobs, since 80% of the presently unemployed in Yugoslavia are skilled, below the age of 35, and waiting for their first job. Employees in social sector companies are most likely to oppose the reform. The opposition to reform is likely to be strongest in large subsidized firms, reflecting both the possibility of losing subsidies and larger layoffs. The opposition is likely to be weaker in smaller firms and firms with better economic performance.

Even aside from well-defined opposition by certain groups, the reform process greatly increases the degree of uncertainty in the system. Individuals and groups are generally risk averse, especially in socialist economies, one of whose main advantages is a great deal of predictability. Our model does not reflect the increased uncertainty and does not model reactions to this increase. To make the reform acceptable, the public needs to be educated that it can be fully compensated in a static sense for the benefits it currently enjoys under the socialist system. The government needs to convince the public that both the details and the overall scheme of the reform are well thought out, internally consistent, and will be applied in practice. Both the government and the program, therefore, need to have credibility. The government also has to have the ability to manage conflict and the explosion of desires and expectations.

In our modeling we have disregarded the role of conflict and expectations in the reform process. Expectations take the form of both desires and fears, and motivate both support and opposition to the reform process. As consumers, the population of socialist countries wants the results it anticipates from reform. As producers, the population fears reform, especially without the sort of legal safety nets built up in the corporate welfare states of the current OECD economies.

Furthermore, as indicated earlier, the population probably does not have an accurate perception of its actual situation. It sees the rationed consumer prices, which our calculations indicate are 15% lower than the rent-or-tax-inclusive prices in the original SAM, while perceiving the living standards of the revealed-MESS-SAM. Price increases brought about by an effort to reveal the consistent picture underlying the existing reality are likely to be interpreted as the beginning of an inflationary spiral. The reform process itself, starting from the revealed-MESS-SAM is deflationary. But people are likely to be aware of the declines in their nominal wages, and unaware that the deflation actually raises their real wages. Scenarios in which workers attempt to defend their nominal incomes and thereby start an inflationary process are therefore likely.

We have modeled the beginnings of such a scenario starting from the 50% MESS-cut with fixed nominal wages (for details see the next to last four colums of table 7). In this scenario, organized workers exert pressure to maintain their nominal wages (step 1). Then, when they realize that their real disposable incomes are 2.5% lower, despite higher real wages, they demand and get nominal wage increases of 2.5%. This, however, leaves them only imperceptibly better off when all is said and done (step 2). But the economy's balance of trade worsens. This invokes macroeconomic intervention by the government: in an effort to maintain the current account balance, the government devalues by about 2% over step 2. This time organized workers anticipate the effect of the devaluation on their real incomes. They demand nominal wage increases designed to prevent the erosion in the purchasing power of their wages stemming both from past inflation and anticipated current devaluation. The result is the same as in step two, but at an even higher price level, and higher balance of trade deficit. The ensuing devaluation and frustrated efforts at recouping real wages set another round of wage increases and inflation in motion in step 4. By this time the price level has jumped by 6.2% and nominal wages by 7%, about twice as rapidly as in the previous step. The process acccelerates even without the effect of expectations and monetary/asset phenomena.

A better approach to maintaining real incomes is modelled in the last column of table 7, in which, starting from the 50% MESS-cut with fixed nominal wages, the government phases out household subsidies less rapidly than other MESS tax/subsidy instruments. While all other MESS subsidies are cut in half, nominal consumer subsidies are only cut by 15%, on average. This succeeds in maintaining real disposable incomes in this scenario at the base level. The decline in non-rural household real incomes in the face of rising real wages, observed in our reform scenarios without capital markets, is, in part, due to phasing-out of consumption subsidies. In rural households the phasing-out effect is overpowered by the large share of own consumption and foreign remittances. In the absence of capital markets, attempts to prevent the decline in non-rural household incomes through the labor market are bound to be frustrated, as our inflationary spiral scenario indicates.

Column 14 of table 7 includes a "government-cold-feet" experiment as well, again starting from the 50% MESS-cut with fixed nominal wages. In this scenario, the government reacts to calm fears of excessive budgetary cost of the reform, of consumer prices getting out of hand and of the trade balance deteriorating, by departing from initially conceived cuts in MESS taxes and subsidies. In designing this experiment, we tried to reflect the traditional socialist biases. Specifically, to protect consumers, the government retains subsidies in basic consumer goods (food, energy, transport, and non-productive services). To pursue the present industrialization and trade strategies, it continues to protect strategic (energy, iron) and "infant" export sectors (textiles, food, and metals) relatively more than other sectors. It also devalues less than in the 50% scenario, from a fear of inflation. Strategic sectors continue to receive relatively greater production subsidies along with some basic consumer good sectors (food and non-productive services). Finally, energy and transportation continue to be perceived as public infrastructure sectors, which deserve relatively higher investment subsidies. In all these departures, the cuts are in MESS taxes/subsidies are 25 rather than 50 percent.

The results are mixed compared to those of the 50% across the board MESS-cut experiment. The effects on GDP are neutral, as minor increases in consumption and investment are offset by worse export performance. Real wages improve less. The consumption-support program injures rural and mixed households slightly. Only urban households benefit relative to the 50% across the board MESS cut. The government deficit is considerably smaller, due to higher tariff, sales and value added tax collections.[7] With these departures from uniform cuts, the government thus trades off a worse external balance for a better relative position of urban households and for the pursuit of its concept of industrialization.

7 Conclusion

Our calculations provide a blueprint for a consistent approach to the reform of commodity and labor institutions of socialist countries. In our paper, we calculate the magnites of distortions introduced by the socialist system of prices and controls, and assign their incidence across the economy. The reform process consists of simultaneously lifting the socialist controls and substituting the MESS-tax/subsidy system for the existing incidence of rents. We then gradually phase out the MESS.(!)

The results of our calculations suggest that a smooth, relatively painless, transition is economically possible. They also suggest, however, that the static economic benefits attendant upon such a transition are likely to be small and delayed. The major benefits to be expected from reforms are their dynamic impact: the continuing productivity gains which the reform will enable to take place.

Our results and discussion also indicate that the transition process is fraught with pitfalls. As in any economic change, there will be winners and losers. Those who anticipate being potential losers are likely to oppose reform and demand guarantees whose granting will make the transition process more painful than it needs to be and whose outcome is likely to be self defeating. Those who anticipate being potential gainers, and who feel blocked and frustrated by the existing economic system, will favor reform. The conflict among potential gainers and losers is likely to be aggravated by regional and ethnic strife. As a result, uncertainty, fear, and conflict are likely to dominate the actual transition process, despite the inherent economic potential for a smooth transition indicated by our results.

Institutions are not only rules and regulations but also behavior patterns and skills. Institutional reform therefore requires a learning process consisting of the acquisition of new behavior patterns and requiring new skills. It also requires the, perhaps more difficult, process of unlearning behavior patterns and skills that were appropriate to the old institutions but are appropriate no longer. Our

---

[7]Sales and value added taxes are ad valorem, and the price level is higher.

modelling effort assumes that this process occurs instantaneously and without friction.

In assessing the real-world import of our results, one should also bear in mind that our model excludes the financial aspects of the transition. Our model does not incorporate the asset-transfer phenomena involved in the privatization of industry and of the housing stock and does not reflect the macroeconomic and financial implications of these asset transfers. We have also not considered the problems generated by the liquidity overhang that characterizes most socialist countries. We therefore substantially understate the inflationary potential of the transition and the likely opposition to the assumption of public-sector-enterprise debt by the government that may be a necessary, but inflationary, component of the transition. This inflationary potential will be reinforced by expectations and by group pressures to maintain present real incomes.

In generalizing our results to transition problems in other socialist countries, one should also bear in mind that they apply to Yugoslavia as of 1987. Yugoslavia is the least economically distorted socialist country; it has the longest experience with the introduction of market aspects and decentralized microeconomic decision making into its economic system; it is internationally more competitive, as it has imported a large proportion of its equipment and technology from the West; and it has recently succeeded in making its currency convertible into hard currency without much of a ripple.

In view of all these considerations, our paper should be regarded more as a "possibility theorem" than as a forecast.

8   References

Adelman, I. (1967) *Practical Approaches to Development Planning: Korea's Second Five Year Plan*, Baltimore: Hopkins University Press.

Adelman, I., D.Vujovic, P. Berck and M. Labus (1990), Adjustment under different trade strategies: a mean-variance analysis with a CGE model of the Yugoslav economy, in J. de Melo and A. Sapir, eds., *Trade Theory and Economic Reform: North, South and East - Essays in Honor of Bela Balassa*, Cambridge: Basil Blackwell.

Adelman, I., P. Berck and D. Vujovic (1991), Using social accounting matrices to account for distortions in non-market economies, *Economic Systems Research* 3, 269-298.

Amsden, A. (1989), *Asia's Next Giant: South Korea and Late Industrialization*, Oxford: Oxford University Press.

Balassa, B. (1990), Perestroika and its implications for European Socialist countries, World Bank Working Paper 428.

Baumol, W.J. and W. E. Oates (1988), *The Theory of Environmental Policy*, Cambridge: Cambridge University Press.

Berg, A. and J. Sachs (1992), Structural adjustment and international trade in Eastern Europe: the case of Poland, *Economic Policy*, forthcoming.

Bhagwati, J.N. (1965), On the equivalence of tariffs and quotas, in R. E. Baldwin et al., eds., *Trade, Growth and the Balance of Payments*, Chicago: Rand McNally.

Bhagwati, J.N. (1978), *Foreign Trade Regimes and Economic Development: Anatomy and Consequences of Exchange Control Regimes*, Lexington: Ballinger for the National Bureau of Econmic Research.

Bhagwati, J.N. and T.N. Srinivasan(1976), Revenue-seeking: a generalization of the theory of tariffs, *Journal of Political Economy* 88, 1069-87.

Blanchard, O. (1990), Elements of a reform program, Unpublished manuscript, Massachusets Institute of Technology.

Bourguignon, F. and C. Morrisson (1992), *Adjustment and Equity in Developing countries*, OECD Development Center.

Bruno, M. (1992), Stabilization and reform in Eastern Europe: a preliminary evaluation, Mimeo, Washington: IMF.

Clague, C. and G. Rausser, eds. (1992), *The Emergence of Market Economies in Eastern Europe*, Oxford: Blackwell.

Commander, S. (1992), Inflation and the transition to a market economy: an overview, *World Bank Economic Review* 6.

Coricelli, F. and R. de Redenza Rocha (1991), Stabilization programs in Eastern Europe, World Bank Working Papers732.

Csaba, L. (1991), *Systemic Change and Stabilization in Eastern Europe*, Dartmouth: Dartmouth Press.

Danji, F. and B. Milanovic (1991), Privatization in Eastern and Central Europe, World Bank Working Papers 770.

Diamond, P.A. and J.A. Mirrlees (1971), Optimal taxation and public production, *American Economic Review* 61, 8-27.

Dornbush R. (1991), Policies to move from stabilization to growth, Annual Conference on Development 1990, The World Bank.

Edwards, S. (1992), Stabilization and liberalization policies for economies in transition: Latin American lessons for Eastern Europe, in Clague and Rausser, eds., *The Emergence of Market Economies in Eastern Europe*, Oxford: Blackwell.

Felix, D. (1991), Reflections on privatizing and rolling back the Latin American states, Working Paper 162, Washington University.

Galal, A. (1991), Public enterprise reform, World Bank Discussion Paper 119.

Harberger, A. (1992), Strategies for transition, in Clague and Rausser, eds., *The Emergence of Market Economies in Eastern Europe*, Oxford: Blackwell.

Hinds, M. and G. Pohl (1991), Going to market: privatization in Central and Eastern Europe, World Bank Working Paper 768.

International Monetary Fund (1986), Fund supported programs, fiscal policy and income distribution, Occasional Paper 46, International Monetary Fund.

Krueger, A. (1974), The political economy of the rent-seeking society, *American Economic Review* 64, 291-303.

Krueger, A. (1992), Institutions in the new private sector, in Clague and Rausser, eds., *The Emergence of Market Economies in Eastern Europe*, Oxford: Blackwell.

Laffont, J.J. and J. Tirole (1990), Privatization and incentives, Unpublished manuscript.

Lipton, M. and J. Sachs (1990), Creating a market economy, *Brookings Papers in Economic Activity* 1.

Lu, M. and C. Wiener (1992), Price reform: China's two tier transition process, paper presented to a conference on reform in China, Center for Chinese Studies, University of California at Berkeley.

Newbery, D.M. (1992), The role of public enterprises in the national economy, paper presented at the Fourth Development Roundtable on Development Strategies.

Newbery, D.M. (1991), Socialist economies, Kiel Institute of World Economics.

Morrisson, C. (1992), Adjustment and equity, policy brief No.1, OECD Development Center.

Sachs, J. (1992), Accelerating privatization in Eastern Europe: the case of Poland, World Bank Annual Conference on Development Economics 1991, 15-42.

Sargent, T. (1982), The end of four big inflations, in R. Hall, ed., *Inflation: Causes and Effects*, Chicago: University of Chicago Press.

Serven, L. and A. Solimano (1992a), Private investment and macroeconomic adjustment: a survey, *The World Bank Research Observer* 7.

Serven, L. and A. Solimano (1992b), Economic adjustment and investment performance in developing countries: the experience of the 1980's, in V. Corbo et al., eds., *Revisiting Adjustment Lending: Policies to Promote Growth*, A World Bank Symposium.

Solimano, A. (1992a), Understanding the investment cycle in adjustment programs: evidence from reforming countries, mimeo, The World Bank.

Solimano, A. (1992b), Diversity in economic reform: a look at the experience in market and socialist economies, mimeo, The World Bank.

Tarr, D. G. (1989), A general equilibrium analysis of the welfare and employment effects of U.S. quotas in textiles, autos and steel, Bureau of Economics Staff Report to the Federal Trade Commission.

Tirole, J. (1990), Privatization in Eastern Europe: incentives and the economics of transition, Unpublished manuscript, Massachusetts Institute of Technology.

Vujovic, D. and M. Labus (1990), *General Equilibrium Models of the Yugoslav Economy* (in Serbo-Croatian), Belgrade: Federal Statistical Office.

Weitzman, M. (1974), Prices vs. quantities, *Review of Economic Studies* 41, 477-91.

Walters, A. (1992), The transition to a market economy, in Clague and Rausser, eds., *The Emergence of Market Economies in Eastern Europe*, Oxford: Blackwell.

Willig, R. (1992), Anti monopoly policies and institutions, in Clague and Rausser, eds., *The Emergence of Market Economies in Eastern Europe*, Oxford: Blackwell.

World Bank (1990), *China: Between Plan and Market*, World Bank.

11

Assessing the impact of environmental protection on industrial competitiveness in Europe[1]

Elisabeth Waelbroeck-Rocha

DRI/McGraw-Hill

1 Introduction

Environmental protection has become a recurrent item on policy makers' agenda, under pressure from scientists worried by the depletion of the ozone layer, by the accumulation of toxic and non-toxic waste and by the waste of non-renewable natural resources, among other factors. Environmental damage caused by non-economic events such as volcanic eruptions put additional pressure on policy makers throughout the world to take action to reduce environmental damage from economic activities. Clearly, however, policy makers are expected to find ways to protect the environment without hampering growth in the industrialised countries nor prejudicing the development of the poorer world regions.

The objective of this paper is not to discuss the likelihood that measures to protect the environment will be adopted by certain regions, nor the form that such agreements might take, but rather to discuss the ways by which such measures can best be modelled in order to:

i) determine their effect on socio-economic structures, as well as on development and wealth in the economy; and

ii) provide the kind of answers that will help policy makers around the world to take the right decisions and achieve their objectives at minimal cost.

[1]The framework of analysis described in section 3 of this article, and the simulation results presented in section 4, represent the combined efforts of various teams of analysts within DRI: the European Industry Service, managed by the author, the European Energy Service, under the direction of Erik S. Sorensen, and the European Economic Service, under the direction of Nigel Gault. Silvia Pariente-David, Research Director at DRI/McGraw-Hill, coordinated the work of the various teams and provided key inputs into the study. Special thanks are owed to Alain Henry, Senior Associate in the DRI European Industry Service, who played an essential role in the industry analysis. Many thanks are also extended to Jean-Marc Burniaux for his useful comments on a first draft of this paper, and to an anonymous referee.

A second objective of this paper is to see, using a framework of analysis that combines econometric and engineering approaches, whether a shift to stricter environmental protection policies in Western Europe can provide the kind of boost to European industry that would reinforce the momentum of the Single Market program. Such a "boost" could for instance result from a "first mover advantage", in that in implementing strict environmental policies ahead of the other world regions Western Europe would develop the type of technologies and products that would be in high demand when these other world regions decide to implement similar measures.

Existing studies of the economic impact of environmental protection measures arrive at conflicting results, depending on the approach that is used. To date, most modelling exercises aimed at analysing the effect of such measures mainly focus on the economic costs of these measures. By economic costs, we mean the cost to society (consumers and businesses) of changing behaviour in order to reduce the negative impact of human action on the environment. These economic costs include the transitional costs of implementing the measures and the opportunity cost due to foregone output and changes in consumer welfare. Indeed, the implementation by economic agents of measures to protect the environment usually translates in the short and medium term into changes in capital and operating costs (for instance through the use of more expensive but "greener" substitutes to certain inputs into the production process, or through substitution of capital for energy to increase energy efficiency). These changes tend to raise production costs and prices and negatively impact competitiveness. Among the studies focusing on the economic costs of measures to protect the environment are most of the analyses of the impact of fiscal and non-fiscal instruments to control CO_2 and other Greenhouse gas emissions into the atmosphere.

In contrast, market studies aimed at assessing the present size and future growth of the environmental protection market generally emphasise the potential economic benefits of actions to protect the environment. These economic benefits include improvements in productivity and in production efficiency (hence lower production costs), increased research and development expenditure leading to the development of new products and processes, increased demand for existing "green" products and lower health care costs, among other. All of these lead to increases in global welfare. Market studies, however, typically ignore the spillover effects of environmental protection measures on other sectors of the economy. These studies have nevertheless created a strong temptation for policy makers concerned by the degradation of the environment to over-emphasise the "market creation" effect and the "first mover advantage", the idea being that the new dynamism created by the accelerated replacement of the capital stock and increased investment in R&D has the potential to become a new engine of growth, strong enough to maintain or revive the momentum created by the Single Market program on industry.

For the sake of completeness, having defined economic costs and economic benefits resulting from action to protect the environment, we can also define environmental benefits as the improvement in the physical environment that is made possible by these measures. The assessment of environmental benefits has seldom been included in past studies, due to the difficulties associated with the monetarisation of these benefits - i.e. in quantifying the increase in welfare that is made possible by measures to protect the environment (such as the increase in leisure time). In this paper also, no attempt has been made to quantify the environmental benefits from the proposed program.

Section 2 provides the background to this paper by briefly reviewing different approaches followed to date to analyse the economic impact of environmental protection measures, and by discussing their relative advantages and limitations. In Section 3, we present a new framework of analysis that combines econometric, engineering and market study approaches to evaluate the short and medium term impact of environmental policies on the economy and on industry. The use of such models in simulation exercises allows to highlight the advantages of the approach but also emphasises the limits to these quantification exercises. These limits result from factors such as the absence or the poor quality of quantitative information on the existing structure and efficiency of the capital stock. In Section 4, we present the results of a simulation exercise undertaken by DRI/McGraw-Hill Europe in its study "Green Europe, Economic Implications and Business Opportunities" (1990). In this study, the impact of a unilateral implementation of a large set of measures to protect the environment in Western Europe is measured in terms of its effect on industrial structures and on the level and composition of output, as well as on changes in market shares of Europe-based producers. The analysis shows that, contrary to what is suggested by modelling exercises which emphasise the economic costs of environmental protection, there are sectors that have the potential to become important winners from the implementation of strict environmental protection measures. Section 5 compares the winning/losing sectors that emerge from the analysis in Section 4, to a list of potential winners/losers from the Single Market program based on the analysis by P. Buigues and A. Jacquemin (1989). Section 6 presents the implications for policy-making.

2   Examples of Approaches to Environmental Policy Assessments

Various types of methodological approaches have been used in the past to assess the economic impact of environmental protection. These are usually categorised as "top-down" or "bottom-up" approaches. As each type of model has distinct properties and features, the type of approach used in any given exercise generally depends on the scenario to be analysed and on the assumptions to be tested.

Below, we discuss the features of some of the key models that have been used in recent policy simulation exercises. A more complete list of the different types of models, including a discussion of their main features, is included in J. Fisher (1991).

2.1 Top-Down Approaches

In this category, we find policy models, traditional econometric models, and general equilibrium models.

Policy models are usually built for the purpose of a particular scenario analysis. These models present the risk of over-emphasising those impacts that the modeller believes will come in play as a given package of measures is implemented. The temptation is indeed strong with such models to downplay impacts not viewed intuitively as very relevant - thus effectively under-estimating the overall effects of these factors on the system. Inter-relationships between sectors, structural changes, wage adjustment functions and demand/supply constraints for instance might be insufficiently developed to provide a complete representation of the underlying economic system.

Econometric models used in simulation or forecasting exercises and that are constituted by a set of equations estimated over the past are also inappropriate to test the impact of developments such as an increase in environmental consciousness, since such developments reflect changes in the behaviour of the key economic agents.

Adopting "clean" production processes for instance, developing new products or implementing end-of-pipe pollution control systems require high levels of investment in R&D and an accelerated replacement of the existing capital stock. Even when market mechanisms, for instance resulting from the use of fiscal instruments, are relied upon to encourage firms to reduce pollution from economic activities, econometric models estimated over the past are not appropriate. The reason is that there has not been much past experience of such changes, so that it is difficult to dissociate the effects of market mechanisms designed to achieve a given objective from other effects that also played a role at the time. Estimating the link between energy prices and investment over the past, for instance, would likely show a negative relationship between these two variables as most rises in energy prices observed in recent history originated from abroad and implied a net transfer of resources from the oil importing to the oil exporting countries. The oil price shocks of the mid 1970s and early 1980s for instance had an overall negative impact on growth and activity, and a positive effect on inflation and interest rates. This depressed the level of investment. Greenhouse gas control measures based on fiscal policy instruments have, however, the opposite aim, as they are designed to encourage an increase in investment, in particular in energy conservation investment. The fact that the additional tax revenue that is generated from the use of fiscal instruments in a given economy is withheld within this economy avoids the negative impact of "external" oil price rises on the availability of funds in the economy. Thus, the level of non-energy related investment ought not to be depressed in the same way as in the case of a traditional oil price shock.

General Equilibrium Models provide a much better representation of the inter-connections between economic activities and the importance of prices in balancing demand and supply than traditional economic models. General equilibrium (GE) models have the advantage over traditional econometric models that the accounting of costs - including transitional costs - is fully consistent and integrated in a coherent framework. All economic agents are assumed to maximise their welfare or a utility function subject to certain constraints. The emphasis on market mechanisms to clear markets guarantees an efficient allocation of resources in the economy. Most existing GE models, however, do not allow for market failures.[2]

The main drawback of GE models, and in particular of sufficiently detailed GE models to appropriately measure the impact of varied measures to protect the environment, is that they put considerable demands on data. Often, important simplification assumptions have to be made to circumvent the absence of data. The fact that the models are calibrated to reproduce the data for a "base year" eases the data collection problem but raises questions as to whether the specific year used as a base year does represents an equilibrium situation, and whether it is a valid starting point to assess the impacts in future years (Fisher (1991)).

2.2   Bottom-Up Approaches

The typical "bottom-up" approaches rely on engineering data and analyses. Engineering studies are relied upon to determine what additional investment is needed to achieve a given improvement in the quality of the environment (for instance the construction of an additional waste treatment plant or a given change in production process). Such studies, however, completely ignore the spillover effects of these measures on the rest of the economy, only providing "discrete" answers from which it is difficult to infer the impact of marginal changes in regulations or in market organisational structures. Engineering studies are thus of little use in telling how much firms will invest as a result of a given rise in energy prices, and what the net impact will be on upstream and downstream sectors. Another drawback of these studies in terms of evaluating the long term impact of environmental protection measures results from the difficulty in predicting technological, economic, managerial and social changes several years into the future. Indeed, many technologies currently under development may never be applied on a large scale, whereas new technologies that are unforeseen yet may be developed in the coming years and radically change the organisation of production in 10-20 years time. Engineering studies are nevertheless more ap-

---

[2]Recent developments in GE modelling, however, now make it possible to take into account the possibility of market failures.

propriate than "econometric" approaches to quantify the impact of regulatory or voluntary measures on direct investment and operating costs.

Because each of the traditional approaches described above has its own drawbacks and limitations in terms of providing readily usable answers to policy makers, we have developed another framework of analysis which is a combination of the "top-down" and "bottom-up" approaches to modelling. This framework, which is described in Section 3, combines econometric models estimated over the past with exogenously imposed behavioural changes that are based on the results of engineering and market studies. This methodology consists of an extension and an adaptation to the DRI models of that used by the Central Plan Bureau in The Netherlands (1989).

3 The DRI Framework of Analysis

The full model used by DRI for its environmental analyses is constituted by three blocks of national models, fully linked both between them and across countries in ways that are described below. The three blocks are formed by the energy models, the industry models and the macro-economic models. The combination of these models for policy assessment purposes was first tested in "Green Europe: Economic Implications and Business Opportunities" (1990), a study whose results are summarised in Section 4 to illustrate the properties of the model and draw conclusions as to the dynamic impact of the adoption of stricter environmental protection policies in Western Europe. These models have since been used in other quantification exercises, including those done by DRI for the Commission of the European Communities (1991), (1992) and (1993).

Below, we describe each of the blocks in turn before explaining how these were linked in the simulation exercises.

3.1 The European Energy Models

The DRI/McGraw-Hill European energy models cover each of the West European countries, and produce forecasts of the following categories of variables:

(i) Consumption of 17 fuel types (8 petroleum products, 3 types of solid fuel, natural gas, 2 additional types of manufactured gas, delivered electricity and 2 types of primary electricity), broken down by 11 sectors/uses (4 industrial, 4 residential/commercial, transportation, the energy sector and power generation);

(ii) Production of the 17 fuel types;

(iii) Net trade in 13 of those fuel types;

(iv) Twelve fuel prices with some information on their constitution, along with a number of other energy cost indicators.

The national energy models also produce forecasts of a substantial number of other variables such as change in stocks, efficiency factors, and other ratios. Altogether, each national model contains over 500 endogenous variables.

The energy models are linked to the national macroeconomic and industry models, from which they take indicators of industrial activity, inflation and other macroeconomic indicators, and to which they supply the energy balances, the price of the different types of fuels and net trade flows in energy. It is the indicators of economic activity which drive energy demand in the energy models.

To take account of the possibility of substitution across fuels, there are a series of aggregate desired demand functions which relate to six end-uses considered to be homogeneous enough to allow a certain amount of substitution between fuels. The six "uses" are: blast furnaces, chemical industry furnaces, boilers and steamcrackers, cooking, water heating and space heating. Desired demand is expressed in terms of useful energy (measured in physical units), and is influenced by autonomous energy conservation emanating from technological or structural change (with coefficients based on past trends in these variables), by price induced long-term energy conservation, by short-term price effects, the level of activity, and special factors such as climatic conditions. Inter-fuel substitution takes place when there are changes in the relative prices of the different fuels.

Fuel prices are determined based on inflation variables, special cost factors, pricing policy parameters, tax levels, and the price of primary fuels. Electricity prices are additionally affected by fuel costs and long-term interest rates. Prices are also influenced by the ratio of demand to supply. Indeed, the demand/supply ratio, taking account of the net import ability of the economy considered, is used in a function that modifies base prices. The model, however, does not reproduce full market equilibrium, as this would result in unrealistic price movements. Thus, for instance, if excess demand for a given type of fuel persists an allocation algorithm is used in order to keep the consumption of the fuel within certain limits and attempt wherever possible to re-allocate the resultant gap.

3.2   The European Industry Models

The European industry models that were used in the case study presented in Section 4 are Input-Output (I/O) based models which describe the evolution of production, prices, exports, imports, value added and employment in 20 sectors of the economy of each of the major four European countries[3] (Germany, France, Italy and the UK). Each model also distinguishes 15 consumer demand categories. The results of the simulation for these four countries were extrapolated to other countries in Western Europe by taking into account the composition of output in each country, and estimates of the present level of environmental damage from economic activities in each country.

---

[3]The models for these four countries have since been expanded to 30 sectors, and new models have been built for other EC countries.

Among the salient features of the models are, first and foremost, the fact that they rely on a modified I/O approach which allows to capture changes in technological coefficients and behaviour over time. This generated output approach allows to endogenize some of the changes in technical coefficients over time thanks to a set of equations which link actual final sales by sector to the "generated demand" by sector which is calculated based on the fixed input/output structure. The changes in technical coefficients that are taken account of in the model measure structural changes such as a progressive increase in the degree of penetration of certain sectors in the economy (such as office and EDP, electrical engineering, or plastics), as well as temporary changes in technical coefficients such as those resulting from changes in the relative price of substitute products, and cyclical factors.

The second main feature of the DRI European industry models is that they explicitly recognise European interdependence through trade blocks that link each economy with each of its partners and with the rest of the world. Each country's exports by sector depends on the level of import demand from each of its trading partners and on relative prices, where competitor prices are determined as a weighted average of the export prices of the country's main competitors on world markets. Similarly, import prices of a given sector are determined based on a weighted average of the export prices of this country's main trading partners. The competitors that are explicitly recognised in the models are the Federal Republic of Germany, France, Italy, the United Kingdom, the US, and Japan.

Similarly to the energy models, the industry models are directly linked to the national macroeconomic models from which they take the forecasts of several macroeconomic variables such as exchange rates, prices and wages, interest rates, investment and disposable income.

The key blocks of the industry models and the interactions between these blocks are illustrated in Figure 1. Behavioural dimensions are captured via a double chain linking prices and quantities. Concerning the quantity chain, the model is fundamentally demand driven. Consumer demand, together with corporate demand for investment goods and government expenditure on goods and services, make up the final demand addressed to each sector. This final demand, together with the induced input/output intermediate demand, represents total generated domestic demand. This variable is then used to determine the level of domestic sales by sector. Exports and imports depend on the level of demand that is addressed to each sector respectively abroad and within the country considered, and on relative prices, and production is equal to domestic sales plus exports net of imports.

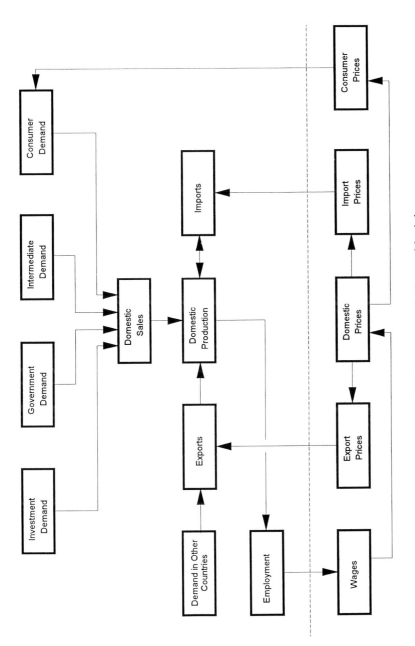

Figure 1. DRI European Industry Model.

The quantity chain is linked to a price chain via the impact of costs and prices on the level of demand from consumers and firms. Sectoral wage rates are determined by assuming that workers, within each industry, adjust their wage demand at different speeds. The speed of adjustment reflects the combined effect of market power on both the labour and product markets, and structural elements such as the growth or decline of the industries concerned. Faced with this industry wage which they compare to the user cost of capital, employers are assumed to select their level of employment according to their production plans. This, in turn, determines unit labour costs. Producer prices are determined on the basis of unit labour costs and a weighted average of the price of the various intermediate inputs that are used. Wholesale prices are a function of producer prices and import prices, where import prices are determined based on a weighted average of the export prices of partner countries. For the purpose of the environmental protection simulations, the producer price equations were modified to take account of the impact on final prices of higher annualised capital costs linked to the new investment.

3.3   The European Macroeconomic Models

The European macroeconomic models provide a complete representation of the main economic variables and of the inter-relationships between these variables. Each national model describes in a comprehensive way the behaviour of the three main types of economic agents: government, consumers, and the corporate sector. Although the models are, similarly to the industry models, essentially demand driven, most also incorporate a supply equation which determines the potential GDP level. The later is then confronted to total final demand in the economy and influences prices.

Each national model is linked to the models of the other European economies and to the models of its other major trading partners through trade, exchange rate and interest rate equations. The exports of a particular country in Europe are determined on the basis of an indicator of overall demand from the rest of the world, which is calculated as a trade weighted average of import demand from its trading partners. Similarly, both export volumes and import prices are a function of a trade weighted average of the export prices of that country's trading partners. This allows to take into account the spillover effects of changes in inflation (and export price growth) in one country on the rate of inflation and the level of activity in each of the trading partners. This is important for environmental policy simulations, as the price effects of energy taxes for instance varies significantly across countries depending on the fuel mix and on present levels of taxation, among other. A given energy tax introduced in all countries in the EC simultaneously can thus lead to important changes in relative prices between Member States, hence influencing the relative competitiveness of the various sectors between countries. This will, in turn, influence intra-EC trade flows.

Each country's exchange rate is determined against the ECU within the limits set by the EMS while the ECU/US$ rate is assumed to be floating. In many European countries where monetary policies are strongly influenced by developments in other countries, interest rates are directly influenced by those in the major EC countries (in particular in Germany), to maintain exchange rate stability.

Prices are determined on the basis of import prices and domestic cost factors (in particular unit labour costs). Supply/demand factors also influence price determination. Export prices adjust to changes in wholesale or producer prices in the economy, and are in many cases also directly influenced by the trends in world prices, especially in small open economies.

Wages adjust to changes in inflation, in a way which reflects past developments in prices and wages in each country. The adjustment of wages to prices thus tends to be quicker and more complete in those countries which have had near perfect wage/indexation systems, and can take place with a lag of up to one year in countries where wage increases are negotiated at given points in time. The labour market situation was often found to have some influence on the growth in labour costs, a rise in unemployment generally leading to a slower growth of nominal wage rates, everything else remaining equal.

Finally, different categories of government expenditure and revenue are modelled and influence the rest of the economy through changes in income levels or profits (for direct taxation, and some revenue transfers), prices (for indirect taxation), and demand (public sector investment, etc.). The cumulated government balances make up the total public sector debt in the economy, and influence money markets.

3.4   Model Changes for the Environmental Policy Simulations

For the purpose of the environmental protection simulations, a number of changes were made to these models. Simulating the impact of "Green" policies indeed requires:

(1) Assessing the additional cost linked to pollution control/abatement, and the nature of the costs (investment in plant and equipment, labour requirements, changes in the composition of inputs).

(2) Identifying the sectors which support these costs (i.e. the sectors which undertake the necessary investment in environmental protection) and the sectors which will supply the material/inputs (machines, services and intermediate input materials) that result from the change in technology. This is where the contribution of engineering and market studies is essential.

(3) Introducing these figures into the European industry models as:
- additional demand for investment goods addressed to each sector;
- changes in demand for raw materials or intermediate inputs, to reflect changes in demand structure resulting from product substitution, changes in

production processes or bans on certain substances; these changes, which imply changes to the coefficients of the I/O matrix, were incorporated as of 1997 to give time to the economy to adjust to the new regulations and undertake the necessary investment;

- changes in the level of employment per unit of output; greater levels of environmental protection can indeed be achieved through improved maintenance of the equipment and a closer monitoring of the production process, and therefore require a greater number of workers to yield the same output; we assumed that half of the additional employment required to comply with the stricter environmental protection standards would be outsourced, hence generating activity in the business services' sector;

- changes in price levels, to reflect the impact of annual taxes on automotive vehicles or of energy taxes on consumer and producer prices;

- other changes in costs, in particular to take into account the additional capital cost related to the "green" investment.

To simulate the impact of environmental protection packages that include a tax on energy, the energy price variables and the energy inputs used by each sector in the industry models were exogenized at the level given by the energy model.

3.5 Interactions between the three models

The simulations of environmental protection policies were done in several steps, iterating between the three blocks of models in order to achieve convergence and guarantee the overall consistency of results for the macroeconomy, for industry and for energy. The iterative procedure is described below:

Step 1

The first step consists in introducing the measures likely to have a direct influence on energy structures (i.e. on energy demand, supply and the fuel mix, among others) in the energy models. Fiscal instruments being an integral part of the models, no particular modelling change was needed to take account of the rise in energy taxes. Regulatory and other changes had, however, to be introduced in an ad-hoc way.

The energy models were simulated to calculate preliminary estimates of the change in energy prices, energy demand, and tax revenues by country. The amount of investment in energy conservation needed to make these savings possible was then calculated, based on an estimate of the unit cost/GJ saved, and the estimated energy saving by sector.

The investment requirements for energy conservation were thus calculated by sector. One such sector is the power generation sector, where the change in investment reflects both a change in the level of investment in new capacity, and a shift away from coal in power generation.

The additional energy conservation investment required was then broken down by type of equipment, in order to identify those sectors that would actually have to produce the equipment (construction, for heat insulation of buildings, electrical engineering, mechanical engineering, transport equipment, etc.). These sectors will indeed see a rise in final demand for their products as a result of the new measures.

Average energy prices by sector were calculated to take account of changes in fuel prices and in the fuel mix, and this average energy price was weighted by the amount of energy saving by sector to take account of the fact that less energy is used to produce the same level of output.

In addition to the market driven changes in energy structures (i.e. those resulting from fiscal changes in energy tax and regulations relative to fuel quality and other supply factors), the package of measures implemented in Section 4 also involved other measures such as the construction of additional waste treatment plants and water purification installations, the extension of sewage systems, waste recycling, and others. These measures do not immediately influence the energy structures but also require changes in investment levels or in the composition of output. They were taken account of in the industry models through exogenous changes in demand levels and through changes in the technical coefficients of the I/O matrix, as explained above.

Finally, allocation rules were decided for the redistribution of the revenue from the new taxes. In the study whose results are summarised in Section 4, we assumed that part of the new tax revenue would be used to finance the environmental investment undertaken by the business sector, thus reducing the annualised capital costs related to this investment. The remainder was allocated to the financing of transport infrastructure projects, to make possible a stronger shift in modal shares, and for the financing of R&D to encourage the development of clean technologies and products.

All these changes, i.e. all the changes implied by the energy model simulations and those assessed by means of engineering and market studies, were then introduced into the industry models that are simulated in Step 2.

Step 2

The first simulation of the industry models enables to calculate the net impact of the rise in energy prices and of the other measures on production costs and wholesale prices by sector, taking into account all the spill-over effects across sectors and across countries. These price and other effects were then passed on to the macroeconomic models, along with information on the additional ex-ante investment requirement and the new tax revenue amounts.

The macroeconomic models were then simulated to calculate the effect of the package of measures on wage rates, on the different demand components and on the overall level of activity, as well as on prices and interest rates. A first iteration then took place between the macro and industry models in order to achieve convergence in terms of levels of economic activity, trade volumes, prices and employment.

Step 3

The net impact of the package of measures on industrial activity, on prices and on the level of economic activity was then re-introduced into the energy models in order to calculate the ex-post impact of the package of measures on energy demand and on emission levels in all countries. Steps 2 and 3 were then repeated, to ensure global consistency of the results.

3.6 Model Limitations

The above framework of analysis has clear advantages over other methods in that it takes account of the full impact (direct and indirect) of environmental protection measures on economic and industrial structures. The main drawback of this approach is, however, that it is not very flexible nor transparent, as it relies on the existence and availability of fairly detailed technical information on ways to reduce or prevent pollution from economic activities, including for "marginal" gains in efficiency or pollution abatement. Comprehensive "engineering" studies, however, do not exist for as varied issues as those that are typically considered by policy makers, so that the number of assumptions that have to be made in this type of study tends to be considerable.

A second limitation of the above approach is that it does not allow assessments of the impact of trading permits between firms. Further changes to the models would have to be made to make such analysis possible.

Thirdly, in their present structure, both the macroeconomic and the industry models are fundamentally demand driven. Although the short-term demand impact of changes in environmental policy stance is important, in an economy working close to full capacity supply constraints are likely to develop if the new investment is not "capacity expanding" investment. This can create pressure on prices and lead to higher imports, both effects that have the risk of having being underestimated with our tools of analysis.

Finally, the indirect long-term impact of environmental protection measures is not yet adequately treated. As indicated above, encouraging "clean" production through the development of new processes and the accelerated replacement of existing equipment typically requires additional investments in R&D and in physical capital. Although this obviously entails higher costs, it can also have long term benefits by allowing productivity and efficiency gains, for instance, or product quality improvements through a better control of the production process. Such effects are difficult to quantify, however. Tighter environmental regulations can also encourage the development of new products, which can have side-effects on the global competitiveness of the economy. All this can stimulate important changes in economic structures, accelerating the structural shift away from degressive sectors into new, dynamic, markets which have the potential of becoming fast growing world import demand categories once environmental consciousness spreads to other world regions.

4 A Simulation Exercise for Europe

This section illustrates the strength of the approach presented in Section 3, by summarising the key findings of a study by DRI/McGraw-Hill Europe (1990).

The assessment of the net impact of a tightening of environmental policies in Western Europe on the economy and on industry relies on the comparison of two scenarios: a Reference scenario, which assumes no change in the present policy stance (this is a "business as usual" scenario), and a Green scenario, in which we assume that all three types of economic agents (government, industry and households) become much more environmentally conscious and implement, either of their own initiative or pressed by the regulatory or fiscal authorities, behavioural changes which can lead to a better quality of the environment.

Five families of measures were assumed to be implemented:
- measures for air quality and protection of the atmosphere;
- measures for water quality;
- measures to control soil pollution;
- measures to reduce nuisance from noise;
- waste management.

In total, about 150 measures were assumed to be implemented, involving different types of actions or behavioural changes. The attached table provides examples of some of the measures that were assumed to be implemented. All of these, once implemented, have an impact on production costs, on the structure of demand for intermediate inputs, on the level of demand that is addressed to the different sectors of the economy, and on the relative price of the different inputs.

Among these 150 measures, a key assumption was the introduction of a carbon tax of 300 ECUs per ton of carbon ($370), phased in progressively between 1993 and 2000. This is much higher than the tax level currently proposed by the Commission (COM(92) 226 final), which is a combined tax on energy and carbon introduced gradually between 1993 and the year 2000 and reaching $10/bbl in 2000 (at 1993 ECUs). The combined $10/bbl energy/carbon tax currently proposed by the Commission corresponds approximately to a carbon tax of $84 per ton of oil, about one fourth of the level assumed in the DRI study. The reason for the choice of a carbon tax of 300 ECUs per ton of carbon is that this was the level calculated at the time (in 1990) as necessary to achieve the stabilisation of CO_2 emissions in the Community, given a projected growth for real GDP in western Europe of about 3% per year on average between 1990 and 2000. In the DRI Reference scenario, CO_2 emissions in 2000 were about 20% higher than the 1990 level. Simulations done recently by the European Commis-

Table 1 Characteristics of the environmental scenarios

	Reference	Green
Economic Growth in		
Western Europe	3%	2.7%
Oil Prices	Increasing rapidly after 1995	Same as reference
Carbon Tax	None	300 1990 ECU per ton
Circulation Tax	Current	Additional Tax of about 150 1990 ECU
Emissions from		
Stationary Sources	LCI Directive	Tightened and Extended
Emissions from		
Mobile Sources	Current Directives	Pre-catalysts Compulsory
Fuel Quality	Current Standards	Significantly Tightened Standards
Energy Conservation	Moderate	Very strong
Renewable Energies		
(incl. hydro)	120 mtoe	150 mtoe
Nuclear Power	118 GW	118 GW
Water Quality	Small improvement	Large improvement in industrial and residential waste-water treatment, extension of sewage networks
Waste Management	Small Effort	Selective collection with: - less landfilling - more recycling - more incineration Prevention of waste Increased recycling
Noise Reduction	Small	High (accelerated replacement of aircraft fleet, noise barriers, noise insulation of buildings, encapsulation of truck engines)
Soil Pollution	Current	Large improvement (cleaning of sites, etc.)
R & D for Env. Protection	Reference	Reference+ 0.5% GDP (financed from carbon & vehicle tax revenue)
Degree of Awareness about		
Environmental Protection	Small	Very high
Rest of World	"Business as Usual"	Same as in Reference

Table 2 Additional costs
(annualized capital costs + operating costs)
in 2005 in "Green" compared to Reference
(Total Western Europe, billion Ecus)

Air pollution control	104
Water pollution control	56
Soil pollution control	39
Waste management	80
Noise reduction	25
R&D	58
Total	362

sion's Directorate-General for Energy, based on an updated (much less buoyant) forecast for economic growth in the 1990, indicate that the proposed $10/bbl combined energy/carbon tax would achieve a 4% reduction in CO2 emissions in the Community compared to the no-tax situation by the year 2000 - not enough to achieve CO2 emission stabilisation. Other measures in the Commission's package, such as SAVE and ALTENER, along with national measures, are thus essential for stabilisation to be achieved.

The DRI "Green Europe" study also assumed the introduction of an annual tax on automotive vehicles, reaching 150 ECUs per year and per vehicle in 2000 (in 1990 ECUs). The revenue from the taxes on energy and on vehicles, which add up to a fairly high figure (up to 2.5% of GDP) was assumed to be entirely redistributed to help finance the investment in energy conservation, infrastructure development and R&D by the business and government sector, as well as the investment in energy conservation by households.

The estimated "direct cost" of the measures is shown in Table 2.[4]

These total costs represent a GDP share of approximately 2.5% in 2005 on average in Western Europe. Table 3[5] puts these numbers in perspective by showing the percentage increase in the environmental protection market (EP market) for each type of product in the major four EC countries, except for soil pollution. In Table 3, the environmental protection markets are defined as the market value of all those types of goods or machinery whose sales are associated with environmental spending to reduce pollution in a given area (for instance, water pollution). The growth rates in Table 3 were calculated by applying our estimates of the rise in demand for each type of product or equipment between

---

[4]Source: DRI/McGraw-Hill, Green Europe: Economic Implications and Business Opportunities.
[5]Source: EC Commission and DRI/McGraw-Hill

Table 3 Increase in the environmental
protection market in the EC-4

	Market Size 1987 (bill. ECUs)	Average Annual Growth Rate 1987-2005
Air Pollution	7.5	11.0%
Water Pollution	16.2	6.4%
Waste Management	9.1	10.0%
Noise Reduction	1.1	17.3%
Total	33.9	9.3%

Table 4 Distribution of the costs linked to the protection
of the environment in the "Green" scenario - 2005

Sector	Percent
Agriculture, Fishery and Forestry	4.0
Fuel and Power Products	3.1
Ores and Metals	6.3
Non-Metallic Mineral Products	3.1
Chemical Products	21.8
Metal Products	2.6
Mechanical Engineering	4.1
Office, EDP and Precision Instruments	0.9
Electrical Engineering	2.8
Transportation Equipment	4.9
Food, Drink and Tobacco	3.0
Textiles and Clothing	0.8
Paper, Printing and Publishing	1.8
Miscellaneous Industries	0.7
Rubber and Plastic Products	0.6
Construction	1.9
Transport Services	14.5
Communication Services	0.4
Retail, Tourism and Finance	5.1
Municipalities and other Government	17.6
Total	100.0

scenarios in the major four EC countries, to the estimated size of these markets in the same countries in 1987.

The breakdown of costs by sector is illustrated in Table 4.[6] This shows the share of total costs linked to the protection of the environment in the Green scenario that is borne by each sector in Western Europe. Table 4 shows that, of all sectors considered, it is the chemical sector, along with the transport services sector, municipalities and other government that have to support most of the costs of environmental protection measures implemented in the Green scenario. The chemical sector indeed bears a large part of the costs linked to waste management and air pollution control, whereas the costs borne by the transport service sector are more directly related to the reduction of noise nuisance and to the control of air pollution through the development of an adequate transport infrastructure that can substitute for road transport. The share of costs that is supported by the ores and metals sector is, in comparison, much smaller (at 6.3%), despite the fact that this is a highly energy intensive sector and that it also has the potential to recycle more waste than it does at present. This 6.3% share is nevertheless significant in view of the sector's share of total value added in the economy, which is just above 1%.

Table 5 shows the percentage increase in the average price of energy paid by the key sectors as a result of the introduction of the carbon tax. Tables 2 to 5 thus give an idea of the magnitude of the shocks that were imposed on the economy.

The impact of the carbon tax on the average energy price paid by the different sectors in each country depends on the actual price level of each fuel, on its carbon content, on the existing tax structure, and on the fuel mix in the sector considered. Fuels used in transport for instance are more heavily taxed at present than energy use by industry, so that the relative impact of the carbon tax on transport fuel prices is comparatively small. The lower part of Table 5 shows the percentage increase in energy costs per unit of output that the various sectors experience as a result of the implementation of the carbon tax, taking account of changes in the fuel mix and of energy conservation. Because energy conservation is taking place, the overall impact of higher energy prices on producer costs is indeed smaller than the energy price increase itself.

The change in aggregate production over time in the key sub-sectors in the economy is shown in Figure 2, while the long term impact on output levels by sector is illustrated in Figure 3.

Real output initially rises in the manufacturing sector compared to Reference, reflecting the impact of the increase in environmental spending on the demand for capital goods and for construction. The change in output compared to Reference however, reaches a turning point fairly rapidly, before falling to a level approximately 2% below Reference towards the mid-1990s.

---

[6]Source: DRI/McGraw-Hill, Green Europe: Economic Implications and Business Opportunities.

Table 5 Increase in energy costs by sector in the four major European economies
(% Difference between the price levels in Green and in Reference, in 2005)
(takes account of energy conservation)

	Germany	France	UK	Italy
Energy Price Increase				
Iron and Steel	146.1	124.5	214.7	145.9
Chemicals	74.1	59.4	115.3	68.2
Other Industry	76.6	64.2	112.2	75.9
Domestic Sector	62.4	26.7	80.7	42.5
Transport Services	36.5	34.7	42.4	37.6
Energy Cost per Unit of Output				
Iron & Steel	96.5	70.4	138.9	78.6
Chemicals	40.4	29.7	59.6	27.6
Other Industry	32.0	31.4	59.3	29.8
Domestic Sector	31.1	5.5	60.1	24.1
Transport Services	30.5	27.6	30.2	31.6

Activity in the service sectors is sustainably boosted by the need for better controls and improved maintenance of equipment in industry, and by higher demand for insurance and other financial services. Output in the service sector thus remains about 1.5% above the Reference level even in the long term. Two sectors do not appear on the chart: energy, whose output falls in response to the drop in demand despite lower imports, and agriculture, whose output also shows a small decrease in the Green scenario compared to Reference due to rises in production costs. The net effect on the private sector is a rise of up to 1.3% in the level of activity in the short term, followed by a fall then a stabilisation of output about 1% below Reference in the longer run.

The rise in fixed capital formation and employment that reflects the need to comply with stricter regulations and from the shift to new, cleaner, production processes, initially boosts activity in construction, pulling with it all those sectors which generally depend on the level of activity in construction, such as non-metallic minerals, and, to a lesser extent, ores and metals. As the construction boom wears out, however, i.e. when the adequate "green" infrastructure has been put in place, the emphasis shifts towards the implementation of clean technologies and a better maintenance of the equipment. This is accompanied by continued energy conservation efforts and a shift to less polluting input materials. At the same time, the rise in inflation progressively builds in and, because we assumed that wages would not adjust fully to the change in inflation to avoid too strong a deterioration in external competitiveness and in the corporate sector's financial balance, real incomes are squeezed. This tends to reduce demand for those goods which do not directly benefit from higher environmental spending, such as food, drink and tobacco, textiles and clothing, and even communication services.

Figure 3 illustrates the long term impact of the package of measures on the level of production in each sector on average in the EC-4. Even in the long term, and despite a rise in the overall price level in the economy of about 7%, there are still sectors which experience higher levels of economic activity than in Reference: these are the mechanical and electrical engineering sectors, retail, tourism and finance, and transport services. Both the electrical engineering and the mechanical engineering sectors benefit from the "increased demand" effect, which reflects additional investment in energy conservation and the modernisation of the capital stock that is taking place in the economy, combined with the fact that Europe is well placed worldwide in these markets and thus can satisfy most of the increase in demand from domestic production. There is thus very little "leakage" of this increased demand to the rest of the world. The increase in activity in retail, tourism and finance, which includes all business services, results from the fact that the greater environmental consciousness and the need to better maintain the equipment and monitor emissions encourages the development of an "environmental services" sector, as most of these activities are being outsourced. Finally, the increased activity in transport results from the shift in transport modes away from private passenger cars to public transport which was made possible by the development of an appropriate public transport network.

The output levels in construction and in paper and printing in the Green scenario are nearly the same as in Reference, whereas the decreases in output levels in most other manufacturing sectors range between 2% and 4% in 2005. The strongest drops in output are recorded in the fuel and power products sector and in the office and EDP sector, the latter being particularly sensitive to the deterioration in relative prices with the rest of the world. The office and EDP sector, which covers the production of computers, office machinery and precision instruments such as clocks and watches and medical instruments, is a sector in which the EC is progressively losing ground both within its domestic market and worldwide, already in the Reference case. The import penetration ratio in this sector is close to 70% at present, and the degree of competition is such that even small deteriorations in the relative price of EC products compared to other world products can mean strong losses in market shares for domestic producers.

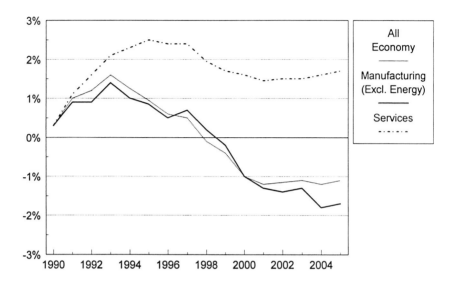

Figure 2. Changes in Aggregate Production.

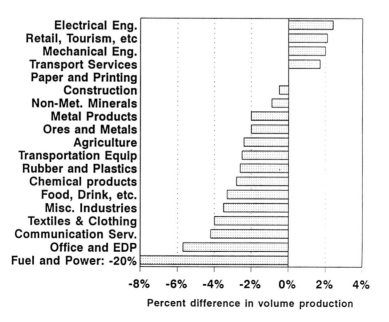

Figure 3. Long Term Impact of the Measures.

Although the office and EDP sector itself is not a highly polluting sector, thus does not need to undertake costly investments to reduce environmental damage from its own activity, it does suffer indirectly from the rise in prices of its key inputs - such as labour, but also printed circuit boards, plastics and other input materials. Producer prices in the office and EDP sector are 4.5% higher in 2005 in the Green scenario than in Reference, and domestic demand for office and EDP products does not increase significantly as a result of the additional investment that is taking place in the economy (NCM and electronic goods whose demand is expected to be boosted by the greater emphasis on clean processes are indeed part of the mechanical and electrical engineering sectors). It is thus the price effect which dominates and explains the relatively large fall in output compared to Reference. The impact on the growth rate of the sector is less dramatic, however, as this is still a fast growing industry: the 6% decline in output levels in 2005 compared to Reference indeed means a reduction in the average annual rate of growth of the sector from 5.5% in the Reference case to 5% in the Green scenario.

These results show that, with an adequate treatment of the demand impact of environmental packages, there are sectors that can benefit from such measures and grow faster in an environmentally friendly economy than in a "normal" growth scenario, whereas others might suffer more than had been initially foreseen in the absence of corrective actions.

Table 6 shows the net impact of the environmental protection package on the market share of Europe-based producers. To calculate the export market share, we had to make the relatively strong assumption that the change in the overall level of world production of each sector is negligible. The second column of Table 6, which shows the overall change in the market share of importers in the EC (including intra-EC trade), points to an increase in the market share of imports in all sectors but office and EDP, where both demand and production grow slower in the Green scenario than in Reference. The strongest increase in import penetration is observed in the non-metallic mineral products sector, where trade is already developing rapidly in the Reference scenario (though starting from a low level) and where imports in the Green scenario are boosted by the faster rates of activity in construction. The fast growth in imports of metal products (which includes boilers) in the Green scenario reflects capacity constraints within Europe which prevent the sector from expanding output in line with the rise in demand.

The changes in export market shares are more varied, as some sectors experience increases in exports (such as the mechanical engineering sector, non-metallic mineral products, and electrical engineering), while others see a fall in exports (office, EDP and precision instruments, and chemical products, for instance). The fall in exports can result either from a deterioration in relative price competitiveness, from a diversion of output away from export markets towards the domestic market (if domestic demand increases significantly, as is the case for electrical engineering), or from a combination of both.

Table 6 Change in market shares in 2005 Green compared to Reference
(Difference, in %)

Sector	Export Market Share	Importers Share of the EC Market (incl. intra-EC trade)
Ores and Metals	0.6	3.2
Non-Metallic Mineral Products	3.8	6.6
Chemical Products	-2.3	1.3
Metal Products	1.7	8.0
Mechanical Engineering	4.1	3.3
Office, EDP and Precision Instruments	-4.9	-0.3
Electrical Engineering	1.3	1.2
Transportation Equipment	-0.4	2.9
Food, Drink and Tobacco	-1.9	0.0
Textiles and Clothing	-1.9	0.6
Paper, Printing and Publishing	-0.4	1.1
Rubber and Plastic Products	1.2	4.5

What Table 6 mainly shows, however, is that the losses in market-share of Europe-based producers are not dramatic, at least if intra-EC trade movements are taken into account. Our analysis unfortunately says little about the relative change in market share on European versus rest of the world markets.

To summarise, even ignoring the potential benefits that could accrue from the development of a more modern, more technologically intensive and efficient capital base in Europe, and ignoring the advantages that the adoption of similar environmental protection measures by Western Europe's trading partners would mean in terms of potential exports, we already find a number of sectors that can benefit from the tightening of environmental protection regulations. Most sectors, however, experience an (albeit small) fall in activity in the Green scenario compared to Reference.

In the next section, we compare the sectors that are potential winners from the implementation of environmental protection measures to the potential winners from the "1992" program, to see whether a shift in priority objectives towards "Green" policies could further stimulate these sectors, or whether, on the contrary, there are sectors to which "1992" gave a positive impulse and which are now put at risk by the rise in environmental consciousness.

5 A comparison of the impact of Green policies with those from the Single European Market program

The list of sectors considered to be respectively "winners" or "losers" from 1992 is based on the analysis by Buigues and Jacquemin (1989). Some adaptation of the sectoral classification used in Section 4 was, however, necessary in order to draw conclusions. In particular, the transport equipment sector will now be broken down into automotive vehicles, aerospace equipment, railway equipment and other, due to the different impact of environmental protection measures on the demand for these various types of equipment in the Green scenario. Similarly, the chemical sector has been broken down into subsectors, and the same holds for the metal products (boilers) and non-metallic minerals products sectors.

The primary objective of the Single Market program was to render the European economy more competitive by eliminating all intra-EC barriers to trade, stimulating a more competitive environment and encouraging concentration in sectors where firms could not fully benefit from economies of scale, or in which growth was hampered by fragmented markets.

In their study, Buigues and Jacquemin (1989) define four categories of sectors based on the possibilities for firms in each sector to differentiate products, and based on the relative advantage of being a leading firm in these sectors. Generally speaking, the benefits from the Single Market program are expected to be strongest in those sectors where there are advantages to being a leading firm. This is the case in sectors such as pharmaceuticals, aerospace, tyres, or electronic components manufacturing (Figure 4[7]).

The type of benefits that the various sectors can expect from the Single Market program, however, vary depending on whether there is the possibility for strong product differentiation or not. In the first case, i.e. if firms can differentiate their products from others in the market, for instance emphasising such and such technical feature or the quality of the product, they will benefit from the creation of the Single Market through the enlargement of their geographical market. The removal of intra-EC barriers to trade will indeed allow them to offer the same "special" product in larger geographical markets than was previously possible. This is the so-called "specialised" category in the upper-right hand quadrant of Figure 4.

On the other hand, in sectors in which there are advantages to being a leading firm but where product differentiation is difficult, firms will only benefit from the Single Market program to the extent that it represents a springboard for global competition (Figure 4). This is the "volume" category in Figure 4, and include such sectors as the motor vehicles industry, domestic appliances,

---

[7] Source: DRI European Industry Service, based on Buigues and Jacquemin (1989)

Figure 4 Industries classified by competitive environment

		Fragmented	**Specialized**
	High	Metal products Mechanical engineering	Pharmaceuticals Specialty chemicals Office, EDP and precision instruments Telecommunications equipment Drinks Printing and publishing
Possibility to to differentiate		*Impact of 1992* Little or no effect on such industries	*Impact of 1992* Enlargement of geographical market
		Impasse	**Volume**
	Low	Agriculture Brick and basic construction materials Nonferrous metals Ceramics Other transport equipment Food Textiles and clothing Pulp, paper and paperboard	Fuel and power products Glass Basic chemicals Domestic appliances, radio, TV and VCR Other electrical equipment for industry Motor vehicles Aerospace equipment Tobacco products Plastic products
		Impact of 1992 Depends on the Community's external policy towards NICs	*Impact of 1992* A springboard for global competition

Low   **High**

Advantage to being a leading firm

radio, TVs and VCRs, other electrical equipment for industry and aerospace equipment, among others.

Among the sectors in which there is no particular advantage to being a leading firm, those firms in market segments where the possibility for product differentiation is high (the "fragmented" category in Figure 4) will see little effect from the Single Market program, whereas firms in sectors where product differentiation is low could still see some benefits, depending on future changes in the external competitive environment (this is the "impasse" category in Figure 4).

When actions are taken to protect the environment, we have seen that the role and importance of the energy sector are such that the winning and losing sectors can be identified based on their degree of energy intensity and on the extent to which they produce goods that contribute favourably to the protection of the environment, at one stage or another of the product's life-cycle. The list of sectors that falls in each of the different categories is presented in Figure 5.[8]

Energy intensive sectors that can benefit from the implementation of environmental protection policies if the demand effect is sufficient are the paper sector (to substitute plastics in packaging), along with glass (for packaging and for use in construction), engineering plastics and cement (also used in construction). The overall winners are, however, the little energy intensive sectors which largely contribute to the environmental protection markets, such as most capital goods producing sectors and the metal products sectors (which includes boilers, structural metals for construction and railways).

In the list of sectors that are neither very energy intensive nor experience a rise in demand as a result of the environmental protection measures, we find most of the consumer goods producing sectors, along with a few capital goods producing sectors such as telecommunications equipment and office and EDP (which includes computers but excludes robots and semi-conductors).

Comparing the winning and losing sectors in 4 and 5, we find that a few sectors, namely electrical equipment for industry, aerospace and other transport equipment, along with glass and engineering plastics, rank among the sectors that are potential winners from both "1992" and "Green" policies. In these sectors, the positive impact on global competitiveness that results from the restructuring and other changes that took place under the impulse of the Single Market program will likely be reinforced by a shift towards stricter environmental protection regulations.

There are also sectors which were expected to be relatively little influenced by the Single Market program (i.e. that are either in the "impasse" or in the "fragmented" categories in Figure 4) but which could benefit from "Green" policies: these are the cement and paper sectors and some segments of the non-ferrous metals industries.

Among the sectors that were potential beneficiaries from the Single Market

---

[8]Source: DRI European Industry Services.

Figure 5 Winners and losers from environmental policies

	High	Boilers Mechanical engineering Electrical equipment for industry Telecommunications equipment Aerospace equipment Railway equipment	Cement Paper Glass Nonferrous metals Engineering plastics
		Impact Strong beneficiary through demand effects	*Impact* Depends on the importance of the demand effect from the EP package
Contribution of sector to the EP markets	**Low**	Pharmaceuticals Office, EDP and precision instruments Automotive vehicles Textile and clothing Drinks and food Printing and publishing	Basic plastics Iron and steel Basic chemicals Ceramics
		Impact Inflationary impact of the package dominates	*Impact* Influenced negatively by own and global price developments

Low   **High**

Energy intensity

program (i.e. in the "specialised or "volume" categories in Figure 4), there are, however, a few which will experience a weakening in demand and/or losses in external competitiveness as a result of the implementation of "Green" policies: these are the pharmaceuticals, specialty chemicals, basic chemicals, office and EDP and domestic appliances, radio, TV and VCR sectors, among others. The negative impact of stricter environmental policies will even be fairly strong in those sectors that are characterised by a highly competitive environment worldwide, as non-EC producers could gain significant market shares in the EC market if the relative price of European products deteriorates . Accompanying measures might have to be designed for these sectors to prevent "Green" policies from eliminating the benefits of "1992".

6 Conclusions

The analysis in Sections 4 and 5 allows to draw a few interesting lessons from a policy-making point of view, and, although based on a different methodology than that used in previous studies on the same theme, confirms the results obtained in some of these studies:

1. The overall impact of environmental policies on the macroeconomy, even when apparently quite extreme measures are assumed to be implemented, is generally small.

2. Even very stringent environmental policies, such as those simulated in this scenario, have only moderate impacts on the sectoral reallocation of output. This result is in line with that of previous studies, in particular those obtained with the OECD's "Green" model.

3. There are a number of sectors which have become more competitive in world markets, or which have benefited from a broadening of their geographical markets as a result of the "1992" program, and which now stand to gain even further from the implementation of strict policies to protect the environment. Among these are many segments of electrical engineering for industry, the aerospace industry, the glass sector and engineering plastics. In these sectors, indeed, the (indirect) effect of environmental policies on demand for these products may very well more than offset the negative effect of such policies on costs.

4. There are also a number of sectors which gained only indirectly from the creation of the Single European Market (through increased rates of activity in other sectors) but that could gain from the reinforcement of environmental policies, again because the likely effects of such policies on demand for these products would more than offset the negative impact on relative prices vis-a-vis the rest of the world. Among these are the paper products sector, cement, and some segments of the non-ferrous metals sector (aluminium, in particular).

5. There are, however, a number of sectors that stood to gain from the creation of the Single Market, but which may be at risk as a result of the

implementation of very strict environmental policies. Among these, the main one is the office and EDP sector, which covers the production of computers and of precision instruments such as clocks and watches. In this sector, Europe-based producers are confronted to very strong competition in terms of price from other world producers. Accompanying measures may thus have to be provided for in these sectors to prevent "Green" policies from eliminating the benefits of "1992".

From a policy making point of view, the main conclusions from the analysis are nevertheless that:

- The concern of policy makers about the competitiveness impact of green measures may be somewhat exaggerated;

- The cleaning of the EC will not give rise to a dramatic expansion of polluting activities in the rest of the world through a major relocation of companies outside Europe, as is often feared.

7   References

Buigues, P. and Jacquemin, A. (1989), Strategies of firms and structural environments in the large internal market, *Journal of Common Market Studies* 28, 53-67.

Burniaux, J.-M., J. P. Martin, G. Nicoletti and J. Oliveira Martins (1991a), The costs of policies to reduce global emissions of CO2: initial simulation results with Green, OECD Working Paper 103.

Burniaux, J.-M., J. P. Martin, G. Nicoletti and J. Oliveira Martins (1991b), Green: a multi-region dynamic general equilibrium model for quantifying the costs of curbing CO2 emissions: a technical manual, OECD Working Paper 104.

Centraal Planbureau (1989), Economische gevolgen van een drietal scenario's voor milieubeleid in Nederland tot 2010, Working Paper, Centraal Planbureau, The Netherlands.

Commission of the European Communities, DG II (1990), Social Europe, Special Edition 1990, *European Economy*, 1-357.

Commission of the European Communities, DG XII, Joule Program (1990), CO2 study - Crash program: cost-effectiveness analysis of CO2 reduction options - Bottom-up approach, a Report by experts involved in the Crash Program, in particular Coherence, Citepa, IER, IIP, ECN and ETSU.

Commission of the European Communities, DG XII, Joule Program (1990), CO2 study - Top-down approach: increase of taxes on energy as a way to reduce CO2 emissions, Problems and accompanying measures, a Report by experts involved in the Crash Program.

Commission of the European Communities, DG XVII (1992), A view to the future: energy in Europe, Special Issue.

Commission of the European Communities (1990), Industrial competitiveness and the environment, in *Panorama of EC Industry.*

Commission of the European Communities (1990), The environmental industry, in *Panorama of EC industry.*

Detemermann, V., E. Donni and P. Zagame (1991), Increase of taxes on energy as a way to reduce CO2 emissions: problems and accompanying measures, a Report to the Commission of the European Communities, DG XII (Joule Program, Models for Energy and Environment).

DRI/McGraw-Hill Europe (1990), Green Europe: economic implications and business opportunities, a multi-client study.

DRI/McGraw-Hill Europe (1991), The economic impact of a package of EC measures to control CO2 emissions, Report to the Commission of the European Communities.

DRI/McGraw-Hill Europe (1993), The economic consequencs of the proposed energy/carbon tax, Report to the Commission of the European Communities.

Fisher, J. (1991), Transition and continuing costs, paper presented at a Workshop on "The Uses and Limits of Economic Models as Tools for Assessing Climate Change Policies," Laxenburg: IIASA.

Nordhaus, W. (1991), The cost of slowing climate change: a survey, *The Energy Journal* 12, 37-66.

OECD (1991), Responding to Climate Change: Selected Economic Issues, Paris: OECD.

Whalley, J. and R. Wigle (1991), Cutting CO2 emissions: the effects of alternative policy approaches, *The Energy Journal* 12, 109-124.

Waelbroeck-Rocha, E. (1991), The outlook for European industry: what market opportunities exist? How can firms take advantage of such opportunities?, *The European Industry Review*, DRI/McGraw-Hill.

12

Life-cycle Consumption and Liquidity Constraints: An Empirical Analysis at the EC Level[1]

Khalid Sekkat, Françoise Thys-Clément

Université Libre de Bruxelles

Denise Van Regemorter

Katholieke Universiteit Leuven

1 Introduction

Since the early 1950's, the life cycle-permanent income theory has dominated research on consumption functions. Broadly summarized this theory considers that consumers plan their consumption over their whole life taking into account present and future resources. Two major implications of this theory justify the interest of policy makers. First the path of consumption over the life cyle is smoother than the path of income. Therefore a temporary change in income should have a weak impact on consumption and the effictiveness of stabilization policy may be limited. Second consumers save in the early stages of their life and disave in the later stages. With an ageing population, as in many European countries, this may induce problems for the financing of future growth.

On the basis of a rational expectations framework, Robert Hall initiated, in 1978, a tradition of empirical tests of the life cycle-permanent income hypothesis (LCPIH) based on aggregate data. The purpose of Hall's work was not to estimate the deep parameters of utility. Rather he tests if the time series of consumption satisfies properties implied by the LCPIH. While Hall's results support the LCPIH, many other studies concerning different countries do not, even when revision in expected income are explicitly modelled : the results show an excess sensitivity of consumption to current income (Flavin (1981), Muellbauer (1981), Bilson (1980), Thys-Clément et al. (1983)). Different explanations have been sought, such as the myopic behaviour of consumers, the

---

[1] We thank Jef Vuchelen and an anonymous referee for helpful comments.

presence of liquidity constraints, the greater uncertainty about future incomes, the stochastic process of income. These explanations have been explicitly tested to track down the causes of the failure of the life-cycle rational expectations model (i.e. Flavin (1985) and Zeldes (1989)). Also, at a more theoretical level, optimal policy rules for consumption have been derived under varying degrees of uncertainty and of liquidity constraints, and under different income processes (Skinner (1987), Deaton (1991)). These theoretical models depart from the basic life-cycle model for the relation between income and consumption, without changing the basic forward looking behaviour of the consumer.

Our purpose in this paper is to test empirically the LCPIH with the explicit possibility of liquidity constraints for different EC countries (France, Germany and the United Kingdom).

The first section gives a brief description of the theoretical model of consumption, both with and without liquidity constraints. In the second section, the empirical approach is developed, the data are described and the empirical results are given. The third section concludes.

2 Structure of the theoretical model

2.1 The model without constraints

The life cycle approach assumes that the consumer chooses his consumption path in order to maximize his expected life-time utility, considering his expected lifetime resources. The problem can be written as:

$$max E_t \sum_{i=0}^{T} \frac{U(C_{t+i})}{(1+\delta)^i}, \tag{1}$$

subject to:

$$\sum_{i=0}^{T} \frac{E_t(C_{t+i})}{(1+r)^i} = w_t + \sum_{i=0}^{T} \frac{E_t(Y_{t+i})}{(1+r)^i}$$

where $U(C_t)$ is the one period utility function (labour is supplied inelastically and the utility function is time separable), C_t is real consumption in period t, δ represents time preference of the consumer, r is the real expected interest rate, at which the consumer can lend or borrow (perfect capital market assumption), Y_t is the real labour income at time t, w_t represents real current wealth at the beginning of period t and E_t is the expectations operator.

The marginal conditions for the optimum are:

$$E_t U'(C_{t+i+1}) = (\frac{1+\delta}{1+r}) U'(C_{t+i}), i = 1, 2, ..., T \tag{2}$$

where $U'(C_t)$ is the partial derivative of U with respect to C_t. By combining (2) for each horizon i with the budget constraint, consumption planned at period t for period t can be expressed as a function of total expected wealth:

$$C_t = g_t(w_t + \sum_{i=0}^{T} \frac{E_t(Y_{t+i})}{(1+r)^i}) \tag{3}$$

where the form of the function g_t will depend on preferences, the discount factor, the interest rate and the age of the consumer.

For the particular case of an isoelastic utility function, $U(C_t) = \frac{C_t^{\alpha+1}}{\alpha+1}$, consumption planned for period $t+1$ will be related to consumption for period t by:

$$E_t(C_{t+1}) = (\frac{1+\delta}{1+r})^{\frac{1}{\alpha}} C_t \tag{4}$$

In fact, in view of new information on income or on the variables determining income, the consumer revises his consumption plans each year and determines a new intertemporal plan. Therefore the observed consumption in t will be related to the observed consumption in $t-1$ by:

$$C_t = (\frac{1+\delta}{1+r})^{\frac{1}{\alpha}} C_{t-1} + \epsilon_t \tag{5}$$

where ϵ_t stands for the revision at time t of expected lifetime resources. The evolution of assets over time is given by $w_t = (1+r)w_{t-1} + Y_{t-1} - C_{t-1}$. At the empirical level, equation (5) is at the core of the tests of the LCPIH.

Rational expectations on the behalf of the consumer imply that the revision ϵ_t is not related to variables known in the period $t-1$. Then if the LCPIH holds, observed consumption in t differs from observed consumption in $t-1$ by a revision that reflects only new information on income or on other determinants of wealth which occurred after $t-1$. Moreover, consumption at a given period is not constrained by the level of income in this period.

2.2 The model with liquidity constraints

The model specified in the preceding paragraph is derived under the assumption that the consumer can borrow against future incomes. If he faces borrowing constraints, the results derived above do not hold anymore. Consumption will be constrained by current income and assets instead of being constrained by the life-cycle wealth. However, this does not reject the forward looking behaviour of the consumer because he is free to save despite the borrowing constraints he faces.

The consumer problem is the same as in the preceding section except for a sequence of constraints on his annual borrowing capacity. Like Deaton (1992), we adopt a very simple form of constraints: current net indebtedness cannot be negative. The model becomes:

$$maxE_t \sum_{i=0}^{T} \frac{U(C_{t+i})}{(1+\delta)^i},$$

subject to:

$$\sum_{i=0}^{T} \frac{E_t(C_{t+i})}{(1+r)^i} = w_t + \sum_{i=0}^{T} \frac{E_t(Y_{t+i})}{(1+r)^i}$$

and

$$w_{t+i} \geq 0, i = 1, 2, ..., T.$$

The Euler equations are:

$$E_t U'(C_{t+i+1}) = (\frac{1-\delta}{1+r})(U'(C_{t+i}) - \lambda_i), i = 1, 2, ..., T$$

where λ_i is the shadow price associated with the borrowing constraint. If the constraint is binding, the shadow price is positive and the marginal utility of the constrained consumption is higher than the discounted expected marginal utility of next period's consumption. The consumer who is constrained in t will consume less during the current year and compensate this by consuming more one year later. If there is no constraint in t, the relation between $t + 1$ and t is the same as in the non-constrained case, even if the consumer expects to be constrained in the future[2]. It must be mentioned that the level of consumption in t and $t + 1$ takes into account the possibility of future constraints: though no closed form solution can be derived for consumption, consumption in $t + 1$ is positively related to consumption in t and to the severity of the constraints until $t + 1$ (this can be obtained by inverting the Euler equations). By analogy with (3), the consumption planned in t for period t (first year of the planning horizon) can be expressed as a function h_t of the lifetime expected wealth (positive impact) and the expected severity of future constraints (negative impact):

$$C_t = h_t(w_t + \sum_{i=0}^{T} \frac{E_t(Y_{t+i})}{(1+r)^i}, (\lambda_i, i = t, ..., T)) \qquad (6)$$

Here again h_t (analogous to g_t) will depend on preferences, the discount factor, the interest rate and the shadow prices of the borrowing constraints. Note that the borrowing constraints will not be binding for all types of consumers. Those with rather low time preference (compared to the interest rate) will have a greater tendency to accumulate wealth and therefore, be less inclined to borrow.

---

[2]This is so because the consumer may save in t to increase his consumption in $t + 1$.

At time $t+1$ the consumer will determine a new path of consumption in light of new available information. This may change his forecast of future income and of future constraints. Then the consumer's optimization problem at time t will lead to a new function h_{t+1} (analogous to equation (6)), linking consumption planned at $t+1$ for $t+1$ to future wealth and constraints:

$$C_{t+1} = h_{t+1}(w_{t+1} + \sum_{i=1}^{T} \frac{E_{t+1}(Y_{t+i})}{(1+r)^{i-1}}, (\eta_i, i = t+1, ..., T)) \qquad (7)$$

where the η_i are new expectations of the shadow prices associated to the borrowing constraints.

Combining equations (6) and (7) leads to a relation between consumption observed in t and $t-1$. This relation shows that the consumption in t will be a function of consumption in $t-1$, the severity of the liquidity constraint in $t-1$, the change in expected income, the change in expected liquidity constraints, and the expectation errors on Y_t and λ_t. In the empirical section we use the following linear approximation of this relation:

$$\begin{aligned} C_t &= \beta_0 C_{t-1} + \beta_1(E_t - E_{t-1})(Y_{t+1}) + \beta_2(Y_t - E_{t-1}Y_t) \\ &+ \gamma_1 \lambda_{t-1} + \gamma_2(E_t - E_{t-1})(\lambda_{t+1}) + \gamma_3(\lambda_t - E_{t-1}\lambda_t) \end{aligned} \qquad (8)$$

The above model is, of course, based on some restrictive assumptions in order to simplify exposition. One of these restrictions that may be crucial given the focus of our paper, is that consumers are homogeneous with respect to liquidity constraints. Indeed the strengh of the constraint may be different between groups of consumers. For instance, consumers who are at an early stage of their professional career may wish to consume more than their current income and wealth. Moreover, their income prospects may be highly uncertain leading to a more severe borrowing constraint. In the estimation we try to pay attention to a possible heterogeneity of consumers with respect to borrowing constraints.

3 Empirical results

Our purpose is not to estimate a structural consumption function. Instead we estimate equation (8) for three European countries (France, Germany and the United Kingdom) and test the life-cycle hypothesis associated with liquidity constraints. The alternative hypothesis is the life-cycle rational expectations model without constraints.

Quarterly seasonally adjusted data on real disposal income and real consumption of non-durable goods and services for France and the United Kingdom are drawn from OECD's National Accounts. Since the same series are not available for Germany, we use total real consumption and real income instead. To obtain per capita series on a quarterly basis, we follow Campbell and Mankiw

Table 1 Stationarity tests (Dickey-Fuller)

	France	Germany	United Kingdom
Levels			
Income per head	-0.66	-375.33^a	-402.54^a
Consumption per head	-0.34	-325.38^a	-239.63^a
Unemployment rate	-1.11	-1.52	-1.29
Credit ratio	-6.25^a	-8.85^a	-6.15^a
First order differences			
Income per head	-8.36^a	-	-
Consumption per head	-11.53^a	-	-
Unemployment rate	-5.33^a	-2.88	-2.60
Second order differences			
Unemployment rate	-	-8.64^a	-10.32^a

[a] Significant at the 5% probability level.

(1991) who construct quarterly population series by a loglinear interpolation of annual data (drawn from I.F.S.). Given that there is no available macroeconomic series for the severity of the liquidity constraints (λ_i) a proxy is needed. The most readily available and commonly used proxies are the unemployment rate and the ratio between the change in credit and the change in income. The unemployment rate was used by Flavin (1985) to test the hypothesis of liquidity constraints on US data. The ratio of credit to income is used by Japelli and Pagano (1991) for different countries. Estimation of equation (8) will be conducted with both proxies. The period of observation is I-1971 to IV-1989 except for the French credit ratio available since I-1978 only.

To model the period by period revision in the expected lifetime income and constraints, we follow the rational expectations approach in assuming that consumers use the stochastic process of the exogenous variables to form their expectations. The innovations in these variables are taken into account by modelling jointly their stochastic process. Equation (8) will be estimated jointly with the VAR (three lags) model generating income and liquidity constraints, using a maximum likelihood method. This joint estimation involves complex cross equations restrictions in order to take into account the direct impact of the revisions in expected income and of the constraints on consumption behaviour. Because of the rational expectations assumption, the revision is uncorrelated with past information. In addition, we consider the possibility of an indirect impact of the explanatory variables on consumption. The unemployment rate or the credit ratio may also affect consumption through the income equation and vice versa. Indeed the innovation in one explanatory variable can contain new information that helps predict the other.

Table 2 Consumption equations

	β_0	β_1	β_2	γ_1	γ_2	γ_3	R^2	D.W	L.R.test
France									
Unempl. rate									
present	-0.27	0.16	0.05	-0.10	-0.11	0.12	0.12	2.18	-
	(-2.21)	(0.70)	(1.18)	(-0.52)	(-0.21)	(0.38)			
absent	-0.26	0.16	0.05	-	-	-	0.11	2.17	0.15
	(-2.12)	(0.88)	(1.13)						
Credit ratio									
present	-0.37	-0.60	8.07	-0.06	0.07	0.04	0.19	2.19	-
	(-2.23)	(-0.11)	(0.13)	(-0.13)	(0.13)	(0.12)			
absent	-0.32	0.02	0.05	-	-	-	0.11	2.10	2.78
	(-2.15)	(0.39)	(0.83)						
U.K.									
Unempl. rate									
present	0.73	0.38	0.25	0.35	1.82	-0.30	0.98	1.87	-
	(8.42)	(1.63)	(2.36)	(1.51)	(1.45)	(-1.06)			
absent	-0.38	-0.30	0.72	-	-	-	0.97	1.04	13.84
	(-5.31)	(-2.57)	(8.17)						
Credit ratio									
present	0.90	-2.72	2.09	-0.01	0.01	0.03	0.99	2.58	-
	(17.71)	(-0.79)	(0.75)	(-0.76)	(0.66)	(0.80)			
absent	0.92	-5.71	4.77	-	-	-	0.99	2.50	6.75
	(18.01)	(-0.78)	(0.75)						
Germany									
Unempl. rate									
present	0.29	-11.71	12.87	212.10	-48.68	-232.51	0.98	1.35	-
	(4.11)	(-0.18)	(0.19)	(0.37)	(-0.41)	(-0.39)			
absent	0.86	0.15	0.31	-	-	-	0.96	1.77	0.33
	(30.90)	(0.59)	(1.85)						
Credit ratio									
present	0.30	-62.35	76.13	0.87	2.00	-1.67	0.98	1.32	-
	(2.89)	(-0.39)	(0.39)	(0.30)	(0.35)	(-0.35)			
absent	0.30	-42.46	46.37	-	-	-	0.98	1.39	41.98
	(4.40)	(-0.55)	(0.56)						

t-statistics are between brackets. The L.R. test is distributed as a χ^2 with 3 d.f.

In order to draw correct inferences from the joint estimation, the time series have to be stationary. Therefore we remove the trends by successive differentiation, when necessary. The Dickey-Fuller test is used to check for stationarity; the results are[3] presented in Table 1. They show that the French series are difference stationary ($I(1)$) except for the credit ratio which is stationary ($I(0)$). Consumption, income and the credit ratio for Germany and the United Kingdom are $I(0)$ while their unemployment rates are $I(2)$.

Table 2 presents the results for the consumption functions. To save on space, estimates of the VAR parameters are omitted. The results for France (model without liquidity constraint) exhibit a poor quality of fit: the R^2 is very low. Hence the pure life-cycle model is rejected by the French data. However neither of the two liquidity constraint proxies can improve the quality of the estimated equation: the R^2 remains very low. This is confirmed by the likelihood ratio tests which indicate that none of the liquidity constraint proxies has a significant explanatory power. This conclusion is not valid for the United Kingdom. While the fit is good without liquidity constraint, the introduction of either proxy seems necessary. Indeed, the likelihood ratio tests show that the unemployment rate has a significant contribution at the 5% level and that the credit ratio has a significant contribution at the 10% level. Moreover, β_0 is negative in the United Kingdom equation without the unemployement rate. While a negative β_0 is acceptable for France because the estimation is conducted on the first difference of consumption, the sign is not acceptable in the UK case because the estimation concerns levels. Thus, both for France and the United Kingdom, the liquidity constraint proxies lead to the same conclusion: liquidity is important in the United Kingdom but not in France. Such a coherence between the results with the two proxies is not observed in the German case: each proxy points to a different result. Note however that the German results have to be taken with caution, because estimation is conducted in terms of income and total consumption rather than in terms of disposable income and consumption of non-durables.

For the United Kingdom, our results confirm those of Daly and Hadjimatheou (1981) who show a substantial contribution of disposable income and liquid assets in explaining consumption. The contrast between the three countries under study does not, however, fit with previous results. Using a different methodology, Campbell and Mankiw (1991) show that, while liquidity constraints may be important in the UK, they are more important in France.

In Section 2, we have stressed the importance of the distinction between young and old consumers with respect to liquidity constraints. In order to take this distinction into account we reestimate equation (8) using the unemployment rate of workers who are less than 25 years old. Quarterly series were constructed by a log linear interpolation of annual data, drawn from Eurostat. The period of observation is I-1971 to IV-1989 except for the United Kingdom where the

---

[3]Similar results are obtained with the augmented Dickey-Fuller test.

period of observation is I-1978 to IV-1989. The results are presented in the Appendix. For France and Germany, they are in accordance with those in Table 2. For the United Kingdom, they are different. This may be due either to the difference in the period of observation or to the fact that the liquidity constraint is less important for young people.

4 Conclusion

In this paper we have tested the life-cycle permanent income hypothesis with the explicit possibility of liquidity constraints for three European countries: France, Germany and the United Kingdom. We used two proxies to take into account the possibility of a liquidity constrained consumer behavior: the unemployment rate and the ratio between the change in credit and the change in income.

Our results show that the pure life-cycle model is not accepted. Concerning the liquidity constraint hypothesis the results for France and the UK are unambiguous. Indeed, on the basis of either of the two proxies, the liquidity constraint is found to play an important role in the United Kingdom but not in France. The contrast between the two countries could be linked to the differences in unemployment benefit systems. The results for Germany are ambiguous: one rejects the liquidity constraint with the unemployment rate proxy and accepts it with the credit ratio proxy.

5 References

Bilson, J.F. (1980), The rational expectations approach to the consumption function: a multi-country study, *European Economic Review* 13, 273-299.

Campbell, J.Y. and N. G. Mankiw, (1991), The response of consumption to income, a cross-country investigation, *European Economic Review* 35, 723-767.

Daly, V. and G. Hadjimatheou, (1981), Stochastic implications of the life- cycle permanent income hypothesis: evidence for the UK economy, *Journal of Political Economy* 89, 596-599.

Deaton, A. (1991), Saving and liquidity constraints, *Econometrica* 59, 1221-1248.

Flavin, M. (1981), The adjustment of consumption to changing expectations about future income, *Journal of Political Economy* 89, 1020-1037.

Flavin, M. (1985), Excess sensitivity of consumption to current income: liquidity constraints or myopia ?, *Canadian Journal of Economics* 18, 117-136.

Hall, R.E. (1978), Stochastic implications of the life-cycle permanent income hypothesis: theory and evidence, *Journal of Political Economy* 86, 971-987.

Jappelli, T. and M. Pagano, (1991), Saving, growth and liquidity constraints, Mimeo.

Muellbauer, J. (1982), Surprises in the consumption function, *Economic Journal supplement* 93, 34-40.

Skinner, J. (1988), Risky income, life-cycle consumption and precautionary savings, *Journal of Monetary Economics* 22, 237-255.

Thys-Clément, F., D. Van Regemorter, and J. Vuchelen, (1983), La consommation privée: cycle de vie et rationalité, une analyse empirique, *Cahiers Economiques de Bruxelles* 99, 327-360.

Zeldes, S.P. (1989), Consumption and liquidity constraints: an empirical investigation, *Journal of Political Economy* 97, 305-346.

6 Appendix

Consumption equations
(unemployment rates for less than 25 years old)

	β_0	β_1	β_2	γ_1	γ_2	γ_3	R^2	D.W	L.R.test
France									
Unempl. rate									
present	-0.24	0.03	0.13	-0.02	-0.11	-0.29	0.11	2.13	-
	(-1.92)	(0.50)	(0.52)	(-0.04)	(-0.41)	(-0.35)			
absent	-0.24	0.04	0.08	-	-	-	0.09	2.17	0.10
	(-1.99)	(1.10)	(0.52)						
U.K.									
Unempl. rate									
present	1.02	-0.05	0.12	-0.03	0.15	-0.03	0.99	2.09	-
	(54.97)	(-0.24)	(0.64)	(-1.16)	(0.40)	(-0.86)			
absent	1.02	0.03	0.07	-	-	-	0.99	2.19	0.10
	(63.29)	(0.22)	(0.67)						
Germany									
Unempl. rate									
present	0.32	30.53	-35.15	-84.78	-9.96	97.61	0.98	1.33	-
	(4.55)	(0.57)	(-0.59)	(-0.56)	(-0.53)	(0.58)			
absent	0.32	-40.72	43.50	-	-	-	0.98	1.40	0.00
	(3.23)	(-0.58)	(0.58)						

t-statistics are between brackets. The L.R. test is distributed as a χ^2 with 3 d.f. The period of observation is I-1978 to IV-1989.

13

Old and New Conjectures on Variables Entering the Household Saving Function

Anne Borsu

University of Namur

Herbert Glejser

Universities of Namur and Brussels

1 Introduction: the issues

Since the mid-seventies, there has been a strong revival of interest in the household saving function. The subject looked almost dried up after the Keynesian and post-Keynesian contributions in the decades 1930 to 1960.

There are several reasons for this phenomenon:

(1) the growing acceptance of the rational expectations approach which has an obvious relevance in a domain where before only present and past values of explanatory variables provided the dynamics.[1]

(2) the theory that myopia, excess sensitivity and liquidity constraints could exert an influence on the consumer.[2]

(3) the argument that one could not dissociate social security provision and corporate saving from household saving as they serve the same purpose. This is the so-called Denison law.[3]

(4) in the same line, the argument that one could not dissociate private from government saving, the so-called Ricardo-Barro hypothesis.[4]

The paper will pay much attention to points (1) and (4) above - and also implicitly to (2):

---

[1] See Flavin (1981) and Hall (1978).
[2] See Hayashi (1985), Flavin (1985), Zeldes (1989), Guiso, Jappeli and Terlizzese (1992).
[3] See David and Scadding (1989).
[4] See Kotlikoff (1989).

- as to point (1), the assumption tested here is that consumers (a) have quite a correct view of the change in future income one year (i.e. $t + 1$) and perhaps even two years (i.e. $t + 2$) ahead of t; (b) modify their saving behavior in t according to the (quite accurate) view they hold of $t + 1$ or even $t + 2$.

- if we can show that the saving ratio adjusts to future income, this weakens to some extent hypothesis (2) above which would entail more rigidity.

- as to point (4), we shall investigate the possible lead or lag and also the likelihood that only large dissaving by government causes the consumer to react.

- we shall pay attention to the demographic evolution as the shares of age-groups have often changed considerably in the West over the last decades.

- finally, we shall look into the impact of unemployment, a variable that has even shown more spectacular changes over the last twenty years: an increase in unemployment could give rise either to a drop in the saving rate if a generous social security redistributes income from rich to poor citizen (redistributive effect) or on the contrary to a rise in this saving rate if the redistribution is rather weak and if the precautionary effect of working people fearing to become unemployed too dominates.

The organization of the paper is as follows. In Section 2, we describe the model. Section 3 is devoted to the regression results and Section 4 to conclusions and scope for future work.

2 The model and the data

We shall consider four North European countries - Belgium, France, West-Germany and the United Kingdom.[5] The data consist first of all of the annual household saving rates for the period 1964 to 1987.

We chose the saving rate $\frac{S}{Y}$ - rather than the amount of saving S - as the dependent variable to eliminate heteroskedasticity and perhaps some autocorrelation and, worse, spurious correlation as the error term in S and ΔY_r could probably be positively correlated.

The specification of the saving function looks as follows:

$$(\frac{S}{Y})_t = a + \sum_{i=0}^{2} b_i(\frac{\Delta Y_r}{Y_r})_{t+i} + cU_t + d(\frac{JP}{P})_t + \sum_{i=0}^{1} e_i(\frac{BS}{Y+M})_{t+i} + u_t,$$

where the lower case letters stand for parameter values and ΔY_r for the rise in real income, U_t for the unemployment rate, $\frac{JP}{P}$ for the share of the juvenile (i.e. 14 years or less) population in the total, $\frac{BS}{Y+M}$ for the government budget surplus as a share of available resources; finally, u_t is the disturbance term.

The rise in real income in the same year would have the traditional non-negative effect b_0 stemming from a possible rise in the saving ratio for a high

---

[5]The three main European economies of the time and one small country.

increase in income the same year. One rationale is that it may take time to know and cash part of the higher income (because of several factual lags[6]) and, more importantly, to make a decision about the new expenses plus possibly delivery delays. On the other hand, we expect b_1 and b_2 to be nonpositive: a higher anticipated income raises estimated permanent income this year and thus raises the consumption rate; this is indeed one *motto* of the paper.

The expected sign of c is indefinite as the redistributive or precautionary effect of U may dominate.

The parameter d is assumed to be nonnegative as the *decrease* in the share of the young in the West during the period under consideration corresponds to a more or less equivalent *rise* of the share of the old (65 years or more), with the intermediate category (15 to 64 years) remaining constant: the theory of the life-cycle consumption would thus predict a decrease in the overall saving ratio, due to the rising share of the old in the total population.

Instead of the share of the young we could thus have taken the share of the old - perhaps even in addition to the former variable but here collinearity is a problem. Later we shall provide another rationale for the inclusion of the variable.

Finally, BS stands for budget surplus: situations here vary a lot with, for some years, a two digit figure found for $\frac{BS}{Y+M}$ in Belgium whereas there is usually less government spendthrift in the United Kingdom and even less in France and Germany over that period.[7]

3   Results

The main regression results are shown in Table 1. The most striking finding is the significance of b_1 (three times at the 0.1% and once at the 5% level). For France, b_2 is also significant at the 1% level. Except for Germany, all the b's have very close values of the order of -.3: this means that an increase in the expectation of the growth rate for the next year (and also the second next in the case of France) by one percent causes the saving (consumption) rate to drop (rise) by three tenths of a point. Compare this result with the average consumption rate which often lies arount 0.8: the ratio is 2/5 (0.3 divided by 0.8).

One should wonder about possible biases in the estimation. The first that springs to mind is a *downward* bias due to reverse causality: an *increase* in the saving rate would cause an *increase* in future income via larger domestic and

---

[6] In continental Europe, yearly dividends, for example, are only known and paid out months after the end of the year.

[7] Sources of the data: $\frac{S}{Y}$, $\frac{\Delta Y_r}{Y_r}$: OECD National Accounts; U (standardized unemployment rate): OCDE, Historical Satistics; $\frac{JP}{P}$: United Nations, Demographic Yearbook; $\frac{BS}{Y+M}$: IMF, International Financial Statistics.

Table 1 OLS estimates of the parameters of the saving function
(variables in %)

Estimates	Belgium	France	West Germany	United Kingdom
a	18.2***	18.8***	5.6*	2.8
b_0	-	-	0.21**	-
b_1	-0.28***	-0.31***	-0.15*	-0.30***
b_2	-	-0.27**	-	-
c	-0.84***	-0.79***	-	-
d	-	-	0.41**	0.13
e_0	-0.59**	-	-	-
e_1	-0.37	-	-	-0.56***
$\tilde{\rho}$	0.72	0.76	0.68	0.00
R^2	0.80	0.87	0.88	0.81
DW	2.08	1.84	1.55	1.41

***: significant at the 0.1% level; **: significant at the 1% level; *: significant at the 5% level. The tests are two-tailed except for e_0 and e_1.

foreign investment. This strengthens our finding. In the same way, errors in the measurement of the growth rate[8], would bias the b's toward zero.

As to the unemployment and demographic variables, it proved difficult to separate their impact: multicollinearity was so strong that the correlation coefficient between the two sometimes ran as high as 0.98. We had to give up one or the other: unemployment over the period ran especially high in Belgium and France for which the regression coefficients hovered around -0.8. As the range of the rate of unemployment was close to 10% in both countries, its negative effect on the saving rate amounted to some 8%.

The demographic variable is significant only for Germany. The positive sign of d is hard to interpret as the usual life-cycle phenomenon of saving. Yet it is also possible that an increase in the share of the very young is conducive to *more* saving. This could be due to the fact that a large number of children obliges the parents to save for a larger dwelling and/or for a second residence; more generally, as Ando, Guiso and Terlizzese (1992) put it, "the existence of future opportunities [a college education?][9] may be an incentive to postpone consumption until those periods in which it yields greater utility." [10]

Finally a significant Ricardo-Barro effect shows, but only for the two coun-

---

[8]They are not negligible; see e.g. Glejser and Shavey (1974).
[9]The interpolation is ours.
[10]See Ando et al. (1992).

tries with large budget deficits over the period, Belgium and the United Kingdom: could there be a threshold effect due e.g. to the greater publicity given to a large deficit? Note also the role of anticipation (again) in the case of the United Kingdom and (perhaps) Belgium. Is it because the budget of next year is usually given more publicity by the media? The Ricardo-Barro effect is of the order of 0.6- except for Belgium, if the nonsignificant but large value of e_1 is taken into account, where one comes close to 1.

4 Conclusions and scope for further research

Our main conclusion is that *future* income changes and not past ones affect the household saving rate. In the future, it may be interesting to check the quality of GNP forecasts of various organizations as using the forecast of OECD e.g. led to the same conclusions as future GNP but with less significant coefficients. We should also correct GNP changes for spurious elements like different lengths in working days.

As to the influence of unemployment: In the United States where benefits are much less generous than in Belgium or France, the precautionary element dominates, i.e. a positive coefficient shows up: this is suggested by the relatively high saving rates of 1980 and early 1981 and also of 1991 and 1992 in the United States whereas a long decline took place in the expansion years in between. Anyway, rising unemployment looks the main reason for the drop of $\frac{S}{Y}$ in Belgium and France due to the redistributive effect.

The demographic influences deserve closer scrutiny - especially if and when unemployment is drastically reduced in the economies so that collinearity is reduced. It does not look as if all the predictions of the classical life-cycle-model come true. There are indications that a decline in the percentage of the very young reduces saving.

Finally the Ricardo-Barro effect seems to exist but it is partial and it is significant only where the deficit reaches high proportions of available resources like in Belgium and in the United Kingdom: there seems to be some lead (1 year) of saving (impressed by the budget figure for the next year?).

We shall also put to a test the predictive power of our model.

Finally a look at the residuals shows them to be sometimes correlated as between Belgium and France. Thus omitted variables for two close E.C. countries would not be independent (assuming normality). This is not astonishing in today's world: SURE estimation should then reduce the standard-errors.

The influence of the interest rate was never significant (as in other studies) and tended to be negative: this is probably because changes in saving are closely correlated with changes in investment which are negatively affected by the interest rate; we have thus a simultaneous equation effect.

5 References

Ando, A., L. Geriso and D. Terlizzese (1992), Young households saving and the life-cycle opportunities: evidence from Japan and Italy, Banca d'Italia Temi di Discussione 164.

David, P. and J. Scadding (1974), Private saving: ultrarationality, aggregation and Denison's law, *Journal of Political Economy* 82, 225-249.

Flavin, M. (1981), The adjustment of consumption to changing expectations about future income, *Journal of Political Economy* 89, 974-1009.

Flavin, M. (1985), Excess sensitivity of consumption to current income: liquidity constraints or myopia, *Canadian Journal of Economics* 18, 219-236.

Glejser, H. and P. Schavey (1974), An analysis of revisions of national account data for 40 countries, *Review of Income and Wealth* 20, 317-332.

Guiso, L., T. Jappeli and D. Terlizzese (1992), Why is Italy's saving rate so high?, Banca d'Italia, Temi di Discussione 167.

Hall, R. E. (1978), Stochastic implications of the life-cycle permanent income hypothesis: theory and evidence, *Journal of Political Economy* 86, 971-987.

Hayashi, F. (1985), The effect of liquidity constraints on consumption: a cross-sectional analysis, *Quarterly Journal of Economics* 100, 183-206.

Kotlikoff, L. (1989), *What Determines Saving?*, Cambridge, Mass.: The MIT Press.

Zeldes, S. P. (1989), Consumption and liquidity constraints: an empirical investigation *Journal of Political Economy* 97, 305-346.